"A Hell of a Place to Lose a Cow"

"A Hell of a Place to Lose a Cow"

An American Hitchhiking Odyssey

TIM BROOKES

ADVENTURE PRESS

NATIONAL GEOGRAPHIC
WASHINGTON, D. C.

Published by the National Geographic Society
1145 17th Street N.W., Washington, D.C. 20036

First Printing, July 2000

Map Artwork by James Noel Smith.
Interior Design by Kathleen Cole.
Printed in U.S.A.

To everyone who picked me up.

CONTENTS

"Let's go for a walk," he proposed. "When you walk, you are much more accurate than when you're sitting down. It is not an idle idea that you should pace back and forth when you try to relate something."

Carlos Castenada

"As I have always held it a crime to anticipate evils I will believe it a good comfortable road untill I am conpelled to beleive differently."

Captain Meriwether Lewis

CHAPTER 1

A Barometer
of Goodwill

The three months that changed my life began on July 1, 1973, when I first saw America. With my traveling companion and soon-to-be-enemy, Richard, I flew over from England on a student charter flight, four guitars being passed up and down the cabin, some of us by sheer habit sleeping under rather than in our seats, all of us drawn toward America like dazzled, half-blind moths. Myself, I was seduced by a vast poster in the window of Oxford Travel, a photo of a Greyhound bus bearing on its destination board a single word that encompassed the infinite adventure of America, its wild past, its endless plains, its mystery: BUFFALO.

I was 20. I had $90 in traveler's checks, a job waiting for me in the tobacco fields of Ontario, and a return ticket for the end of the summer. I was in love with an Iowan girl I'd met at Oxford with extraordinary qualities that I'd never seen in anyone else, qualities that I took to be quintessentially American: optimism, vitality, spontaneity, courage, a lightness of heart that illuminated everything she looked at. "The future is pliable," she said, contradicting everything England had taught me. "We can make of it whatever we want." It was 1973, and I believed her.

Richard, the friend of a friend, was tall, skinny, with wild black hair, and full of wild enthusiasm. I met him just once before leaving—a major mistake. "You're going to the States," he cried. "Can I come too?" And that was that; as casual as going to the pub. At 45, I'm starting to see how important that casualness is, how it is the necessary ingredient for both disaster and miracle. It's a gift of youth.

For £90 the British Universities North America Club— BUNAC—arranged our visas, flew us over, and put us up for our first night in the United States at the Royal Manhattan Hotel. Everything from that summer now seems like a damaged home movie, vivid short sequences spliced together bridging unknowable lengths of missing footage, but the New York sequence seems the most intact. We arrived after midnight to find the walls of Kennedy Airport covered with posters depicting a skeleton with a syringe climbing in through a window. "KEEP DRUGS OUT OF AMERICA. COOPERATE WITH YOUR CUSTOMS OFFICIAL." A squat, grizzled customs man pawed at my bag, which contained a change of socks and underwear, a nylon rain jacket, a sleeping bag, a single-volume complete works of Shakespeare, which I had to read before the autumn term began in October, and my asthma drugs. I was terrified that the last of these would be mistaken for heroin and babbled out an explanation to the agent.

"Azzma, huh?" he grunted. "That's too bad. " He shoved the bag back at me. "Next."

Dazed, our BUNAC mob were led outside and loaded on a streamlined bus with back-slanted aerodynamic-looking windows. Even muttering at the curb, the bus looked faster than prim, upright English buses. It was after 1 a.m. when we made our way into Manhattan. The city seemed to be uniformly awash in a curious dead light, not the expected big-city jazz of neon but a lifeless midnight sun. Hookers lounged on corners. We watched agog as a car the size of a swimming pool created a parking space by ramming the car parked in front, then the one behind. Everything I'd heard about New York was true.

The Royal Manhattan Hotel, skulking somewhere down in Lower Manhattan, put us up in a triple. The third bed was already occupied by a young guy from Sierra Leone. He told us that he had lost his money and passport and was trapped in a ghastly bureaucratic limbo, spending his days at the Sierra Leone embassy and his nights at the Royal Manhattan, unable to go home or go anywhere else in America. The streetlights burned in through the flimsy paper shades, and the room was astonishingly hot. On television, American hotels had air-conditioning. We opened the window, and the surf of traffic pounded over us. Somehow, we fell asleep. At one point I woke to a room full of pulsing lights and a weird *WheeoowWheeoowWheeoow* sound. I thought the flying saucers had landed. Toward dawn Richard felt the young Sierra Leonean groping at one of his hands tucked between his legs, hoping to fondle him, perhaps, or steal his watch.

In the morning, we found that the Leonean kid had vanished and we had missed our complimentary continental breakfast. We hoofed it down to the hotel ballroom for orientation, an obligatory BUNAC activity. BUNAC theoretically worked as a cultural exchange—and if we did not attend orientation, we were told, we would not get our visas. It turned out that orientation was simply a movie made in the fashionable if confusing quadruple split-screen format showing a bunch of kids traveling around America in a VW bus, to a soundtrack of bluegrass banjo.

"Any questions?" called the student organizer; then we were out on the streets.

The streets were the strangest part of Manhattan, cracked and steaming, bordered here and there by vacant lots being used as primitive car parks. The famous skyline—at one time, the silhouette of the future—was ragged with rooftop shanties and leggy water towers. New York City was both epic and tragic. It seemed to have been invented as a fantastic idea, the idea of the century, rather than as a place where people could actually live. I was petrified, excited, appalled—but not in the least deterred. America was the world's amusement park, and New York was simply, as billed, its scariest, most death-defying ride. The rest of America would be...well, I had no idea, really, but four years of hitchhiking had taught me that whatever it was, I would conquer it. Besides, not knowing was what it was all about—hitchhiking, the trip to America, the world.

Richard knew someone in Boston, I knew someone in Evanston, Illinois, so we split up, agreeing to rendezvous in Des Moines, Iowa. Having heard that it was illegal to hitch in New Jersey, I caught a bus to Stroudsburg, the first stop across the Pennsylvania line. As I was wandering from the tiny general-store-cum-bus-station through a neighborhood of maple trees and neat wood-frame houses toward the interstate, trusting my sense of direction, I passed a postman kneeling beside a mailbox, emptying it. He looked up at this total stranger, this kid wearing a backpack with a Union Jack flag tied to it, carrying a cheap classical guitar in a plaid vinyl case, and called out, "Hiya, buddy!"

Coming from a country so reserved toward strangers, so constrained in its affections, I was astonished. For years to come, when people asked me why I had emigrated to the United States, I told them about the postman in Stroudsburg and a vision of an America of morning sunshine and dew barely off the unfenced lawns, of egalitarian cheerfulness and a future as full of unbounded possibilities as the continent itself.

Hitchhiking was always magical to me. When I was 17 I left my family's home in Worcester to hitch down to London, where my older brother was at college. I went via Stratford-on-Avon, miles out of my way, just because that was where the first lorry driver that picked me up was going. As I walked across the Avon bridge, I saw a large green road sign in the distance bobbing steadily nearer, a sign that showed the roundabout ahead and the roads springing away from it like a compass radiating directions. As the sign grew larger, I was filled with a growing sense of horizons and of awe, of the novel sense of unlimited choice. I could go anywhere from here. It was as if all the lines of latitude and longitude converged at that crossroads, and as soon as I set foot on the magic crux I would be catapulted clear out of the realm of my narrow, tame experience into places unimaginably exotic.

Insofar as I had a plan for my life, it had something to do with hitchhiking. I came across the Japanese proverb "It is better to travel hopefully than to arrive," and took it as my mantra, holding it in my mouth like a piece of fruit, the word "hopefully" provoking a little saliva each time I repeated it. I didn't know what arriving would be like, but I thought I could guess from my father, slowing down as he passed through his mid-40s, putting on weight, irritated more and more easily by change and novelty, developing an almost irrational suspicion of closed doors. What if we could travel all our lives, I thought, and never arrive?

At first, miraculously, everything went according to my planless plan. At the end of the summer of 1973, I flew back to England. With a naivete so great that it amounted to both genius and utter idiocy, I applied for teaching jobs at the colleges and universities in states I had hitched through, just so I could say, "Last summer I traveled through Iowa City/Berkeley/Seattle and was very taken with the place." My naivete, though, opened locked doors: Even though I was still an undergraduate, and every college teaching job in the U.S. routinely attracted a thousand or more applicants with master's degrees or doctorates, I got a job at the University of Vermont.

You'd think that after such startling vindication I might have held on to my Zen navigation principles. Somehow, though, over the next 25 years, they slipped away. By the spring of 1998, I'd had two books published and two rejected, had taught countless introductory writing and literature courses at the University of Vermont, had surgery on both knees, had become the father of two wonderful daughters, had survived two less-than-wonderful divorces, had founded and lost a magazine, I had coached championship soccer teams, my hair had gone gray, and I had shaved off my beard. By the standards of the day, I had grown up. Yet if this were true, I wasn't much of an advertisement for the adult life. I'd spent a decade or more trying to be a good husband and father, trudging grimly through the valley of the shadow of debt. I had a mortgage, I paid child support, I had credit card debts. I was working 50 or 60 hours a week, exhausted by the chronic clutch of anxiety. When I found myself night after night washing dishes under a fluorescent tube, eyes burning, my wife and the girls already asleep, or climbing the stairs with yet another basket of laundry to fold, I found myself imagining that I was hitchhiking beside some highway out West—desert on both sides, mountains like red teeth nibbling the huge horizon, the road itself peeled back and open to the sky.

If this was a midlife crisis, it wasn't just mine. The whole of America seemed to have lost its youthful imagination and vigor. Art and music were stagnating in a spiral of recycled ideas, politics had sold out to business, everyone was downsizing. A new millennium was approaching, but nobody seemed to be looking forward to it with much hope. A new, meaner spirit seemed to have taken root. The end of the Cold War had brought neither peace nor the long-hoped-for peace dividend. Instead conservatives had turned their attack from communism abroad to liberalism at home, to such effect that even while our kids were rediscovering bell-bottoms and tie-dyed shirts, their once-radical parents were renouncing the most exciting time of their lives as a series of youthful indiscretions, abandoning the faith.

I was damned if I would give up that easily, and between fantasy and anger I formulated a plan: Go back on the road. Compare it to my previous trip. Find out what America was really like now.

I toyed with the idea for months, then approached NATIONAL GEOGRAPHIC magazine. What if I were to retrace my 1973 journey, starting at Stroudsburg and heading west to Chicago, Des Moines, Boulder, Salt Lake City, Reno, San Francisco, Portland, Seattle,

Vancouver, Calgary, Winnipeg, Toronto, into the tobacco fields and then back through New England? What if I tried to track down some of the people I'd met a quarter century earlier, find out how their lives and America had changed since those days when, for me at least, America was so vital, so full of life and hope?

The GEOGRAPHIC called me on my 45th birthday to say yes. They would pair me up with a Polish photographer named Tomasz Tomaszewski, a stocky guy with an impish grin, a degree in physics and a rich, self-taught command of English who had been active in the Solidarity movement. He had shot pictures (and been shot at) all over the world, but he had never lost his fascination with America. I'd write, he'd shoot pictures. Every couple of days I'd call his cell phone and we'd rendezvous at some cheap motel and swap notes. We'd wax philosophical about America from our vantage point as outsiders, exchange droll European ironies, maybe travel together every so often. We'd have a road trip.

To my surprise, everyone I knew, including Barbara, my wife, thought I had gone mad. All the men and almost all the women had hitchhiked 20 or 30 years ago, and given a sliver of encouragement, they would launch into their road-trip stories, their eyes lighting up, their faces glowing—yet everyone ended with "I wouldn't do it now, of course...."

"Why not?" I'd ask, and at once the clouds would roll over their foreheads. Sure, everyone hitchhiked back in the sixties, they said, but now America was a far more dangerous and terrifying place. Fear had edged in like dusk, and the land had filled with dark shapes: religious cults with private armories, Nicaraguans marching up through Texas, neo-Nazis, psychotics with shotguns in fast-food restaurants, satanists in the daycare center, pipe bombs in the mail and more psychotics in the mail room, poisoners and perverts, teenage drive-by gang shooters, rapists in pleasant parks and on leafy campuses, sharks in the shallows, and chainsaw killers up the dirt roads: monsters for every age and every political persuasion. It was common knowledge that all hitchhikers were murdered—that was why nobody hitchhiked anymore—or, conversely, were murderers, so drivers were too scared to have anything to do with them. Several people advised me to take a gun. "Nobody in their right mind will pick you up," one friend warned. "You'll be a target for every wacko and werewolf from here to San Francisco."

I was stunned by their vehemence. My God, I thought, this is the America they think of when they make political decisions. No wonder they vote for mandatory sentencing, and buy the wife and kids car phones for Christmas. Or handguns.

Bollocks, I said. America is actually safer now than it was 25 years ago. I cited some of the latest violent-crime statistics: Between 1990 and 1995, network coverage of murder rose by 336 percent, even without including the O.J. Simpson case. Over the same period, real murder fell by 13 percent. Even the roads are safer: twice as many vehicles but, even so, fewer injuries and deaths.

Facts didn't matter. People clung to their fear as if to an electric fence. The entire country seemed to be suffering from a kind of patriaphobia. What happens, I wondered, when we become afraid of our own country? When we were teenagers we went out on the road to disprove our parents' anxieties, I thought; maybe now that we are parents we should go back out again to disprove our own.

CHAPTER 2

Anywho

Like most hitchhikers, I began planning my route by sticking little flags in a mental map: Places I Can Crash (a word I hadn't used in two decades). Gail, my first wife, in Seattle. Barbara's ex-boyfriend Andy in Utah. The trip began to seem like Harold Pinter's play *Betrayal,* in which each scene goes back in time, taking place earlier than the previous one. Maybe if I were on the road long enough, I'd turn back into a teenager.

There were eight people I wanted to find whom I'd met en route in 1973 and hadn't seen since. To track them down I whistled up www.anywho.com, a digital bloodhound. Anywho, which I'd never used before, turned out to be a scary commodity. When I tested it out on myself, it not only knew my name, address, and phone number (which it would dial at the click of a mouse), but choosing the map icon threw up a detailed map of the little valley I live in, with my house highlighted and arrowed. Yikes! Technology might be making my job easier and the past more accessible, but I wasn't sure I'd want to be so easily accessed.

Uncomfortably, I turned Anywho's nose toward Mitzi Porges. I met Mitzi—a tall, brilliant art student, all blond hair and angular cheekbones—when she was hitchhiking through Europe in 1972 and dropped into Oxford to see her childhood friend Steve Block.

Offering Anywho the name Porges in Evanston immediately produced Mitzi's parents. Alberta Porges, Mitzi's mother, said yes, of course she remembered me, and told me I should stop in if I passed through Chicago. Mitzi, she said, was in Oakland: The art student had become an artist and art critic. When I visited her in 1973, she took me around the Chicago Art Museum. Now she was writing guided audio tours for museums all over the world. She seemed to have inherited a life already waiting for her.

I called her, and we began to catch up, but the conversation seemed to consist of two currents—one warm and familiar, the other eerie and unreal. Our mutual friend Steve Block, she said, was now teaching at Princeton. Steve, a hyperactive kid with a Jewish afro, taught me how to play "Ain't She Sweet?" and "Has Anybody Seen My Gal?" on the guitar, and when his draft notice arrived, he and I burned it in the frying pan. When Mitzi and I hung up, I called up the Princeton molecular biology web page, and there was Steve's photo. He had thickened a little around the waist, but still had the same slightly evil, Pan-like grin. "My research interests lie in biophysics, particularly with the problem of cell motility....My lab has pioneered the use of optical tweezers (laser-based optical gradient force traps) and other advanced methods...to make physical measurements of macromolecular assemblies, such as the torsional stiffness of bacterial flagella..."

How did we ever acquire such gravity?

Other names came drifting out of the phone as more or less familiar voices. The two brilliant, radical sisters I stayed with in Vancouver were now married with children, and less radical. Larry van de Maele, the son of the tobacco farmer I'd worked for, was now living down the road in London, Ontario. His wife, who had never met me, insisted I visit. Two others seemed to have vanished off the earth. All the same, I found this rediscovery very reassuring: a time that seemed as remote as a dream was being verified by independent witnesses, and it felt as if part of me, too—a part that I particularly liked—was also being authenticated.

But of all the people from my 1973 trip I wanted to meet again, the most elusive was Kathy, the love of my young life, and the reason I'd come from England in the first place.

She was an enigma. On one hand, she was the woman who changed my life. I could show you the photos: blond hair, ski-jump nose, radiant. More importantly, she made me open my eyes. It was as if, after spending all my young life looking down, I glanced up and found a realm as vast and deep as the night sky. My favorite times with her weren't about sex, which was still new and uncertain ground for me, but about discovery. On her narrow bed, looking up into the dark ceiling, our arms round each other, it was as if everything in the universe had spun out from that tiny box of a room and all we had to do was send out a line of thought and it could reach anywhere.

On the other hand, I was also furious at her. After I had bought my ticket, planning to spend the whole summer with her, she dumped me. I never knew why. But there was still hope: when I came to America, she said, I must visit her in Des Moines, which I did. We had four days together. I spent a quarter of my traveling pittance on a dress for her made of silk scarves. One evening she drove us down to a lake to eat watermelon (which I'd never eaten), and we watched fireflies (which I'd never seen) dance like fairies in the enchanted darkness. When, against impossible odds, I got the teaching job in Vermont, she wrote to say how wonderful it was, that she'd love to come and visit, and was there somewhere her boyfriend could stay? I wrote an angry letter, a hurt letter, and a sad letter, but she didn't reply to any of them, and I hadn't seen or heard from her since.

Now, in the back of my mind, was the hope that somehow on this nineties trip I'd find out what had happened to her, and between us. In a sense, she was the whole story—not just my reason for being in America but my reason for being myself.

Anywho was baffled by Kathy. Her mother had written me a letter in 1976 saying that Kathy was marrying an Episcopal minister named Cramer, or Kramer, but all the Kathys and Kathryns and Heins and Cramers in Iowa were either disconnected or the wrong person. No sign of her parents, Marv and Peg Hein, in Iowa, nor in Minnesota, where they'd owned a summer cabin. Colorado College, Kathy's alma mater, claimed never to have heard of her.

I called the Episcopal diocese of Iowa, who said that they did indeed have records of Kathy married to an Alfred Cramer, but that he had remarried in 1988 and moved out of state. No mention of what had happened to her. Maybe she'd remarried and moved. Maybe she'd died, I thought, suddenly struck with horror. I called the *Des Moines Register* to try searching for her in their obituaries, but by now, they said, the records were too old to be readily accessible. This business of rediscovering the past started to seem no longer a game, and the eerie authority of Anywho looked shallow and threadbare: If she had died, what would it have to offer about her? Information is just information. The map is not the territory.

On the shelf in my office I still have a letter addressed to a detective agency, containing a check for $75 and the few details I knew. Just before I mailed it, I decided to try one last lead, and called the Episcopal archdiocese in New York. "Alfred Cramer?" the secretary asked. "Just a moment...Yes, he's in Vermont."

Anywho gave me two numbers for Alfred Cramers in Vermont, both in the southeast of the state, possibly work and home. I left messages on both machines. Within two hours, I got a call. This is pretty weird, I admitted to him, but I'm trying to track down a mutual friend. I believe you knew Kathy Hein?

"Kathy?" he cried. "Bless me! Well, well, well. Yes. I was married to her. Do you hear the piano in the background?" Beethoven, played quite well. "That's our son."

He gave me her phone number in Texas. She had remarried, he said, and lived in Austin. I walked around all day with my heart in my throat. What would I say when I called? Why would she want to talk to me? Would she think of me as an old friend or a stalker?

At about 5:30 that evening, the phone rang.

"Tim? This is Kathryn Lewis. You may remember me as Kathy Hein." Her voice came unchanged out of the darkness.

"Kathy!" I cried. "This is wonderful. So Al Cramer told you I called him?"

"Al?" she asked, puzzled. "No, I haven't talked to him in months."

"How on earth did you get my number, then?"

It was very odd, Kathy said. Her husband had taken a call from someone at Colorado College who said that a Tim Brookes was trying to get in touch with her, and they had his number if she wanted it.

Wait a moment, I said. When I called them they said they had no record of you at all. I spoke to two or three different people, I e-mailed, they said they'd never heard of you.

"That's not the strangest thing," she said. "When I called the college, nobody there knew anything about you, and nobody knew who could possibly have called me. They kept saying, No, we don't have his number. We don't have any record of anyone of that name calling. I kept begging them to check again, and they kept saying no, until someone happened to glance down at a desk and saw your name and number on a Post-It note on the desk. Nobody knew who had written it down, or how it had got there." The universe seemed to be conspiring to put us back in touch.

I told her about my road trip; she understood immediately what it was all about. She herself had recently started wondering about her time in Oxford. She had managed to track down her girlfriend from those days, and had been wondering what had become of me.

"I wish I could make it as far south as Texas on my trip," I said, "but I can't see how I'll have the time."

"Maybe we can meet somewhere nearer you," she offered. Her new husband worked for the *New York Times*, she said, and they were coming up to spend a couple of weeks in the city.

"Well, that's possible, I suppose, but it would have to be pretty soon. I'm starting my trip from New York on July 20th. When are you planning to get there? "

"Wait a moment," she said, "I've got it written down somewhere. Here it is. July 19th ."

CHAPTER 3

Clothing Technologies

I n 1973, the only gear I bought was a sleeping bag and a rain jacket from an army surplus store for under $25. Now I was in the contradictory position of hitchhiking on a generous expedition budget. I rubbed my hands together gleefully and ran off to the climbing/camping/hiking shops that have sprung up all over Burlington like tents on Everest.

After five minutes in Eastern Mountain Sports, though, I was paralyzed. They had different socks for light, medium, and heavy hiking. They had sneakers that were more like boots and boots that were more like sneakers, and two dozen different types of sandals including some with grooves that would draw water (or sweat) away from the soles of my feet. They had backpacks with dozens of pockets, and an entire range of stick-on pouches for the accessories that couldn't fit in the pack. Nothing cost much less than a hundred bucks, and when I'd finished I might as well buy a Range Rover to chuck them all in.

The EMS outfitter urged me to buy *Medicine for Mountaineering and Other Wilderness Activities* and *Everyday Wisdom: 1001 Expert Tips for Hikers*. All I wanted was insect repellent and a snakebite kit. The outfitter frowned. The conventional wisdom about snakebite kits, he said, was that they didn't really get much of the venom out, and you were better off trying to get to a hospital. If you got to the hospital in time, the bite didn't matter; if you didn't get to the hospital in time, nothing mattered.

I wasn't a very good shopper. I turned down the cutting-edge lightweight microfiber zip-away pants because they made me look like an unemployed circus clown, and I could imagine a Nevada trucker taking one look at them and beating me to death with a tire iron. I did buy a microfiber shirt ("This uses clothing technologies that are barely two years old") for close to 60 bucks because it had a neat invisible vent in the back that kept you cool and more importantly could be washed at night and would drip dry by morning. I went with the sandals that also worked in water and the ecosensitive bug repellent, but I reached a point of diminishing greed when the Gore-Tex rain jacket cost more than my entire trip in 1973. The very idea of good equipment collides head-on with the tradition of hitchhiking. It's not just that hitchhiking is a function of poverty and relies on a certain sympathy for the poor, ragged sod beside the road; it's that ostentatious displays of wealth—say, six-color backpacks and self-inflating sneakers—would make me a target. I imagined getting mugged just for my incredible Dri-Stride light-hiking socks ("...the magenta line indicates the buffer where our patented, anatomical design interface produces the comfort benefits...").

The best stuff was all bright and peppy. I wanted something good but unobtrusive, a state-of-the-art superlight 48-pocket backpack that looked as if it had been dragged behind the bus all the way from Casablanca to Marrakesh. In the end I bought a bottom-of-the-line pack in black and royal blue. "Good choice," he said. "When you're all packed and ready to leave, come back and we'll fine-tune all the straps."

The plan for the expedition was that Tomasz and I would carry cell phones. Though I balked at first, having never owned a one—and couldn't imagine anything more daft than standing with my thumb out while talking into a cell phone—after a while I began to see that the idea had possibilities. If I was on an interstate and saw the highway patrol coming, I could quickly dial 911 and call in a ten-vehicle accident in the other direction. I could have pizza delivered. If I got really desperate beside the road I could dial 900 and have phone sex. Good deal. I stuffed the phone into one of my daughter Maddy's thick socks for protection, and it became the Sock Phone.

I bought a tent, but I had no intention of camping. Camping was permanently tainted for me by the summer of 1975 when I finally lived out the dream of driving around Europe with a girlfriend and sharing a tent. This fantasy of lust and freedom turned out to involve a mosquito-prone tent, shockingly hard ground (this was the days before self-inflating sleeping pads) and a relationship going sour by the mile. A tent to me means sleepless nights, the whine of insects hungry for blood, nylon walls closing around my throat. I'd rather sleep in roach-infested motels and crash on people's kitchen floors.

At the last minute, I bought a large newsprint-quality paper pad and a black magic marker for making destination signs. I toyed with the idea of taking a complete Shakespeare again, but decided on something more suitably American: the journals of Lewis and Clark. And the day before I left, a packet arrived from my brother in England containing a Union Jack flag to tie to my backpack. Unfortunately, the only one he'd been able to find was about six feet by four feet. I could have used it as a blanket.

My father, who was in the Army Reserves, had taught me how to pack, so I shoved everything small and loose—inhaler, EpiPen syringe, antacids, cortisone cream, antifungal shampoo, inhaled steroids, antihistamines, Tylenol, Lemon Zinger tea—into my sneakers. They became my "Pharmacy Shoes: The Perfect Apothecary For The Middle-Aged Walking Hypochondriac." I ended up using all the antihistamines, as every motel cleans its carpets with stuff that would take the paint off the space shuttle, but otherwise I never needed any of my drug supply.

The night before I left, I was delighted to find that everything fit into the pack, just about, and that I could actually lift it off the ground. But the only way I could keep the pack on my back was by unclipping a serious-looking strap apparently designed to hold my shoulder blades together, and at six the next morning, when I swung it up to my shoulder, I nearly fell off the porch. It was like wearing a house.

≈

CHAPTER 4

The Road to Jericho

There is no definitive history of hitchhiking, but the first recorded hitchhiker is Philip the Evangelist. Philip was walking the desert road from Jerusalem to Gaza when he was passed by an Ethiopian "man of great authority"—the Queen of Ethiopia's treasurer, in fact—riding in a chariot. The Ethiopian was reading aloud from Isaiah as his charioteer drove him along. At the prompting of the Holy Spirit, Philip called to him: "Do you understand what you are reading?" The Ethiopian invited Philip to ride with him and explain the text, which he did to such good effect that the Ethiopian asked to be baptized. They never saw each other again: The Ethiopian "went on his way rejoicing," and Philip made for Caesarea (Acts 8:26-40).

What I find fascinating about this story is that the spiritual benefit falls to the one in the vehicle, not the one on foot. The wealthy man may possess the vehicle and the opportunity to be generous, but in the Bible, the wise one is the poor man, the one on foot, and similar figures—gods in disguise as beggars—appear in many of the world's religions. Hitchhiking may seem to be simply about kindness in the giver, but this story, if we take it as a parable, suggests that the giver receives, too, though it's a gift he didn't expect, and certainly not from the anonymous pedestrian, the stranger in the dust.

In early July, when my trip was only a few days away, for no obvious reason I drove home through Essex Junction instead of taking the back roads, as I usually do. Standing by the road on the way out of the town, wearing a puffy ski jacket, jeans and a small pack, was a hitchhiker.

I pulled over. I wanted to quiz him on how easy or hard he'd found it to get rides, how far he'd come, what people were like to hitchhikers these days. Besides, what terrible karma it would be not to pick him up, right before I hoped for the same kind of generosity from others.

"Where are you headed?" I asked.

"Great!" he said. "I'm doing great. Just went into Burlington to help someone out. Haven't had a drink, don't worry. Thanks a lot for stoppin'." He leaned across and shook my hand. "It's my birthday," he said. "I'm 40 years old. I'm still young. I've got my life ahead of me."

His breath smelled of beer and fruit-flavored Lifesavers. My heart sank. I asked him how long he had been waiting for a ride. Somehow the question led him elsewhere, and he gestured at his rosy face.

"I been takin' medication for my thyro," he explained. "Makes my face get all puffy, and I get all hot and cold."

I sympathized. I had thyroid problems myself once, I told him. The strange thing about the medication, he said, was that it meant he'd never get drunk. "I could take any man from round here and drink a case of beer with him and not get drunk."

He thought of something. "Do you ever drink a beer?" he asked, as if he were merely curious. Yes, I said, I liked a beer with my dinner.

Suddenly he was very interested. "Would you like one now?" He reached into his small pack.

I declined hastily, saying something about cops and open-bottle laws. He nodded wisely, and settled back into his seat.

I asked him again about his journey. He said it had taken him three hours to get from Jericho to Burlington; he had done well. My heart sank again. *Three hours to do. . .what, 15 miles?* I tried to find out what he had been doing in town, but he slipped past the question as if dodging a shadow, and was off somewhere else. I remembered something I'd been told by a friend who worked in a bike shop. "You get a lot of mentally ill people coming in," he said, "because they're not allowed to drive cars, but they can ride bikes." Or hitchhike, I thought gloomily.

"Did you lose your driver's license, or do you just prefer not to drive?" I asked.

He shook his head. "Never had one," he said. "I'm 40 years old. I've got my whole life ahead of me."

"I turn off just up here," I said, pointing ahead to the light.

He was galvanized into action. "Could you take me on to Jericho?" he pleaded. "I can pay for your gas." He pulled a bunch of small bills from his pocket. "That's where I live. I'll pay for your gas."

I calculated quickly. It was no more than 15 minutes out of my way. "Sure," I said. He pressed money on me. I waved it off; he offered again. I declined again. We were through the light and making for Jericho—and a strange thing happened. As soon as

I was beyond my rut, my commuter track, driving at this odd customer's behest, the day suddenly seemed lighter, as if I were sneaking a quick vacation.

He was embarrassingly grateful. He shook my hand several times, and talked some more about his thyro. I told him about my hitchhiking plan, and he drew back in astonishment. "Well, if you can do that, you must be Superman," he said. "You must be Superman."

Within minutes, we were in Jericho. He pointed to the church as we passed it. "I'm affiliated with that church," he said. "Minister's a good man. I been shovelin' his steps all winter. He pays me 75 cents."

He kept shaking my hand. "You're a good man. You're a good guy." He lived behind the bank on the left, he explained. Maybe he told me he lived with his parents, or maybe I just guessed it.

I waited for the oncoming traffic, then pulled up in front of the bank.

"Hey, thanks a lot," he said, shaking my hand again. "I'll see you in heaven."

By now something had happened: I felt light-headed, and a little off-balance. My glibness was being worn away. "That's the plan," I said, half joking, but he would have none of it.

"Thanks again," he said, shaking my hand one last time. "I love you, brother."

∼

CHAPTER 5

Searching for That Wonderful Tribe

July 20 — New York City

At 6 a.m. on July 20, 1998, backpack swaying alarmingly above my head, I lurched up the driveway to a taxi that would take me to the airport. By 10 a.m. I was ringing the bell outside the apartment where Kathy was staying. Footsteps came to the door, the lock turned, the door opened and I saw a middle-aged woman—a stranger.

It was Kathy, but it wasn't. At 21, she hadn't worn makeup or jewelry, and her hair and skin shone. Now she wore heavy silver bracelets and had the slightly dry look of someone who has spent too many years in the sun. She asked me to call her Kathryn; no one had called her Kathy for years.

She was equally nonplussed to see me. At 20, I had a full beard and chestnut hair down to my shoulders, but the man that she saw was clean-shaven and greying. When she produced a sketch she'd done of me playing the guitar on the sands of South Wales in 1973, only my forearms and my long, pointed nose looked familiar. She and I could have sat next to each other on the subway, and we'd never have known each other. In that door-opening instant, I got the first inkling that my entire project was sunk: No matter how intimately I had known the America of 25 years ago, I wouldn't recognize it now.

We talked in the apartment, in Central Park, in a restaurant over lunch, and back at the apartment. The stories came flocking back with warmth and color: searching every greengrocer in Cornwall because she discovered I'd never tasted a mango (a mango, in Cornwall in 1973!); camping out in Wales and nearly freezing to death, ending up in an all-night laundromat. Gathering mussels on the beach below King Arthur's supposed castle in Tintagel, then accidentally leaving them under a seat in the rental car so it smelled so ghastly we barely dared to return it. Dropping books and papers to hitch down to London; trying to find the Tate Gallery, getting lost but knowing that wherever we went we were always finding things, and finding ourselves. Getting up at two in the morning and walking down to the Thames to watch the swans by moonlight. Kathy told me that her mother had recently discovered a stash of old Oxford photos. "In all of those pictures, we were posed something like the Beatles in *A Hard Day's Night.*" She laughed. "Every picture I have...making pyramids. There wasn't a straight photograph in the bunch."

We were both laughing giddily, finishing each other's sentences. "So what happened to you after you went back to college?" I asked, and then time began again, the path forked.

Her sunny, American optimism had evaporated once she was back in America. Back at college for her senior year, she fell into a black depression. Trying to find her way in the darkness, she got entangled in some confused relationships; within a couple of years she was a Des Moines mother, in graduate school, and working. "In that year in Oxford I was never lonely," she said. "When I left to go back to the States, I was very lonely. I was always searching again for that wonderful tribe, that group of hilarious, spontaneous, bright friends, and I never found it."

After nearly twenty years, she divorced, then remarried, and her life began again. It was as if she had surfaced like a submarine long overdue, rocking and bobbing uncertainly while the crew threw open the hatches for fresh air. What she had gained from that long detour, she said, was two wonderful children, and her own successful graphic design business; I didn't ask her what she thought she lost.

As she talked, she became a separate person. The grievances that I'd held against her seemed ridiculously petty against the long, slow wavelength of time; but by the same token my own presence in her life seemed incidental. The more complete she became, the less I mattered. The shared past dwindled to a small, bright point.

I asked her why she had dumped me. It was too much, she said. Both of us were younger, more fragile, and less experienced in love than the other thought; both of us were looking for the other to lead the way. I wanted her to be my America, my new-found-land, my spiritual guide. She couldn't carry that load. Nobody could. She had dropped me because I was just too much weight.

The afternoon, too, seemed to be getting heavier under the burden of my expectations. I wanted her, once again, to give me answers, yet if we met now, for the first time, we'd probably have nothing to say. The past was visible, all too clearly—but it was under glass twenty-five years thick. It was like those tantalizing visions of the Holy Grail offered to the Round Table knights who were good, but not perfect: This is all you get. You're lucky to be granted a glimpse of it, and that glimpse in itself may energize and inspire you, but you can never have it.

The reunion was almost over: we had to meet Tomasz to shoot some pictures, and then Kathy, her husband (who seemed to be deliberately keeping out of sight), and her daughter were going out for the evening. We took a cab to Times Square, where Tomasz showed up with his grin and his camera. Kathy and I goofed around, back doing those *Hard Day's Night* poses again. We had touched on that third rail of shared silliness—then it was over, we did the good-friends hug-and-kiss-on-the-cheek thing, and she was gone.

She became my guide after all. She showed me that I couldn't go back, that I would find my own path, through America, through everything. Just as I did then. She cut me loose again. At the time I didn't see that, though. The teenage boy in me had been brought back to life, and he was crushed, all over again. To hell with the past, I thought. You can't get there from here.

The following morning I woke up in a hotel in Chinatown that was surrounded by shattered streets and sidewalks, with garbage bags piled up in their dozens, and corrugated storefront shutters spattered with paint as if by small-arms fire.

Tomasz met me at the breakfast table. He raised an eyebrow. I explained.

"To tell you the truth," he said ironically, "I was surprised to see you yesterday in such a good mood."

I shrugged helplessly.

"You idolized her," he said. This was the second time I'd met the guy. Was it that obvious?

"I've always tended to idolize women," I said gloomily.

He shrugged and grinned. "Everybody does."

"That's right. The Polish are notorious romantics too, aren't they?" I said, thinking of Chopin, and of the Polish Army trying to stop Hitler's tanks with cavalry charges. He chuckled.

Breakfast done, Tomasz went off to find his rented car, and I went off to find . . . well, everything, really.

CHAPTER 6

Been a Long Time Since I Did the Stroll

July 21 — Stroudsburg, Pennsylvania

The Port Authority bus station was a dam rupturing: smartly dressed men and women poured out of every door, flooding the sidewalk in both directions, surging onto the street, scowling and waving for taxis. I picked my way through them in shorts and backpack, fighting the tide.

A guy built like a running back, head shaved, one gold earring, collapsed into the seat next to mine. He told me that he was a merchant marine and had driven 40 hours straight to catch the bus. He'd been around the world seven times. After a while, he said, every port and island had started to look the same. Now he just ran coastal routes. He had a house in the Poconos but was thinking of moving to Nevada to escape taxes. He fell asleep minutes outside of the Lincoln Tunnel, leaving me wondering what kind of omen this was: The first person I met was a world traveler who was sick of the world?

On the other side of the aisle sat a young African-American businessman whose cell phone went off, embarrassing him, as we turned onto the interstate. A quarter century ago, a half-empty bus left I-80 and bumped through rundown, dusty Newark, home of race riots. On one grubby street I had seen a single slender tree enclosed in a metal cage, as if to keep it from escaping. A van had passed, advertising "Electrified Water—Every Glass Full of Health." America's doorstep now seemed slicker and faster, the road in better fettle, bearing twice as much traffic as it raced past huge malls and billboards:

SNEAKER STADIUM

CIGARS: 450 KINDS IN STOCK

INNOVATION LUGGAGE

Not so much a road as a shopping channel.

The bus station in Stroudsburg still doubled as a store, though. I looked for signs to I-80, maybe half a mile away, past white wooden houses under maples barely changed since 1973. There were no mailmen around, but an elderly gent coming out of the *Pocono Record* office nodded and smiled. I found the interstate roaring through the valley like an asphalt river. I shrugged off my pack, hung out my thumb, and settled into my spot by the guardrail as if I had never left it. I was doing nothing, and I was doing exactly what I wanted. Anything was possible. I had arrived.

Within five minutes, two young guys in a red muscle car pulled off the interstate and paused opposite me at the head of the ramp. "Need a ride?" one called out. "Yeah!" I called back, though I couldn't imagine that they were going back onto the highway, having just pulled off. He screamed an obscenity and gave me the finger. *Guys*, I thought, *do you have any idea what a cliché you are?*

Almost at once, a blue Buick Skylark that seemed to have missed its exit off the interstate came to a halt at the bottom of the on-ramp. Must be lost, I thought. It paused, then began to reverse up the ramp. It had Virginia plates. Must be seriously lost, I thought. To my amazement, the car stopped beside me. *No! Surely not!* The window rolled down. The driver leaned across the passenger seat. It was Tomasz.

"How did you get here so quickly?" he asked, grinning in bewilderment. It was the first sign that he was used to a leisurely, time-consuming prowl, looking for the right conjunction of subjects and the perfect light, whereas I was moving at the speed of the interstate. Our coordination was already starting to fall apart.

We shook hands as if this, rather than our clownish photo-shoot in Manhattan, were the real start of the journey, and he headed off into Stroudsburg to look for small-town America. He had barely completed the complicated and illegal task of reversing up the rest of the ramp, peering around and disappearing down a maple-lined street, when a pickup pulled over and an ex-Marine, now driving for UPS, picked me up. I was on my way.

Thinking of the long trip ahead, I asked him if there were other hitchhikers on the road, or whether I was as much of an oddity as I felt. "Oh, I see a few," he said. "A couple of years ago I was working as a security guard on a construction site where they were building a mall. I picked up this hitchhiker coming east from California and he didn't have anywhere to stay, so I took him over to the construction site and found him somewhere out of the way to sleep. I always wondered what happened to him, and then, guess what? I picked him up again two years later, heading back west."

He dropped me off a dozen miles later in Tannersville, where a new mall had been carved into the woodland. "Seems like it's happening all over," he said, shaking his head. Then he was gone.

A short ride, but it was still before noon, and above all, the journey had begun. Yes, I thought, pounding the guardrail with the flat of my hand.

Ten minutes later, it was Jeff, a calm, bearded young guy, also driving a pickup. He worked for a lumber company, assisting one of their chief salesmen who was blind—and at once I imagined him feeling the clean rectangularity of a well-planed board of ash or maple, smelling the rich tang of sawdust. I wondered if, for him, smell had a hint of color—if he could detect the dense redness of cherry, the soft breezy amber of pine.

As we drove west, the Pennsylvania woodland rose and fell in gentle waves. "How has America changed over the last 25 years?" he mused. "I'd have to say that people are moving farther away from God." He cruised through the calm morning sunshine, as comfortable in his faith as he was in his driver's seat. Anyone who disagreed with his church's beliefs was damned, it turned out; discussion was Satan's way of trying to confuse and pervert the faithful. He fascinated me, though. I'd never met anyone quite like him, yet in a way he seemed no different from so many Americans I know: goodhearted but deeply mistrustful of other Americans. His stern faith seemed to be a kind of spiritual agoraphobia.

He turned off after about 30 miles at White Haven, where the interstate had a familiar everywhere-and-nowhere geography: tarmac baking in the midday sun, stubby grass, a gas station where I belatedly bought a map. All I ever saw of White Haven was a yard full of Hi-Reach cherry-picker vehicles looking like mechanical giraffes, next to which I set up my pack. I still felt uneasy beside the road. I expected that I looked like an oddity, or just a fool. I examined my clothes and fiddled with the British flag my brother had sent me. Under the pretense of conducting a scientific experiment, I strapped the flag onto my pack for 20 minutes, then took it off for 20 minutes, then gave up altogether because it was a kind of fraud: I hadn't come from England this time. I'm not really English anymore.

My next ride was in another pickup with a blue-collar guy who had his own industrial cleaning business—scouring out giant boilers and furnaces, cleaning up toxic spills—but we talked mostly about hospice, as both of us had mothers who died in that calm, luminous care.

When he let me off at a rest area after 50 miles or so, it was 1 p.m. At this rate it would take me a week to cross Pennsylvania, which I remembered vividly from my earlier trip as the first hint of the unimaginably vast breadth of America: wooded hill and valley after wooded hill and valley, the greenery interrupted only by giant yellow Sunoco signs. I love the woods, but this was just too much. I could imagine the early pioneers driven mad by struggling up to ridge after ridge and still finding no break, no view.

Overhead, the sky had been getting steadily darker, and a brisk wind had sprung up. A guy in a construction truck leaned out of his cab and said, "You might want to stick around here," meaning the rest area, which at least offered shelter. "There's a severe storm coming. Might get your ass wet."

My only fear, before I left, had been of lightning. Planning the trip I imagined myself out in one of the Great Flat States— Nebraska, say—with one of those horizon-to-horizon purple thunderstorms approaching, and the only vertical item in the entire landscape being me. What should I do? Was I safer on the road or the grass verge? Would the lightning be attracted to anything metal in my pack? Should I carry a collapsible metal pole—like a tripod, or a music stand—so that if the thunder was right overhead, I could plant it 50 feet away as a lightning rod?

"I'd get down on my knees and pray, honey!" chuckled the woman at the National Weather Service, when I called to ask. She thought about it a bit more. "No, I guess I'd dig myself a hole and jump in it." We threw jokes back and forth nervously for a moment, and then she discovered that she had a pamphlet on this very subject right on her desk. She faxed it to me.

It was called "Thunderstorms and Lightning—the Underrated Killers!" and was a fascinating document. Twelve pages long, the pamphlet spent the first nine pages convincing me that storms were much, much more dangerous than I had thought ("The air near a lightning strike is heated to 50,000° F—hotter than the surface of the sun!"), and it wasn't until page ten that I reached "What YOU Can Do!"

In the case of my Nebraska Lightning Nightmare, it boiled down to:

• wait until I feel my hair stand on end
• squat down to make myself a small target, but
• rest on the balls of my feet to minimize my contact with the ground so the lightning passes through me as quickly as possible (The longer the charge stays in your body, the more damage is done.), and
• place my hands on my knees with my head between them, but another authority—was it NOAA?—said to clasp my hands over my head to prevent contact burns to my skull.

No suggestions about packs, keys, or portable lightning rods. Of course, with my bad knees I would probably lose my balance as I squatted, fall over backward, and present the lightning with a perfect target, a rich, ripe place to set its forked foot. Next day I read about a guy in Georgia who ran into a portable toilet during a storm and was killed when the toilet was struck by lightning.

Behind me and to my left the sky turned purple. Lightning struck, first in the distant hills, then closer. Rain smashed against the road in large, ballistic drops. When confronted by the real thing, I was strangely unafraid. I pulled out my rain jacket, which I had packed near the top of my pack, and a black plastic garbage bag, which I had intelligently packed in a small mesh side compartment. I put the jacket over me, and the bag over my pack, which now looked like a large stuffed grape leaf.

The rain began falling steadily. With a bit of luck, I thought, the poor-drowned-rat-sympathy-effect would kick in. Sure enough, another pickup pulled over. I threw my grape leaf in the bed, and jumped in. No sooner had we started than the rain tripled in force, pounding the pickup, bouncing off the road. Traffic slowed to 25 mph.

Nothing creates intimacy like sharing your car with someone. There's an added intimacy when the outside world turns to liquid, running down the windows. He was a retired newspaperman with the *Philadelphia Inquirer*. As we passed a General Motors plant, he told me how GM became the nation's top car company because of World War II.

"All the automobile plants went defense. They even dug up trolley tracks for the steel and put the trolleys out of business, just to get the steel. GM jumped the gun because they knew Truman was going to drop the atomic bomb on Japan, and they started converting their plants back to automobile production six months before the war ended. That's how GM beat out Ford and became number one. Hudson and LaSalle, they couldn't compete. It took 'em a year to retool and die, and—*boom!* American Motors had to merge with Chrysler and was kicked out of the big three."

He was the first person I heard call the stripped tires beside the road "alligators," or "gator skins," and explained that these were faulty retreads: in reconditioning the tire, a new tread is sealed onto the old. As it heats up, the seal can give way, and the whole tread rips off like duct tape. He also spoke the arcane language of highway department signs, with their cryptic terms and abbreviations. This section of highway, with its blue signs "Minimal Restoration" or "13 Inch Overlay Rubblize" was a test section: The state was trying different forms of road surface to see how a layer of shredded tires under the top stratum of asphalt affects the life of the highway, its grip and its dynamics. I never found out what "Saw and Seal Joints" meant, or "Brake and Seat," but it helped to bring alive the road, the least animate feature of the landscape, to show it rippling and changing beyond our limited perception, slower than the grass but faster than the rocks.

He dropped me off at 3:30 p.m. at a rest area near Snow Shoe, Pennsylvania, a little beyond Jersey Shore, which is neither in Jersey nor on the shore. Every ride so far had been in a pickup. An hour later, I got my first ride in an 18-wheeler truck.

In 1973, I got only one ride in a truck, and that was from a guy who had actually been a successful accountant and had dropped out to drive truck for a year to get his head together. The trucker's world had been summed up for me by a graffito I saw on the wall of a gas station men's room in Iowa: ALL THE HIPPIES AND ALL THE COMMIES AND ALL THE NIGGERS IN THE WORLD AIN'T NO

MATCH FOR ONE ALABAMA TRUCK DRIVER. In England, lorry drivers had impeccable working-class credentials and were thus part of the great socialist alliance between students and workers (though this came as a surprise to many of the lorry drivers). In the U.S., they were the enemy.

But this guy was perfectly amiable. "How has trucking changed in the last 25 years? The technology, most of all," he said. Trucks are easier to drive, ride better, last longer (more than half of the trucks his company owns have more than a million miles on them, he said), get better mileage (up to eight miles per gallon, as opposed to three or four) and are more comfortable to live in: he had CB, a cellular phone, and a small television, whose antenna cable draped over my right shoulder, out through the window, and up to the roof of the cab.

The storms were still not over, and I told him my Nebraska Lightning Nightmare. He took lightning seriously. His father was a dairy farmer and had two cows killed by lightning, which struck the outside of the barn, ran inside along the milk pipe and through the milkers still attached to two of the animals. "The cows just dropped," he said.

He let me off in the late afternoon at DuBois. The on-ramp was littered with fragments of rock and concrete, bottles and cans, a dead pigeon. Women in passing cars stared at me as if I were in a zoo. Perhaps I am an endangered species, I thought.

The sun was getting low, nobody looked like they'd be stopping, and I was still in Endless Bloody Pennsylvania. After an hour or more I gave up on the ramp and climbed up onto the interstate, the open concrete stage where it was just the trucks and me. And perhaps a state trooper. After ten minutes, I was picked up by a Penn State student named Erik in a new candy-apple-red Jeep.

He was wearing fashionable bug-eye shades and holding a CD player, which he'd hooked up to the Jeep's sound system. This was my chance to find out what today's twenty-somethings listen to. I cocked an ear.

"Isn't that The Doors?" I asked him, puzzled.

"Yeah, man. They're the best," he said enthusiastically.

He was headed to a county fair to help some friends of his, who were playing in a band, set up on stage. This sounded like fun; I asked if I could come along. "Sure," he said. "That'll be cool." He was just launching into more praise for Doors albums I'd never heard of when he broke off. "Oops," he said. "Oh, well. I just missed my turn. I was supposed to pick up some of the guys back there." Did he want to go back? "Nah. They'll figure out some other way to get there."

The Jefferson County Fairgrounds were carved out of a wooded hillside near Brookville. The band, rather generically called Label, was setting up on stage in a corrugated shoebox in front of a scattering of picnic tables and benches. Half of the musicians weren't actually there because the bass player had forgotten his bass, and had set off on the one-hour round trip to get it. They had also forgotten their bug spray.

"They won't need it," Erik told me. "Mosquitoes are afraid of noise."

While they waited, I explored the fair. Not many backpacks here, not many sandals. The lemonade stand pumped two shots of pure corn syrup into my dixie cup and the juice of half a lemon. The young Army Reserves recruiter hailed me, having seen me earlier beside the interstate. He was at a disadvantage, he explained, because he didn't have any tanks or howitzers for the kids to clamber over. "The [National] Guard has those, but we don't get along with them." So his tactic, he said, was just to corner folks and talk about $40,000 toward the cost of college.

My favorite part of fairs is the animals, and my favorite animals are rabbits and chickens. The Jefferson County fair had an extraordinary chicken with the face of a Pekinese surrounded by a startled ruff of feathers. THE SULTAN, the cage label read. The world must see this chicken, I decided, and I pulled out my camera.

I've never actually done any photojournalism, but Tomasz impressed on me that the first rule is to take good notes so you can write up the captions. No caption info, no photo. I diligently wrote down the details from the cage labels: BUFF ORPINGTON #1118 SEX C (this baffled me for a long time, wondering what the other sex was after M and F), WHITE SULTAN #1118 SEX C, BUFF SILKIE #1119 SEX C-H (even more baffling). I got the soft evening light falling across the cage, the row of cages fading away out of focus to suggest the scale of the event. All that was left was to focus on the bird, point, and shoot.

I focused, pointed, and shot. Nothing happened. Instead of the usual green light, I started getting a combination of flashing yellows and oranges, as if my camera had been designed by an out-of-work traffic engineer. I tried changing the flash setting. OFF was clearly not right for in-tent shots. AUTO seemed to be having fits. The only one to work was something labeled AUTO-S, but that seemed to suffer from performance anxiety, as it gave a series of small, stuttering flashes, and then went off when I had given up on it. Still, this one, however eccentric, at least flashed, so I crouched down by the Sultan and focused.

The Sultan had clearly been bred for show, as it had developed a bizarre feeding-and-display-in-one dance. It drew itself up to its full height, looked around haughtily, abruptly ducked its head and pecked half a dozen times at the corn, then shot back up again and minced a few steps down the cage as if being watched by the MTV fashion editor. This was too good to miss. I focused on its head, pecking around on the cage floor, and pressed the shutter. The fill in flash started blipping. At once, the Sultan shot up and began mincing, the flash went off, and I had successfully photographed its feet.

All right, I thought, and focused on its head. It stopped mincing and froze. I pressed the shutter. The flash began blipping. The Sultan ducked swiftly and pecked at the corn. The flash went off, and I had successfully photographed an empty cage. This went on for about 20 frames, by which time I was frenziedly changing the flash setting every shot and pounding the shutter over and over until the flash went off. I no longer cared about composition, or even if the bloody animal was in the bloody frame: just getting the camera to go off was an achievement. Eventually I ran out of film, thank God. I threw the camera in its expensive little clip-on protective pouch and went off in search of another paper cupful of lemon-flavored corn syrup.

In front of several hundred people in the grandstand, a well-built young woman sang the national anthem. "Heather and 11 others will be competing in the county talent show on Saturday night," said the announcer, and then it was time for the tractor pull.

The Antique Pull, quaint little tractors with slanted pairs of front wheels, went first, then the Farm Stock, the big machines, shooting up more smoke than a steam locomotive as they heaved at their huge concrete sleds. The 4500 class appeared to have pulled without anyone measuring them. One tractor managed a long but very, very slow pull. "I was late for work the other day," said the announcer, who had the unruffled and laconic humor essential for county fairs, "and I *know* that was the tractor I was behind." The waiting tractors lined up around the back of the clearing, idling, giving the place the atmosphere of a cigar bar. One tractor had something wrong with its timing, and blew enchanting clusters of smoke rings out of its chimney, then backfired sharply and shot sparks backward out of its exhaust like a muzzleloader.

Meanwhile, Label had finally assembled, tuned up, and started playing Hendrix's "Red House." Twelve people were watching, their view impeded slightly by a half dozen healthy young saplings that grew between the seats and the stage. Dave "Goober" Renwick sang Eric Clapton's version of "Crossroads," though the words were not quite in the same order as when Robert Johnson wrote them. The bass player, wearing a 99 Gretzky shirt and a baseball cap, played with his back to the audience. The songs tended to peter out rather than end, but there was no doubt that Jim Kassip—if it was indeed Jim playing lead guitar—knew what he was doing. The question was what I was doing, nodding along to the songs of my youth played by kids half my age. I felt both at home and a million miles from home.

They had just started into Led Zeppelin ("Been a long time since I rock and rolled,/ Been a long time since I did the stroll"), and time was bouncing back and forth unnervingly, when I realized that I was exhausted, and that I couldn't imagine waiting three hours for them to finish so I could beg them for a place to crash. I had to get out.

But that was the catch. The cheery folk on the gate told me that Brookville, just down the hill, didn't have any kind of a motel (it says a lot about my attitude toward camping that I didn't even remember I was carrying a tent, sleeping bag, and pad), but there were several just along the interstate at the next exit, no more than four miles away.

The first problem was that no traffic at all was going onto I-80 at the Brookville exit. The second was that evening was falling, and by the time I climbed up to the interstate, it was already dark enough for drivers to think twice about stopping even if they saw me. Oh, well—I'd walk it. Four miles, call it an hour. I'd be there by 10:15, maybe 10:30. I set off along the shoulder, at first with my thumb out, then just trudging over the crown of the hill and down the other side.

It was a pleasant evening, warm and calm. The woods down to my right, deep in shadow, would have made me uneasy at 20, when darkness occasionally terrified me. That all changed when my second wife told me that she was pregnant. To my surprise, fatherhood settled around my shoulders like a coat that had been made years before and had just been waiting for me to grow into it. My fears of the dark vanished as if they had been loneliness unable to express itself.

The highway had a nice broad shoulder, so the traffic was ten or twelve feet away. After a while, I made out the rectangular shape of the next exit sign, across the valley where the road started back uphill. Four miles? It must be less than three. I'd be in bed by ten o'clock.

As darkness fell, trucks seemed to outnumber cars, and they seemed to be coming in convoys: for every singleton, there was a massive cluster of two passing three, a solid phalanx of heavy metal.

After ten minutes or so, I was close enough to the foot of the hill to realize a third problem with my plan. Where the interstate leveled, crossing the dark, wooded heart of the valley, was a bridge—a long bridge, maybe a thousand feet. The bridge had no shoulder.

The trucks, which couldn't see me, were now slamming past two or three feet away. I thought quickly: among all the clothing in my pack, did I have a single item that was reflective? No. I looked over the parapet, which was barely thigh-high. The river was a hundred feet down, and looked shallow. If I hit that, I was dead.

Curiously, I wasn't frightened. I was alarmed, certainly: The seriousness of the situation got my attention, no mistake, but it was clear what I had to do. I started running as hard as I could, the pack lolloping from side to side and threatening to topple me over the edge. I heard the next truck coming up behind me, and at the last moment I squeezed down against the parapet, trying not to stumble off the bridge. As soon as the truck had passed, I jumped up and ran again, stopped again, crouched again, then ran again, sweating hard. By the time I reached the middle of the bridge I found to my dismay that as the trucks passed, the bridge bounced. The traffic seemed to intensify. Sometimes there was so little gap between one cluster and the next, it made no sense to run on, so I just stayed huddled against the parapet, waiting for a decent break. At last the road behind me cleared, and I ran the last 20 or 30 yards, passed the end of the parapet and lurched to my right onto the shoulder, which seemed as wide as a tennis court.

Yet, it was now that I started to worry, because about 30 yards ahead of me, where the interstate began to climb again, a truck had pulled over. It looked evil, its flashers blinking, its engine idling, the cab, of course, in complete darkness. It seemed not parked but crouching. I had seen enough movies: I didn't want anything to do with it. I walked past it like a kid passing a graveyard, believing that if he didn't look, and kept repeating that he didn't believe in ghosts, he would be all right.

I'd got maybe a half dozen paces past the massive front end when I heard a short hit on the horn, not a blast but almost a quiet *ahem*. I turned round, walked back, and looked way up at the cab window. It was dark. There was nothing else for it: I put one foot up on the sill, hauled myself and the pack up to the door handle, and opened it.

The driver, a short, ordinary guy in jeans and shirt, looked across at me.

"You'd better get in before you get yourself killed," he said.

He had stopped to rescue me. This would be the pattern for the trip: I would always be afraid of the wrong things. People would turn out to be friendly; my most dangerous enemy was myself.

I'll call him Bob, as many drivers can get in serious trouble for going against company policy and picking up riders. Nothing has changed since Tom Joad was picked up by the trucker in *The Grapes of Wrath*. "Didn't you see the "No Riders" sticker on the windshield?" asks the trucker. "Sure—I seen it," Tom says. "But sometimes a guy'll be a good guy even if some rich bastard makes him carry a sticker."

Bob told me about the trucker's life, which comes down to the loads you get. Some loads pay more per mile than others—three dollars a mile is good; a dollar twenty-five is not—but a long load that pays only a dollar seventy-five may be more worthwhile than a short load that pays two twenty-five. In this respect, every trucker who works for a company is at the mercy of dispatch, universally pronounced *dis*-patch. Dispatch didn't like him, he said, because he'd complained about this and that, so now he only got shitty loads. He had family in Texas, and once in a while a load went down there, but he never got it. He was thinking of buying his own cab so he could become more independent; that was the only way to go in the long run, but he'd need bobtail insurance (a bobtail is a cab without a trailer; when you work for a company they'll insure you only while you're pulling their load) and the owner-financed deal he was looking at, buying a used cab from a fleet owner, sounded pretty shady: If he missed a single payment, ownership of the cab would revert to the seller.

I offered to buy him a cup of coffee and a piece of pie. He thought about it for a moment. "I wouldn't say no," he said, and we pulled up on the weedy fringes of a huge truck stop lot that looked like a giant warehouse, the trucks all virtually the same shape and size, chrome crates stacked side by side. Inside, all the tables had phones—another innovation since 1973—and a remarkable number of truckers were using them, calling wives and family, calling dispatch.

He told me some of his own army hitchhiking days. Much of his travel had been in the South. I told him I had avoided the South. "After seeing *Easy Rider*, I was convinced that some redneck'd shoot me."

He chuckled. "Won't shoot you," he said. "Might run you over." He was hitching somewhere in the South and was passed by a cop. A couple of hours later the same cop came by again. He called Bob over and said, as cops do, "Son, you got a choice"—but this was an unusual choice. "Either you let me get you a ride, or I arrest you." It seems some wacko had been swerving off the road and hitting hitchhikers. So the cop got on the CB and said, "This is Smokey the Bear. I'm at mile so-and-so. I need someone to pick up a hitchhiker," and explained why. A few minutes later a semi pulled over, and Bob was on his way.

He was less lucky in West Virginia, where a cop threw him off the freeway and wouldn't even drive him to the next exit, but made him bushwhack 150 yards through woods and undergrowth down to a little country road running parallel to the highway. "I was lucky if there was one car an hour, and that wasn't going anywhere because he lived on that road and was just going home." His luckiest trip, he said, was Jasper, Texas, to Bangor, Maine, in 45 and a half hours. If there were a Hitchhiker's Hall of Fame, that would put him in it.

Back in the cab, the CB kept up an intermittent speckled chatter. In that strange dark industrial world of Bob's cab, lit only by his instruments, within the equally strange world of a midnight interstate lit only by vehicle lights and flanked by orange barrels, the CB was the voice of those who worked overtime while the rest of America slept.

"Can you smell burning?" I asked Bob near the Ohio border. He sniffed. "Smells like brakes," he said, though it smelled more like rubber to me. He ran a quick internal check. "Not coming from me," he said, meaning his truck. He got on the CB. "Anyone out there smell burning?" he asked. A no and a yes from other voices, running somewhere close to us in the darkness. The smell kept up. "Must be someone up ahead," Bob said. "Hasn't got his CB on."

For ten or fifteen minutes we continued to smell something burning; every so often the CB would alive with another invisible trucker saying, "Yeah, I smell it too." An ad came on for what sounded like a body shop and tattoo parlor, which I thought must be a wonderful combination business, like a gas station and charm school.

Finally, just into Ohio, Bob's headlights fell on some big vehicle, an SUV or a pickup, towing a trailer with a large inflatable pontoon boat on it. The truck was slowing down and pulled onto the shoulder. The smell was so strong it was amazing nothing had caught fire.

Passing the truck, we plunged through the darkness toward the Ohio line. Bob dropped me off well after midnight at Truck World, just across the state border in Hubbard, Ohio. It was an enormous truck stop, the largest I saw on the whole trip, with its own small motel surrounded on three sides by parked trucks. I staggered in, as filthy as I've ever been in my life, dried sweat on dried sweat on dried sweat. The guy running the motel was a chubby, graying Indian gentleman.

"Please tell me you've got a room," I gasped.

"No," he said.

My jaw fell, aghast.

"Just kidding," he said.

It was a decent room, in that the bed was horizontal. I found dried blood all over my left knee from a two-inch gash. I had no idea how it had gotten there. I fell asleep to thunder and lightning, and the distant rumble of idling diesels.

CHAPTER 7

The Vagabond, When Rich

July 22 — Hubbard, Ohio

I f there's one thing that has changed in 25 years, it's truck stops. Truck World had a game room, an ATM, and a booth offering Internet access for a quarter. It also had its own curious highbrow streak, expressed in a series of maxims neatly painted on boards hanging in the restaurant:

LIFE IS A CAFETERIA: HELP YOURSELF

INTELLECT IS INVISIBLE TO THE MAN WHO HAS NONE

And my favorite:

THE VAGABOND WHEN RICH IS CALLED A TOURIST.

Paging through my notebook over eggs and corned beef hash, I found that I had already forgotten the faces of everyone who had picked me up. When you hitchhike, you get to know the drivers who pick you up in a nonvisual way. You plough on mile after mile, looking ahead, the white line flicking under you like a hypnotist's pendulum. All that you see of each other is a glance of profile every few miles. Every time I get a long ride and we stop for a bite to eat, I make sure that I take a long look at the guy's face as we climb out, stretch, and amble over to a restaurant. I've found out things about this guy that I don't know about my best friend, but, if I take my eyes off him, I'll spend the next fifteen minutes wandering from table to table trying to find someone who looks familiar.

I called Tomasz on his cell phone. He was somewhere north, closer to Lake Erie. You've got to see this place, I said.

So he motored over and we ate breakfast together, while Tomasz stared in fascination at a couple of giant, hairy truckers—the exception, not the rule—wondering where they got their tattoos.

He asked me how the previous day had been different from what I remembered of my trip in 1973. Was hitchhiking harder now? Easier? More dangerous?

No, none of the above. More interesting, I said.

This was a surprise to me. After all, novelty had left that first visit permanently endowed with the brilliant visual clarity of a dream. What adventure could compete? Yet, looking back, it seemed to me that I'd just sat there passively and let it all roll by. I had the shallow fascination that only a visitor can afford: I'd come to conquer, not to fit in. Besides, I was traveling with Richard. Hitchhiking with a companion is safer, but leaves you less open to chance. When the two of us were on speaking terms we were a small, traveling England, resisting the Americanness of America; when we weren't, the wait seemed longer and there was half as much space on the side of the road. It was when I was on my own that I felt circumstance peeling me open.

Beyond that, in 1973 we encountered our own kind—to such a degree that I can't remember ever speaking to someone of color on the whole trip. It seems to me now that I had very little sense of other people's kindness and tolerance, or curiosity about how they lived and what they thought. I got one ride from Lincoln, Nebraska, to San Francisco in a VW bus with a bed, eight-track, baby fridge—the whole nine yards—five male hitchhikers, one female driver called Robin and her big white dog Shantih (Sanskrit for "peace"), yet I can't remember anything interesting that anyone said during the entire 1,700 miles. I whiled away most of the time reading an enormous stack of DC and Marvel comics. No wonder it all seemed so golden and carefree. We were like children given an entire continent as our sandbox.

In 1998, I was meeting working America, and it seemed a less privileged, more real encounter. I was meeting people who were nothing like me. I loved it.

So much, in fact, that I decided to head off next to Cleveland, the epitome of blue-collar cities, butt of a thousand jokes. "I think I come with you," Tomasz said thoughtfully. Well, that was easy, I thought. Hitched a ride just sitting here eating breakfast.

Bill DiLillo, my tennis partner in Vermont, grew up in Cleveland. I called him while I was on the road; he alerted his dad, and Tomasz and I were off in the Skylark. We found Tony DiLillo in a dim retirement home on the outskirts of Cleveland that smelled of resignation, with an Indians cap on his settee and a copy of *Inside the Vatican*, a lavish photo book, on the coffee table. "This was shot by a friend of mine," Tomasz said, fingering the gilded pages.

Tony, now widowed, was a strong man only slightly bowed by time. He had been born and brought up in Little Italy. With a little prompting he agreed to join us in the Skylark and show us the neighborhood. He told us about the Italian-American Brotherhood Club, where the political deals were made, with boxing in the back room. "Some of the best lightweights that ever fought fought there."

We dragged west toward the city past mall after mall until the road took a sudden twisting dive, and we were in the narrow, colorful streets of Little Italy. Here, as in other American cities, even the poorer Italians built walled, sunny gardens behind their houses, filling them with peach and pear trees and grapevines. The DiLillos bought rather than grew their grapes, but they did have their own press, and Tony had helped his father press the grapes and make the wine. After six months of fermenting, the wine was ready, and at once friends and relatives would start to drop in. "We always had two bottles of wine on the table, growing up."

Over there was the corner where he sold papers, 65, 70 years ago. "Two cents a paper. I made 25 cents, 30 cents." He showed us Guarino's restaurant—"This used to be a pool hall. I used to play pool in the back"—and the Holy Rosary Church—"That's where I was baptized and got married."

Outside the church, a cheerful stout woman was selling raffle tickets for the Feast of the Assumption, when the Virgin is carried in effigy around the streets of Little Italy. A local drunk—bottle in brown paper bag, only one tooth in his head—was talking big, saying he was going to steal the poor box. "If they have a poor box, I might as well take it. I'm poor."

The cobbled streets and idiosyncratic little brick houses and shops of Little Italy are a prime target for gentrification. "We used to have all kinds of grocery stores, hardware stores, dry goods stores," Tony said. "Now it's all art stores." We passed the cemetery where his wife was buried. "And this is where I will be, when the time comes."

Having nothing much else to do, Tony agreed to spend the next few hours with us. He climbed back into the front seat and directed us through a series of increasingly broad and well-landscaped streets, past the city's palatial civic buildings toward the hot, flat, decrepit industrial downtown and the West 25th Street Market. A cluster of long, narrow, old, brick buildings, the market seemed European rather than American, its cluttered geometry bringing vendors, customers, and produce together in a proximity that suggested a relationship rather than a transaction. In the meat-cheese-and-fish building, for instance, I could smell what everyone was buying, especially the bracing salty halloo of fish, 56 kinds gazing one-eyed from the slabs, their names written up on the blackboard, including some that I'd never heard of, like buffalo and blackfish, the chalk handwriting itself a developed art, and one nearly lost to computer graphics and the uniform printed signs of franchises.

Finally, Tony took us to the most arrant and cynical manipulation of time and memory, what Tomasz called, "This pyramid of nonsense": the Rock and Roll Hall of Fame and Museum. Perched on a fabulous, and fabulously expensive, plot of groomed grass overlooking the lake, it was like an expensive oldies-theme-restaurant-and-gift-shop, but without the food.

No Photography signs hung everywhere. Tomasz disappeared to try to get permission to shoot. Tony and I wandered aimlessly, scowling at Annie Liebowitz's photographs, snorting at the aisles of T-shirts and CDs and gift trinkets. It was Graceland without the kitsch. No juice, no guts, a representation of rock-and-roll without the spirit. If it could really embody rock 'n' roll, it would be an electrifying disaster: Pete Townsend jamming his guitar through its ceiling, Bill Haley's fans tearing up the seats, Hendrix setting fire to it, Grace Slick slipping acid into its water coolers, Jim Morrison exposing himself in it, Brian Jones dying in its pool.

Tomasz came back. No dice. We gotta get out of this place, I thought, even if it meant missing the Flying Elvises, due to parachute down on the Hall on August 8.

We dropped Tony off at his gloomy retirement home, and headed off into the unknown. As soon as we were heading back east along two-lane blacktop in search of Amish territory, the country seemed to shrink and flatten. I began to wonder why I was already bored, when Tomasz pulled off the road at a garden statuary business, fascinated by an 18-foot fiberglass giraffe. I was walking along between gnomes and bambis, when a wasp stung me. My hand must have brushed it in midair, because by the time I felt it and looked down, the insect had gone. I found one of a dozen assorted ornamental ponds and laid my hand under the cool running water. It wasn't especially painful, and after a few minutes it seemed like the perfect way to spend this hot, dull day—sitting on a low wall, letting the water run over my arm.

Amid the pleasant open fields of Amish country, we stopped to visit a cheese factory. I'd love to do an *Across America by Cheese* book, except that I'm almost completely uncritical. Doughty Valley: very nice. Middlefield Swiss: very nice, if a bit sweaty after five hours in a car. Full of romantic potential, though: "Excuse me, ma'am. I'm doing a story on the Cheeses of Madison County. You wouldn't happen to have a glass of lemonade to go with this chunk of Bakersfield Brie I've been keeping in my shirt pocket?"

Tomasz spotted a beautiful, shy, 19-year-old Amish girl leading her horse to the barn and found out that she was going to a friend's 20th birthday party. We followed the little buggy at ten miles an hour along a series of lanes, the Amish cornstalks with their curious braided crests glowing in the low sunlight. When we arrived, though, the mother of one of the Yankee (the Amish word for all outsiders) girls at the party threw us off the property, made uneasy by our stalker's pace, our intrusion. "People pick on the Amish because they're kind of backward," she said forcefully. "Please leave."

"Saturday night in Toledo is like being nowhere at all," Tomasz read from *Road Trip USA*, which he had bought in an increasingly desperate desire to find photogenic America. But as we skirted Cleveland to the south, trudging through one stoplight after another in the rain, past bank after bank advertising its drive-through ATM and an endless succession of convenience stories offering cut prices on soda and cigarettes, everywhere was nowhere at all.

"I went to the woods," Thoreau wrote, "because I wished to live deliberately, to front only the essential facts of life, and see if I could learn what it had to teach, and not, when I came to die, discover that I had not lived."

But going to the woods no longer works. In some respects, I already live in something of a 20th-century Walden, in my unassuming little house on ten acres in Vermont with a small wood and a beaver stream, but it's no longer the retreat it might have been in 1845, or even in 1965 when the first of the hippies began moving up here from the big, rotten apple. Planes from Burlington airport climb the violet morning sky, the New York train moans from across the ridge, the world rushes in by Federal Express truck, telephone and modem. Those of us who moved to the woods did nothing to solve the problems of the greater society and everything to hasten them by removing our money, our intellectual capital, and our goodwill. In the end this came back to haunt us, in the form of an America that sends a new suburb or a Wal-Mart steaming into the fields around us like an aircraft carrier while we howl impotently. It's impossible, these days, to be as isolated as Thoreau, that old proto-hippie—except, perhaps, by being Amish and running the risk of being stared at or stalked. In the long run, we're much better off going back into town, getting elected to the planning commission and making sure that in 50 years time there still are woods, not merely rows of little semi-dwarf crabs and sand cherries planted between Circuit City and Toys 'R' Us.

We crawled toward the outskirts of Sanduskie, Ohio, where the air stank of bitumen, then started looking for a motel with ground-floor rooms that opened directly onto the parking lot so Tomasz could back the car right up to the room, and not carry his equipment more than 15 feet. He traveled with three cameras (four, after he bought an old Brownie at a junk shop), tripods, lenses, special suitcases—probably more than 50 pounds of stuff in all. Once he was shooting in Spain, he said, and his entire back seized up from lugging so much weight around.

The air inside the hotel was acidic; whatever chemical they had used to clean the carpets was still hanging around, and at once began to go to work scouring the linings of my sinuses. Tomasz tugged at cigarette after cigarette as he worked out the day's expenses. I tossed and turned for two hours, feeling wretched, not knowing why. At one in the morning I woke from a half-sleep with the revelation that I had done nothing all day of my own free will. I had not been a vagabond: I had been a tourist.

To hell with it. I'd go and have a swim in the motel's tiny pool. I woke Tomasz to see if he wanted to come too. He stared at me in disbelief, through one eye—"What the ...? Am I dreaming? What time is it?"

On the flagstone walk sat a large toad. The toad, I seemed to remember, was a Hopi symbol of wisdom. I squatted down and looked at the toad, which looked at me for a moment. Then I padded off to the pool. The gate in the three-foot-high chain-link fence was locked. This was the funniest thing I had ever seen. I hopped over it, watched the parking lot lights swaying on the almost still water, and slipped in.

CHAPTER 8

"Public" Being a Dirty Word

July 23—Sandusky, Ohio

"A*gh*," Tomasz groaned from under his bedcovers. "You are one of those born with the propeller in the arse. You have to move all the time."

It was true. I wanted to get moving, as I always like to in the mornings, to get the day on the road. "Morning is when I am awake and there is dawn in me," said Thoreau. Over a quick breakfast, I chatted with a couple from Erie and their two preteen daughters. They were all on their way to the amusement park at Cedar Point, which the father had last visited 20 years ago. Must have changed a whole lot since then, he said, they added all sorts of rides. What's your favorite music? I asked the girls. "The Beatles and the Beach Boys," they answered.

We arched north through to the shores of Lake Erie in the hope of a photo, but everything was buried in fog. "Drop me at a rest area on I-80," I told Tomasz. The overcast sky and the dulled green of the alluvial fields made me feel trapped. As we made our way southwest, Tomasz told me that by his calculations he had narrowly missed death 14 (I think) times. In El Salvador, he was in a helicopter with eight soldiers. The pilot, who was drunk, hit a 700,000-volt power line. Luckily, it wasn't live—there had been an earthquake, and the grid was down—but the chopper still came down. Four were killed instantly, the others died later, one of whom had had both legs cut off above the knee by his metal seat. It was an hour and a half before help arrived.

Then there was the Coast Guard flight he was supposed to be on, but he got delayed on his way to the airport and it left without him. Forty minutes later it crashed, killing everyone on board. Or the time he was shooting a story on the St. Lawrence River for NATIONAL GEOGRAPHIC. He hired a light plane to do some shooting, got on very well with the pilot, and agreed that he would come back later to shoot more pictures. Shortly afterward, a mutual friend hired the same plane and the same pilot. The plane crashed, killing both of them. Or the time he hired a helicopter with a very young Indian pilot who neglected to mention that this was his first flight since getting his license. They flew into fog. The pilot panicked. They ended up landing blind—and discovered they were in the courtyard of a factory. They had missed a solid metal gantry by a very small margin. When a more experienced pilot arrived to retrieve the chopper, he was afraid to try taking off, and decided to remove the rotors and truck the chopper out. I made a mental note never to travel with Tomasz in anything other than a car.

He drove a few miles up I-80 and dropped me off where he could also get gas, cigarettes, and more coffee. Gasoline vapor wafted over from the pumps. I petitioned truckers in their cabs and got a series of silent head-shakes. The morning had become hot and sweaty under a dull, glazed sky of no color at all. A cop, racing past on the interstate, honked angrily and pointed: hidden behind a parked truck was a sign saying, NO HITCHHIKERS. This had been my fear before I left: that after three weeks I'd still be stuck in Ohio.

It was over an hour before a courteous, elderly gentleman pulled over in a Lincoln Town Car, possibly the only Town Car in the world at that moment with three bricks in the trunk. He was George Persinger, and he was restoring Toledo Cathedral. Every brickyard, he explained, produces a slightly different brick. One of his jobs for the day was to take the bricks around every yard in western Ohio until he found a match for each of them.

We drove into Toledo with George explaining to me that dirt doesn't penetrate limestone, so you can scrub it clean with a wire brush, but it penetrates sandstone to a depth of up to three-quarters of an inch, so it needs sandblasting. And that decorating a ceiling with gold leaf isn't as expensive as it sounds: an ounce of gold, beaten to the thinness of leaf, should cover an acre.

He was one of a family of 18. "All we've ever done is mason work," he said. He's been doing restoration work since he was 25, and it goes far beyond bricks and stone: In the cathedral he'll raise tile, put up netting to keep pigeons off the statues, replace wood sheeting with cedar to resist rot and insects, replace wiring, heating, ducting, insulation....In one place, he found that the heating ducts had never been hooked up, so for years the vapor in them had been simply piped into an attic, where the condensation had rotted all the sheeting. "I spent 24 days in that attic," he said.

We circled the cathedral, and he showed me the nearby storage building, guarded by a Rottweiler, where they keep $50,000 worth of copper for the flashing and gutters. "This isn't the best end of town," he said dryly. The other day someone had broken out all the windows of five parked cars, and then the following day had come back and done the same to thirteen more. A diocesan report on the cathedral wrote: "Locks on doors seem to be jimmied regularly.... In our choir door entrance, two stained glass panels have been vandalized...one entirely and one with bullet hole."

He parked on a leafy street on the good side of the cathedral, and met his sons Tim and Chris, who reported on progress, then all three took me on a tour. The stone steps had previously been mended with up to six inches of caulking, which traps water, instead of mortar, so the rain had worked gullies all round the caulk. That all had to be replaced. Between the stones of the cathedral itself, someone had used caulking covered with a thin veneer of sand instead of mortar; George got out his penknife and scratched at it, and the solid-looking joint made a dull rubbery noise instead of a healthy scrape, leaving the gray caulk exposed.

He opened the main door, and in the darkness of the interior, all I could see were several blue stained glass lights from a window somewhere on the far side of the building, swimming like celestial fish.

He threw on some lights. It was a fine building, smaller and younger than the European cathedrals I'd known, but majestic, well proportioned, and decorated to the hilt in the Catholic fashion. I counted dozens of different marbles in one flight of inlaid steps alone. At the same time, the full scale of the restoration job became apparent: 150 light fixtures to be cleaned, repainted, the cheap plastic fittings replaced with brass "candles," the cracked marble above the heating registers to be replaced. Limestone was shipped in from France, marble from Italy. The pulpit—all wood, pins rather than nails or screws—and made of wood from the Black Forest had to be entirely rebuilt, and, up on the ceiling, a tide line showed where the first few sections had been cleaned and repainted (from a scaffold, like Michelangelo) while the rest remained dull. I had a sense of parallels, of a faith built soul by soul, a cathedral built stone by stone.

The walls and windows, especially above the votive candles, were so black with soot that the parishoners didn't know they were stone. Such restoration changes entirely the emotional tenor of worship. The stained-glass windows before cleaning were solemn; afterwards, they were joyful.

George's son Chris was stripping and repainting wooden carvings and reliefs. "They get that from their mother, who's very artistic," George said. The boys have been doing restoration work since they were in high school. He sent them off to do work at Mary Wood College in Scranton, Pennsylvania. "I told them, 'Get in the truck and drive it around, so they know you're at least 16,'" he chuckled.

One of George's brothers was now on the job, too. "I know I can trust them," he said. "I could call in someone who says he's been doing something for 50 years, but that still doesn't mean he's going to do it right."

Before we left, George chatted to one worker who had just come down from the roof. He had been way up in the battlements, trying to work loose a large piece of carved stone in a space so tight that he could only use his fingertips.

"Show me your hands," I asked him.

He held out the large, rough hands of a mason.

"Turn them over." Two of his knuckles were grazed and oozing.

He grinned. "Most days I skin a couple of them," he said cheerfully.

Despite my resolution to travel in the present rather than the past, I did decide to make for Evanston, Illinois, just north of Chicago, where Mitzi's parents, Karl and Alberta Porges, still lived.

On the map, Chicago seemed to extend in a blotch of suburbs and townships from South Bend, Indiana, halfway to the Iowa border. Major cities are always a headache to hitch through: on the way in you're always being dropped off in some out-of-the-way suburb; on the way out nobody knows where you want to go, so you're faced with what John Dos Passos described as "the walk out of town with sore feet to stand and wait at the edge of the hissing speeding string of cars where the reek of ether and lead and gas melts into the silent grassy smell of the earth."

Besides, I was falling behind schedule, haunted by my fear of never getting farther than Ohio. George offered to take me to the Greyhound station, where the manager behind the ticket desk warned me not to throw my receipt away. My credit card number was on it, and someone might root through the trash, find the one and use the other. We must be close to some level of desperation, I thought—and sure enough, two women arrived to harass him loud and strong over something that happened the previous day. This was the bus as public transport, "public" being a dirty word in America.

The bus driver was a short, sharply dressed young African American whose name was James E. Carter. As soon as he pulled us onto the highway, he ran through his own version of Greyhound's house rules in a cool amused tone.

"There will be no smokin' or drinkin' on the bus, and no snortin', injectin' or hallucinatin'. If you smoke or drink, I'll pull over at the next service area and put you out. If you're snortin', injectin' or hallucinatin', I'll pull over at the next service area and *I'll* get out." He skillfully paused for effect. "Just messin' with you. My name is James. I'm not the driver for this trip. Your driver for this trip is our heavenly father."

Soon the greasy sky of Ohio was gone, and we were in Hoosier farmland. A hawk circled over a swamp. I saw my first triple trailers, and James advised us to set our watches back to Central Time. In the fields, long insectlike irrigation crawlers were parked alongside the roadside fences, not needed at the moment because of the recent torrential rain—three inches in an hour, the same downpour that had hit me in Pennsylvania. The corn was as high as an elephant's thigh.

We pulled off for a fast-food break at a service-area restaurant. "If this bus should peel off and leave you," James warned us dryly, "it might take six hours for Greyhound to find you and pick you up."

We clambered off and back on with our Styrofoam lunches, turning the bus into a dining car. A woman with a Tennessee twang, sitting across the aisle from me, confessed, "First time I've eaten today."

She was traveling with a young boy, who was sitting in the seat behind me. She was loving and attentive; he was well behaved. They were from near Elkhart, Indiana. She was his aunt, or perhaps his grandmother. They had been on the bus for more than 23 hours. "Where are you coming from?" I asked. "Barre, Vermont," she said happily. Barre is an old quarrying town, remarkable mainly for its place in the history of industrial safety. It was in Barre that the Italian anarchists, stonecutters, and skilled monument carvers held out against the bosses because of the lethal conditions in the cutting sheds, where marble and granite dust filled their lungs, slowly killing them.

The boy, whom she called TJ and who was just going into sixth grade, had done a school project on Vermont. Fell in love with the place. So they took a week's vacation, two days each way on the bus, three nights and two days in central Vermont, seeing Barre, Montpelier, a granite quarry, and a mall.

Did they see the mountains? From a distance. Lake Champlain? The state house? No. "We found all kinds of things on the Internet," she said, "but in the end we didn't get round to any of them." He wanted to buy a CD to add to his collection of three, but they ended up with everything but: T-shirts, ashtrays, mall souvenirs of Vermont. Then back on the bus. Now he wanted to go back when there was snow on the ground and learn to ski.

To me there was an epic quality to their trip—two days on the bus each way! It made hitchhiking seem spoiled—but there was also something sad. When they arrived in Vermont, how on earth were they supposed to get to the Green Mountains, or the lakes, or even the Ben and Jerry's ice cream factory, now the state's top tourist attraction? It's a small state; but even so, nothing is within walking distance. And if you wait for a train or a bus, you'll die waiting. The mall makes perfect sense. It's one of the few American public spaces designed for pedestrians.

I spent the next hour chatting with a young Baptist—a nice kid, clearly, as he had chatted to TJ about CD's, in flagrant violation of the teenage rule that you never talk to kids younger than you. He was coming back from Connecticut: he'd just up and gone off to see a girl he knew, a friend. Twenty-four hours on the bus each way. "It gets cold on the bus at night," he said. Cleveland had terrified him. When the bus took a layover, he had made it only as far as the crust of humanity at the entrance of the Greyhound station, where guys had begged money or offered to sell him drugs, and women had offered to sell him something more. His parents had been hippies and hitchhikers, he said, so maybe he inherited their wanderlust. The greatest time of his life, he said, was last summer when he went with a group from his church, more than a dozen of them in a van, telling stories, singing songs, sleeping all over each other, all the way to Mexico to help build houses for the poor. Yet it might not happen again. The church might throw him out, as they had done to a girl he knew, for secretly listening to his rock-and-roll CD's.

"What should I do?" he asked.

"Well, what do you believe?" I asked back.

He couldn't say. Instead he repeated what he had been taught, and as he spoke he seemed to lose his youth and his vitality. You either believed the true faith, he told me glumly, echoing Jeff the lumber salesman, or you were damned, and the true faith was as follows....

He's a good kid, I thought, but his church is going to lose him.

A narrow stack of skyscrapers rose over the horizon, and freeways struck at us from all directions. It must have been somewhere near here, back in 1973, that the truck taking me from Wilkes-Barre to Evanston broke down beside the Edens Expressway, and, knowing virtually nothing about automotive repair, I crawled underneath, waggled a few wires, and fixed it.

The bus extricated itself from the interstates and chugged into the South Side of Chicago as if into the Third World. The overpasses were rickety, the pavement shattered, the small buildings the urban equivalent of tarpaper shacks. Billboards advertising $50 divorces and bankruptcy lawyers sprouted among them like weeds. Every fourth building, it seemed, was a storefront revivalist church, and I found myself thinking of the Toledo Cathedral. Respect for materials is a close cousin to respect for spirit—which is perhaps why the devastated landscapes of South Chicago were a sign of injuries to the spirit and why there were so many revivalist churches.

Before long James was on the mike again. "On your right, you'll see a very tall building. That's the Sears Tower. For those of you wanting a fine view of Chicago, it has an observation deck on the 103rd floor..."—a well-timed pause—"If that's a little too high up for some of you, a little farther over you'll see the John Hancock building, with the two red antennae. That has an observation deck on the 60th floor. If that's still a little too high for some of you, you will now see on your right the Greyhound building. That has an observation deck on the first floor."

The sad moment had arrived, he announced, when he must part company with us. "Greyhound hires only professional and handsome drivers. Ladies, if over the last eight hours you've fallen in love, become infatuated or been seized by passion, please, please, please control yourselves when leaving the bus." He offered thanks to the Light of the World for a safe trip.

I stepped into the tiny subway station and was immediately out of my depth. I needed to take three or four different-colored lines, apparently, but there was no map immediately visible and no sign of how much this would all cost me. By the turnstiles, a chuckling knot of three guys spotted me and beckoned me over in a small explosion of welcome. A short round one, who seemed to be the station manager in the sense that this tiny tiled antechamber was his stage, gathered money from my hand, fed it into a ticket machine, and fed the ticket through the turnstile while introducing a taller, skinny guy as "The Mayor."

"Pleased to meet you, your Honor," I said, recognizing one layer of irony and sensing others. We shook hands, and I was ushered through the gate toward the trains—but at once I heard calling behind me, and The Mayor (whose name, I gathered, was George) was running to catch up with me and volunteering his services to walk me through the kaleidoscope of lines that I apparently needed to take. As we walked, he launched into a story so fluid and convincing it couldn't possibly have been entirely true, or entirely false. Could I guess where his accent was from? he demanded. He bet I couldn't because he had worked in 17 states doing track repair for the railways, and even when he was down in Atlanta they thought he was from Georgia, or something....They called him "The Mayor" because he was always giving food or money to those who needed it, his daughter was getting her Ph.D., but he had been downsized, but that was okay. The only problem was that now he lived 67 miles away and his train was leaving in half an hour and he needed $17 for the fare....He glided with me from Clinton to Belmont and from one subject to the next with the fluent fiction of the rural auctioneer. Here was my platform, with the three guys playing drums, percussion, and guitar; here was my train. I gave Mayor George $10 for his guidance and his entertainment, and considered it money well spent.

"All aboard, step up, step in, doors are closing." And the train slid off, above ground now on its carnival erector set of rusted scaffolding, impossible to take seriously. The most enchanting feature of the Chicago's elevated trains is that they are so clearly an afterthought, passing barely ten feet from the windows of the little brick houses and the third- and fourth-floor balconies and decks set out with chairs, barbecues, even a hammock, as if the train were a sunset over a lake, with trout leaping for flies.

I was making for Evanston, where Karl and Alberta Porges still lived, and where I spent my first Fourth of July all those years ago, astonished and vaguely disturbed by the weird draft-the-kids militarism of the parade and the unself-conscious flag-waving, just when the country seemed to have come to its senses and decided to back out of a war nobody wanted anymore. Astonished also by the spaciousness of green American suburbia, the gray squirrels—rarer in England—running through the yards. As the light began to fail I found Judson Avenue, named for the redoubtable Philo T. Judson, the first treasurer of Northwestern University, and was surprised all over again. This is no ordinary suburb but a regatta of magnificent wooden houses with deep porches, fronted by tall, mature trees and with no less than ten paces of grass between the sidewalk and the road. Even this was a little threadbare, Alberta said, since the Fourth of July tornado last year, which had brought down so many trees the city had to come and cut her out of her own house.

Both Alberta and Karl were bent over in considerable back pain, and moved with difficulty, but even so Alberta made me the best meal I had eaten in five days. Afterward she and Karl fought to tell me the history of Evanston, whose first house was a tavern on the Green Bay Trail but ironically became the home of the Women's Christian Temperance Union, which promptly made it a dry town. "Chicago" was an Indian word for a foul-smelling swamp plant, skunk cabbage, or wild garlic. Every agricultural product, in the days before railroads and refrigeration, had to be both portable and imperishable. Hogs were cured into ham, corn was distilled into bourbon, and logs were made into rafts or barrels. The settlers floated the rafts down to New Orleans, broke them up, sold the logs, and then walked back to Illinois.

Karl, recently retired from a career in nuclear physics, told me of a college roommate who had hitchhiked around the world in the late 1930s. He set off at the beginning of summer, rode the rails to San Francisco, worked across the Pacific as a stoker, worked in Japan as an English-language reporter, and rose to become a fashion editor; bought a ticket on the Trans-Siberian Railway, took a ship from Gdansk to New York, and arrived in Cambridge a week before term restarted.

My days are parabolic, I wrote in my notebook. *In the morning I'm young and optimistic; by evening I'm the middle-aged man falling to earth, missing his family. If I were 20 I would be making awkward and futile attempts to get laid. I seem to prefer middle age.*

CHAPTER 9

In the Silverware Drawer

July 24—Evanston, Illinois

I woke up with my left knee in agony. This was the knee operated on two years ago. While lying on the table, cheerfully stoned from the spinal, I heard the surgeon curse, and knew that things were not going well. The pain, I thought, was probably caused by tissue, swollen from several miles of hiking on Chicago's hard streets, pressing on a nerve. If so, I should rest it, and with luck the swelling would subside in a couple of days, I told myself firmly, trying to ignore the voice of middle age—constantly alert for signs of that final crash into decrepitude—yelling, *It's finally happened. The cartilage has ripped right out.*

I decided I'd call Tomasz and hitch a ride with him for a bit. Did this constitute cheating? Well, yes, of course, but I had six weeks to make it around America, and in any case, perhaps I should accept the luxuries of middle age along with its liabilities.

It was a glorious morning, leafy and quiet with the sun falling through sprinklers, so I left a thank-you note, tiptoed out of the house, and limped into Evanston. I was up so early the only place to have breakfast was a Starbuck's. I despise Starbucks, which has succeeded in making the most iconoclastic of public spaces, the coffee-house, both pretentious and generic. As I sat in the window nibbling on an expensive muffin and keeping one eye on my laundry going round in the laundry across the road, one espresso drinker timidly approached another. "Good morning! Heard you the other night, the Beethoven Ninth. Really liked it." Heard as in attended the concert, it seemed. The musician, clearly one of the star soloists, immediately launched into an appraisal of his own fine performance and bemoaned the trials of working with the numbskulls surrounding him, including another soloist ("she's renowned for her hissy fits"), whom the concertgoer had praised, but not including James Levine, whom the soloist called "Jimmy." A blond girl crossed the street, a coffee in each hand, to where her blond friend, sunglasses atop her head, was waiting in a Mercedes.

When my laundry was dry I refilled my pack, shuffled to the station, and took the El into Chicago, where everything was three and a half painful blocks away. At Union Station—vast, magnificent and empty, a cathedral to a forgotten religion—I was told that trains don't go to Des Moines, or Iowa City, or in fact most anywhere. Then more limping to the post office, apparently designed for track-and-field events, where it took me four or five minutes just to reach the escalator. I caught sight of my knee in the oceanic plate-glass window, and the double glazing made the bulge look grotesque. Then another three and a half blocks to the Greyhound station. A tall, thin guy looked me up and down: "Man, I sure hope you ain't plannin' on goin' far," he said.

After some unsuccessful punching at the sock phone, which I had already discovered to be useless when I was out in the country near mountains, or if there was a cloud in the sky, I found a pay phone and got through to Tomasz. We agreed to rendezvous in Iowa City, which I remembered fondly as the place where I first had a Reuben sandwich. He sounded more cheerful: He had found a building near Peoria completely covered with hubcaps. "It is quite fantastic, I think." Later he would shoot a replica of Stonehenge made out of junk cars—"This is really very interesting. History as junk as art."—the Liberace Museum, and a coffin maker who customized caskets in the shape of furniture.

This is a European's America, glittery and bizarre, but also flamboyantly free from tradition, common sense, the tyranny of good taste. When I first saw it, I felt a strange mixture of emotions, half-mocking, half-fascinated by the excess of light and energy, the outsized hypertint. Now, Tomasz's friendly mockery just made me uneasy: I felt as if he were making fun of me, too, for staying here and digging in rather than for laughing and leaving.

In the ticket line ahead of me at the bus station, a beautiful young woman with broad shoulders and a tight, worried jaw carried her huge Nike bag as if it weighed nothing. In my imagination she was a college track star. Nowadays, when I see gorgeous women running, I look at them longingly, envying their knees. Across the crowded hall was a middle-aged woman who might have been the depressing surprise of some tabloid "World's Biggest Bust!" come-on, wearing cutoffs and a huge Florida State T-shirt, her breasts pouring out and down, out and down until they finally stopped somewhere below her navel. She was a pyramid on chubby legs. For the 750th time my water bottle fell out of its handy little net pocket on the side of my pack, was retrieved by a kindly stranger who could actually bend down, and I decided that whatever the experts said about the importance of rehydration, the bottle was going in the trunk of the Skylark, to join the tent, the sleeping pad, my writing portfolio, and a few other odds and ends. I was getting lighter all the time.

A young Italian couple with a child were having trouble with the Greyhound authorities: tickets but no seat. The mother, holding a pink heart-shaped mylar helium balloon on a stick, poked at the stout African-American Greyhound employee and shouted *"Fark* you!" The father was wearing denim shorts so low I could see the top three inches of his white underwear, over which the strap of his money belt hung like a tail. In the end the the Greyhound employee stayed calm, and the Italians got on, handshakes and smiles all around.

Part of me admired the Italian woman for speaking her mind, not caring who turned a startled head or what anyone thought of her. My soul tosses in mid-Atlantic. Half of me, the half I think of as American, is confident and outgoing, but half is middle-class English, brought up on politeness and self-conceal-ment, and I can easily imagine a fatal collapse of initiative, a sudden shriveling of spirit, and then I'd be spending the rest of my life saying, "Of course, sir. Certainly, madam." My habit is to sort through my thoughts like a butler going through a drawer of silverware: Some may be worth considering, perhaps polish-ing a little, but some...well, it would be unthinkable to present them. Most unthinkable would be simply to say what I think on the spot. What is the source of the world's suffering? asked Gaston Bachelard the French philosopher-postman. It lies, he decided, in the fact that "we hesitated to speak.... It was born in the moment when we accumulated silent things within us."

We passed a hitchhiker, the first I'd seen on the trip, sitting next to I-88 on a small pack, thumb up, barely noticing the traffic, looking weather-beaten and stoned. In the old days, these would have been attractive qualities to some; he might have been thought mellow, mysterious, perhaps even sexy, well traveled, at peace with the universe. Perhaps he was.

As we neared Davenport, the Midwestern sheet of cloud broke into smaller and smaller clusters, until we were under the Iowa sky I remembered: cornflower blue, full of light. The corn here was as high as an elephant's ear. You know you're in Iowa when you see a billboard advertising windows installation, and it actually means windows, not Windows.

The driver, Barbara, had a book on tape, *Petals on the Wind* by V. C. Andrews, which judging by the box would comfortably last her from Chicago to Fairbanks. She was chubby and nervous, talking out loud to herself when she couldn't find her way through Davenport. I was ready to look down my nose at her until she got into a conversation with a blind girl sitting in the front seat, claiming that she spoke seven languages—and to judge by some of the offhand observations she made about German and Russian, she did.

I read for a while, too, and began compiling a list: Top Ten Things Lewis and Clark Encountered in The First Six Weeks of Their Expedition That I Haven't So Far:

BEAR

WOLVES

FRENCHMEN

BUFFALO

QUICKSAND

CURIOUS PAINTINGS AND CARVINGS ON LIMESTONE INLAID WITH

WHITE, RED, AND BLUE FLINT

THREE VERRY LARGE SNAKES

300 LBS. OF GREASE

TICKS (thank God)

BOILS (ditto)

DEASSANTARY (ditto)

But my pack needed still more lightening, and in Iowa City Lewis and Clark would go into the trunk of the Skylark.

When the bus dropped me off, I happily sat down on the sidewalk, my back against a wall. A guy with graying hair curling down over his ears bicycled past me. I was clearly in a college town, and felt immediately at home.

Tomasz picked me up a quarter of an hour later and gave me a wan smile. "I must say, this is one of the hardest assignments I have ever done. I am getting up at six in the morning when the light is still quite good; I am driving for twelve hours a day staring out of the window of this car looking for pictures, and I am finding nothing. So far I drive maybe 2,000 miles and I have maybe one frame, that's all. Normally I would spend two, three weeks in one place looking around, talking to people, before I start shooting. That is the only way to find something of quality. But this driving, looking out the window, is impossible. It's madness. I am permanently exhausted."

He had been living off a diet of hamburgers, coffee, and nicotine. Poor bastard. I would take care of him. I'd even help with the driving.

From the two-lane blacktop the undulating wilds of Iowa were not nearly as flat as they had seemed from the interstate 25 years ago. Quiet folds of greenery lay tucked into the small, neat river valleys cutting through the farmland. Tomasz shot the small, terraced huts of a pig farm silhouetted on the grassy hilltop against the late afternoon sun. We pulled over in North English, one of the tiniest villages in this or any state. A woman outside the convenience store saw our Virginia plates. "You've got to be lost if you're in North English," she remarked cheerfully. And yet even in this tiny, peaceful spot, the newsstand selling the *Gazette*, "The Newspaper of Eastern Iowa," was trying to attract readers by advertising that the paper would carry "Unsolved Murders Sunday Through Wednesday." Two guys in bib overalls, leaning on the bed of a pickup, looked in our direction. If we were in a movie, I thought, this would be the first hint that shotguns were just out of sight, chainsaws waiting to be tugged into action.

By the end of the day we reached the small town of Indianola.

Tomasz and I were cracking jokes with desk clerks and waitresses like young traveling salesmen let loose on their first territory. ("I wouldn't accept that credit card if I were you. It isn't even in English..." "In those pants you look, if I may say, *radiculous*...") We ate at a Country Kitchen, and met the hands-down national winner for Best Waitress Humor—blond, middle-aged, cheerful but nobody's fool.

Two guys, one in a John Deere cap, asked her what the catch of the day was. "Crocodile, I think," she offered straight-faced. They looked blank.

She watched while Tomasz insisted I sit with him in the smoking section. "Tell you what," she said helpfully. "I'll bring you a coupla straws and you can stick 'em up your nose and round the corner into non-smoking."

I suggested we could attach the straws to some kind of tube running over to the salad bar.

"Great idea," she said. "That'll probably get us into the Country Kitchen newsletter."

Or the web page?—

"Yeah!" she shot back," Hotcakes dot com."

Letting my dinner digest, I browsed through the local *Recreational Review*. Wipers and white bass, I learned, were to be caught below the dam at Saylorville by casting jigs tipped with minnows. At Saylorville Lake, the catching of crappie—pronounced "croppie"—had slowed down due to high water, the result of the storms that had hit me in Pennsylvania, but there were still a few being caught along the rocks at the marina, along roadbeds and in parking lots that had been covered by the floods. This, not unsolved murders, was the real news of the region.

CHAPTER 10

Dysgeography

July 25—Indianola, Iowa

I t was fair season. The huge Iowa state fair, with its celebrity country singers and hot-air balloon launch, was still a couple of weeks away, but the Warren County fair was opening barely a mile down the road. We parked on the vacant grass while the sun was still slanting low over the trees, before anyone was there to charge admission. This is my favorite time at a fair. Farmers and their wives and kids were setting up, coaxing the sheep and goats into the stalls; three handsome Swiss cows were staring thoughtfully toward the back of the grandstand; wood shavings in the horse stalls were still clean and smelling sweetly of cedar; and the 4-H kids were setting up their exhibit, "The Dos and Don'ts of Baby-sitting," illustrated with Barbies. Not yet the sticky smell of elephant ears, nobody yet charging $2 for lemonade that is half water, half corn syrup; not yet the louche carnies offering BB rifles with bent sights and plastic darts that barely stick; no chicks-on-the-Harleys posters nor hats proclaiming "51% angel, 49% bitch."

The merry-go-round with the American flag was shining, its empty chairs, slightly rusted, shifting on their chains in the breeze. The carousels and miniature trains were silent; the fast-food carts, locked up, smelled of nothing. Only the flags and the fringe stirred on the red-yellow-and-blue canopy over the toy motorbikes and rockets. It all seemed hokey yet miraculous, as if our chief accomplishment as a species was to produce a series of artifacts so angular and bizarre. A great, dignified cottonwood leaned over the video arcade tent.

"Pretty quiet this morning," said a passing farmer wearing blue jeans, blue cotton shirt, and a blue baseball cap. "Couldn't get much better, could it?"

Outside the 4-H tent an elderly woman was taking no guff from an elderly guy. "I got taters at home that weigh a pound and a half, pound and three-quarters," he grumbled, as if affronted by the pitiful specimens on display inside.

"Well, go get 'em, then," she replied briskly.

Kids hosed down white-faced cattle. A trailer went by full of black-faced close-shorn sheep looking like a bench of magistrates trapped in a freight elevator. A woman beside the Farm Bureau stand told her friend a bad-weather catastrophe story regarding the recent rains: "Thank goodness I had my old flivver instead of the decent car."

For the rest of my trip I'd remember how healthy and attractive the children and young teenagers all looked, how unself-consciously cheerful. Indianola came to represent that old-fashioned heartland calm, the evidence that sun, local food, and hard work in the open air might not be the secret of life, but they'd do until the right answer came along.

Steve Beckley, who owned a Buick franchise but had moved out to the country to become a gentleman farmer, helped his daughters Laura and Stephanie and their boy, Christopher, unload the animals: Nubian goats, chickens, Peking and Cayuga ducks. Christopher held a duck called Boomer as if he were holding a set of bagpipes.

Steve recommended the figure-eight racing—in other words, racing where the track crosses over itself and a collision is a good possibility every lap. "The funniest thing are the women. They get so revved up about it." Once last year there was a crash, and the race marshals put up the red flag, "but they wouldn't stop. They had to block the track with old tires or those gals'd have been racing all night long!"

We climbed into the Skylark and headed west, Tomasz looking from side to side for photogenic curiosities. He found a man mowing his lawn with his poodle on his lap, and shot half a roll—always a sucker for dogs, he explained. Back in Warsaw he and his wife founded an organization that takes in strays, and currently house over 150. We stumbled onto one of the bridges of Madison County, which Tomasz insisted on shooting, art imitating art imitating art. But the bright promise of the morning clouded over and turned into another car day; and a car day in the Great Flat States is like dying slowly of oxygen depletion—very like my case, as Tomasz alternated between cigarettes and pipe.

There's nothing like a road trip for making enemies. Traveling with Tomasz was actually a breeze compared to traveling with Richard, who by the time we reached Boulder had abandoned his energetic, sunny self and had sunk into a black melancholy. He had dark hair and dark eyes, and day by day seemed to shrink into a cave beneath his eyebrows from which he stared out, at first moodily, then bitterly, emerging every so often to deliver a muttered sarcasm. Traveling with Richard might have been an education, a chance to try out new tactics for dealing with people I didn't like but was stuck with, but I just kept going, thumb out, hoping things would get better. As I was still doing years later when I was married and things didn't seem to be working.

We stopped at a rundown middle-of-nowhere gun shop, whose owner gave us the usual line: media prejudice and government interference were ruining business, but he added that competition from the likes of Wal-Mart and K-Mart were hurting small dealers like himself. One of his sons took me out front and showed me a genuine antique, parked right by the road because they didn't know what else to do with it—a cast-iron King fairground shooting gallery, badly rusted. Step on up and shoot the ducks gliding across on a cog belt, or the eagles or bull's-eyes! Hit the smoking pipes or the little stars, and make them spin. What about ricochets? I asked. Apparently the .22 bullets would have been made of powdered metal, disintegrating on impact with a solid ping. There probably wasn't even a prize, he said, just satisfaction—and compared to that, trying to win a cheap soft toy with an air rifle with bent sights does seem a poor substitute.

Griswold, Iowa, had an eerie, abandoned quality: nobody in sight, a half dozen cars parked on the main street, shop windows vacant, silent, bleached, and dusty. Only a bar and a bank looked new. Tomasz decided to try some shots in front of what looked like a dilapidated hotel. It was actually a daycare facility, according to the small, handwritten signs, but there were no signs of life.

Later I called Shirley Ward, owner of the Sleep Well Motel and president of the Griswold Chamber of Commerce, to ask her why the town was in such sad shape. Part of the reason was the flood, she said. They got 13 inches on June 14. "The crick overflowed, it flooded out my whole motel, it flooded downtown, and people's basements. I'm still dealing with the effects of the flood. We had FEMA and the Red Cross and the Small Business Association in here, and let me tell you, some of those organizations are not all they're cracked up to be." The flood closed the bridge on 92, and "thanks to certain persons not getting the applications in properly," she said darkly; it would be a year or even two before the bridge was open again.

Other, deeper causes: the opening of a Wal-Mart in Council Bluffs, 40 miles away, had an impact on the town businesses, adding to the general economic decay. "My personal opinion is that the city council hasn't done a damn thing to help it....They do not cooperate with the Chamber of Commerce to get things going on Main Street."

I wished her luck. "Okey-dokle," she said, and went back to the tough business of revitalizing Griswold.

Kerouac, like us, passed through Council Bluffs, where "the great wagon parties...held council there before hitting the Oregon and Santa Fe trails. And of course now it was only cute suburban cottages of one damn kind and another." I wish! Our road was a dead gray artery of gas stations and car dealerships, with the wind tossing a million flickering blue-and-white plastic pennants separating moving cars from the sticker-priced, queued cars facing the road.

Tomasz's daughter, Maryna, inheriting her parents' taste for adventure, had just left Poland to visit China for a month. As we hauled ourselves through Council Bluffs, Tomasz tried to call her in her hotel in Beijing, having spent the previous ten miles trying to subtract time zone by time zone and calculate whether it was tomorrow morning yet. He stood at a phone booth outside a gas station bellowing *Hello? Hello?* across the world to a hotel functionary who spoke no English. I slumped moodily in the car, suffering a strange dysgeography, thinking that this ghastly urban landscape by Route 92 in south Omaha with its gray half-finished, untenanted concrete homes and a steady stream of cars up and down the hill by the gas station was in China.

Tomasz came back over to the car and examined his coffee in disgust. "We are entering 21st century and we still drink this horrible brown liquid," he grumbled, having not yet learned, it seemed, what Amoco coffee tastes like.

As we dragged west in steady drizzle along Route 92 through a series of small, desolate Nebraska towns, the concrete slab cracked and weedy, little sign of business to be done or pleasure to be had, the whole country seemed bleak and shattered. We ground to a halt at York, a service excrescence growing on the artery of I-80. The Super 8 motel advertised a donut bar but didn't have any vacancies. "It must be because of the donut bar," Tomasz observed wearily, reaching for another cigarette. My lungs were burning. In a week the Skylark would be uninhabitable. When he turned it in, back in Washington, the rental agency would probably just sell it for scrap.

As evening falls, I wrote in my notebook, *I always feel farthest from home.* I was exhausted. The people of York, or Shelby, or Griswold were probably perfectly happy—far happier than I. I was bored, and suffering from oxygen deprivation. The very idea of playing journalist, of going on the road and reporting back about the state of the States, seemed ridiculous. The America I found was an America I was creating. Staring out of the window into the darkness, I saw my own reflection.

CHAPTER 11

Missile Silos Would Make Great Condos

July 26—York, Nebraska

The next morning it was drizzling, but I was up at six. After two days in a bus and Skylark, I was more than glad to be on my own, limping out onto the weedy roadside in the early morning rain.

The traffic materialized out of the wet mist under the overpass, roared past, and vanished in the drizzle to the west. Rain beaded on my expensive rain jacket, and every few minutes I'd shake my arms and shoulders to throw off the drops. My shorts were more of a concern: Once I was inside a car, they would dry in a few minutes, but already they were clinging and clammy. Yet not a soggy molecule of me wanted to be anywhere else.

In less than half an hour a truck pulled over, and I ran-hopped 60 yards to catch it. It might be a hoax, and my knee wouldn't take many little sprints like this, but not many truckers would

waste all the gas and brake lining involved in stopping just to jerk
me around.

I'll call him Chris. He worked for a trucking company in Cincinnati, and was hauling 18,000 pounds of assorted electrical components through Wyoming and Utah to Boise. What a stroke of
luck, I told him. My wife's old boyfriend lives in Ogden, Utah.
Chris looked at me and raised an eyebrow.

"No, it'll be fine," I said. "I already e-mailed him, and he said I
should drop by."

"O-kay," Chris said doubtfully, working up through the gears.

Through gray, damp Nebraska, Chris talked about trucking and
weather hazards. Once he came along I-80 soon after a tornado
and found pieces of a barn on the road and pigs rooting around on
the median. Another trucker he knew, driving late at night near
Grand Forks during the Red River floods, came across a three-
story house in the middle of the road. In snow, he said, he may
have to use chains, but they're a pain in the ass. A semi usually
needs eight sets, and putting them on can take an hour and a half
in good conditions. "It can take two and a half to three hours
under your trailer with snow dripping down your neck." And then
another hour to take them off.

Like three-quarters of the guys who had picked me up so far,
Chris had done a stint in the armed forces, where he'd done a fair
amount of hitchhiking. But it wasn't only from standing beside the
road that he'd learned the value of patience, and the futility of
worry. Once, for example, his squad was ordered to report for
transport in the middle of winter, and had sat in sleet for an hour,
waiting for the bus. "What are you going to do?" he asked me
rhetorically. Complaining wasn't going to make the bus come any

quicker. "If you can wait it out for the duration, you've learned what patience you'll need later in life."

The Army had also taught him to take care of himself, which may be one reason why he wasn't afraid of picking up hitchhikers. If anyone wanted to steal his load, or anything in his cab, he was planning to take the Buddhist route. "If they want it bad enough, they can have it. You can always get it back—you got it in the first place."

Mind you, he wasn't entirely without protection. He had a remarkable communication device, a kind of 21st century pager. It was essentially a small computer hooked up to an antenna in a bubble on the roof of the cab, which connected via satellite to his company headquarters in Cincinnati. It not only sent out all the dispatcher's messages and various communications from the company, like a cross between e-mail and a newsletter, but it enabled him to send messages back—and given that the company employed more than 1,000 drivers, that was a lot quicker than a phone line, and less likely to get backed up with calls. Two more features: The satellite pinpointed his position so he and the company always knew where he was to within 30 feet; and he could also send a shorthand distress signal that would be automatically relayed, along with his location, to the nearest police station.

Hitchhiking shows you only the narrowest ribbon of country, and one disadvantage of this long ride was that I wouldn't be able to see a place I'd noticed on the map and fascinated me: Massacre Canyon, near McCook, Nebraska.

Massacre Canyon was where, in August 1873, the last major intertribal Indian battle between the Pawnee and the Sioux took place. A group of 300 Pawnee warriors and 400 women were on a buffalo hunt along the banks of the Republican River, in Sioux territory. They camped on the north bank of the river on August 4, and the next morning a band of Sioux, which outnumbered them four to one, happened upon them. The first to die was Sky Chief; after his death the Pawnee raised a white flag and a rider rode it toward the Sioux, but his horse was shot from under him. The Pawnee fled into the canyon where the greatest loss of life took place as the Sioux rode down the walls and fired upon them. As the Pawnee were attempting to cross the river at the bottom of the canyon, the U.S. Cavalry arrived and the Sioux fled.

The incident at Massacre Canyon marked an end, not just of an era but of a history. Within two years, the Pawnee would be herded onto a reservation in Oklahoma; as an active, independent people with their own culture and traditions, they effectively ceased to exist. This is what nowadays is called "ethnic cleansing." Within three years the Sioux would be crammed into roughly a third of South Dakota, their sacred territory in the Black Hills, but when gold was found there, they would be shunted again, onto three much smaller reservations. There would be no more inter-Indian conflict because there would be no more Indian nations; and there would be no more fighting over buffalo grounds because there would be no more buffalo. In 1800, there were more than 60 million buffalo in the U.S. and Canada. By 1900, there were fewer than a thousand.

As soon as we forked north on I-80, leaving I-76 to cut southwest into Colorado, everything changed. The agriculture at once became more varied, the endless corn giving way to fields of different colors: dun-colored bare earth, spring-green shoots coming up in a haze, golden stubble...Then we were in a country that was all bare hills and undulating grassland. The rain stopped at the same time, the sky cleared, and the dappled shadows of a flotilla of small clouds rose and fell across the dimpled plain. The skyline near Potter, Nebraska, was broken by a huge howling coyote sculptured in sheet steel.

As soon as we crossed into Wyoming, we saw the first cattle, the first artesian wells, the first nodding donkeys. Power lines stapled the horizon, cattle clustered around wells and feed bins, and to our surprise there were ore and coal trains everywhere, a half dozen in no more than 20 minutes. The on-ramps were now gated so that the interstate could be closed for snow, then cattle grids appeared by the gates. Both the railway and the highway were periodically lined with snow fence sections looking like flimsy bleachers. "Nothin' to stop it for miles," Chris observed laconically. We saw first an antelope at a stream, then a spotted deer on a hilltop.

Bluffs appeared on both sides of the valley, then pines on the bluffs. The West was starting to look western, and even to adopt a certain cultural self-consciousness, as if aware of its obligations. We saw our first stetsons. Truck stops rented audiotapes of westerns: *Lady of No Man's Land; Treachery at Triple Fork.* Wonderful rock formations like piles of chocolate chips grew above the small rivers.

Chris had a stronger sense of history than most of the people who picked me up; world events had an odd habit of reaching for him. He missed the war in Vietnam, but his English teacher brought a Vietnam veteran into class—a daring thing to do in Bible Belt

Arkansas, even in 1975—who told them about the war in graphic detail. "He told us this story of when he was in a foxhole with his lieutenant. All he saw was a bright flash of light, and next thing his lieutenant wasn't there," said Chris, and for the first time, some of the class began to ask themselves questions.

He also had a clear view of the end of the Cold War. "North of Tucson, in a city called Catalina, there was a Titan base, or silo, right across the street from this little shop my friend owned. Trucks came in; they opened up the top of the silo, and a crane came in and picked up the warhead. They picked it up, put it on a flatbed, secured it, and carted it off. They went ahead and drained the second section of all the propellant, took it up and laid it down on a cradle, and did the same to the final section. They left the silo open with the sections on cradles for 30 days so that the Soviet satellites had a chance to come by and verify that they were putting nothing back in, and that it was dismantled. They took the sections to Davis-Monthan [Air Force Base], cut them up, took the rocket engines out, and the Soviet observers were watching at Davis-Monthan for part of the time when they cut them up. It was the first time the Soviets were on a base in the States. We saw the Aeroflot that they came in on. Then they took all the rest of the equipment out of the silo, back-filled with rubble, concrete, sealed 'er. Let the Soviets verify that for 30 days.

"I always thought missile silos would make great condos," he added as an afterthought. "Put a dome over the top and you could have one hell of an indoor garden."

Yet, the end of a war isn't always what it seems. Just as the end of the Cold War robbed American conservatives of their favorite enemy, forcing them to turn their fury on domestic liberalism, so the end of the Vietnam War defeated America's brief flirtation with leftist politics. The antiwar movement declared victory and went home, and at once my generation lost its coherence and lost its way. I don't think we've found it since.

Chris agreed. "1973 was a time of hope," he said. "I think a lot of people have lost hope—that tomorrow will be better, that the weekend will be nice," Chris said as we approached the Continental Divide. Everybody had come to want things to be larger than life; our faith in the value of the ordinary has been lost. "My grandfather's idea of a good day was waking up, having a cup of coffee, scratching his dog behind the ears, and being able to go out and see horses. And that's not bad. We get oversold on larger-than-life. Life has gotten real simple for me lately, and it's going to get simpler. I've done the rat race." Chris liked gardening, he said, and pottery, and he'd like to know the constellations, so he'd have something to look for in the night sky.

As we began the long, slantwise haul up the Continental Divide, he told me of being estranged from his father for most of his adult life, then reuniting. I told him about the ghastly summer of 1982 when in the course of three months I tried homesteading, got married in secret, developed a fear of flying, and began to go gray. The journey was slipping into balance: Instead of driver and hitchhiker, we were fellow travelers. We found ourselves in a strange high desert, with reptilian ranges stretching off out of sight on both sides. Scrub brush, a few cacti, and tough clumps of grass more brown than green. A billboard for Jubitz, a big-deal truck stop, announced, "Rejoice! Only 1,094.2 miles!"

"It's in Portland, Oregon," he explained. "Beats me why someone hasn't taken a shotgun and shot the hell out of that sign."

For me, this was a part of America where the myths had not yet been kicked out by brusque reality. Nowadays the word "California" no longer means to me what it did in 1973, when it was a place wholly without substance outside the imagination, and when I burst out singing "I'm going to see the folks I dig,/ I'll even kiss a Sunset pig,/ California, I'm coming home" as we crossed over in Robin's VW bus from Nevada on I-80. Oddly enough it really did feel as if by coming to California we were coming to the home we ought to have, as opposed to the old-and-cold-and-settled-in-its-ways isle that I would soon leave for good. The West, too, wearing its young but vivid history on its sleeve, seemed more myth than map. Laramie, Rock River, Elk Mountain, Fort Steele, Red Desert, Table Rock, Bitter Creek, Point of Rocks, Green River—the names themselves a chronicle of discovery, of hope and disappointment. Butch Cassidy worked in a butcher's shop in Rock Springs—hence the "Butch," some historians think—and the Hole in the Wall itself is a natural gateway through a red canyon wall on Buffalo Creek, just away to the north of the interstate. I had no desire to see the replicas of old jails or boot hills, advertised at every turn in the road, or even the real ones. For the time being, I wanted to carry on savoring the soft explosion of astonishment that I was actually here in the place of myth, the land of *Gunsmoke*.

It was around this time that Chris pulled over for gas and got out of his cab. As I was idly flipping through his road atlas, I found his gay pornography.

I barely saw it—a large playing card, perhaps 4-by-6 inches, bearing a black-and-white photo of a guy in a leather cap and a leather jacket open to reveal his bare torso. I shut the road map and dropped it on the floor. Half of me remained perfectly calm. The other half panicked.

The panicking half ran screaming around my head, yelling, "Do something! Do something!"

The calm half said, "Think about this. The guy has shown you absolutely no ill will. You're actually bigger than him. Besides, does it really make sense to throw away a good ride?"

The panicking half, meanwhile, had gotten in touch with its inner homophobe and was not going to let him go. Chris might have good reason not to want the trucking fraternity to find out about his private life. If he knew what I knew, and felt threatened by the possibility of being exposed, who knew how he might react?

After several minutes, Chris got back into the cab and set us back on the road. By now I was calming down a little and had reasoned that I was learning some valuable things about fear, and about violence. For one thing, this was not a credible fear. I have gay friends of both sexes and never feel threatened by them in the least. No, this was an old worm, a deep, deep serpent of fear, one that hadn't surfaced for decades, and it had taken the extra vulnerability of hitch-hiking to bring it to the surface. This was an interesting journey of self-discovery: I wondered what other worms might surface before the trip was over.

And yet this don't-ask-don't-tell policy, hatched at the behest of yammering anxiety, was ridiculous. Within 50 miles or so I realized that I was getting exactly what I deserved. I had left myself to gnaw in silence on my fear, thereby guaranteeing that I would never know even whether the photos were in fact Chris's or, more interestingly, what it was like to be a gay man in the trucking trade. Besides, he and I had steadily been getting to know each other better, and now that stopped dead. I was now cautious and a little distant. My fear, my loss.

By early evening Chris had used up all his legal hours for the day and needed to take a sleep break. He pulled over at the Flying J Travel Plaza in Rawlins, Wyoming, and after a bite of dinner he went off to sleep in the truck's cab. I ordered more coffee and began writing up my notes. At the table behind me, a group of truckers were telling hitchhiker horror stories—this guy getting his load stolen by someone he'd picked up, that guy getting killed. Intellectually, I thought yes, well, this is the climate of fear, everyone afraid of everyone else, but deeper down I was laughing in a mixture of amazement and relief. These truckers, these tough-looking characters, were afraid of me. After ten or fifteen minutes of this I got out of my seat and squatted down at the end of their table. "I couldn't help overhearing what you were talking about," I said, "and I thought you should know I'm one of those killer hitchhikers."

They broke into embarrassed laughter. "No, man," "We didn't mean you, man."

They asked me to join them. The most vocal was Jason, a young blond guy with a military mustache and a habit of making his points emphatically with a finger leveled like a rifle. Next to him sat a marmalade blonde who may have been his wife. Across the table sat a magisterial dark-haired guy, quieter than the others and perhaps in his early 40s, who drove high-end removals for top executives, and a short, round, balding guy in his 50s who offered a series of cheerful, rude remarks and dirty jokes. From them I learned that an entry-level trucker such as Jason might make $30,000 a year, but if you were carrying cars or doing removals, you could easily make four times that amount. The schoolmasterly trucker acknowledged modestly that he had made well into six figures the previous year.

Freedom of expression is a trucker's job benefit, almost part of the job description. Everyone said exactly what was on his or her mind—a spirit fostered by the constant use of CBs, perhaps—and accepted everyone else's right to free speech. The roly-poly guy, who would have got on my nerves at once, was tolerated like a wicked uncle; his coarse cracks were taken in stride by everyone, including the woman, who was gloriously unoffended by everything, and while she clearly loved Jason had no hesitation in telling him exactly what she thought of him when an occasion arose.

They restated the trucker's creed—Everything You Own Came By Truck—with a certain militancy born of knowing that America looks down on its truckers. Jason told me the story of driving 18 hours overnight through a blizzard to deliver a shipment to an auto parts store. He had to get a signature for the delivery, so he went around front and into the store, which had just opened. The clerk was serving a customer, who asked for a part he'd desperately been waiting for. The clerk looked it up on the computer, and said it had just come in; it had been part of Jason's load, in fact.

"Thank God!" the customer cried out. "Thank you so much for getting it in."

"What the hell did he do?" Jason yelled at the customer, pointing at the clerk. "He finished work last night at six o'clock and went home to bed! Why don't you thank the trucker who drove all night in a frickin' snowstorm to bring you that part?"

"Who is this guy?" demanded the customer.

The clerk said, "He's the trucker who drove all night in a frickin' snowstorm to bring you that part."

As the guys were packing up to leave the table, they asked me if I wanted a ride, but they were all headed East. Jason gave me his name and address, and as an afterthought told me that I really ought to check out the annual Harley-Davidson rally that took place just down the road from his place, in Sturgis, South Dakota. It started around the second week of August, he thought, but the partying went on for the whole month. Bikers were part of my anxiety, and I had dared myelf that before the trip was over I'd go into a biker bar and start interviewing. Sturgis sounded like a biker bar with a quarter of a million bikers. "It's wild, man," he said. "You gotta see it if you're seeing America."

Then I was on my own—but that was all right, too. No hitch-hiking trip is complete without being forced to stay up all night in a truck stop somewhere, waiting for a driver to wake up or just waiting for dawn, eyes stinging, nose itching from cigarette smoke, folding your arms and putting your head down on a Formica table. "Thirty-nine years old and I had four back injuries," complained one trucker. "Last one put me out for five months. Last week and a half I been eating a bottle of Tylenol a day." The big-screen TV in the drivers' lounge had been out because the satellite dish had been hit by lightning—from the same storm system I had been tracking backward across the vast flatlands of America. The steady background sounds were country music on the PA system, the grunts and thuds of kung-fu games from the video parlor, and, all night, the prerecorded announcements from the ablutions host-ess: "Shower number 237 is now ready. Shower number 238 is now ready."

CHAPTER 12

A Frontier Planet

July 27—Rawlins, Wyoming

Gray-green ranges lounged like iguanas on the horizon; mesas like elephants' feet lined the dry valleys. The entire landscape, coming off the divide into western Wyoming, was barren except for oil and gas flares, chemical plants, and soda mines. It was utterly without shade as far as the eye could see; and when we reached the horizon, we'd find another barren and bizarre landscape as far as the eye could see, then another, then another. Completely beyond human scale. It was not only hard to believe this was the same country as Vermont; it was hard to believe it was the same planet. Winding down beside the interstate was the longest train I've ever seen—150 cars just in the section I could see. I never did see either the beginning or end. It was a forever train.

Then another chemical plant, and another.

"Where do their kids go to school?" Chris wondered. Exactly. How far do the people who live and work here have to commute?

Where's the nearest public library? Where is civilization? This was a frontier planet. Who would willingly come here, except miners, thieves, and whores? "The world's largest deposits of trona, the rock that produces the industrial chemical soda ash, are west of Green River," says *Roadside Geology*, but this makes the region sound as if it's a rational landscape: Here are the minerals, so here we mine. The fact is, this was some of the most inhospitable land I've ever seen, dry, savage, impossibly alkaline. Off to the left, a badlands area looked as if a giant had hacked up the ground with a cutlass.

Just as strange as these natural sights were the man-made ones. Many of the small towns had no landscaping at all, presumably because water is too expensive, so the front yard of the boxy modular home was just fenced-in sagebrush. The whole place seemed to have been dropped from midair. There was nothing to make the houses seem settled and woven into its landscape, to suggest a shared history. In one town—Green River, I think—the only place where I saw grass (thanks to a spattering of sprinklers) was the cemetery, which we like to think of as the place of rest, as a final home.

For several hundred miles we'd seen signs for what looked like a hotel called Little America. Between Green River and Evanston, where the desert had flattened out a little but was still as bleak and uninviting as ever, there it was: a small cluster of brilliantly clean, new buildings (supersize convenience store open 24 hours, laundry facilities, ATM, U.S. Post Office, 24-hour auto-and-truck-repair garage, and a service station) surrounded by a cluster of valiantly watered trees.

"This traveler's oasis," reads the brochure—the photos all shot in a tight close-up to hide the fact that beyond the fringe of trees, around the pool, lies nothing but soda—"was conceived by a local sheep rancher who became stranded overnight in a blizzard, miles from nowhere. He dreamed of creating a place of warmth & comfort on that spot with a cozy fireplace, comfortable beds, good food and congenial atmosphere." Little America was the ultimate service area; it even had its own interstate exit sign, as if it were a town. Yet it was so alien to this strange, barren land that it was, in effect, its own country, a little America, a foothold on a forbidding continent.

I was struck by the vulnerability of the place. Everything must have been trucked in from hundreds, even thousands of miles away. No use could possibly have been made of indigenous elements, unless they served the guests heaping piles of baking soda for breakfast. How would this "oasis" hotel survive hard times? Several months later I was driving through the Anza-Borrego Desert, west of the Salton Sea in southern California, and saw other adventures in desert investment: an abandoned motel, a driveway winding off to the weedy beige waste, a pair of ornate gateposts with nothing but sand beyond them—the sense that a civilization had sent its emissaries here but they had been shipwrecked on the dry shores. Most of the West, I'm convinced, is a series of valiant (and often crooked) attempts to put humans where humans were never intended to be, a few successful, most not. Little America looked like a ghost town waiting to happen.

It turned out that Andy, my wife's former boyfriend, lived just up the hill from the McDonalds where Chris dropped me, on the northern fringes of Ogden. I didn't want to be a burden to Andy, so I thought I'd rent a car. I had the massively misguided notion that I might drive out to Dinosaur National Monument and be back by the time he got home from work, forgetting that this was the West, and two inches on my pocket road atlas was actually 200 miles. The nearest car rental place, however, was at the airport, which turned out to be virtually in a different state. I called a cab.

While I waited, studying the decor in McDonalds, I noticed an ad for the Ogden Eagles, a semi-pro football team that was scheduled to play that night. For more information, call 737-9024. Good deal. I'd never seen small-town football. I copied down the number.

The rear side window of the cab I took to the airport was decorated with two stickers: a fake bullet hole and a notice—"Warning! Driver Only Carries $20 Worth of Ammunition." The ride cost me $25.

Utah's Second Busiest Airport featured the Best Lil' Airport Terminal in the West, home of the Taildragger Cafe and Budget Rent A Car. Budget Rent A Car was not in. According to a note at the desk, he had gone to the other Budget branch to return a vehicle, and should be called at a number that was illegible. I tried calling various number combinations on the sock phone, but by now the wretched thing was routinely telling me that the number I had dialed was not available to me, or in a fit of higher mischief was telling me that I should enter my secret access code, and when I entered it told me that I should disable the secret access code and try again without it.

I gave up on modern weaponry and used the pay phone, standing in the airport's tiny lobby and looking across its small, empty forecourt up at the dry, almost vertical Wasatch Hills, the final range of mountains beyond which Brigham Young stopped his long trek, pointing at the vast lake ahead of the Mormons and saying, "This is the place." Then they discovered that it was salt, and stank, but all the same they built their new capital by the Great Salt Lake, like an illustration on the cover of a science-fiction novel.

I called both Budget and Hertz and was told they had no cars for at least a week. I called the Ogden Eagles' number and was told that it had been disconnected. Suddenly, the sock phone rang. Nothing could have surprised me more: it was like being attacked by a fried egg. It was Tomasz, whom once again I had left behind, meandering through western Nebraska. At once our conversation was interrupted by the sound of a phone on the line, ringing so loudly neither of us could hear the other. I called Tomasz back using the pay phone, and after a while we worked out that our plans to travel in tandem were bollixed up almost beyond belief: we had the entire state of Colorado between us. He wanted to take me to see Bryce Canyon, which he had seen on his first visit to the U.S.; I wanted to see Las Vegas, which I'd missed the first time around. We agreed to meet next day at Beaver, Utah, near where I-15 going south through Utah meets I-70 coming west from Colorado. Hitchhiking more than 200 miles to a rendezvous is always tricky; I decided to take the bus.

Now all I had to do was call the cab company back and pay another $25 to take me back to Andy's, where I had started. The cabbie had his fiancée in the front seat with him, keeping him company. Both were African American. They'd moved to Utah from the Bay Area, which was getting just too dangerous, they said, but they were finding that Ogden was a hard place to fit in. Well, Utah is a very white state, isn't it? I asked. No, it's not just a matter of color, they said. They knew white newcomers to Ogden who said the same thing. Well, what was there to do in the evenings? They looked at each other and laughed. Not much, it seemed, especially if you were an outsider. "I just drive up into the mountains," she said, pointing up at the Wasatches towering right in front of us, "find some jazz on the radio, lie on the hood of my car, and look up at the stars."

Andy had the strangest address I'd ever seen: 608E, 2650N, Ogden. Once again, I felt as if I were on another planet, navigating by grid references alone. Not so far wrong, he explained when he turned up an hour later and found me asleep on his front lawn. The whole of Utah (and parts of eastern Idaho, Arizona, and Nevada) lives by Mormon geography. Street addresses are based on a grid that in turn is based on one's position relative to the intersection of Main and South Temple Streets in Salt Lake City. It all seemed faintly Arabic to me. I imagined road engineers putting in a new development turning toward their latter-day Mecca, squinting through the theodolite and writing "15700 South" on the clipboard.

I'd never met Andy. When I called Barbara and told her I was going to be dropping in on him, she reeled. "My worlds are colliding," she said. Andy was in his early 30s, with a goatee and long blond hair pulled back in a ponytail, talked in that slow valley drawl, attentive and playful with his young daughter. He taught computer art, and was an exquisite connoisseur of contemporary Americana. He was both hip and retro. For example: Every year he and a group of friends hold a golf tournament—not that Andy actually can play the game, or would do anything so tiresome as go to a country club. No, they drive out into the desert and play at night, using luminous balls on one of the dry salt lake beds. The surface is so flat, a good drive will send the ball half a mile. It's near an Air Force base, and one year a military satellite picked up their lights and interpreted them as a landing strip for drug runners. "Before we knew, it there were helicopters and all kinds of shit chasing us around the desert."

He was exactly the person I needed to tell me what I should see in Las Vegas. The thing I had to understand, he stressed, was that the casinos had evolved from cheesy gambling dumps into hotels-cum-theme parks. I had difficulty picturing this, so as we hung out in his kitchen, looking out on the tidy Mormonic front yards of suburban Ogden, he ran down a few of his favorites.

The Stratosphere: "I haven't done it yet. There's so much to do in Las Vegas, you always run out of time. Anyway, this guy built this big tower, definitely the tallest thing in Las Vegas. It's got a revolving restaurant and a casino and all that stuff, but the really funny attraction is on the very top—you know how they have a needle on top of those towers? They have this thing. It's, like, seats that go up in the needle, and they strap you in there and then they fire you off! You zoom up at, I don't know, five g's, or some crazy thing, and then fall down. And you're just surrounded by air. And there's a roller coaster up there, which I hear isn't all that great, but that also goes along the edge, like, way up high. Apparently this guy is like this Las Vegas legend and he, I don't know, shoehorned this thing in there with some kind of leveraged money that he got somehow. Anyway, it's going bankrupt. That's what I hear."

The Luxor—he giggled in delight or disbelief, I wasn't sure— had a concrete Sphinx. "It's really cheesy." Circus Circus, it seemed, had its own amusement park inside a pink glass dome. Treasure Island had a show in front where they sank a ship every hour. New York, New York was the only place in Las Vegas where I could get really good coffee, "But I can't imagine it'll last too long. Everything in Las Vegas is made to be disposable. In a few years it's going to be so dirty and dusty and hideous, it'll be a nightmare in there."

Caesar's Palace had statues of Bacchus and all his attendants, and if I stood there long enough, "the lights dim, there's a big thunderstorm in the ceiling with lightning and stuff, and then the statues all come to life and dance around and sing! We were in town once right after a Grateful Dead show, so there were all these Deadheads in there, camped out. They weren't moving. They were just watching that thing all day."

His only concern was that I might be arriving at the same time as the annual Comdex convention, the biggest computer gathering in the world. "They're all computer geeks, right? So they never spend any money at the gaming tables. All they want to do is go to the titty bars on the outskirts of town and watch the strippers." He laughed. "They'll be lined up ten deep trying to get into those places!"

His final comments, though, were warnings: Some cheaper motels were drug-connection motels, and I'd hear people coming and going all night, shots in the parking lot. And as soon as I got a room, I should check the lock on the door, make sure it works. "The scam is to check out, take the key, and, because the cheap motels don't change their locks, then break back into the room and rob whatever is in it. The electronic locks are much safer."

Fully briefed, I went with him into town to pick up his daughter Abigail from daycare and then to Farr's for homemade ice cream. Farr's offered an array of flavors hitherto unknown to man: licorice, play dough, raptor ripple, named after the local baseball team (in turn named after Utah Raptor, who was left on the cutting-room floor when *Jurassic Park* was being edited), pineapple upside-down cake, grape, ambrosia sherbet, and spaghetti-factory spumoni. This was the kind of Americana Andy loved. I shuddered.

CHAPTER 13

"A Hell of a Place to Lose a Cow"

July 28—Ogden, Utah

My friend the cabbie with the fake bullet hole drove me into town. He, too, had moved here to escape the fear of crime—in his case, in New York. He dropped me off at the Greyhound station at 6:30 a.m. The ticket office was closed. We could pay when we got to Salt Lake City. Greyhound was clearly a lot more relaxed here than back East.

Ogden has had a very peculiar past. Founded as a small Mormon community, it was swooped up and whirled around when the Union Pacific and Central Pacific Railroads met nearby. Ogden became a railroad town. The three blocks of 25th Street between the city and the railroad became a red-light district known as Electric Alley, all the more rowdy as prostitution was legal, or next to it. One of Ogden's more famous madams was hired away by Salt Lake City to set up a brothel there. To Mormon eyes, this was appalling—

but as the religion still condoned polygamy, it suffered a strange impotence: dominant in numbers, but politically powerless.

With the collapse of the railroads after the Second World War— Andy took me down to the switching yards, where only a few tracks were still active on land that had once clearly been laid out for dozens—the town lost much of its income, and much of the area down by the tracks was still semi-derelict. But at the same time, the city fathers had been investing heavily in the city's rebirth, albeit largely along Mormon lines. As a result, Ogden has a downtown that is half yuppie, half Bowery. In one two-block stretch of 25th Street, flanked with new antique street lighting and neat, little saplings like ruffed choirboys, I found a biker bar, pawnshops, a brew pub, a flophouse hotel, a coffee shop (which had to be new, as coffee was not to be found in Utah until recently because of a Mormon prohibition on caffeine), vacant storefronts, antiques shops, a comedy cafe, a beauty salon, a place selling pool tables and dart supplies, a club full of Beatles paraphernalia (bars, too, were not to be found in Utah until very recently, alcohol being as unacceptable as coffee, but private clubs flourished), and a Chinese restaurant, the Star Noodle, with a neon sign so spectacular it had appeared, according to Andy, in several movies. Rumor had it that renovators discovered a network of tunnels under the old downtown that enabled the Mormon elders to visit houses of ill repute; but I was unable to verify either the tunnels or the houses of ill repute, so sadly this must remain a rumor.

On the corner, waiting for the bus, I met a frail-looking middle-aged black guy named Robert. His eyes were bloodshot; he had perhaps a day of white stubble on his chin, and he clutched a plastic grocery bag. He had just ridden into town on a freight train.

"I rode most all of them," he said. "The Union Pacific, Conway, Rock Island, Burlington Northern, Chicago Northwest..." He'd recently come from Newport, Rhode Island, he said, where his ex-wife lived.

Wasn't riding the rails dangerous? He shrugged and nodded at the same time. "You have to know what you're doin'," he said. "You pick up a spike, put it in a door so it won't close on you. But some people out there, they don't know what they're doin'."

He scratched the plastic hospital tag on his wrist. "I just been in the hospital for my kidneys," he said apologetically. "Had to be on antibiotics. Some of them antibiotics'll kill you." He was on dialysis, he said, but at another point he said he took his kidney medicine with him.

I told him what I was up to, and he asked me about hitchhiking by road. When I told him I had started in New York, his eyebrows rose. "Hey, I might try that," he said. He'd once asked some guys about road hitchhiking and they'd said he might have trouble because of his color. "I said [to them], 'I ain't havin' nothing' to do with that. *I* ain't prejudiced'."

Now, writing this, I realize that hitching by rail is also a significant step closer to the dangerous edge—to the metal. You don't have to be white to get a ride, or look reasonably presentable. The train doesn't care about your race, or your clothes; but, then, it doesn't care about you at all. If it slices your leg off, or leaves you trapped in a freight car to die of heat or cold, it won't look back.

"I'm lookin' for a ridin' buddy," he said. "I don't trust some of those guys." I thought maybe he was looking at me hopefully. This is the kind of hitchhiker who is more likely to get killed, I thought, not some tall white guy. His death wouldn't even make the nightly news. He couldn't defend himself. All I could do was give him $5 for breakfast, and then I got on the bus.

When I set out, I had hoped to get to Salt Lake City and relive one of the most amazing moments of my 1973 trip. I was in Robin's VW bus. Two of the hitchhikers had got out in Boulder; the other hitchhiker, Chas, was driving while I rode shotgun. Richard was asleep on the bed. We skirted Salt Lake City around 10:30 at night. As we headed west across the Great Salt Lake, Chas asked, "Have you been to Salt Lake City before?"

"No," I said, "this is my first trip to America."

"You mean you've never seen the Great Salt Lake by moonlight?"

"No," I said, wondering what this was all leading up to.

Right there and then, on the interstate, he killed the lights. All around us, the moon reflected off a billion tiny crystals of salt, and we were sailing on an ethereal sea, glowing soft silver, waveless and insubstantial, as far as the dim horizon, where dark mountains rose like whales.

In the past week, something happened to that previous trip. Far from wanting to retrace it, I wanted to avoid it. First novelty, then the burnishing effect of memory had created scenes that glowed in the darkness like the Salt Lake, part fact, part imagination. They were among my most precious possessions. Why would I want to risk destroying them?

The bus headed south through Provo and slowly climbed between scrawny pines into high, dry country dotted with scrubby sagebrush running up to the distant, arid mountains. I was in the desert.

Or rather, I was in an air-conditioned bus looking out through polarized windows at the desert. I wondered what the air outside smelled like. Maybe it would be like the south of France, dry, hot, and resinous with pine—and perhaps a hint of sage.

We stopped on the outskirts of Fillmore, Utah, and I bought a gas-station tuna sandwich that turned out to be several shades of brown in the process of evolving into a more complex life-form. A grizzled grain-elevator worker from Fargo, North Dakota, chewed next to me on the baking asphalt by the bus. A pickup crawled by, its bodywork apparently made up of parts reclaimed from every other pickup in Fillmore. "That's a five-tone paint job," he remarked.

I was stunned by the light. It was hot, yes, a clean, pure heat that lay on my skin without wringing the sweat from my vitals, but what struck me more was the light. I found myself remembering *Paris, Texas* and *Baghdad Café*, films set in the desert but made by Europeans, and how in each case the opening sequence was drenched in light, as if the desert light were in itself a character and a plot point. The sky was a brilliant blue virtually untroubled by clouds, lucid, as if to encourage clear thinking as well as clear vision. It made the eastern light and European light seem complex and equivocal, untrustworthy. No wonder there's a tradition of coming to the desert to tell the truth, or hear the truth. No wonder, too, that the desert is a filmmaker's medium rather than a novelist's. Every sentence would have to contain the word "light."

The Greyhound stop in Beaver turned out to be the El Bambi diner, a classic aluminum-and-Naugahyde joint standing alone in the noonday desert sun, a Disney deer on its sign. I sat on the low cinderblock wall out front, trying to generate some melanin.

Twenty minutes later, Tomasz pulled up in the Skylark, looking dazed. "I must tell you, this is something completely new for me," he said. "I drive 18 hours to see someone who is neither my lover nor my wife nor my child. This has never happened to me in my life."

As we turned east toward Bryce Canyon, the soil turned a vivid orange-red, the result of oxidized iron and manganese deposited by streams 60 million years ago. Spectacular chimneys and spires climbed away among the pines on both sides of the canyon, while a little stream ran chattering down beside the road. We pulled over to shoot pictures, and I got to talking to a woman from New Jersey, her nails painted in an Art Deco pattern in black on lilac and cinnamon, who had just come from Las Vegas and couldn't say enough good things about the Rio, where you could take part in the show and have your photo taken with the cast.

I wondered again what the desert smelled like, and stepped off the road into the sagebrush. It did smell like the south of France, hot and resinous with pine, with a hint of sage. Maybe I'd finally get to see a rattlesnake. I looked more closely at the red earth around my feet and saw something long, narrow and cream-colored. I picked it up. It was a section of snakeskin. I put it in my shirt pocket and stepped smartly back onto the road.

But this was just the prelude. The canyon road wound along for several miles, not especially deep but utterly beyond belief in its livid redness and the unearthly carvings rising all around us, then climbed a little, dropped us in a small grove of pines with the usual National Park signs, and Tomasz announced excitedly that we had arrived.

What we saw from the guardrail, elbowed by Germans and shouldered by Italians, was the remains of the Paunsaugunt Plateau, part of the Colorado Plateau that ten million years ago was thrust almost a mile up, shattering and fracturing. As it rose, a river now known as the Paria and its tributaries carved swiftly through the rock, leaving a bowl about three miles across and several hundred feet deep filled with thousands upon thousands of slender ridges called "fins" and individual pinnacles called "hoodoos"—yellow, red, brown, pink, beige, salmon, peach, even violet, filled with entrenched shadows, timeless yet breathtakingly fragile. Hawks soared over it; down in its depths, a small party of horses wound between the hoodoos, following a stream long dry.

Here was a place unlike anywhere on earth, so the first thing everyone did was to try to make it like something else. The Paiute legend was that the canyon itself was full of "Legend People," half-human animals turned to stone by Coyote. People around me saw family groups and birds. A German said, *wie Kirchen*, "like churches." But the challenge of this place was to see it without metaphor, to be dumbstruck and just take it in. Not so easy, as a car alarm went off back in the parking lot and tourists squabbled and chattered. I backed away from the railing and tried to stay with my own perceptions, feeling a cool breeze springing up, lying down on a half-tree bench looking up through the pine branches at the scudding clouds. Then watching a beautiful young Italian girl of perhaps ten or eleven, her face framed by long dark hair and a baseball cap, trying to handle the frisky water fountain, drinking with the jet running all over her face and off her chin.

I didn't want to follow the crowd; I didn't want to follow Tomasz's directing, as he tried to set up a portrait shot. No wonder hitchhiking appeals so much to adolescents, or to the adolescent in me: It's full of decisions we make, at our own behest, and the discoveries that come with them. I found myself remembering climbing the Malvern Hills at 16, on my own for the first time, discovering the breeze and the springy turf as if I'd never been up there before, as if nobody had every discovered such a place, or felt such strong and unnamable emotions. I watched in delight as a western magpie laid its head sideways on a puddle to drink out of the corner of its beak. The guy behind me said to his girlfriend, "They're magpies. Heckle and Jekyll were magpies—you know, the cartoon characters."

After a while I confronted Tomasz, who shrugged and said, "If you don't want me to shoot you, I won't shoot you. You can do what you want. What the hell? We are just two guys."

I calmed down, and only then did it strike me that finally, after more than 3,000 miles of driving and God knows how many cigarettes, this was Tomasz's first real day of work. He shot again and again, pausing only to say "This is incredible," then shooting again, then shaking his head. He pulled in an elderly southern lady so he could shoot her and her beige umbrella, then held his camera upside down above his head so he could squint up through the top viewfinder and shoot four college girls in shorts leaning in a line on the rail, their bare legs at identical angles, a study of landscapes within landscapes as he was shooting down at the canyon below them. Ah, America: girls in shorts and T-shirts, their muscular legs promising competence and go-anywhere adventurousness. This stunned me when I was first meeting American girls. They all rode ten-speeds, they could all swim well, they could all drive, they'd all look you in the eye. Of all my reasons for leaving England, this was up near the top.

Tomasz shot a guy looking at the viewfinder of his digital video camera as it panned across the canyon. I looked over Tomasz's shoulder, seeing the view of the view of the view of the view. He had earned this day.

We found a plaque explaining that Bryce was named after a Mormon farmer named Ebenezer Bryce who had settled in 1875 on the flatlands at the foot of the canyon. He sounded like farmers have always sounded: When asked for his impressions of this incredible place, he said laconically, "It's a hell of a place to lose a cow."

Afterward, Tomasz and I strolled into the little tourist village that had been tacked on to Bryce like a necktie on a peacock. Tomasz had his photo taken in full western gear, sitting on a stuffed bull. I had ostrichburger for dinner at Ruby's Canyon Diner. It was tough and a little dry, but that's probably what meat tastes like if it's had an active and fulfilled life.

~

CHAPTER 14

Red Wind at the Mirage

July 29—Bryce, Utah

"I f America were run by Europeans in the European culture," Tomasz asked seriously, "do you think it would be improved?"

We were driving east from Bryce toward Escalante in search of a petrified forest, under a brilliant sky, winding between solitary bluffs and small, raggedly scalloped mountains heaving themselves out of the desert. We had eaten breakfast in the little village of Tropic, at the foot of Bryce Canyon, which had grown out of the farmstead of Ebenezer Bryce himself. Tomasz seemed to have stopped eating altogether and was living on coffee, cigarettes, and his pipe. I worried about him, and gave him all kinds of grief about his diet until he grinned and said, "Shut up and drive." A pickup was parked outside the restaurant; on the trailer attached to it lay the head, skin, and entrails of a cow.

I imagined a gaggle of Brussels bureaucrats looking around at the parched grass beside the road, the slabs of slanting rock studded with rough and hardy juniper, pinyon, and ponderosa pines. The English delegate was fanning himself weakly with the *Sunday Telegraph*, the Frenchman complaining loudly about the lack of decent coffee. Utah seemed to have nothing in common with Washington, D.C, or Indianola, or Stroudsburg, let alone with Europe. "I think they'd all give up or shoot themselves," I said. "It'd be madness."

It was hard to imagine anywhere farther from civilization. The road itself seemed scratched along the desert's margin; the road crews laying hot mix seemed tiny and irrelevant against a landscape so inhospitable, so completely abandoned. They also made me feel guilty: I was here because I wanted to be; they were here because they had to be. Even rubble and weeds have majesty on this scale. *You could not build anything one-hundredth this size,* the desert says. *Your Hoover Dam barely fills one wrinkle in my endlessness. You cannot destroy me, because I am already laid waste.* I had found the physical equivalent of the Bachelard Principle: The landscape that is not afraid to speak. *My geography and history are transparent, unafraid. This is what I am,* not even bothering to add, *Take me or leave me.*

In the end we found no petrified forest, but, hidden on the parched valley floor behind a screen of trees was an artificial lake on which one girl was driving a motorboat and another was water-skiing behind her. O America, burning your natural resources like the runner carrying the Olympic torch, with every other country pounding along behind you, trying to catch up.

We had lunch at Mount Carmel Junction in The Best Western Thunderbird Resort, in which everything was fake except the hanging plants at the front consuming half the region's water supply. Out of the corner of my eye, I thought I saw a long green snake among them. When I looked again, it was a hose.

We were just finishing lunch when a Harley roared past. Not just any Harley, though: this was a Harley trike, with flames painted on the two rear wheel covers, and it was being driven by a woman, with a guy on the back. I immediately thought they might be able to tell us more about Sturgis; Tomasz immediately thought picture. We leaped into the Skylark and shot off after them.

Almost at once, the road began to wind uphill, hugging the mountain. "Pull up beside them! Pull up beside them!" Tomasz yelled. Well, that was my plan, but I couldn't help thinking that once they saw they were being followed by two maniacs yelling and waving at them from a car, then even if I did manage to avoid a head-on collision and even if we managed to get them to pull over, they might kill us. "Faster!" Tomasz yelled, frantically waving me on. After a few moments, when we hit a relatively straight stretch, I managed to pull out alongside them, but to my horror Tomasz, instead of calling out something neighborly like "May we take your picture?" shouted "Pull over! Pull over!" and pointed off the road. To my amazement they did. I pulled up behind them at a safe distance, in case they got off and came after us with a chain and a tire iron. Tomasz armed himself with a few pounds of cameras. I waited in the car, trying to hide under the dashboard.

Their names were Reggie and Sharol, and they were from Royal, Arkansas. He was tall and burly, she was slight, and both were tanned and leathery from the sun. They wore T-shirts from the Broken Spoke Saloon, Sturgis, South Dakota. Both were well into middle age. She worked in a convenience store.

"He's on disability," she explained. "His eyes are going."

"Only reason I'll let her drive," he said, in mock disgust.

They'd set out two weeks previously; they'd been to see Lake Powell and Zion Canyon, now they were heading off to Colorado to see her dad, and some friends. The whole trip would be 5,000 miles before they were done.

The Harley was immaculate.

"Got 2,000 miles on the shine job, mind you," Reggie pointed out, tongue in cheek. They'd bought the bike-to-trike conversion kit from Canada by mail; it had cost them $15,000.

As I asked questions, Tomasz sprang into action, shooting me by the bike, by the couple, with my notebook out, chewing my pen, behind the bike, in the back of the bike behind Sharol, in the back of the bike behind Sharol with Reggie's enormous forearm in a hammerlock around my neck. Then order was restored, and Reggie climbed over the fenders and into his place in the back.

"Could I ask you to please put your arms around her?" Tomasz inquired. Reggie reached around Sharol and squeezed her breasts. She grinned.

"This is a very American thing," Tomasz said afterward—the Thorolds' trip as an expression of freedom, that is, not the squeezing of breasts. What I thought was especially American about them was not so much their outlaw spirit—every nation has its bikers—as their goodwill.

It was at this point that I began to wonder if Sturgis wasn't a kind of Woodstock, in a very specific, chrome-and-leather way, or perhaps what Woodstock might have become if it had been held every year, and admission had always been free. I couldn't wait to get there.

Zion Canyon consisted of two quite different halves. The first was shallow and pink, and the rock on each side of the tiny road, winding between vast boulders, seemed to have been scoured into a series of rippling horizontal grooves, leaving it looking curiously soft and fleshy. After an umbilical tunnel, the road emerged at mid-height into a valley of magnificent mountains and then zigzagged downhill step after step after step, and with each descent the mountains on each side grew still taller and more overwhelming. At the western end of the canyon, someone had put up an IMAX movie theater. "YOU HAVE SEEN THE PARK NOW SEE THE MOVIE."

Every town in southern Utah, it seemed, had its fake western saloon, its fake jail, its fake livery stable. It all had a strange quote-of-a-quote quality, as the architecture they were echoing was itself the desperate false-front pretentiousness of a century ago when every western main street building, and many eastern ones, was little more than a shed with a much taller rectangular frontage to make it seem bigger, grander, and older. In a speck-on-the-map called Virgin, the "Indian store" itself made no bones about being just a big metal box, but out front sprouted a bizarre set of pint-size Wild West buildings, bent and exaggerated like a Warner Brothers cartoon. The fakery reached a glorious peak in a little buy-your-fossils-here bend-in-the-road called Orderville, where outside an odd building like an upturned pot stood a strange white skeleton. "What is that?" I asked the proprietress. "It's a cow, a deer, and a horse," she said. With its fossils and dinosaurs, this was in some respects the very oldest America, yet nowhere did America's history seem less genuine.

Maybe everything seems false when it exists without a context, I wrote in my journal. *Maybe it's just that this is a desperately poor region, and everything has to be turned into a commodity. And to be a commodity, it needs to be recognizable, which is why inside the upturned pot building, the exotic minerals and the delicate, bony fish fossils cost twice as much if they have also been carved into coasters, or bookends, or just geometrical shapes. No commodification without representation.*

We saw Las Vegas from the north, a bowl of smog in a valley of gravel. As we neared the city, an AWACS plane flew overhead, looking for trouble. Both sides of the interstate were littered with so much trash and broken glass it looked as if the entire population of Nevada spent its Saturday nights cruising up I-15 getting drunk and chucking longnecks out of the window. Las Vegas lay like a mirage, offering the promise of fiscal redemption, a beacon for the nation's illusions, but all around was the wasteland of a poor state. It was like being back in the eighties all over again. One stroke of bad luck out here and you'd flame down into the gravel wastes and all that would be left would be the fragment of your humanity, holed up in your wreckage under the merciless sun.

Or at least that was my vision of Nevada—a paranoid concoction of my hatred of fiscal conservatism, my conviction that the place is still run by organized crime, and an irrational fear of the Nevada police, which must have been left over from the *Hitchhiker's Guide to North America*. I couldn't buy into Andy's amiable view of Las Vegas as colorful and fascinating; I was bracing myself for trouble.

Like all sizeable American cities, Las Vegas' characteristic glamor-sights are a tiny portion of an unremarkable whole, most of which was being torn down or built up. The taxis sported ads for—we're talking about the same ad, now—doctors who made house calls and strippers. When we peeled ourselves out of the Skylark at a gas station that tried to charge us twice for the same tank of gas, we were suffocated in a kind of air I'd never tasted before—an evil, hot, angry air. Raymond Chandler wrote a short story called "Red Wind," and I knew at once exactly what he meant.

As soon as I stepped inside the Mirage I could see what Andy had meant about a theme park. Kids, parents, grandparents, singles, and family groups—all had that Disney World look, the head revolving on the neck, eyes wide as oysters, determined not to miss a sight, not the white tigers, not the wolves or hippos, or whatever other jungle attractions the hotel offered. Most hotels don't see that much lobby traffic during a fire. The front desk had a 20,000-gallon aquarium, featuring live sharks and tropical fish. What it didn't have was a desk clerk. I eventually attracted the notice of a small, dapper man impersonating a French waiter, who told me that the hotel was full. I could have told him that.

Tomasz defied death by making two U-turns on the strip, dropping me off at the first hotel that advertised vacancies: the Casino Royale. I liked the Casino Royale immediately because it didn't pretend to be anything other than a casino with rooms on top of it. It was so modest its restaurant was a Denny's. It had no gift shop, so the guy who asked Julie, the desk clerk, if he could buy a Casino Royale sweatshirt was disappointed. It had only four floors, unlike the Mirage opposite, which seemed to have several thousand. The view from my window encompassed a large parking lot flanked by a small, uninviting kidney-shaped pool and a long Pepto-Bismol pink wall punctuated by the word "Casino" in red neon over a small door; on the right, by an unfinished hotel-casino the size of Belize; and between them lay a very tall crane. Behind the crane stood Treasure Island, a new hotel-casino-theme park in the shape of an open book standing upright.

There were no laundry facilities in the Royale. I could have my laundry picked up, but Julie warned me against it: "I had a man send his laundry out and it came to $80." I had the overwhelming urge to watch TV and suck my thumb, but no: I would shower, don my least smelly clothes, and go out to look for dinner and live sharks.

By the time I left my room, though, Las Vegas phobia had started getting to me. All the muscles between my shoulderblades locked so tightly that I felt shooting pains up and down my back and I could-n't turn my head to either side. My first stop was the aptly named Mirage, across the road, where the first sight was a tank decorated not at all like a temple in which a white tiger was lying with its back to the four-deep throng at the glass frontage. It seemed stuffed; everyone near one of the video monitors watched those instead, where the video tiger cubs gamboled and played.

This thoroughfare led (of course) into the main casino, where the hostesses wore short red velvet dresses caught in the clefts of their buttocks. The ATM, if I understood the screen correctly, charged $7.99 for credit card withdrawals between $25 and $50. I became so convinced that I was being watched on camera that I started sneaking into the men's room to take notes in a stall: *Waitresses @ Mirage have little tails.* Every second I expected a security guard to grab my notebook and tear all the pages out.

I found a tropical-theme grill, but froze in my tracks when I saw the three-piece band playing between the fake palms. A girl with the exact expression of a magician's assistant was playing light percussion and shifting her weight back and forward almost, but not quite, as if she were dancing. An aging male model played congas; an aging rockabilly hipster played a steel-drum line on a Yamaha keyboard. All had clearly been dead a long time.

I ate noodles in a Chinese restaurant (all this was still in the Mirage, by the way) with fake ferns and bird-of-paradise flowers, followed by decaf in a coffee-and-pastry shop next to a man who looked unnervingly like Billy Graham but sounded like Fred Rogers. I thought of getting my nails done in lilac and cinnamon at the Spa and Salon, but it was closed, the door guarded by two bronze Dobermans. The whole area was nothing but a mall, the dullest of all human creations. I retraced my steps to the casino...

...where the strangest thing happened. I was strolling between the slot machines and the blackjack tables, trying to look as if I were an undercover agent from the IRS and giving the dealers my best steely gaze to make them, rather than me, feel uneasy, when the whole clanking, flashing, glittering place seemed to pale, as if someone had undone a valve under the carpet that let all the color drain away, and left the room and all of Las Vegas seeming no longer threatening but utterly irrelevant. A guy sat at his slot machine while it paid out 145 quarters like a mechanical orgasm, but his success, and the failure of the college student losing steadily at the blackjack table, just didn't interest me. This place wasn't about dreams and depravity and greed and glitter, it was only about making and losing money, and as such I had already seen it all over America. I found myself thinking of the biker couple from Arkansas, and their 5,000-mile escape, blasting through the southwest to get away from the convenience-store job, and next to them Las Vegas seemed lifeless and unimaginative.

I left the Mirage, whose name now seemed to have taken on yet another layer of meaning. As I waited at the light to cross the street back to the Royale, a bald-shaven guy with an earring and a fire department T-shirt pointed down the street to the darkness beyond the city limits, the darkness above the desert, where a massive bolt of lightning split and vanished. "It's a storm coming," he said excitedly. "A big one." Before our light changed, two more bolts split, lighting up the purple sky. This was the real thing, I thought. This might be worth watching. One lightning strike could knock out the lights of this entire city, melt the computer credit-card links, fry the satellite dishes. Even a modest downpour, Julie had told me, and Las Vegas floods. Beside me, an elderly woman snapped a photo as the Mirage's fake volcano erupted.

CHAPTER 15

Another Casualty of the Sixties

July 30—Las Vegas, Nevada

Tomasz wanted to spend a couple of days together in Las Vegas, photographing the Liberace Museum, but I'd already had enough of the place. I had the wild idea that I'd take a bus up Route 95 to Beatty, hitch west along the tiny National Park road through Death Valley, just so I could boast that I had done it (I had the whole thing worked out. I was going to buy an egg, crack it onto the road where I was thumbing, and see if it would fry), then cut north through Yosemite and make for Oakland, where I could crash with Mitzi Porges. I caught a cab to the bus station the next morning.

The cab driver, a transplanted New Yorker, affectionately described Las Vegas as a "friendly little burg." All the same, he went on to say that he worked the 4 a.m. shift because the night shift was too dangerous for his liking. "When they hold you up at night, they have a tendency to kill you." Downtown Las Vegas, I had discovered, is like a barbell, with a glitzy center around the Golden Nugget and a glitzy center around Caesar's Palace with a nasty, decrepit strip running between the two. As we stopped at every light down this strip, the dispatcher put out a call to some apartment building behind the Stratosphere, but nobody answered it. "That's where the druggies hang out. You go in there and you won't come out." Still, he was a cheerful soul and a Boston Bruins hockey fan. It's amazing what will take root in the desert.

The bus station, like most, was not remarkable for its cleanliness or charm. I couldn't see them hiring George Persinger to restore it. Behind me in the line for the Reno bus was a curious couple. She was short, slight, pretty in a tired way. He was a big guy, six three, perhaps 240 pounds; small mustache, long graying black hair slicked back off his forehead and falling down onto his collar; stubbled and gap-toothed, with a deep smoker's cough. He spotted my accent right away, with none of this wishy-washy "English or Australian?" stuff, and told me I reminded him of an English judge in the St. George, Utah, misdemeanor court. "Thirty days," he said, in passable English tones.

They got on the same bus as I did, and sat across the aisle and one row back. "How much do you weigh?" he asked, looking her up and down.

"Hundred and fifteen," she said.

He laughed. "Hell, my leg weighs a hundred and fifteen." I couldn't quite work out their stories, especially hers, since he did most of the talking and had the louder voice. She was going to San Francisco to see her kids, and had been traveling for several days straight. He said something to her about a jail pass, but that might have been a joke. He seemed to have been thrown out of Las Vegas for drunkenness.

"Them girls with the slick pantyhose and the short skirts come around and give you free drinks. I'm not a gambler, but I sat there and fooled around with a dollar, two dollars of nickels for about four hours, had about fifteen drinks...."

He had been in the Army for 18 years, and threw some jokes across the aisle to me about places he'd been stationed in England, about spending most of his time getting off base and getting stoned. "Get out the hashish and fire that baby up!" He said he'd been married "for three years to a bitch from hell," and he'd never do that again.

The bus stopped at Lathrop Wells, Nevada, where a miniature western town—lockup, saloon, gallows, etc.—was just the frontage for a convenience store. Not every convenience store, though, sells postcards of Death Valley tarantulas as big as your hand (which didn't do much for my confidence) or displays a sign saying THEY'RE BACK! BROTHEL T-SHIRTS.

Brothel? A sign outside had said Adult Entertainment, and when I investigated, it seemed to point to a small cuboid building set back from the road calling itself the Cherry Patch Ranch II. I suspected this had little to do with fruit trees, but as everything was closed in the late morning heat, I would never know.

This weird little storefront set me thinking back to *Baghdad Café* again. No wonder outsiders find these desert roadside buildings so compelling. Out in front is the road, the passing of time, the route to the civilized world; out back is the desert. It's as if all of humanity is wedged into those few yards of frontage under the brilliant sun. Anything might happen.

Back on the bus, I noticed that the conversation across the aisle from me had taken on a hint of urgency. He was going to get out at Beatty and try his luck hitching to Reno, or maybe spend the night at Beatty and then try hitching tomorrow; and as we got closer to Beatty he began hitting on her in a gentle—almost courteous—but persistent way, trying to persuade her to get off at Beatty with him. She kept on not quite saying no, talking about her daughter who was expecting her, changing the subject. She asked him what he would do if he won the lottery—buy a Ferrari? He laughed his deep laugh, and perhaps coughed his deep cough, too. "Ferrari? I'd have me a big old black whore about eight feet tall." I liked him. He was loud and coarse, but he spoke his mind and misled nobody. He was a magnificent wreck.

More desert went by, and still more. Every so often a narrow, dusty road would wander away like an ill-advised out-of-stater, to die of thirst somewhere out of sight. It was inconceivable that there was anywhere near here for a road to go to—though somewhere beyond the dry mountains off to the right was Groom Lake, a.k.a. Area 51, the most secret air base in America (that we know of).

The two of them were still talking, but he had half-turned toward her now. Something was going on. "I been reading a lot about the male menopause," he said, "and how once we start realizing that we're not going to live forever after all, we start thinking about what we've done with our lives. And when I look back at it, the fact is, I ain't done a lot with it. I had a lot of fun, but I haven't done much that was any use. My daughters say, 'Look at your grandchildren. They're something.' I tell them, I didn't have anything to do with them. My daughters say, 'We couldn't have had them without you,' but..." He shrugged that argument away. "When I was young, I thought I was going to change the world, but it never happened."

He paused, chewing on what he was about to say. "I'm sorry to get all philosophical on you, but—well, it's been on my mind a lot. Fact is, I know I'm goin' to go to hell."

"Why do you think you're going to hell?" she asked.

"Because I killed a lot of little yellow people." He was young and gung ho and All-American, he told her, and Lyndon Baines Johnson told him to go, so he went. Now one of his few consolations seemed to be that he would meet Lyndon Baines Johnson in hell.

"The worst part of it all," he said somberly, "was that I didn't have any reason to kill them. Hell, the only reason they were shooting at us was because we were in their country. It wasn't like they were in California."

She tried to reassure him, and told him that everyone had committed sins of various kinds. She certainly had. He said, "Yeah, but you didn't kill a lot of little yellow people. Shit, if I were God, I'd send me to hell."

This is the thing that I regret most about the whole trip. I wanted to cross the aisle, sit in the seat in front of them, turn, rest my forearms on the seat backs, and offer some kind of consolation—but I didn't. My own personal theology is still so new and unspoken, and I fell back into that English reserve. So I left him staring into the heart of darkness, his own heart. He had been tested more than many of us will ever be; he had been thrown into a program of accelerated learning—a basic training of the soul.

When I got off at Beatty, they both got off too, though I don't think he even noticed me. When I had set my pack up on Route 374, the side road to Death Valley, he appeared and marched heavily past me on the other side of the road as if heading out of town. He didn't recognize me. After 15 or 20 minutes he reappeared, calling out to me, "Where's the liquor store at?" I spread my arms and shrugged. By the time I went into the hotel-casino to take a break from the sun, they were both at the bar; he was drunk, and it was too late. He was already with his demons, another casualty of the sixties.

Beatty wasn't much more than a bend in Route 95 with a few buildings staggering up into the hot, dry hills surrounding it. The junction where I set up my pack featured a tiny bank on one side—I kept thinking the Beattians pulling over at the ATM were stopping to pick me up— and a tiny Nevada Highways Department depot on the other. A few yards beyond me was a tiny hut, the size of an outhouse, labeled BEATTY MUSEUM, which was closed, and a Death Valley ranger station, which was also closed, but at least offered a map of the region. Beatty fell between Bare Mountain and the Bullfrog Hills, and in the Bullfrogs was Rhyolite, a ghost town where Shorty Harris and Ed Cross had found gold and which, in its heyday, according to the brochure, had three water systems, three train lines, over 50 mines, one daily and two weekly newspapers, an opera house, a symphony, baseball teams, tennis courts, swimming pools, two undertakers, two hospitals, eight physicians, two dentists, 19 lodging houses, 18 grocery stores, over 50 saloons, two churches and Tom Kelly's Bottle House, made entirely of bottles. It sounded wonderful. Somewhere in Death Valley was Zabriskie Point, the Devil's Golf Course, Bad Water, and Salt Creek, which has flowing water and popfish, whatever they are.

I decided against the fried egg. Out here on the fringes of Death Valley, it wasn't that hot—no more than 95 degrees, say. The wind was warm but light, not unpleasant—a yellow wind. All the same,

I was uneasy. The few passersby stared. The sheriff prowled past. "People are strange when you're a stranger," Jim Morrison said.

In order to get past this unease, I tried a tactic I'd never used before: I nodded once, briefly, at everyone who passed. A nod is a simple thing, far less demanding than a smile or a wave, and almost impossible to resist. I nodded, and everyone nodded back: the guys in the Nevada Highways Department pickups, the little old ladies, even the sheriff. After half an hour, I found myself warming to Beatty more than virtually anywhere else I passed through. It was a wonderfully hospitable little town. Everybody nodded.

In more than two hours, I was passed by at most 40 vehicles that were actually going into Death Valley, most of which were expensive out-of-state sport trucks packed to the roof with expensive climbing/running/camping/hiking/orienteering/scuba gear, with mountain bikes hitched to the hatchback and streamlined Thule containers on the roof full of more scuba gear. Maybe it was the heat or the disappointment, but I began to be pestered by a scene that kept rising out of my imagination and wouldn't be dismissed, a scene in which a group of freaks in a VW bus would pull over and yell "Hop in, man!" tossing baggage into a corner to make room, stashing my backpack in the way back. We'd tool over the mountains and down through Death Valley telling stories, laughing outrageously, comparing travelers' tales. We'd all fall silent when we first saw the valley, then breathe "Oh, wow. Far out. Look at that!" We'd look for Zabriskie Point, and someone would say, "No, it's farther over that way, man" and we'd argue over our recollections of the movie, and someone would try to hum the Pink Floyd music from the soundtrack. Then north to Yosemite, where we'd camp out, and from somewhere under the mountain of luggage one of them would haul out a guitar....

No freaks any more, I wrote in my notebook. *No VW buses. I can't afford such dreams. They make me bitter. I need to stay in the present. Stop all this low-percentage stuff. Get some lunch, switch over to 95. Make for Reno.*

Yet no sooner had I thought this—well, no sooner than another 90 minutes of hitching in the midday heat outside a gas station visited solely by Germans going to Las Vegas—than it came true, or at least a version of it came true, translated into the idiom of the late nineties: I was picked up by Hank, an artist from New Mexico driving a Subaru going all the way to Oakland.

I offered to help pay for gas. Sure, he said. "Isn't that what people used to say? Gas, grass, or ass?" His words jarred me like the bow wave of a truck. Once again, I'd stumbled into the traffic in another corridor of time. Is that really what they used to say? Not in England.

"So, you're from New Mexico. Ever seen a UFO?" I said, joking. To me, the whole southwestern desert is an eerie place, the stories of UFO sightings and of top-secret air bases blending in my mind and the public imagination until the flying saucers are next-level Air Force prototypes and the government is run by aliens.

He looked at me as if it was my turn to startle him with a casual comment that arrived like a brick through a window. "As it happens," he said slowly, "I have. Just the other day"—though that encounter turned out to be part of a larger story, a story that seemed to arise from the desert around us and follow us, hovering almost visibly in the hot, dry air.

"I went to a fleamarket in Las Cruces," he began, "and there's this very distinguished-looking old man, 88 years old, selling these wonderful paintings, and he introduces himself and he says that he's the former senator for New Mexico, Joseph Montoya. I'm with the mayor of the town that I live in, and she remembered his name. So we asked him, why was he selling these paintings? Well, he doesn't have his house any more, his wife died, blah blah blah. So we started talking, and I realized that he was the senator from 1945-1949, right during the 1947 Roswell incident. So we wound up buying all of the paintings, because they were great paintings, and we took him to lunch because I wanted to pump him for information about his UFO experiences, because the mayor and I had just had one no more than two weeks before that."

"What? What had happened?"

"Well, we were driving back from Albuquerque at 10:30 at night and a string of white lights on a diagonal line was following us across the desert. It would surge up on us really, really fast—and I had her car going to the floor, I was going about a hundred miles an hour, and this thing would go *whoom!* Just like that. It was a diagonal row of white lights, that's all you could see. And then it would zoom back. It would zoom away."

"Wow. How far off the ground?" I asked.

"The lights looked as if they went right to the ground, but I couldn't tell how high up they were because I couldn't tell how far back it was. There was no way of getting any perspective because it was a dark, dark desert night. But this thing was gaining on us and moving away, gaining on us and moving away. Finally I said, the hell with this, I'm going to stop. And as soon as I took my foot off the accelerator, it just went *whoom!* back, shot out of sight and the lights went out, gone. Then we stopped the car. We were right at the back entrance to White Sands missile base, you know, the proving-grounds base, and within two minutes they scrambled I don't know how many jet planes and helicopters one after another—they scrambled the entire base in the direction that we saw this thing go zooming off in. It was unbelievable. We were pissing in our pants. Then I was afraid to drive the rest of the way. Not one car passed us on that road that night between San Antonio and Saragosa. It's the deadest road in the world."

We turned left at bleak, dusty Tonopah, which I'd always assumed existed only in the mind of the Grateful Dead. Tucson to Tucumcari, Tehachapi to Tonapah—how could these desert names be part of anything but a long, strange trip?

"So then we meet the senator, right? We're at lunch, have a couple of glasses of wine and I had to ask him, 'Joe, you were there at Roswell....' He looked at first a little uneasy, but then he looked at us and figured, well, we're certainly not with the government, and he told us he had been warned not to talk to anybody, over and over again for many, many years, or he would lose his Social Security, he'd go out into a shallow grave in the desert, all this sort of stuff. But he told us that he was there. And saw it, saw the bodies, was in the hangar." The four alien bodies from the UFO that crashed on Mac Brazel's ranch on July 4, 1947, that is, and the fragments of the weird craft made apparently out of tinfoil, collected from the desert hillside and taken to the Air Force base. "Not only did he see it, but a guy around the corner in Truth or Consequences was also on the base as an officer in the R.A.F. who was stationed there, is still alive, now has cancer and wants to talk about it.

"So I go to the Roswell U.F.O. museum, right? and I tell the director this story. He's very, very interested. Very interested. And he wants to speak to Senator Montoya, and this other officer. So I gave him all the information on how to find them, blah blah blah.

"About a month later, a man calls me from Pennsylvania. Pennsylvania, of all places. And he says he's with, quote, the U.F.O.

museum. Gave me some name like Dan Smith. And I had no reason at first to question whether he really was or not. He said 'I'm a researcher and I'm attached to the Roswell thing'—but no one had mentioned his name at that Roswell place. He started asking me all these questions about what happened, what did [Montoya] say, where were you when you had this conversation, and you could tell he was taking all this down, word for word."

Hank broke off to get gas, which I paid for in a small barnboard shack of a gas-station-and-quick-stop, west of Tonopah. In one corner, a crusty old local was holding forth about Clinton's wickedness while the other two or three people squashed into the narrow aisles did their best to ignore him. It was the only time all trip I heard anyone discussing national politics. (The same was true in 1973: I can remember only one person discussing Watergate.) Television, radio, and the newspapers seemed to have their own arena, existing everywhere yet nowhere, in which their own matadors fought their own bulls. For the first time, I understood that this disembodied dimension was what people getting on with their lives out here in America meant when they said "Washington."

He continued when we got back into the car. "The next time I spoke to the people at the Roswell museum," Hank said, "they had contacted Joe Montoya. He'd moved from Truth or Consequences, and he wouldn't talk to anybody because he had been approached by somebody from the government again because of the conversation that we had. Now, how did they find out? The guy at the Roswell UFO place thinks it's his own telephone that the government's tapped. Of course, it sounds totally paranoid, but I wouldn't put anything past this government."

We passed small salt pans amid the sagebrush, and headed toward the chain of mountains at the Nevada-California border.

Hank told me that his wife had died in a car crash; he was very close to his two daughters, now high-powered and magnificent in their own right. He himself lived in what sounded like a high-class condo by a ski area, and did what might be called southwestern art, which was selling rather well at the moment.

Though I didn't know it at the time, that was the last I'd see of the desert, and to my surprise I would come to miss it. My experience of the desert was an oddly social one: I was always in a car or a bus, talking with someone about what I saw, or listening. Now I wish I had spent more time walking, vulnerable to that sense of brilliant and cruel indifference.

At Benton we turned west on Route 120, the most interesting road I traveled all summer and probably one of the most interesting in the country. The first thing that happened, though, was that Hank, who had been complaining of hunger for some time, started muttering, "Hot springs. We'll get something to eat at the hot springs." The sun's got to him, I thought. He's beginning to hallucinate. But the road jumped off the valley floor and suddenly, in a little grove of cottonwood and aspen, appeared a small wooden house surrounded by strange metal carcasses that had once been farm machinery or instruments of multiple torture. This, it turned out, was the town of Benton Hot Springs. Well, this and the tumbledown hotel-and-garage building opposite where someone was mending junk cars by the time-honored method of standing them out in the sun and then retiring for a little nap. Benton Hot Springs' leading citizen seemed to be Uncle Bob Schmidt, droll, semi-shaven proprietor of this antique emporium, ice cream shop, and hot tub spa.

The five hot tubs were out back, each in its own little grove by the little hot stream that, Uncle Bob told us, rises in the canyon above at a scalding 137 degrees, though by the time it runs through his property it is only slightly too hot to take at 124 degrees. (The stream looked innocent enough, though in winter, he said, it steams.) Uncle Bob had jury-rigged a number of hoses, shower-heads, and other miscellaneous adventures in plumbing to draw water from the stream and spray it into the hot tubs, which looked like well-aged whisky barrels. The showerheads were not because bathers liked showers, he said, but because the water was still too hot, and needed more exposure to air to cool it. He'd had the water tested, he said, and claimed it was as pure as any spring water in the world, though high in sodium. "See how it has that slightly greasy feel? That's salt, Mother Nature's water softener."

From this micro-resort, 120 rose into a cradle of hot, dry little hills, turned north, and began skipping along a series of rapid bumps and hollows: driving it was like dry-land powerboat racing. We spent half the time in midair. Then west again through the Inyo National Forest, but almost at once we were cresting a hill and looking in astonishment down to our right at Mono Lake, the strangest body of water I've ever seen.

"In the middle distance," wrote Israel Russell in *Quarternary History of the Mono Valley,* 1889, "there rests upon the desert plain what appears to be a wide sheet of burnished metal, so even and brilliant is its surface. It is Lake Mono. At times, the waters reflect the mountains beyond with strange distinctness and impress one as being in some way peculiar, but usually their ripples gleam and flash in the sunlight like the waves of ordinary lakes. No one would think from a distant view that the water which seems so bright and enticing is in reality so dense and alkaline that it would quickly cause death of a traveler who could find no other with which to quench his thirst."

Russell's "in some way peculiar" might go on to include the fact that the original Paiute residents of the region were known as the Kuzedika'a, or fly-pupae-eaters, because they ate flies—or, more accurately, the grubs of the alkali flies that breed around the lake. Or Russell might have had in mind the strange black cliff of volcanic ash rising down the far shore. Most likely, though, it would be the bizarre gray excrescences rising from the water's edge looking like stalagmites made by dribbling wet sand through your fingers. These are called tufa. The lake is fed by warm underwater streams laced with limestone particles. As the streams hit the cold lake water, they precipitate out, depositing tiny granules of lime that cluster and build up. In past years, when the lake's level was higher, they were invisible; now, as the lake falls in what some see as an environmental catastrophe in the making (caused by the theft of the lake's tributary streams by the Los Angeles Department of Water and Power), the fantastic tufa gardens are exposed like coral at low tide.

You should think of eating at the Mono Inn at Mono Lake, Uncle Bob Schmidt had said, because it is owned and operated by Ansel Adams's granddaughter Sarah. We found the Inn, perched above the lake just north of the oddly named town of Lee Vining. Leroy "Lee" Vining crossed the Sierras in 1852 in search of gold, built a sawmill and sold lumber in Aurora, Nevada, where he came to an odd end: As a shootout developed in the Exchange Saloon, he left the building and started to walk up the street. Somehow his gun went off in his pocket, shot him in the groin, and he bled to death.

The sun was already declining. If we wanted to see Yosemite before dark, we wouldn't have time to wait for dinner. We looked around the room of Adamsiana on sale. We looked around the art gallery, its panoramic window overlooking the lake, while the party ahead of us was waiting for its table. Sarah swept in, tall, beautiful, athletic, to tell the party that their table was ready. This was a magazine moment, a quest moment, one that miraculously granted me access to one of the epic figures of the west, someone who had helped to define America.

But at that instant I suffered what might be called a crisis of time. The past, with its epic photographer, vanished, and in its place I saw a busy woman getting on with her own life. Why should I interrupt her? Besides, I know nothing about Ansel Adams except that when I saw his big show in New York I went the wrong way around it because of my deep revulsion for shuffling along in a crowd. I passed on Uncle Bob's greetings, she smiled, and vanished with her guests down to the dining room.

The sun was barely above the mountains of Yosemite as we climbed up through the switchbacks at the park's eastern gate, crowning the peaks with gold as the shadows crept up from the wooded valleys. We started out giddily, taking turns standing up through the sun roof to shoot photographs while careening under precipices and around blind corners, but after a few miles we reached the first ranger post and were told politely that all the gas stations in the park were closing.

This was when I began to realize that Hank was one of the most anxious people I'd ever met. At once, his high spirits started being nibbled away by the invisible mouse of anxiety. He had a quarter tank. It was at least 20 miles back to the last gas station we had passed. Well, we'd push on. Surely we'd find something. Besides, how far could it be to the other side of the park, anyway?

The first gas pumps we passed were closed. We ran into another ranger. Well, she said, the pumps father west stayed open a little longer, so we might get lucky there. How far were they? Oh, a good 40 miles. *Forty miles?* How big was this park, anyway? Oh, about 120 miles across.

Hank started worrying in earnest—a serious, professional anxiety of the kind that transforms the entire world into one ghastly, undulating threat, and all incoming data just goes to prove that your worst fears were right after all. It was now dusk, and the forest-and-mountain landscapes were dark, winding tunnels. The fuel gauge was just above empty, and we had at least 35 miles to a gas station that might well be closed. To take his mind off all this, I asked him if he had been to Woodstock. To my delight, he had.

"It was a nightmare. Ah, Jesus. The mud. The rain. It was freezing. This black friend of mine, Marianne, bought two tickets, and she forced me to go." He chuckled at himself. "She didn't have a car, and I did....It was our senior year in college. She just laid a guilt trip on me. She said, 'You'd take me if I was white!' And I thought, well, if you're going to go to Woodstock with anybody it should be with this outrageous black woman, with her Afro.

"I don't remember the names of all the bands we heard. Jimi Hendrix. Uh...There was a lot of folk people there too. Joan Baez. You name it. Everybody who had a record at that time was there. Oh, God, who was that black musician?"

I racked my brains rapidly over this faint hint. "Ritchie Havens?"

"That's it, Ritchie Havens. Oh, God, I can't remember who else.... There must have been a hundred bands. I can't remember one. I think I must have Alzheimer's. I wasn't even into that music, that's the weird thing."

"Who were you listening to?"

"I was listening to jazz. I was listening to, like, Stan Getz. I didn't even like the Beatles."

Me, I was 16 and in the wrong country when Woodstock took place, but I remember the British music papers panning the event as musically mediocre and self-indulgent. I asked Hank whether, at the time, it seemed like a significant occasion, or just a mess?

"It was a significant mess. It got so far out of control that the people who thought they could control it finally gave up. Once that happened, it started to be more fun. At first there were signs, there were fences, there were directions, there were guards, there were nurses," he said, as if he were talking about life itself. "There were police, there were all kinds of things. But after a while, it got so out of control that they just gave up. That's when it became a party. And it just went on all night long. Girls on guys' shoulders so they could see the bands, naked or at least topless. It was the era of free love, and there was a lot of that going on. Men and women, women and women, men and men. Of course, the drugs had a lot to do with it, too, but there was a sense of freedom, as if you left the rules of social behavior at the roadside when you entered that farmer's field. Anything went.

"The announcements were funny. 'The blue Pluto acid is no good. Don't take the blue Pluto.' They were warning people about a lot of the, uh, products that were being distributed among the crowd, and acid was a big problem because a lot of people had never tripped before and were freaking out. They had tents set up for people on bad trips, and the tents were filled to overflowing. I wasn't into drugs at the time, thank goodness, or else I'd probably still be there.

"Not everything that happened was good. I heard about people being raped, and being sexually assaulted by strangers because they were passed out facedown in the mud. It wasn't all pretty. For me it was odd, because I was very prudish. This was the most naked people I had ever seen partying at one time. I was from New Mexico, I wasn't used to this kind of thing. Baptist, on top of everything else." He shook his head and grinned ruefully.

"What I liked about it was that it was as out of control as you could get without killing someone, although I think somebody did die of an overdose—of what, I don't know. [Marianne and I] weren't that wild and crazy. I think we were both restraining influences on each other. I was too uptight, she was not going to take off her clothes being with a white guy. She was a black militant woman. If she was with a black guy she might have done it, but here she was with me, this white, blond, Baptist, Nazi-looking guy!"

I asked him what they were talking about as they were going, thinking that they might have been raving over the "three day nation," the sense of love and peace.

He laughed. "Well, we had an argument. She was pissed off because she paid for the motel in advance, and when we got back there finally, of course they wouldn't refund any money just because she didn't show up for the room. They rented the room to somebody else who walked the three miles or whatever it was back to the motel. And it was expensive. This was the closest motel, and they took advantage of that and charged I think about $75 a night, which was a lot back then. She had prepaid that, and she was furious that she didn't get her money back. So we left in a bad state of mind. Terrible hangover. I had slept in the back seat of somebody else's car. It was just parked there. The doors were open. She slept in the front seat. The worst that could happen was that somebody would ask us to get out. I don't know where the owners of the car were. They never showed up. And a lot of cars got stuck in the mud, because people had pulled off the road into the dirt and the grass, and people were helping to get them unstuck.

"If Woodstock were to happen again now, I think there'd be more deaths. We're darker now than we were in the sixties. That was a real innocent time, in many ways. You know, they redid it just a few years ago."

"Did you go?"

"No."

"Did you even think of going?"

"I did. I thought of Marianne—she lives in Buffalo. Woodstock is right near New Paltz. I was in New York at the time. I thought, well, gee, I should call her up. But, you know, the truth is that we were so miserable. We really didn't enjoy it because it rained; it was cold, we were uncomfortable, and I was trying to enjoy myself while drinking Lancer's."

Hank seemed to have drifted somewhere else. "When I see the movie *Woodstock* now, I can't even imagine I was in that. Seeing a movie of Vietnam and being a Vietnam vet, you probably have the same feeling. There's an unreal quality. When I watched the movie, I recognized certain people that I had seen because they were being outrageous, and those were the people they filmed, but looking at it now it's like it never happened. I wasn't there. It was like a dream state, or something."

And my own movie, my recollections of my cross-country trip: If I saw it now, would I even know the lanky, puppyish kid with the chestnut hair?

When we finally reached it, the gas station, a small pool of light among dark trees, was closed. People were inside, sweeping up, but they had turned the pumps off and would not turn them back on. Hank pleaded with them. They swept on. Now he was worrying about bears. This seemed a little excessive to me: We both had sleeping bags, I pointed out, and we could easily sleep in the car. His cell phone even had an automatic distress signal built in that would alert the gendarmes, but he was not soothed. "You don't understand, it's a technique," he said frantically. "If I worry about something, then it won't happen."

Down, down, down, curve after tight curve in the darkness, the headlights falling on countless tree trunks, Hank now convinced that the whole of American society was falling apart, that the kids with their Gothic body-piercings and dark clothing were all main-lining heroin. Then on the right, a patch of light: a little store with a gas pump out front. We fueled up the Subaru and our spirits, and as we broke out of the park and saw the whole of coastal California laid out in front of us in a carpet of tiny lights, Hank asked me shyly if I would mind looking at his poetry.

Who could not love this guy, this world?

~

CHAPTER 16

Between Me and the Basted Egg

July 31—Oakdale, California

Early-morning thoughts, 5:25 a.m.

Any spontaneous decision has about it not only joy and energy but a mysterious kind of truth. Any spontaneous act involves abandoning self-protection.

Oakdale is the home of the basted egg. "It's exactly the same as poached," said Melissa, the waitress. "Don't ask me why we call it that."

I knew right away that I was in California because the roads had become very serious and professional. Oakdale wasn't even on our map, but it had a five-lane street between me and the basted egg. But then anyone's roads seem well-funded after Nevada's.

Hank and I set off westward, through walnut and almond groves, past a ridge of a thousand windmills, their arms churning like a race of stationary swimmers, and it began to sink in that I was back in California again—the name itself still thrilling even though it's one of the few states outside of Vermont where I travel a couple of times a year—and I found myself remembering my arrival in Berkeley in 1973.

For a hip place, Berkeley seemed remarkably ugly. Robin dropped us off on a hot, dusty street of almost identical, charmless houses with address numbers in the tens of thousands. I'd never seen house numbers go that high. We walked several blocks, the numbers mounting in their hundreds like an auction, until we found the number Mitzi had given me.

I haven't the slightest recollection of the guy who opened the door, except that he was young and gave off the air of lived-in slovenliness that was always a good sign. "You don't know us," I began, "but I'm a friend of Mitzi Porges, whose brother Tim used to live in this house, and she said we might be able to stay here." He looked at us. I imagine him scratching his chest through his T-shirt. "Tim who?" We compared domestic genealogies, following the house's recent ancestral descent through its host of transient inhabitants, and came to the conclusion that Tim had moved out before this guy moved in. We waited on the step, he lounged in the doorway. Impasse. Then he caught sight of my guitar. "Hey, you got an axe? Come on in, man! Let's jam."

Richard and I trooped in. The guy picked up his electric guitar, which was lying on the couch like a stoned friend. I took my cheap travelers' classical out of its tartan PVC case. Richard settled in a corner. We tuned, more or less, and began to play.

Musically, the early seventies were a time when virtuosity was beginning to overcome cohesion. It was no longer cool for a band to be tight; individual display was where it was at. Album-length tracks replaced the two-minute single, and In-A-Gada-Da-Vida was born. People would compare concerts by the length of the guitar solo or the drum solo, and nothing was a better sign of artistic integrity than the long, self-indulgent jam session. The next hour and 45 minutes were some of the most boring of my life. I had no idea what he was playing or where he was going, and even if I tried a standard 12-bar chording pattern, he would wander off into keys of his own. I could barely play lead-guitar-style riffs, but it didn't matter: he had no interest in listening to what I was playing anyway. Richard adopted his by now familiar scowl, punctuated with even dirtier looks and jerks of the head to let me know that we had paid our dues and could I please shut up now? But the guy never looked up, and never stopped playing. You might think he was stoned, but I'm sure he wasn't. Narcissistic numbness was a respectable posture of the times; dope was just one way of getting there.

Eventually he stopped. "Far out, man." He told us we could sleep in the walk-in closet behind the front door.

Hank dropped me off in Walnut Grove, a wealthy suburb east of the Bay Area. It looked like the kind of place where the kids of 1973 Berkeley would live when they grew up and started software companies or chic health-food restaurants. One Jaguar driver gave another the finger. In a bookstore, the guy ahead of me in line must have been a lawyer: he was carrying a book titled *Big Deal,* and he had mastered the art of ordering his latte while talking on his cell phone so quietly that nobody else could hear what he said.

I was almost within sight of the Pacific—but how was I going to get there? In 1973 it was easy: Everyone lined up along University Avenue in Berkeley, two dozen, three dozen people in singles or groups with their thumbs out, and by nine in the morning they were all gone as the counterculture rapid-transit system picked them up in ones and twos and took them into the city. In 1998, the only person waiting at the freeway entrance was a ragged man with a sign— "Purple Heart No Income Small Change Anything Will Do Please Help"— calling inaudibly to the cars as they accelerated up the ramp. I was tired, my neck and shoulders still hurt like hell from Las Vegas, and I deserved a break. I was 45, dammit. I walked to the Walnut Grove Marriott, which had its own Avis desk like a baby in a kangaroo's pouch, and rented a little white car. As the computer reeled out the paperwork, another customer swung by and dropped off a couple of posters for the Avis staff. They were an artist's representation of a project under way at the National Ignition Facility. "He works at Lawrence Livermore," the manager explained. "He's making a star."

I zipped out into the traffic, thinking *You're not really in California unless you're driving*, something in me reaching out for that Joan Didion ecstasy, the fast, supple rhythm of the freeways, making for Oakland and Mitzi.

The rhythm of the freeways, though, had changed since Joan Didion's day. Now it was fast, slow, crawl, stop, as the lanes died and the orange barrels squeezed like a sphincter. So it was a few seconds before I realized that the patch of brilliant silver sunlight on the western horizon was the Pacific. It had taken me 11 days to cross America.

CHAPTER 17

Laundry on the Freeway

August 1—Oakland, California

Mitzi and her husband Bill lived in a sunny bungalow perched on the shoulder of a hill in Oakland. Mitzi herself looked completely unchanged after a quarter of a century—though warmer, less like an intellectual hawk—but now asked to be called Maria.

She showed me the little outbuilding she'd converted into a studio and some of her current work. She collects old-fashioned glass bottles, makes molds from them, then recasts them in colored beeswax, so the objects are beautiful, light, slightly unreal-looking. Then she plays with other characteristics of bottles: what they contain, the fact that they're supposed to stand upright, and the very fact that they're supposed to contain something at all. She engraves the bottles—in delicate copperplate gold writing—with the names of their supposed contents, but her bottles are full of abstractions: Fertility, Devotion, Lust. Their shapes, too, defy bottledom. Some have round bottoms, so they can't even stand up, some are joined at the side or bottom like Siamese twins, so the contents of the two would be bound to escape and mingle.

She made me up a bed on the floor of their basement/office/library, and I sank into it. By morning, though, the fear-of-Las-Vegas pain in my shoulders had migrated up to the back of my neck and I could barely turn my head. Maria made an appointment with their friend Doctor Dave, the cool chiropractor, at his office on Lombard. As he went to work with the ultrasound and the manipulations, he told me his own 1973 hitchhiking story.

He had been in Europe. He had $105 in his pocket one day, when he walked past a travel agency in Amsterdam offering a special to New York for $99. He figured he'd better grab it while he could, and flew back. "I called this girl I'd met in Greece, who lived out on Long Island. We'd become really good friends—very platonic, but very good friends. So I went and stayed with her...actually, her mother was dying of cancer, and I think I helped the family a bit because my mother had died from cancer, so we had long talks. Her father ended up really liking me, even though I had long hair and a beard and at first I think he was a bit intimidated by me.

"When I left, he drove me to the George Washington Bridge, and offered to pay for my trip back to San Francisco on an airplane, and I said no. Then he offered to lend me the money for the plane ticket, because he thought I didn't want a handout, and I said no, I'd rather hitchhike. Then he said, Well, at least let me give you some money, and I said no. So I took my five bucks and hitchhiked back across the United States."

omasz claims I was nine hours late for our first rendezvous in New York (I deny this)
o he walked around the city looking for visionary moments. For him, he said, New
ork is both a city of gold and a city of the dead, where the future rises glittering above
he past (TOP). It's also a conjunction of opposites, though this example (BOTTOM),
as an artificial one, part of a TV commercial being filmed downtown.

Photographs by Tomasz Tomaszewski

I found George Persinger and his sons in Toledo, Ohio, working to preserve the faith not only in the cathedral's statuary (ABOVE) but in its very bricks and mortar. Tomasz was often impressed by the way African-American churches, such as the Second Canaan Missionary Baptist Church in Detroit (OPPOSITE, TOP), played a vital role in holding their communities together. We both saw the family farm, too, as an American icon—though where but in America, Tomasz asked, do you see exhibits, like this one in Woodstock, Vermont (OPPOSITE, BOTTOM), to teach children how apple trees work?

ɔmasz arrived in South Dakota a few days before I did, and when he wasn't shoot-
ng bikers at the annual Harley-Davidson rally in Sturgis (OPPOSITE, TOP), he was
etting up before dawn and driving several hundred miles a day among the state's
nall towns, finding a panorama of the history of the plains on the main street in
Aitchell (OPPOSITE, BOTTOM). Well, not quite the entire history: there doesn't seem
ɔ be any sign of the Lakota Sioux. We found them on the Pine Ridge Reservation,
here Trevor and Godfrey Chipps improvised a shower on a sweltering day (ABOVE).

"The thing you forget about America," Tomasz said, "is that it's not a country, it's a continent. It has landscapes enough for a dozen countries." Jim Curuchet and Antonio Rodriguez, shepherds from the Basque lands in Spain, were brought over to work under the vast Wyoming sky (OPPOSITE, TOP). Mount Rainier National Park (OPPOSITE, BOTTOM), for Tomasz, was another region not yet cannibalized by progress. Ebenezer Bryce farmed a century ago at the foot of the canyon (ABOVE) that was later named after him. "It's a hell of a place to lose a cow," he said.

I left Las Vegas after less than a day, much to Tomasz's amazement. He couldn't understand why I wasn't drawn to Elvis impersonators on Fremont Street (TOP) or the Liberace Museum. While I saw wings on sale in a sex shop in Chicago, he went one better and found people actually wearing them (BOTTOM): just another day on Castro Street in San Francisco.

He made it in a dozen rides or so, running the usual gamut: a serviceman on a two-day pass driving 1,500 miles to see his girlfriend, a Kansas lawyer who casually pointed out that they were driving past an entire field of pot, a couple who invited him to join them for a threesome, a group of hippies who were so stoned they asked Dave to drive for them ("I drove for six or eight hours, until they came down from whatever they had taken, then they dropped me off, turned round and went back. I think I'd driven them hundreds of miles beyond where they were going"), and a fatherly, blue-collar guy who forced him to accept five dollars. "People in general were pretty darn nice," he concluded, as if it had only just struck him, and I thought, Yes, that's true: As adolescents, we're so self-centered we have no idea how much kindness people show us. That's probably the most significant difference for me: In middle age I no longer take generosity for granted.

"For my last ride, I got picked up by this hippie bus, with three or four people in it, just an old school bus with wooden bunk beds and curtains and posters on the ceiling, and tie-dye stuff, and they were burning incense—pretty colorful, but the thing was so darn slow it drove me nuts. So I saw a girl at a gas station. She had a Chevy Impala convertible. The top was down. I asked her where she was going. She really didn't know; she'd worked for Kodak in Rochester, New York, and just wanted to get away from home for a while. I just said, 'Why don't you come to California and stay at my parents' house?' So she did. No romantic thing between us at all. We slept in the car together in campgrounds. She slept in the front, I slept in the back. We drove for a couple of days, got to my parents' house; I introduced her to them, asked them if she could stay, they said yes and I said goodbye to my parents and went over to my girlfriend's—and didn't come home for two days! She ended up staying with my parents for a few months. She married a guy, and she still lives in California."

Listening to him, I realized how much the word "road" had changed. For me, in 1973, it was an enchanted word. It was the crucible where the elements toughened you up and your encounters changed you into something leaner and wiser, but it was also a kind of circus, full of people from every walk of life who had uprooted themselves and were now, as Cat Stevens put it, "on the road to find out."

Since then, the road has become narrower and harder; a "road warrior" is now a professional business traveler. Everyone travels more than they used to, by whatever means. The lonesome moan of the train whistle and the boats watched from the dock of the bay used to be exotic because nobody left the farm, or the neighborhood. I didn't travel outside England until I was 13. I didn't fly until I was 16, and at that point the longest car journey I had made was less than 200 miles. Hitchhiking was my first real means of travel, period. At 11, my daughter Zoe has crossed the Atlantic a dozen times. But everything is also safer, more convenient, more predictable. Everyone travels, but not everyone explores.

On 101 south all the traffic slowed down, and I couldn't figure out why; then I saw that there was clothing all over the freeway. It looked as though someone had been carrying their laundry in a bag, perhaps on the back of a pickup, which had burst, scattering probably three or four dozen pieces of clothing across the asphalt.

It was bizarre, because it felt as if I was in danger of running over a person—and presumably others felt the same, because we all slowed down to a crawl. A pinkish-red check shirt, probably a woman's size, lay on the road in front of me, and I swerved to avoid it. It was as if the people who lived here, on this place of no people, had vanished, and left only their shapes. Some very deep drama of the road and the city was being enacted in our strange, jittery driving behavior: the freeway is the place where we last expect to see people, and it's disturbing to see even the shapes of people. The clothes represented a strange archaeology, as if here at last was evidence that once people had lived here, before a catastrophe—the building of the highway—had startled them, and they had fled.

Maria and Bill recommended a tiny Mexican restaurant down at the foot of the hill, right beyond the headquarters of the Oakland Hell's Angels. It wasn't a war zone, but it was barely demilitarized. By the time I'd gotten to the bottom of the hill, all the trees had disappeared—had fled, probably—reminding me of the study that found that the fewer trees there are in an area, the higher the crime rate. As I waited for my meal, along with a Mexican family watching a game show in Spanish on the TV and a trio of young African-American women with their kids, a ragged guy came in and tried to bum ten bucks off me until the owner caught sight of him, rolled up her sleeves and threw him out.

As I left, two police cars and a motorbike cop raced past, sirens screaming. Just down the road there had been an accident. Glass was littered everywhere. A crowd had gathered and stared, as if watching television. A couple of blocks farther along, two more motorbike cops peeled down the hill and raced off ahead of me, heading for some other disturbance of the peace.

~

CHAPTER 18

Don't Start Singing Before the Money Gets Through

August 2—San Francisco, California

"Check. One two two two. Check. One two."

Glide Memorial United Methodist Church on Ellis Street was packed. An usher in a road-crew reflector vest directed me to the far wall. "There's room for two on that windowsill," he said. I waded through a pew to climb onto the sill. It was astonishingly hot in the church—this was San Francisco, after all—-and other ushers were passing out purple paper fans with slim wooden handles. On one side, the fans read

REVEREND CECIL WILLIAMS & GLIDE CHURCH

OVER 30 YEARS SERVICE

UNCONDITIONAL LOVE

TRUE DIVERSITY

COMPASSION

On the other, an invitation to "Contribute to Glide and empower us all!" listing a few of the church's 35 programs: Computer Learning Center, Job Training/Placement, Recovery Programs, Feeding the Hungry, Scholarships for Kids, HIV/AIDS Project.

As soon as I reached the Pacific, something had changed. I had done the hard part, the thing that everyone said couldn't be done anymore, and now the tight fist of duty was relaxing. I had a day or so to spare waiting for Tomasz, who had left the Liberace Museum and was somewhere in southern California trying to shoot a single field of 100,000 cows.

I had been longing to see a gospel service, partly because I'd never seen one and partly because of a story Tomasz had told me about shooting a gospel baptism at a Baptist church, a total-immersion service in a river in Florida, during which the congregation had to keep shooing an alligator away.

The band—bass, synth, percussion—warmed up. More people were squeezed into the cracks between the church's bricks. Downstairs, another 250 people were watching the service on live video. *Another* 250. Badgeworth Church, next to the group home for boys from broken homes that my parents ran, was lucky if it saw 250 people a month, even though every Sunday all 40 boys and a half dozen staff trooped in a line through the gate in the high yew hedge, all clean knees and clean handkerchiefs, destined for a boredom close to living death.

A slim, dark-featured man with earrings, close-cropped hair and a shadow of a beard climbed up next to me on my sill. Whatever homophobic dread had seized me in Wyoming seemed to have vanished. We shook hands. I was very happy.

The choir came in, swaying and clapping in their purple-and-gold robes, the most ecumenical choir imaginable, all colors, all races, all ages, everyone cheerful and rocking. Me, too, though whether because this collective spirit was something I'd been missing on my trip or in my life in general, I couldn't tell. Within minutes I was being warned not to jump up and down on the windowsill—not because the usher disapproved of such behavior, but because I was apparently jumping up and down on a heating register set into the sill that might collapse at any second.

Cecil Williams, beaming, rotund, bespectacled, bearded, his hair thinning, called out "Yeah! Oh, yeah! We *lurrrrve* it when it's hot!" Everyone laughed, cheered, and fanned harder. He called on three members of the congregation to take cordless mikes from the ushers and offer prayers, and the synth player picked up the rhythms of their voices and turned them into quiet and holy songs.

On stage next to him was an interpreter for the deaf, who had a permanent grin installed from ear to ear and interpreted in the visual equivalent of inflected English, or perhaps inflected music, drawing out his signs as Cecil drew out a word, bending them like a harmonica player bending a note. He moved with the music like Joe Cocker.

Badgeworth Church meant ponderous hymns echoing off chilly gray stone, rows of elderly ladies in Sunday best hats, the cassocked vicar, his mouth opening and closing like a sanctimonious oyster, droning "...and Jehosophat begat Temeculah, and Temeculah begat Tempeh, and Hashish, and Hazzamarazzamatazz..."—nothing to do with life as I knew it. At Glide we were holding hands and singing "Amazing Grace" and three or four other songs in succession—the service had more songs that your average CD—ending with "God will take care of you."

Yes, that's it, isn't it? I thought. That kind of reassurance is anxiety's opposite, and its antidote. It's also very, very rare. Where in the modern American urban landscape is the reassurance that anyone will take care of us in this land of competitiveness and greed, with a third of its people in poverty and holes in its safety net the size of small countries? And isn't it precisely the absence of such reassurance that creates most of the anxiety in the first place? "You're at the right place," Cecil said. "You're at the right place to be loved." Yes. Yes.

Announcements: a call for donations to the American Red Cross for tsunami victims in Papua New Guinea. A call for Glide volunteers by a woman who described herself as a Christian lesbian working in a Jewish day school. "Glide is about the only place where I fit in," she chuckled. Then Cecil climbed back up on stage, having been down visiting the 250 in the basement. "Now I want you to listen to this song," he said. "It's the second time we've done it. It's a great song, with great music, great words, and a great soloist. So I want you to listen to it." He paused. "I'm extendin' my conversation so they can finish takin' up the money." Everyone laughed, and he beamed. "I got wisdom enough to know that you don't start singin' before the money gets through."

More wonderful singing, a great trumpet solo by the keyboards player, then Cecil's sermon on spiritual openness and closedness, using the central metaphor of a jar. He had a lot of fun riffing like a jazz player on the qualities of jardom and the word jar (jarring experiences, remaining ajar), he called out, "How'm I doin?" and we all cheered, then more songs, more rocking, more cheering, whistling, jumping up and down and all the other forms of behavior never seen in the precincts of the Church of England. Then we were done, and Cecil was helped off, clearly exhausted. It was the first church service I'd ever been to that was worth it for the clothes alone, or for the beautiful women, or for the great dancing by the handsome young guy on stage at the end. It was empowering, it was wild, it was sexy, it was full of human warmth and compassion, and it was the first place on my trip where I had felt collective hope.

A different prayer of mine was answered, immediately afterward: The San Francisco 49ers were playing a pre-season game against the New England Patriots at home that afternoon. Surely, I thought, this is a benefit of travel: you see in person, things you would see only on TV. And the 49ers are my team. For me, the only cultural artifact of any value to be created during the eighties was the passing of Joe Montana, the outstretched hands of Rice and Taylor appearing like a miracle from the corner of the TV picture to gather in the ball like a sacrament. Besides, this would make a nice echo: The only other time I'd seen a pro football game was on my previous American road trip, when I saw the British Columbia Lions inflict a rare defeat on the Edmonton Eskimos under lights in Vancouver. At the time it was like an astounding circus: Whenever B.C. scored, a pair of motorcycle cops roared around the running track.

So within two hours I found myself in another building for collective worship: 3Com Park, formerly Candlestick Park, and a very odd and contradictory place it was, too. The blunt, massive concrete ramps and walkways suggested a mass-appeal sport, but the $50 ticket price implied the opposite. The whole place, in fact, rebounded back and forth between these contradictions. The concessions stands offered gourmet junk food. I bought a Gordon Biersch Export Ale and a plate of garlic fries that together cost $10. To my surprise, they were both very good. I had another Biersch just to be sure. The vast, ugly concrete rampways offered Internet access. Forty feet above ground, my beer in one hand, I logged on and got the cricket scores: England had won a historic victory over South Africa. The men's room, on the other hand, offered the curiously old-fashioned opportunity to piss in a sloping trough. I could have been a teenager playing club rugby again, except that the walls were clean.

Game time was approaching. I made my way toward my seat, taking care to obey the injunction not to bring in "cans, noisemakers or hard fruit." The first contest was not a game of football but The Bark In The Park, a series of dog obstacle races. I rubbed my eyes and examined my empty Gordon Biersch plastic cup suspiciously. The public address system informed me that the 49ers cheerleaders, the Gold Rush, would be unveiling, if that's the right word, their all-new uniforms at the home opener. "Stay tuned for this exciting new look." Actually, the cheerleaders looked disappointingly fifties, like the Rockettes. Well, if their role hasn't evolved since the game began, it would be hard to expect their dances to have done so. Maybe the new uniforms would help.

The middle-aged guy in front of me heard my accent and decided to turn around and be helpful. He and his wife were from near Sacramento. They made a 280-mile round trip to see every home game, meeting for drinks before, during, and after the long bus trip. "If you have any questions, ask the mouth," he said, gesturing toward his wife. He repeated the information that the announcer had already given us, that the game would feature no Jerry Rice, and several other 49ers and Patriots were injured or being rested. "It's pre-season," he said. "It's a very experimental game. They try a lot of experiments. Like the British did at Dieppe. Sorry. Couldn't resist that."

The Rolling Stones sang judiciously edited excerpts from "Jumpin' Jack Flash" and "Start Me Up" from the digital scoreboard, a plane flew overhead towing a banner reading "Pizza Orgasmica. We Never Fake It," and the game began.

My instructive neighbor yelled a steady barrage of insults at the field, and took great pleasure in calling one of the 49ers team, whose name sprouted vowels and consonants in unexpected combinations, "Alphabet." "Alphabet, you boob!" he yelled, as the guy dropped the ball.

Tomasz arrived from Los Angeles, smiling wearily as he slogged up the concrete steps, still exhausted and anxious about how few pictures he had of me, and how few good pictures altogether. None of us had realized beforehand how slippery serendipity would be. It was like Heisenberg's Uncertainty Principle: Interesting, random things would happen to me only when I was unobserved. Conversely, when he was with me or racing to catch up with me, his own charmed movement halted, and he lost momentum and energy. Heisenberg squared. After our trip, he decided, he would go back around America on his own, to allow his own serendipity a chance to exert its own curious forces.

We gave up on the game just after half time. I was losing interest—in the game, in my team, in football as a whole—and Tomasz was afraid of losing the evening light, now falling through yellow toward the perfect soft pink. He badly wanted to shoot the city and the Golden Gate Bridge. One problem: He couldn't remember where he'd parked the Skylark.

It was hardly surprising. The complex of parking lots, the size of a small town, had its own strange and dangerous laws of nature. One car, an enormous bronze Cadillac, had sprouted a steer's horns above its radiator grille. By one of the fences, I found a dead cat. Someone had written EX PAT FAN on a Styrofoam fast-food box and stuck the box under the cat's head.

The Skylark, meanwhile, was nowhere to be found. Look, I said, we'll find it much more quickly by car. I'll get my rented car, you look for a few more minutes and then I'll meet you by this exit here. I trotted off to get the little white car, but by the time I'd found it, catastrophe had struck: The game had ended, or, more likely, the game had nearly ended and everyone had decided to bag it and leave. The roads now became a one-way system heading away from the parking lots. There was no way to get back to Tomasz.

What saved us was the sock phone, useful at last. I called him. The phone worked, and he answered. He had found the car and was somewhere in the effluent traffic, but he had virtually no gas left. Okay. I would try to get on ahead and scope out some gas and call him. I crawled out into the northbound traffic, which was going nowhere. I called him again. He was somewhere behind me on 101, but his gas needle was looking up at empty. Okay. I'd go on ahead and listen for his call, and if necessary buy a can of gas and come back to him. I managed to fight free of traffic, barreled into the city, and called him again. He had miraculously found gas. Okay. I'd shoot onward to the bridge and see if it was fogbound, and he'd catch up to me. Five or ten minutes passed at lights and stop signs, then he called me. He had fueled up, but was now lost. As it happened, that didn't matter: At that instant I caught sight of the bridge, which was fogbound. We'd have to shoot the city from some other vantage point. Okay. I'll come back and find you, I said—but I was in three lanes of traffic on 101 heading north, barely 200 yards short of the bridge, with no cross streets and three lanes of traffic coming the other way. I took a deep breath and shot into a U-turn, barely avoiding the far curb and a slew of suddenly furious oncoming cars.

This was getting to be fun. I called Tomasz back. He was still lost, somewhere near Van Ness. I know where you are, I said. Hold on. He called back: He had found himself again and would wait for me at the intersection of Van Ness and Market. I called him back barely a minute later, giddy with the power of the communications age, solely to give him my ETA. Zeroing in, I realized he was headed the wrong way up a one-way street, and called him again. The sock phone was blistering. A minute later I slithered to a halt outside a car wash, and five seconds later Tomasz appeared out of a swirl of traffic to pull up behind me. It was technology's finest hour. We dashed in convoy over to an outcrop known to rock climbers as The Crack Above Castro, jumped over the fence, and hiked up to the top, from where the city lay like a perfect idea in the evening sun.

He found a hotel near Chinatown. Back in Oakland, I found that Maria had had enough of this intrusion. I said my goodbyes, packed up, and hauled myself back into the city and a small hotel where the desk clerk turned out to be from Vermont, another young man setting off to find himself and landing for a while in San Francisco. I was delighted. " 'We haven't seen that spirit here/Since 1969,' " I said, quoting the Eagles' "Hotel California," and he laughed.

As I turned out the light in my room, I realized that for some time I had been hearing a steady roar, like a plane standing on a runway one and a half blocks away. I couldn't figure out which direction it was coming from. It was as if the city itself was idling on full throttle; then it abruptly stopped, whatever it was, and all I heard was half a dozen young men and women laughing on the street under my window.

∾

CHAPTER 19

Fundamentally Nomadic

August 3—San Francisco, California

"Oh, shit," Tomasz said. He and I were heaving ourselves up two of San Francisco's steepest long blocks in search of a trolley—he with 15 pounds of camera equipment; I with my pack, my bad knee threatening to collapse.

He shot Chinatown. He shot trolleys. He shot Fisherman's Wharf, half of which was an area of trinket shops, the other half of which was a working dock, rich with the smell of fish. I wandered off among the boats, where tuna was selling for two dollars a pound. The fishermen, a weathered, unromantic crew, and I discussed the possibility of buying a 15-pound tuna, so that every time I got hungry on the roadside I could grab its tail, whip it out of my pack, and take a nibble. "Sell you some ice," one guy in well-worn yellow waders suggested. Looking for Tomasz, I wandered off the dock through a narrow, dark passageway, a wormhole between the universes of the working America and the leisured America, and found myself surrounded by tourists buying T-shirts and sipping latte.

The morning was heating up, but to Tomasz this meant that the fog might be burning away. He had been hoping to shoot the towers of the Golden Gate Bridge rising out of a sea of fog. We grabbed a taxi whose driver told us that Avis had a drop-off right by my hotel, and now everything was haste: back to the hotels, pack up, haul the pack to the garage, rescue the car, clean it out, drop it off, meet Tomasz who had the Skylark muttering by the curb; race through the small streets that I finally understood, driving like a rally crew, me yelling directions, Tomasz hitting 65 mph between one stop sign and the next, diving onto Lombard and in the distance seeing the bridge still in fog, racing out into its cool dampness, then up the little roads that lead to the Marin headlands, guessing where we'd find the best view, rounding a corner and pulling up hard on the sandy overlook knowing we had arrived.

Clouds from the open sea flowed through the bridge and under it, and died in streamers in the San Francisco Bay. The fog rose and fell, changing all the time in a slow, cold boil. Sometimes we could see the cars on the bridge, sometimes just their lights, sometimes just the supports themselves, floating on a pillow of white cloud. Invisible freighters moaned like whales.

The city was vanishing; the past was closing. You were here, but you are not now, the fog said. In future, any vision of this city you have, looking back, will always be misty and perhaps completely obscured. You can be sure only of the here and now, the tawny hillsides of the headlands in bright sunlight, the boy finding a lizard among the rocks, and the hawk circling above the bay, wingtips raised like fingers, and now even that has come and gone back into the mist.

Tomasz and I split up. He would cut inland to shoot Lake Mono and the high plains of Wyoming, I'd follow the coast to Seattle, and we'd meet at Sturgis. Around 2 p.m. he dropped me off just above Sausalito, in the heart of wealthy Marin County, where the traffic came off 101 to take the coast road, the legendary Highway 1, which I hadn't taken in 1973 and had regretted the choice ever since.

I left even more of my baggage in the trunk of the Skylark. Being out on the road not only provided constant novelty, it taught one to adapt to novelty, to thrive on it. I was feeling more and more drawn to Bruce Chatwin's argument that humans are fundamentally nomadic, and the habit of building houses, then cities, cut us off from a crucial range of experience, eating the foods of the season and the place, moving with the buffalo, so to speak. Who in his right mind would spend winters in Vermont? Or summers in Galveston? Civilization was starting to seem like a massive accumulation of weight, an infernally complicated infrastructure to bring goods to us because we wouldn't go to them, and then another infrastructure to carry our wastes away. I thought of the paintings of Columbus or the conquistadors encountering bronzed, feathery natives, and thought how heavy the Europeans looked, as if their armor were already part of their collective soul.

I looked around for somewhere to stick out my thumb, but I didn't like the look of the place. Two sets of traffic were blending at just the wrong spot; it would be hard for them to see me and dangerous to pull over, and I felt scruffy and out of place among the rich. As always my anxieties were unnecessary. I got one short ride in less than ten minutes, and another within five more—but the second guy, a college student going to camp out with his friends on Mount Tamalpais, apologetically left me where Route 1 winds up into the hills, one skinny lane each way between steep grassy banks, with the eucalyptus hanging right over the road and a blind curve every 30 yards. No shoulder; nowhere to stop except tiny passing bays every so often. I started walking—and in a quarter of an hour met my first hippies.

I wasn't even thumbing, as there was nowhere for drivers to stop. A faded blue VW bus—Oregon plates, a bumper sticker with a picture of Einstein and "Imagination Is More Important Than Knowledge" passed me, the vastly underpowered VW engine clattering like eggbeaters against the side of a mixing bowl. It pulled over at once, but the passing bay was so small, the road so narrow and the grassy bank so high, that I couldn't get in the side door. The driver yelled something and pointed to another bay on the opposite side of the road. He puttered over; I ran after and they let me in.

Or perhaps on. The interior was stacked high with boxes, cases, bags, and bundles; and the only way to settle myself was to squeeze my pack into the last remaining floor space and lie on the bed, raising myself on one elbow and jamming my head sideways against the roof.

They called it the Blue Moon Bus, they being Leilea Satori and Aaron Longshore, both young, skinny, and blonde. The Blue Moon was a vintage 1971 with a 1200 cc engine, Aaron fighting it around every corner, pulling into a passing bay every few miles to let all the traffic pass that had built up behind us. Leilea and Aaron loved the bus, but conceded that it was impractical. They'd broken down in

Santa Cruz and had put in a new generator. "You get up close and personal with your Volkswagen," he said. "But it's such a small engine, it's easy to work on." A Westfalia pop-top, sleeping four, would give them more power and more room, but to a true VW buff, the Westfalia might as well be an RV.

He was from Colorado, she was born in Maui. Both of her parents were hippies. Her father sailed to Maui in 1969, lived there for 18 years as a musician, then moved to the mainland and started selling his paintings on the sidewalk in New York; now he has several galleries exhibiting his work, she said. He encouraged her to do whatever she felt was right for her (which turned out not to include going to college), and so far his advice seemed to be working. Leilea and Aaron had a number of shops on the West Coast that took anything they made and sold it out every week. They'd traveled the mainland, and they'd traveled around Europe and Asia together. They set up their studio on Bali, where they rented a house for $340 for the year. They even had Internet access there. They were modern, global hippies. When in the U.S., they were based in Colorado, but for all practical purposes they were living in the bus, just as Ken Kesey would have recommended. When I told a friend about them later, he said, "They can't be hippies, can they? They're imitations." In a sense the past is past; in a sense, though, it merges with what we think of as the present. That's how we should judge an era: not by its eccentricities, which glow in their own strange light and die, but by what survives.

They took me to Point Reyes, where a shop owner who sold tie-dyes and candles and other such sixties paraphernalia had invited them to stop by. I made them unpack the back of the Blue Moon bus and show their wares: blankets with sun-moon-stars and tropical-island designs, pants with diamonds or fishes or colorful

Chinese characters. I bought trousers for Zoe, Barbara, and me. They didn't have small children's sizes for Maddy. It seemed a good idea to have a little of this color and spirit in my life. I'd wear them when I was writing.

So far I'd made only about 40 miles, but for once it didn't matter. I was ahead of schedule (or so I thought). I could look for adventure instead of looking for a 300-mile ride. A short lift up along the shore of long, slender Tomales Bay with a builder—a Marin County builder, who used environmentally sound building techniques—left me opposite an unpretentious little seafood restaurant called Tony's. A gentle onshore breeze carried the smell of fish and the sound of small ripples collapsing on the beach.

A middle-aged woman and a well-seasoned, white-haired guy appeared from a rough driveway just back up the road. She was carrying a bottle of water, he a bottle of Anchor Steam Ale. "We passed you earlier," she said apologetically, "and felt bad about not picking you up. So when you showed up here, we thought you might be thirsty. Would you like water or beer?"

"Well, that's very kind of you," I said. "I've reached the age when if I drink beer on a hot afternoon, I get a headache, I'd be very grateful for some water."

"By the way," she said, handing me the water, "My name's Jan, and this is Ramblin' Jack Elliott."

Yeah, I thought, and I'm Frank Sinatra. But it was. It was Ramblin' Jack Elliott, the man who learned from Woody Guthrie and carried the portfolio of the American folk music tradition to Bob Dylan and to England, where he inspired Mick Jagger, Keith

Richards, and countless other young would-be musicians to pick up a guitar—including, indirectly, me.

We tracked into their pleasantly unmown yard and sat at a rough picnic table under a tree outside Jack and Jan's little house, which was as ordinary a place as you'll ever find a saddle, lariat, and boots tucked away in a corner, or a Grammy next to the TV. How did you end up in England? I asked, and for the next eight hours he told me some of the chapters of the story of his life.

"I've always been in love with the sea, and a lot of it was nurtured by those articles in the NATIONAL GEOGRAPHIC about sailing around the Horn in various square riggers, and around the world in the schooner *Yankee*. Captain Irving Johnson and his wife Electa made about seven trips around the world. The first *Yankee* and the second *Yankee*, about 92 and 96 feet. Then he had a 55-foot ketch that was built in Holland, and he cruised the canals of Europe in that...."

And there it was, that dock-of-the-bay excitement, the thrill of an inconvenient world not yet Frommered and Hiltoned, when people still went around the Horn instead of taking the red-eye. Jack himself was born Elliot Adnopoz in Brooklyn in 1931, a doctor's son, but somehow that assignment seemed to have been a clerical error: As early as he could remember, he was down at the docks.

"You couldn't go anywhere near the boats without permission, but as a youngster I could slip through. I once went on board a Norwegian liner, the *Oslofjord*, without permission. I just pretended to be delivering something. I went up the gangplank when no one was looking and saw all these gorgeous women. I'd never seen gorgeous women before. They didn't have them in Brooklyn, I guess," he chuckled slyly. "They just sort of strolled around as if they owned the place. Norwegian gals. Come to think of it, [the crew had] just unloaded some interesting cargo, including a boat that looked like a miniature Viking ship...."

Somehow this story got supplanted by the story about the seal that had swum up the culvert behind Jack's house and got stuck. Jack had played and sung to it to keep it calm until the official seal-rescuers arrived and scolded Jack saying, incredibly, that you mustn't sing to seals because they're tone deaf and it upsets them. And from there he told me how he first went to England in 1955, though the story, like all good journeys, started out in the opposite direction.

"I got married, having been traveling around with Woody Guthrie through 1951, '52, '53, '54—four years with Woody. Woody brought me out to California on a trip, with two other musicians, Brew Moore and Billy Faier. Brew was a tenor sax, modern jazz bebop player from Miss'sippi. He was a very cool guy. I didn't know him at all before we started the trip. We were introduced as we were getting into the car with Woody. The person who was driving was Billy Faier, my old banjo-player friend from New Orleans. Woody and I were pretty tight by then. I'd spent the better part of 1951 and '52 with him, and '53 intermittently, and then in '54 we got together to go on this trip. We'd made a trip down to Florida in my Model A Ford, which cost $25. Woody spent $50 fixing it on the way down, so I gave him the car and went on my way hitchhiking.

"I was playing guitar and singing. I let Woody write the songs. He was so good at it. In fact, hanging out with Woody Guthrie has prevented me from learning how to write songs. Him and a bunch of other good songwriters I've had the misfortune of meeting," he said dryly, with the courteous manner and the understated humor of the old-school cowboy. "Guy Clarke, for instance. He's such a great writer, I'm intimidated by him. Bob Dylan followed me around after I came back from Europe. We met visiting Woody in the hospital the day after I got off a ship from Europe. The S.S. *Liberté.* Fifty-five thousand tons. Took about seven days to get across the Atlantic. We were held up the first two days by a storm. I was one of three people who lived on deck through the storm. The 2,000 other passengers stayed in their cabins."

By this point, we had at least two stories going: the trip to England and the trip across country with Woody. "We should probably get back to one of the stories," I said.

"Either that, or use two tape recorders," he suggested. "I usually have two or three stories going at once."

He had a way of ending his sentences with a pause, as if it would just be a second or so before he'd think of something else to say. I began to think of what he was saying as not stories but a story, the story of his life and pretty much everyone else's from that time. The story branched like a road, and branched again, or picked up apparently from nowhere. He was wandering around in the deep background of my life, not even in its shadows but in the adjoining rooms, saying things that struck a distant echo, a name or a song title that I hadn't heard in 30 or 40 years, or things that connected to things that connected to things, and suddenly a small light went on under a door. He had met everybody, and people who had always been just names in the music world— Ewan McColl, Peggy Seeger, Seamus Ennis, Big Bill Broonzy, Donovan, John Mayall—now stepped briefly out into the third dimension and said one thing, or did one thing, and for me would never again lie flat. For what it's worth, this is how the brain grows. We are born with all the neurons we'll ever have; intelligence consists of the connections that grow between them, connections that we encourage to grow simply by curiosity and experience. I had the sense that if I stayed there long enough, everybody would connect up with everybody else and it would all make sense.

I asked Jack if he'd ever ridden freights.

"I rode one freight and I didn't like it at all. It was one of the kind of cars that smart hobos would never ride on. It was an empty boxcar, and they bounce. They go up and down about eight inches at a rapid rate, and it's hard to keep your footing. So I sat on my suitcase. It was a beautiful sunny day in Arkansas. Went from Texarkana to Little Rock, and when the train stopped in Little Rock I got off, never to ride again. I hitched a truck. Got a ride in a truck that was going up through the Ozarks to Missouri. That was the last time I ever rode a freight train. I like trucks," he said wistfully. "When the motor home dies, I want a nice big solid Peterbilt truck. Convert the trailer.

"Four days to California in a new Buick," he went on, back with Woody. "A delivery job: We didn't own that car, we were just delivering it for the owner. Woody disappeared a day after we arrived at Topanga Canyon. He had a restless nature, and he felt ill at ease. I think he felt unwelcome because he'd absconded with someone else's wife, a 21-year-old, rather a pretty girl. Her husband was a big handsome man, looked sort of like Gary Cooper. He was an actor named Dave Marshall. Everybody liked Dave, including myself, but somehow his wife fell in love with Woody, who was a tiny little guy with a lot of hair and a beard, just an old hobo, very sun-dried, very rustic, but very poetic. Very romantic...he stole away and they drove to New York in a Terraplane car....So when Woody disappeared from Topanga Canyon, he hitchhiked all the way across America, and was put in a hospital in New Jersey, and he spent the next 13 years just gradually wasting away. Terrible disease.

"After he disappeared, I met June, who was destined to become my wife. We fell in love, we got married in June, and we bought a ticket to go to England."

"Why?"

"National Geographic! June was raised on National Geographic too. She became an actress, and traveled all round the country on a truck. She was the navigator. She always wanted to see things...."

I was amazed. The story had linked up—three of the stories had linked up, in fact—but only after touching on a dozen other stories that cried out to be told, and probably would before nightfall.

Jan brought out a guitar, an Epiphone. It was hers; not surprisingly, her own musical career had fallen into the shadow of Jack's, and now she was his fiancée/manager. "When I was a young guitar player," she said, "I went to one of his concerts in 1980 and he said, 'Would you like to run away with me?' I said, 'Can I go home and get my toothbrush and my guitar?' and he said 'No, I'm in a hurry.' So I moped around Los Angeles for six months playing Ramblin' Jack Elliott songs....We got together about six years ago, up here. I thought I was losing my mind. I was working for a newspaper in Sausalito, and I was looking out of a window one night—I'd been working a double shift, 12- and 13-hour days—and, God, I see Ramblin' Jack Elliott looking in through the window at three o'clock in the morning. He was at the shipyard, 50 yards away from my office, visiting friends, and they set us up on a blind date...."

I had been waiting the whole trip for someone to bring out a guitar. Jack asked me why I hadn't brought my own. I told him I thought nobody would know the songs I sing any more, and felt rather sad about it. Now I had ended up with people who knew almost every song ever written.

We had sung several of them by the time word arrived that Dave and Tamara, neighbors of Jan and Jack's who had built their own trimaran, had sail up, and Jan drove us in the old, old Volvo half a mile to the dock, Jack telling me how at 15 he ran away from Brooklyn ("no place for a cowboy") and joined the rodeo for two dollars a day, slept three feet away from the horses' tails, and learned guitar from the rodeo clown....And somehow that slid into the story of singing the "Mule-Skinner Blues" and other slightly risqué songs at a command performance for Princess Margaret and a hundred of the hipper young members of the British aristocracy.

Dave and Tamara sold organic wine, which we drank along with cheese and crackers, and more stories. Dave, who had a long, bushy, graying beard and the gentleness that often grows in people who work carefully with their hands, had built the trimaran over 15 years; it had been in the water barely a month. The rest of the crew were Jan and Jack's "car czar," Chris, who restored antique wooden speedboats and their engines, Chris's mother Daphne and his daughter Jesse, who at twelve said "I'm working on a equestrian career."

As the sun went down the water was suddenly full of hundreds of medusas, pulsing alongside like small aquatic ghosts, and it was at this point, while it was being generally agreed that swimming was not recommended in Tomales Bay, someone added that the mouth of the bay is one of the West Coast breeding grounds for the Great White Shark. "Remember Tony's," someone asked me, "where you were hitching opposite? Someone caught a 15-footer off their pier a few years ago."

"Ready about!" called Dave.

We picked up an Irish friend of everyone's, who had restored a boat and planned to sail to South America, a born storyteller, roaring with laughter at his own tales, and all the while the three-quarter silver moon rose higher and higher above the bay, above the peninsula where Jesse Colin Young of the Youngbloods had his house before it burned down in a fire that left the whole hillside bald. This was exactly my 1973 feeling, that I could scarcely believe what was happening and felt as if I was constantly blinking in stunned amazement, that all I could do was just grin foolishly and be grateful. The weather was part of this experience, too: The brilliant light and warmth created a haze that was not a haze, just an overflowing of sensations. The impossible was happening. My job was simply to be open to it.

Jack said he wanted to write his memoirs, but he was having trouble, not because of his memory, which was extraordinarily precise, but because one story just sort of rambled off in any three other directions. Later, when people asked me if there was anywhere on my trip I wished I could stay, the only place I was really tempted was Marshall, so I could hang out with Jack and help him write his memoirs, go for a sail every so often, and acquire a taste for Jim Beam.

CHAPTER 20

An Overlapping Assortment of Fantasies

August 4—Marshall, California

The following morning Jack drove me in his motor home—
it was like being in a furry brown box—up to Bodega
Bay, where *The Birds* was filmed. I wouldn't have recognized the
place, but then I barely recognized San Francisco; I must start
thinking of memory as being entertaining rather than useful. He
told me stories about a fennel forest and a nude beach, about his
friends the boatbuilders who seemed to sprout in every crack and
cranny of the coastline, and of how he got his limp, which was
not an old rodeo accident but, of all things, a skateboarding
injury. He dropped me off at a nice straight stretch—a rarity on
the coast road—outside a horse ranch, and we wished each other
well. I gave him my Union Jack. He seemed touched. "England's
been very good to me," he said.

After 20 minutes of watching hawks circle on the updraft from
the cliffs, I got picked up by a tall, lean surfer in a wetsuit driving

a venerable faded blue VW bus, who was going a few miles up to Salmon Creek. As the beach wound into view we could see surfers in the morning mist. "Gnarly waves!" he cried. The mist was a good sign, he said: the waves get sloppy when the wind picks up.

Five minutes later I got a ride almost all the way to Seattle.

His name was Jay, and he was driving a new Nissan Pathfinder that was, as they say, loaded. Digital thermometer and compass. Global Positioning System (GPS) that told him the heading and distance to any destination he punched in. He was, by all appearances, an American success story: He had retired at 36, had bought himself a boat and a motor home and the Pathfinder and the GPS, had taken up scuba diving, and now he was just tooling around, doing whatever he pleased.

In late 1990, he said, five friends and he, with no money, founded Wizards of the Coast. "We didn't even have a business plan, just six people in the basement of a house." The company designed and sold games, role-playing games. They were, in a sense, professional fantasists. In July 1993, their game Magic: The Gathering was released. "We hocked ourselves to the eyeballs to do Magic. By July '97 sales in 52 countries were well over $100 million a year. We had 500 employees, four overseas offices, the product was being made in ten languages, and the rulebook was being printed in 30 languages. There are Magic leagues, and a professional tour," not to mention one and a half million a year in prize money for seniors and scholarship money for under-18s.

I was immediately a little defensive. It's hard to be a financial failure in America, especially if you're sitting next to someone rich; and although I was eight years older than Jay, I instinctively felt somehow his junior, and started asking him groveling questions about his philosophy of life, as if I were writing for a money magazine.

The road started rising up the cliffs in a series of hairpins. "By the way," he threw over his shoulder to reassure me, "I am a graduate of a number of professional driving schools." Before he got rich, in fact, he was a limo driver. Once, he said, he did a 360 at 40 mph. on a freeway in fog, and managed to keep control of the car. "The client thought it was cool. He wanted to tip me 50 bucks to do it again." The Pacific was invisible, unfortunately, behind a fogbank that hugged the foot of the cliffs. Still, it was one of the most beautiful roads I traveled, skimming the line of the cliffs and then darting inland through groves of pine or eucalyptus, rising and falling as it crossed the innumerable small streams headed for the ocean, surprising a small coastal town and then dodging back into the woods again.

"Why don't you pick out a CD?" he asked, passing me what looked like a thick floppy photograph album. I opened it up. It was a CD book. I had never seen so many CDs in one place outside a record store in my life. They were almost all of music 20 years old: The Beatles, Led Zeppelin, Jethro Tull, Billy Joel; various heavy metal bands whose music I didn't know but whose names I associated with violent pain behind the eyes; Enya (presumably as an antidote) and, of course, Pink Floyd. There was no question. If he had a sound system this good, we were going to listen to *The Dark Side of the Moon*—an album that dates back to 1973 but is still selling several thousand copies a week. I play a couple of the tracks on my guitar, and for some time my daughter's favorite rock song was "Money," which she could name at the age of four from the ringing of the first cash register.

No road trip is complete without a soundtrack. One of my most vivid memories of 1973 is gliding through the cool, dim evergreen forests of the Rockies, while on the eight-track stereo Paul Horn played flute runs into the perfect echo of the Taj Mahal. People stuck in a car together who otherwise have virtually nothing in common can be united simply by listening to the same music—or other shared cultural artifacts. The following day we spent half an hour quizzing each other on Star Trek: Who was the only actor to play four different species in the original TV series? Popular culture is an overlapping assortment of fantasies, some spontaneous, some cultivated. And music can become both the journey and the inhabited space. After a while I stopped seeing the passing landscape, as the music itself had become the scenery.

In a surprisingly literal way. Hearing is, in fact, a specialized form of touch: What we take in are vibrations that strike us in different ways. Jay's was such a good system that after he cranked the volume up more than halfway, the sound didn't seem to get any louder, just more powerful. Every bass note kicked me in the back. Instead of coming out of the speakers, the sound seemed to exist everywhere in the air, and I found myself in the middle of it, each sound having virtually a solid presence and color that nudged me or slid past. It was like swimming among a school of whales. I heard features of composition or orchestration I'd never noticed before. "Look," Jay said, pointing. With each kick from the bass, the rearview mirror twitched. As a teenager I was too self-conscious to be a head-banger, but now I was screaming with the guitar solos, and by the time we reached Fort Bragg, shivers were running from my neck all the way down my legs. "Damn, this is strong stuff!" I yelled to Jay, who nodded happily.

After a while I started to notice that Jay's depiction of himself, as the Man Who Got Rich and Retired Young, was wearing a little thin here and there. For one thing, he had a curious neck-and-shoulder twitch. At first it made me uneasy. We English are taught that it is rude to stare, but in not saying anything about it I couldn't stop looking at it, and looking at it I couldn't help wondering if this was actually a sign of deep-rooted mental illness, and at any moment he might leap across the seat and try to brain me with his GPS. The Bachelard Principle was at work. After a while I started to get annoyed at my own hand-wringing, and asked him about it. He was quite open: He'd been in an accident, and some of the nerve tissue had been damaged. As a result, nerve impulses would fire unpredictably and cause the twitch. It didn't hurt, and he didn't even know it was happening, most of the time. *Pouf!* as they say in France. Another anxiety gone.

All the same, I liked these qualities, which made him more human, more like someone I could travel with. We cut inland through the coastal forest, and by the time we hit Route 101, which runs up through the redwoods, the digital temperature had risen from 59 degrees to 106. Jay had a map that identified dozens of trees that should be visited by any fan of tree giantism, and we started off as if he meant to see all of them. We drove through the Drive-through Tree—officially, the 315-foot Chandelier Tree, thanks to the elbowlike angularity of its branches. We visited huge trees lying down with houses in them and standing up with gift shops in them. There seemed to be no indignity that had not been visited on the silent giants, all of which had to be given names and identities that made them something other than trees. No commodification without representation. Luckily, Jay's determination to obey the guidebook began to flag, and at last I persuaded him to get out of there and head north. Long after dark we hit Coos Bay, Oregon, whose principal feature for me was the cheapest motel room to date: $27.82, and not a roach in sight.

~

CHAPTER 21

Trodden by Rogues

August 5—Coos Bay, Oregon

At Tillamook, Oregon, which boasted not one but two cheese factories, we went wine tasting. A just-for-show wine bar had been set up at one end of the specialty-products salesroom, and a wealthy blonde sipped from a wineglass with the corners of her mouth down. For a couple of bucks we could sample the local vintages—or rather I could, Jay still being the professional driver. This was clearly to be my next book: *The Hitchhiker's Guide to the Wines of Oregon.*

First, a Secret House White Pinot Noir, which struck me as slightly puppyish and eager to please, but light and fruity. For the hitchhiker, an ideal traveling wine, full of the possibility of getting a hundred-mile ride with a blond cellist in a VW Rabbit convertible.

Next, an Elk Cove '95 Chardonnay, fermented (I'm told) in small oak barrels. Dry and crisp, and existentially rigorous—a wine that knows its place in an uncertain universe. A good wine for a long wait by the road on a cool, windy day with the possibility of rain.

On to the reds. I picked out a Rogue Valley Ashland '95 Merlot, not on the strength of its silver medal or its 87 points in the *Wine Spectator*, but because I liked the sound of Rogue Valley, and grapes trodden by rogues. The wine was dry, inky, and unremarkable, but worst of all it was clearly bad headache material. The thought of hitching at 2 p.m. on a hot afternoon after a bottle of Rogue Valley sent a shudder up my spine. I once hitched west across England after an all-night party where I drank a pint (Imperial, not American) of scotch and ate fried egg sandwiches for breakfast, and I could barely keep my eyes open, let alone my thumb up. I ended up catching a bus the last dozen miles, fell asleep, walked off the bus in Worcester still asleep, and woke up standing in the middle of traffic. That's how hitchhikers get killed.

Finally, dessert wines, at an extra 50 cents per sample. I chose the Hood River Marionberry—19 percent alcohol by volume— solely because I'd never heard of marionberries, or salmonberries for that matter, until the previous day. A port-style wine, said our hostess, making me think fondly of Steinbeck's winos drinking port at Monterey and Brautigan's winos drinking port in San Francisco. The wine came out of the fridge in a long, thin bottle that suggested a seasoned olive oil. This wine can be kept for a year after opening, the hostess added, which should have tipped me off. I sipped. Blood and sand! This stuff was death on wheels! Now I knew why winos drink port: One sip of this, and you can chew on it for days. I could imagine having half a glass of this and waking up seven hours later in a police station with perfect little caps on all of my teeth, made of pink crystallized sugar.

By now I was feeling merry and thoroughly irresponsible, so I bought a packet of salmon jerky because I couldn't imagine what it might taste like, and we rollicked up the highway into the next cheese factory, where the cheese curd was nice. The medium cheddar was nice. The colby jack was nice. The jalapeno pepper jack was nice. I had reached the West Coast, and my cheese trek was over.

Jay asked if I wanted to stay at his place in Tacoma for a few days, or go on to Seattle. I was looking forward to Seattle, partly because I would be able to stay with my first wife, Gail, and her family, but also because of Seattle was another place where I'd had almost a visionary experience in 1973.

We'd spent two days in the city, getting drunk, sightseeing and crashing at the apartment of a girl who stayed up literally all night arguing that Richard Nixon was insane, with the unflagging fervor of someone who herself is completely nuts. When we arrived at the docks, bleary and exhausted, to take the early morning ferry to Vancouver Island, the waterfront was lost in fog. After a few minutes the ferry honked and pulled away from the jetty, and I gradually became aware that everyone on board had stood up and was looking toward the stern, pointing in a concerted fashion that suggested something more than saying farewell to dogs and loved ones. I struggled to my feet and looked back at the docks.

The mist had cleared just enough for the summit of Mount Rainier to appear above the city, an eerie silver-white in the morning sun. Somehow I had managed to be in Seattle for nearly two days without seeing this huge, ghostly, brilliant mountain, apparently floating in midair ten miles, or perhaps a thousand miles away. I left Seattle staring, my mouth open.

When I told Jay I'd prefer to head on right away, he seemed deflated. For all his talk of successful retirement, he seemed lost; he had defined success by work, and he was no longer working. He was divorced ("We got married too young, too quickly, for the wrong reasons, and we didn't work hard enough at it"), but he seemed to miss his marriage, and his former stepdaughter. Since then, he had had a difficult time with women: His uncomplicated background and his all-too-visible money were at odds with each other, and at least once he had been strung along by a woman more in love with the money than the man. Sometimes, he said, he thought of giving away everything he had and going back to some blue-collar job in which he felt more at home. It can't be easy, I thought, to be a fantasist, but no longer a wizard.

We crossed the endless Columbia bridge at Astoria, the Shell station at one end offering little booklets on how to escape from a vehicle that has plunged into deep water, and wound through the river flats and marshes. Jay pointed out espresso stands even in the tiniest damp villages, a sure sign we were nearing Seattle.

As we got closer to Tacoma, slicing through darker and darker woods—where signs by Weyerhauser proudly announced the company's replantings, though were oddly silent about the clear-cuttings that had taken place first—Jay talked more about his house, which had been on the market for nearly a million but which he and his friend Emiel had bought for a quarter of that by shrewd businessmanship. With all the renovations they'd done, it was probably worth $750,000, he said. View of the Puget Sound. Pool room. Games room. Tennis court. Hot tub...He invited me to stay a day, a couple of days. Much as I like playing pool, I couldn't see myself staying: I get uneasy lounging with the rich, and start to feel like a poodle.

The house was as remarkable as he had promised: hardwood floors, cathedral ceilings, deck overlooking the sound. What I hadn't expected was that a band would be cutting a CD in the basement. Kareem, Emiel's younger brother, played sax, and he had hired some local pros to back him up on a selection of his tunes. We tiptoed across the shag carpet, decided to forgo the pool table because of the noise, and ended up with little more than a guided tour and a beer. It was a strange homecoming, in a way: The only part of the house that really seemed to reflect Jay was down in the games room, where he showed me his collection of fantasy-game pieces, not toy soldiers but gorgons and knights and dragons and a whole medieval bestiary, the children of J.R.R. Tolkien.

Kareem and Emiel's mother, who also shared the house, lit the gas fire, the blue flames playing over authentic-looking logs. Kareem finally finished, and reappeared, saying he was pleased, that those guys were really good. Emiel, his brother, had not appeared, apparently still closeted in his room. You should meet him, they said. Emiel's a trip. He owns a .50 magnum Desert Eagle, Jay said, one of those enormous handguns that will stop a horse. Emiel came downstairs and lay down in front of the fire, shirt off, his young body already a little soft from good living. We were introduced.

"I'm curious," he said. "I can't understand the appeal of hitchhiking. Whenever I travel I go by limo and stay in five-star hotels."

"The problem with that kind of travel," I said, "is that you're never vulnerable."

His eyebrows went up. "Why should I want to be vulnerable?"

"Because otherwise you'll never feel grateful for anything. You've got to make yourself vulnerable before you need something from someone else, and you've got to need something before you can feel gratitude. And unless you allow yourself to be vulnerable, you never have any chance encounters. All the most remarkable people I've met on this trip, I've met by chance."

On consideration he was willing to see the appeal, he said, but he wasn't going to try it any time soon.

He talked blandly about the hurdles involved in opening a casino through a loophole in state law, claimed with a smile that he wasn't afraid of "illegitimate competition"—my euphemism for organized crime—and said he'd always wanted to be in the hospitality business. This struck me as an odd way to describe gambling, which in the next breath he described as "pardon my French, a license to steal."

When he heard I needed to get to Seattle, then to Sturgis as quickly as possible, he swung into the persona of the connected man. He was going into Seattle on business in the morning, he said, so he could take me. And as for Sturgis, he had a friend who owned a plane. And he'd fly me there? I asked, astounded. "He'll do it if I ask him," Emiel said. "I'll make a call."

~

CHAPTER 22

The Last Don

August 6—Tacoma, Washington

Around 8:30 Emiel drifted downstairs, looking pale, puffy, and fragile. He ate breakfast: coffee and two Pepperidge Farm Selection de Choix cookies from a newly opened box, like a dealer working with a new deck. He disappeared upstairs to shower and dress, and Kareem—lean and eager, young but disciplined—told me about learning from Joshua Redman and Wayne Shorter, Miles Davis and Cannonball Adderly and others whose names I recognized but don't know. He's learned that the important thing is to take something from all kinds of music but to remain himself, he said. He was 19.

Emiel reappeared. "The last don!" Kareem cried. Emiel was dressed for Coppola, wearing a dark-blue suit with a black shirt in the Italian fashion, shades, the beginnings of a goatee. He gave Kareem orders as if talking to the houseboy—do this, clean up that—and then it was time to go. I was expecting a BMW or a

Porsche, but no, Emiel had gone all the way: a brand new Cadillac Eldorado, the sporty model, tinted windows and all. He laid my pack in the open trunk on top of a pump-action shotgun and a saber in a studded leather scabbard. He let the trunk lid fall gently, and it paused a half-inch open as if to show that it could close itself better than any human could, settling with a faint sigh and clicking shut.

We pulled onto the road and at once Emiel was on the phone, setting up a meeting. "Welcome to my life," he moaned when he had finished. "Without a cell phone, a comfortable car, and a pager I'd be a dead man."

He cataloged his real estate interests: he owned several duplexes, and the house in Tacoma....Wait a minute, I said. I thought you and Jay bought it together? He shook his head bluntly. "Jay's money is as good as anyone else's," he said, "but he pays me rent." I felt more sorry for Jay than ever. To think yourself a successful young entrepreneur, and then to wind up living with someone younger and arguably even more successful?

Emiel's last few building purchases had all been of that no-money-down kind I've never understood, with the seller picking up the closing costs. He got into real estate by meeting a mortgage broker, the father of an ex-girlfriend ("dumped the girl, kept the father"), and together with a realtor they formed what he called "a dastardly trio," with him as the finagler and wheeler-dealer. Now they were trying to raise two million to exploit a loophole in the local laws and open a casino, the first in Tacoma. Hell, why not make a quick detour? And he took me to see his palace-to-be, a nice slim four-story brick building on Broadway, across from the theater (convenient for the after-the-show crowd) and a small park (aesthetic and therefore classy). He imagined a New York-style awning out front with a small tree on each side. He wanted to attract an older, more affluent, more respectable crowd than most casinos—which would make him not only a good neighbor in Tacoma but also a guilt-free one. "I don't want people to be spending their welfare checks. I want people who can lose $500 or $1,000 and it's play money. I don't feel bad about skimming the rich."

Then he was back on the phone, talking to a business broker of some kind about the business plan. "You're hired. I'll pay you up front. Check? Hell, I'll give you cash."

He hung up. "I'm having to do a lot of fancy dance steps," he told me. "All I have at the moment is an idea, and to get people to put up two million for this idea is hard to do, especially if you're 21 years old." To illustrate the point, he picked up his business proposal from the floor of the car and flipped it open. The first four pages were devoted to brief biographies and photos of the major players involved. Aha, I said, noticing that many of the faces, even those who looked like bit players, exuded the gravitas and respectability of prosperous middle age. "Exactly," he said. "I'm not stupid."

Something about this reminded me that he had forgotten to follow up on the promise to get me flown across the Cascades. He called his friend Mike and left a message.

Most people's problem is that they don't know how to handle money, he said, and they're afraid of it. His father, he said, though coming from one of the wealthiest families in Iraq, worked as a mechanic all his life making $35,000 a year. Emiel didn't want any part of that. "I hooked up with a bunch of Italians at a very young age, and they taught me how to live good." He grinned. "I tell people I'm Arabic by birth but Italian by choice."

By now we were at Pike Place Market. Emiel hauled my pack out of the trunk, dodged an invitation to explain the shotgun and the sword, promised to follow up on the plane business, shook my hand with genuine warmth, and then, getting back into the car, found he'd been hedged in by the cars behind him. As I hoisted my pack onto one shoulder, I imagined him fuming impatiently behind the tinted glass, and gave him an extra wave. Emiel's either going to go through a cycle of making it and going broke, making it and going broke, said his mother, or he's going to really make it. I've got to do this trip again in ten years' time to see what happens to all these characters, I thought, even if I'm in a wheelchair.

Six weeks later I e-mailed him, half-expecting his "godfather" e-mail address to be a joke. But Emiel is nothing if not serious: He e-mailed me back saying he had his money. Construction would begin in nine months.

At the entrance to the Pike Place Market was the fish stand, fronted by a chunky, aproned guy with a magnificent whisky mustache.

"Clean 'em up, head on!" he yelled to the crew behind the counter, flinging a couple of large fish across the counter.

"Clean 'em up, head on!" they chorused back as the nearest guy caught the fish neatly in waxed paper and wrapped them.

A tall, skinny African-American cyclist with a shaved head, wearing shades, bike shorts, black and yellow sneakers, and an Alcatraz Swim Team sweatshirt, inquired about the smoked salmon. Mustache pointed them out to him, and yelled, "Jail-bird's looking at the smoked!" to alert his colleagues. I decided to take some dinner home to Gail, who had offered me a couch for the night.

"Two pounds king filet!" he called, hurling my fish across Seattle.

"Two pounds king filet!" they called back in unison, catching, cutting, and wrapping. I walked around the cases, admiring rows of crab, an avalanche of shrimp, and a migration of lobsters across the chipped ice, when I heard his voice again, right behind me.

"Three tilapia!"

"Three tilapia!"

I ducked as the fish flew one after another past my right ear.

I found Gail in a small, sunny house in a settled-looking neighborhood of bungalows up on Queen Anne Hill, with plenty of trees, the houses themselves all slightly different, sprouting gables and porches, the sidewalk grass dug up here and there in favor of tiny box-gardens, with pumpkins, rosemary, sage, peas, and tomatoes. Her house was full of light and healthy plants. Two kittens lay asleep in a basket, their paws around each other's necks. Gail and her husband Hal owned an old Mercedes. I was shocked. I thought that anyone who knew me was condemned to a life of poverty.

Gail and I have been in regular contact over the years, and we've formed a collective identity beyond marriage: I think of her as something like a cousin, or perhaps a sister who has gone out to make her way in a different part of the world. She has decided that having been married gives us the right to be honest with each other, and if that had been the only outcome of the marriage, it would have been worthwhile.

Talking about our marriage and my trip, and how things had changed between one and the other, it was only natural that we should come around to the issue of parenthood, and how being a responsible parent affects our freedom and our bravery. When I first knew Gail she had worked in jails as a paralegal, she was becoming a fearless investigative reporter, she had stood up to the Special Branch in London while they smashed everything in her boyfriend the anarchist's flat. Now her priorities were more domestic. Over the clatter of the salad spinner and the percussion of chopping vegetables, she talked of caring for two children in a school system that seemed to be leaderless and vulnerable to copycat crimes. Whether by coincidence or some deep repercussion of a constant, low-level anxiety, she had developed a fear of heights.

Her daughter Gabrielle, she said "is now coming into her fear and vulnerability as a female, in middle school and as a preadolescent. I'm trying to figure out how to help her stay secure and strong. I don't want fear to dictate to her in ways that are destructive, but at the same time I want her to be smart and savvy, which involves a certain exposure to risk. She's asking to watch *Scream 2*, and I'm saying, 'I don't think that's going to help with this issue!' But I think there's a real appeal for girls to watch that stuff because it validates their fears."

She told me a story about a friend of ours named Alice, back in Vermont, a woman with a strong spiritual grounding. "Alice took me to this waterfall," Gail said, "and I asked her if there was anything she wished she had done differently in bringing up her children. She said she wished that early on she had made it clear to them that whatever happened, they were safe. I said 'What do you mean by that?' She said, 'We're all spirits. We're all safe.' That's what it comes down to with Gabrielle. When we play out 'What's the worst that can happen?' we realize that our spirits are always safe. And when Gabrielle looks at things this way, she suddenly feels this enormous inner strength. If you can't do that, you've lost this incredible potential and your reason for being here."

I'd have liked to stay for a couple of days, but it turned out that Jason, the trucker who had recommended I see the Harley rally at Sturgis, had got his dates wrong: the rally ended on August 9. If I didn't leave at once, I'd miss it all—and even now I'd have to cover a thousand miles, a third of the country, in two days, three at the most.

I'd already set up a ride in the cab of a train going east through the Canadian Rockies, and planned to hitch down from Calgary, but now there just wasn't time. I'd have to cut due east and miss western Canada altogether. Which was a pity, because I'd seen little enough of it last time across. After a terrible time on the Trans-Canada Highway in British Columbia, stuck for five hours at a place called Hope, where the slipstream of a semi knocked over and cracked my guitar, we cut south and crept along just above the border. That night, riding in a VW bus owned by a forest ranger who had fallen asleep in the back leaving Richard to drive, I saw one of the most bizarre and frightening sights I've seen. It was well after midnight. We had passed through a small town called Trail and made a right turn by a wheat field when the headlights picked up a post of some kind, perhaps 12 feet tall, just ahead on our right. Whatever was at the top of the post—a sign, presumably— was wrapped in some kind of sacking. Richard started to pick up speed as we approached this pole. It was a slightly odd sight, in an odd place, serving no apparent purpose, and without saying anything we both looked up at it as we got nearer. Just as we passed it, the sacking moved slightly and an arm reached out.

We stared at each other. "Did you see that?" I asked, and Richard nodded, looking white. We said nothing else about it. Nothing would have made us turn round to find out what it was.

The following evening we made it to Calgary and called Ben van de Maele, the farmer, and he said, "Season's starting early, boys. Be here by the first of the month." That was four days away. By our calculations, we needed to make 550 miles a day.

After a sleepless night in the youth hostel, where we shared a stifling bunker of a dormitory with a dozen other guys including the loudest snorer I've ever heard, we were on the Trans Canada at 6 a.m. We made 600 miles the first day, crashing on the floor with some Yorkton kids who insisted on staying up until 3 a.m., drinking and smoking dope, then another 600 miles (including a drenching in Thunder Bay) on the second day; but late on the third, we got stuck at Marathon, Ontario, with 800 miles still to go and nothing in town but a rail junction—closed by a strike—and a gas station. Then a pickup pulled in for gas. Yeah, he'd take us. Where was he going? London, Ontario—right down the road from the tobacco fields. He drove all night and all the next day, and I rode those 900 miles or so sitting in a tire in the back, my own built-in suspension. We got one last ride from Port Burwell (pop. 600) right to Ben's farm, arriving just as the sun went down.

These are the stories hitchhikers tell to each other, reminding ourselves that we once had daring, and that we once found adventure and kindness wherever we went, as if those were the reward for our daring. This was the weird and tragic contradiction of my contemporaries, those I talked to before I left. Given the chance to tell their stories, everyone who had hitchhiked began to soften and melt, to stare away over the horizon and tell me their own epics, eyes glowing, the years falling away, the fire at their core visible, perhaps for the first time in years, telling tales of a lost youth, or the lost youth of a country.

Before I was ready, I was heading back. The idea of backness, of heading East toward the increasingly familiar, depressed me. America would start to repeat itself: I'd start meeting the same people and hearing the same conversations. I was heartily sick of the word Sturgis, and wished I'd never suggested going there.

Only two things kept me going, both of them lessons I'd learned on the trip: a bleak outlook is usually just a sign I'm tired; and whenever I think something will be dull, I'm always wrong.

CHAPTER 23

Idiot A, Idiot B, and the Journey Back East

August 7—Seattle, Washington

Emiel's friend didn't call. There was a bus that went from Seattle through Sturgis, but it was a 29-hour nonstop haul, and I didn't think I could handle that. The following morning, as it happened, Gail and Hal were driving a hundred miles east on I-90 to pick up Gabrielle from camp, so I asked if I could ride with them.

Before we left, Gail took me around Seattle to see what I remembered of it. Virtually nothing. Well, Proust had his blind spots, too, and invented as much as he remembered. Young transients were still drawn to the university, just as Richard and I had been, settling on University Avenue like a small flock of ragged birds: some in dreadlocks, some with piercings, some in Gothic black, some in baggy clothing the colors of dust, hanging out on sidewalks or sitting against walls. They seem so lost, Gail said, and I remembered that Maria had said exactly the same about the young hippies by the freeways around the bay. And our parents probably said just the same about us, all those years ago.

We ended up at Uptown Espresso on Lower Queen Anne Avenue South, Seattle. No Starbucks, this: it had character. Lively chatter on both sides of the serving counter, and their homemade marionberry torte was the best pie I had on the entire continent. Slipping into the local dialect, Gail ordered "a single short wet cap 2 percent."—"If they get it right, they get to keep the change."—I wanted a café au lait, only to discover that Uptown Espresso seemed to have evolved beyond mere coffee. They had reached a quality of life where it was espresso drinks or nothing. I gave in and ordered a cappuccino. She sipped her short wet cap and pronounced it excellent. The trick is to get the foam right, she said. I kidded her that this seemed to me the perfect Seattle remark: We were earnestly discussing something that had style but no substance. No, she argued, but it has texture. Good foam is like velvet.

On the drive east from Seattle, Hal, whom I've never known well and who tends to present the benign cream-of-wheat public face of the professional psychotherapist, began to open up, as if having me dumped on the household was making him revisit his own past. He told us about the commune he had helped to found in Vermont between 1974 and 1977 in a bankrupt girls' summer camp. They lived in the cabins, year round. In the summer it was idyllic, right on the shores of Lake Champlain; in winter it was cold, and they sat around the wood stoves telling stories, playing cards, drinking beer, and getting high. "We had our own paradise, full of energetic, creative people with their own idealism. Anyone who came just stayed because it was so wonderful." Everyone did whatever he or she could—carpentry, farming, cooking—but the collective enterprise evolved, like many other collective enterprises of the time, into an alternative school. This gave the commune purpose and focus, but ultimately destroyed it. Making things up more or less as they went along, they did such a good job with the maladjusted but essentially well-intentioned children of the wealthy that the state started sending them more and more children in state's custody, who had a different set of needs entirely. "We were trying to deal with them based on hippie ideals of togetherness and love and trust, when what they really needed were discipline and locks. That was when I left. I didn't get anything back from my initial investment—it all went to pay off bank loans and debts."

If life in Vermont was an adventure, so was getting there. He was hitching across from the West Coast, making for Hartford, Connecticut, and was picked up in Wyoming by two young guys who turned out to be—or perhaps turned into—robbers. The first inkling of trouble came when they stopped at a topless joint somewhere in the Midwest, where a husband and wife were stripping to music from *The Good, The Bad and The Ugly*. The two young guys got into a fight, and when one of them stormed off to the bathroom, the other grabbed the keys and said, "You'd better come if you're coming, because I'm outta here." Hal went off with him, and after about 15 miles persuaded him to turn round. When they got back to the strip joint, there was his buddy standing outside waiting for him.

Money began to run short. The two had some traveler's checks, but they were headed for New Hampshire, where they planned to live off the checks until they found work or, perhaps, a small rural bank with a geriatric security guard. So they stopped off somewhere in Indiana and robbed a convenience store. One went in and bought beer, using their own money, while the other looked around the place, then they produced a gun and held up the clerk, taking whatever was in the till including their own money. They did this twice while Hal fretted over what he should do. If they were all arrested, he could hardly claim he was just a hitchhiker, and an innocent bystander. On the other hand, he felt a certain responsibility: If he just said, "Drop me off," then these idiots might kill someone sooner or later.

He came up with a fascinating and creative plan. Look, he told the idiots, sooner or later you're going to get caught if you keep holding up convenience stores and gas stations. I know a better way to make the money you need. You (he said to Idiot A, who owned the traveler's checks) give the checks to him (Idiot B, who presumably was sitting with his mouth open wondering what was going on). You (Idiot B) sign them and you both use the money. Then, when we get to Hartford, you (Idiot A) go to the police and tell them your traveler's checks were stolen. They'll see that they were signed by someone else and reimburse you, so you can spend the money now and still have it when you get to New Hampshire.

The idiots thought this was such a good idea (and, apparently, a successful one) that they unanimously elected Hal to be their leader, like a bad *Star Trek* plot, and by the end of the trip they were asking him to make decisions for them—Should we stop here? Should we take this road? Hal went with them as far as southern New England and ended up in Vermont, counseling unmanageable teenagers.

Gail and Hal dropped me off on I-90 in mid-state, feeling as if they were abandoning me to starve in the wilderness. By now, though, the road felt like home. I found myself leaning into the traffic as if this area was my force field, and the cars were passing into it and couldn't help being affected by it.

I was picked up within ten or fifteen minutes by Al Montgomery, a custom builder. A few years previously he and a hired man were working for the U.S.-Canada border commission, clearing a strip of open ground all along the border, the Mason and Dixon of their day. A helicopter would drop them off, they'd work with their chainsaws all day, and their last act would be to cut an open space at the end of the day's strip big enough for the helicopter to land and pick them up again.

Some pretty strange people live right up on the border, he said. One day, he and the hired man were on their lunch break and decided to do a little target practice, shooting off a little bridge that someone had built over a creek. After a few minutes a guy appeared out of the woods and asked them if they'd mind not doing that, as there were children around. Al and his partner immediately obliged, and the man invited them for a drink up to where he lived, which turned out to be a sort of commune, buried in the woods on the border. The newcomers were welcomed into this odd little community, and offered some pot. The hired man accepted; Al declined, feeling there was something strange about the place, wanting to keep his wits about him. He sat with the rifle next to him, while the others lit up.

Looking around, he noticed a newly dug open grave and, next to it, an open copy of Stephen King's *The Dead Zone*. Well, I think we'd better be getting back to work now, he said, picked up the rifle and the hired man and got out of there as quickly as he decently could.

Then another first: I was picked up almost at once by a girl.

Her name was Tove; she had the fresh-air complexion of a skier. Not only was she unafraid to pick me up, she was unafraid to pick me up even though she had all her worldly goods in her Subaru, as she was moving to Mount Hood and then down to Mammoth. No big deal. A lot of my friends hitchhike, she said. She was a true daughter of Title IX: broad-shouldered, self-confident; she looked like someone who could recover from a fall.

The only drawback was that she had to turn off almost at once where 82 split off from 90 and peeled south. I was stuck on the sliver of shoulder between two interstates—never a good spot. After ten minutes of being knocked sideways by the bow wave of every passing truck, certain that I would get hassled by the police, I saw a Washington State Patrol cruiser pulling onto the shoulder toward me. To my surprise, the cop took off his shades and grinned at me. "How're you doing?" he asked.

I had no idea how to answer. I was ready for anything except friendliness. I thought of saying, "Fine until you came along," but that seemed a little churlish, under the circumstances. "Okay," I said cautiously.

"You getting rides?" he asked. Now I was completely off balance, and for want of anything sensible to say, I told him about my trip. He seemed genuinely interested. Almost apologetically, he came round to business. "I guess you got dropped off here by someone going south on 82?" he said sympathetically. I nodded. He took my name down in his log, and I took his—Trooper Mel D. Sterkel—and he allowed as how he'd have to ask me to walk back to the last exit.

"It's one of the best exits around," he said earnestly. "You've got all the traffic coming out of Ellensburg, you've got all the long-haulers...." He sounded like a field reviewer for the *Hitch-hiker's Guide to North America.* "Make sure you walk way off to the side," he said in parting. "I want to read that book of yours."

Of course, this meant a two-mile hike over the usual roadside rubble, but even so I wanted to sponsor him for some community policing award. Back in 1973, the police were the enemy.

At the Ellenburg exit, though, the pendulum of police conduct swung back. I was leaning on the sign announcing the entrance to the freeway, and this was apparently too close to trespassing: a jerk in a cruiser coming up the opposite lane screamed something inaudible over the traffic, scowling, making threatening gestures, and pointing back toward the beginning of the ramp. So much for modern policing methods.

I was rescued by Blaine, who had just finished his engineering degree and was working in construction—not a dropout choice but a sound business decision. Housing values in Seattle have gone up 27 percent in the last year, he said, as we passed the strange black river cliffs of the Columbia and then the golden stubble and rippling vanillafudge hills called the Palouse, lying like suede and soft corduroy on the undulating ripples of the land.

He dropped me off at 8 p.m. in Colfax, due south of Spokane. If only I could cover that last 50 miles, I could stay with a friend of Gail's who was writing a book on the Y2K computer threat—but the traffic was failing with the daylight. At the Chevron station across the road, a chubby girl emptied the soapy water from the squeegee tubs and turned out the lights.

~

CHAPTER 24

Hate Kickin' This Thing out of Cruise Control

August 8—Colfax, Washington

I awoke in Colfax's only motel at 4:30 a.m., anxious to get going, still uneasy from a waking dream: I was back in Vermont again, and Barbara was calling the wife of Redmond O'Hanlon, my favorite travel writer, to ask "Is it always like this?"

"Oh, yes," came the reply, pitched between stoicism and resignation. "He gets home, sleeps for a week, and just when you think he's becoming human again, he says that now he can't wait to start writing about it all, and disappears into his study. You get used to it."

The sun was well up when a teenager pulled over in a pickup, a big old farm boy with fingers like bunches of pink bananas, up early to work on the harvest. Or so I thought: I had to learn again each day that my assumptions about America would always be wrong, as if night healed the gaps that had been torn in the landscape of the mind and it would take the day to break them apart again. Yep, he said, he'd been harvesting all of 'em, wheat, barley, lentils, peas.... Peas? Yes, those were peas on the left there, crawling across the ground rather than climbing up neat little trellises, drying to the same desiccated gold color as wheat and then scooped up and winnowed. Not that he actually knew much about farming; he just drove the truck that took the crop from the combines and drove it down from the fields to the Snake River, where it was floated on barges down to Portland.

So you're not a farm lad, then, I ask, walking into it with my chin out. No, he laughs. All his bulk came not from farm food but from the college weight room: He's a shot-and-discus thrower. He's already got the best discus throw in college this year, and the fifth best in the whole U.S., 211 feet, 5 inches. He hopes to make the Olympic team for Australia in 2000. He's been there already with the U.S. juniors a year ago, he says casually. Give me your name, I say as he drops me off at the Flying J in Post Falls, Idaho, so I can watch out for you. Ian Waltz, he says.

At the Flying J, I asked the manager if she'd make an announcement over the p.a. for me—that I was writing a book about hitchhiking around America, that I needed a ride east on 90. She looked very doubtful, but a couple of truckers standing nearby said sure, why not? Where was I going? Sturgis, I said. Hell, we're going right through there, they said. Just let us grab a bite of breakfast and we'll be on our way.

Over breakfast, unfortunately, they called dispatch (I could have told them this was a bad move) and were told that the principal driver had to be with the company 90 days before they'd let him take a rider, and as he had only 30 days, it was no go.

Still, it might be worth hanging around the truck stop anyway, I thought, and asked a few drivers passing in and out. An ancient, speckled guy with a cane, sitting at a picnic table, told me that the embassy bombings in Kenya and Tanzania the previous day were just the beginning. "A lot of people are sick of the government," he said in disgust. "Soon that'll happen in this country."

"I thought that had already happened in Oklahoma City," I said evenly.

"That was just a little one," he said. "There's going to be a big one."

I gave up on the Flying J, walked across under the interstate, and set up on the bottom of the ramp. After about a quarter of an hour, a well-ridden pickup pulled over, its bed full of storm windows, bicycles, steamer trunks, and all kinds of miscellaneous effects. The driver, who introduced himself as Kevin, was a wild-looking guy in cut-off sweatpants, his blond hair combed back from a receding forehead to fall down over his shoulders, his chest and thighs tattooed, a front tooth missing. He had a curious sidelong look, a cross between a grin and a glower. We threw my pack in among the stuff in back, and as I climbed in I saw two things on my side of the seat: a small, suspicious-looking Dalmatian, who seemed altogether unhappy about having to give up his spot, and a wallet. I handed over the wallet—a great opportunity for a good-faith gesture—and climbed in, the dog turning this way and that to get settled, occasionally digging a claw into my bare thigh.

Kevin spoke in a high-speed mumble, in clusters of words shot out of the corner of his mouth. "Seatbeltsdon'twork," he told me. It took me a second to work out that this was in fact four separate words. "I kinda throw one over my shoulder." He demonstrated, looping the useless belt over his left shoulder and letting it fall down at his side. "Gives the cops something to see."

He had just come from a museum somewhere, he said, selling them a horse-hair bridle. (I thought he said "horse-head bridle"; I had no idea what that was, but he didn't seem to pay much attention to whether I was listening or not anyway.) Two thousand bucks. He'd just sold another one to a different museum, and two to some rich guy for 1,500 apiece. Fifteen thousand bucks so far this year. And he'd only started making them a few months ago. Wow, that sounds like a pretty skilled trade, I said. Where'd you learn that? In jail, he said.

O-*kay*, I thought. I'm just going to let a suitable amount of time pass before I ask what he was inside for. In the meantime, he was occupied by something else: He inadvertently cut off a woman in a red Mustang, and spent the next ten or twelve miles checking in his mirror to see if she was still behind him. "Jesus," he said, "Maybe I should let her pull up alongside so I can apologize. Shit." I was rather touched by this. For all his wildness, he had an odd, tender streak—actually, he seemed to consist entirely of odd, contradictory streaks. His great-grandfather, he said—and I'm not sure I'd want to try to verify all this, even if I could—donated the land on which Oberlin College was built, and came west with a wagonload of books. Kevin himself seemed to love books. "I got all kinds of books in a foot locker back there," he said, gesturing back toward the bed of the truck. "Longfellow. Whittier. Bibles a foot thick. I gotta Dr. Jekyll an' Mr. Hyde that's so old it hasn't even got a fuckin' date in it." He hadn't read it yet, he said, because he liked just looking at it and feeling the cover.

It was a different ancestor, a grandfather, I think, who came to Yakima, Washington, as a tramp and was treated unkindly by some major figure in town, perhaps the most prominent junkyard owner. "He treated me like dirt," went the family legend. He vowed to break the guy, or die trying, and by the time he died he owned the largest junkyard in central Washington, and his widow became a paper millionaire. Some of this didn't quite add up—if there was so much money, why was his mother working in a Wal-Mart?—but I didn't mind. His parents were divorced, but he clearly adored his mother, and his dad (by which he may have meant his stepfather, I was never sure) often made this trip from Washington to Montana with him. The guy was as deaf as a plank now, and just sat behind his newspaper for the whole trip, "except for one place where he always puts his paper down and just looks at me," Kevin said. "He's sure we're going off the road."

Kevin had been inside, it turned out, for possession of marijuana with intent to sell. "Ten years for possession?" I asked, sympathetically. "Did a year and a half, violated parole, ended up serving nearly six years," he glowered. Actually, he didn't seem to mind: jail had taught him the value of things, he said, though I was never quite clear what values he had learned. He grew up around dope. "My dad had sinsemilla plants seven feet tall, peeking up over the garage," he said. "When he went off to Sturgis one year he said, 'If those plants dry out and die I'll kill you.' By the time he came back they were all lying on the ground from overwatering. I watered them four or five times a day and my sister watered them, too. He'd have killed us if we hadn't."

The road had imperceptibly climbed up to a pass between the Coeur D'Alene mountains on the left and the Bitterroots on the right, and from now on, as they say, it was all downhill. He settled himself in his seat with an expression of grim glee, and set the cruise control on 84. "I used to be a cocaine addict," he said. "Now I'm an adrenaline junkie."

Let me tell you about Montana. Much of the state is wild and beautiful, the interstate running alongside streams and rocky rivers, up between pine-covered mountains and then down to meadows. This section was a genuine mountain pass. On the one side, as Arlo Guthrie sang in "The Motorcycle Song," there was the mountain. On the other side there was nothing.

We wound downhill for several miles, and Kevin passed the time by pointing out how Buddy would've made an amazing surfer, leaning professionally into each turn, and by telling me the story of how his father, who seemed to be a trucker, had not long ago taken a rig, "brand new rig, seven hunnerdnfiftythousand dollar rig, the cab alone was worth a hunnerdnfiftythousand," up over a mountain pass and as soon as he'd started downhill had realized the brakes weren't working properly. Before he was even up to twenny-five, Kevin said, he just opened the door and jumped out. Your heart must've been poundin', Kevin said when his dad told him the story. Not at all, his dad replied calmly. I was just hoping I'd stop tumbling in time to see her go over the edge. And he did: The truck's near-side wheels must have caught in the ditch because she rounded a couple of curves, picking up speed, before breaking free and going over the other side. "Landed in 150 feet of water. They just salvaged the cab. Didn't even bother with the trailer."

So this tale was in the back of my mind as we barreled down into the steepest, tightest curves in the pass. There wasn't much traffic, but every so often Kevin would steam up behind some slowpoke passing some other slowpoke at only 70 or 75, and he'd thump the wheel and say, "Damn! I hate kickin' this thing out of cruise control!"

But there wasn't any traffic worth speaking of when we hit the three curves to end all other curves. The first was a right, so if we flipped we'd just go into the sheer rock face on Kevin's side, which seemed infinitely preferable to me. I braced myself against the g force, and as I was plastered against the door (which, it occurred to me at this very second, was probably in the same shape as the seat belts and might fly open at any pressure), I found Buddy doing the same; his head appeared under my chin.

An insane calm fell over me. At this speed, it didn't matter whether the seat belts worked or not. Everything came down to one roll of the dice. I remembered my friend the psychic, who is always right about the important things, telling me before I left that I wasn't in any danger on this trip, that I was quite safe in cars and with mechanical devices in general; and I thought, *You've just got to let it go.* So I did, and we were around the first bend.

The second bend was a left, the bad kind. The gorge rolled up beneath my window as we hit the curve, the guardrail looking laughable, as flimsy as tin ribbon. For the first time in my life, all the most crucial information in the world—the feel of the road, the grip of the tires—came to me through my buttocks. The truck felt high and loose, the tires impossibly fat and soft. It felt as though the slightest extra pressure, the touch of a toothpick, would flip us over, and then straight over the edge. I realized I was still hanging onto the useless strap of the seat belt. Let it go, I thought. Let it go. Then we were round, and heading back the other way. The third curve, though just as tight, was almost a relief.

"My God!" I breathed, as we straightened out.

"Yeah," he said happily, with his sideways grin. "That's the place where my dad puts down his paper and looks at me. The hard part is, I have to say something to him to show I'm all confident, but I have to turn right round to look at him or else he can't read my fuckin' lips, so I have to stop looking at the road. And meanwhile my heart's pounding. Shit," he added, feeling his chest, "my heart's *still* pounding!"

From then on, he just had time to tell me about his brother being shot—not fatally—by some assholes he threw out of a party, which led to an interesting ethical predicament because he wouldn't give the cops the satisfaction of testifying against the assholes in court. In the end, the assholes copped a plea and ended up doing four and a half years apiece, and we were pulling off the interstate in Missoula, Montana.

I bought him lunch at a chain restaurant. He gave me his card— well, someone else's card, with his name scrawled on the back—so that when I saw his work hanging in some gallery in London next to a Picasso, I could check the name and know that it was his. Oh, yeah…He was struck by a thought, and led me outside to the truck. He rummaged around in the bed, hauled out one trunk, his prison muscles flexing, then another. I thought he was going to show me his beloved books, but he seemed to have forgotten all about them. Instead he threw open the last trunk and produced one of his bridles. It was tightly and expertly woven in what to my untutored eye looked like a series of Navajo designs, tassels on each end, the kind of thing I can readily imagine a rich person wanting to see on a fine horse.

He made a last couple of aslant come-ons to the young waitress, who brushed them off as easily as stray wisps of hair, then he was gone. The place seemed almost unbearably pale and dull without him. I clambered over to the rubble of the work-in-progress interstate exit, where I felt much more at home.

To my amazement, for the first time I had competition. Two hitchhikers, both guys around 20, were already in position; or rather they seemed to have found their position and fallen over it, like a drunken actor looking for his mark. One was sitting on a small, disintegrating vinyl hold-all, surrounded by a raft of plastic one-gallon milk jugs filled to varying degrees with water. The other had given up on verticality and was slumped beside the road—possibly a good move, as it made him less visible, and what there was to see of him was not generally inviting. He was pale and meaty; he had shaved his head; and he was dressed in undershirt, camouflage trousers, and combat boots. Both had large-caliber chains swinging from their pants pockets. They might as well have stuck up a sign saying, "Will Accept Rides Only from Members of White Supremacy Groups."

At first, they put their lack of mobility—it had taken them two days to get a truck ride here from northern Idaho—down to bad luck and other people's fear or hostility, but once we began talking, it became clear that they hadn't a clue about hitchhiking. As soon as they heard how far I'd come, they pressed me for tips. "Well," I said, trying not to sound condescending, "when I'm hitching I never sit down. It makes me look as if I don't care whether I get a ride or not." They nodded and straightened up. How could they not know this? I thought, amazed, but we're at a strange point in history when the idea of hitchhiking has survived but the culture of hitchhiking has not. There was nobody around anymore to set them straight.

We discussed equipment. The senior partner, who was slimmer than his friend and had a buzz-cut, cursed himself for having bought this cheap pack, but at least he'd had the foresight to bring water, he said. This was the half-dozen milk jugs. "I don't know," I said. "I started out carrying water but gave it up. I've never been anywhere yet where I couldn't buy some juice. And all these jugs just make you look messy. You want to look serious about what you're doing."

"Yeah," said the meaty one with surprising bitterness. "When'd you ever see a fat hitchhiker?"

We discussed appearance, and they allowed as how it might be a good idea to put away the chains. They asked me about signs, and whether they should stand facing this way or that way. I asked them if they'd thought of going across the road to the gas station or restaurant and asking for rides. No, this had never occurred to them.

"Where are you trying to get to?" I asked. Alabama, they said. My jaw dropped. The older kid had been visiting his girlfriend, who lived in Idaho, and in a couple of weeks they were going to get married down where he lived. My God, I said, that's the perfect story. Go into that restaurant, over there, where everyone's pulling off the highway for lunch, and tell people you need to make it to Alabama in two weeks for your wedding. Someone's bound to help you out." There was also a Greyhound every day around noon, I told them—it had never occurred to them to take a bus, even though they had money—and it was bound to pull off and stop somewhere around here.

They looked uncertain. They hated this spot, where they had been for four hours, but they hated to give it up. "Okay," I said, "the rules of hitchhiking say that I can't step in front of you, so I'll just go 20 yards farther up." No, no, they said, they wanted a break anyway. I could have their spot; they'd try over at the gas station. We shook hands and wished each other luck. They stumbled off across the rubble. After a few minutes I looked across and saw that they had sat down with their backs to the side wall of the gas station. They didn't go in. They didn't go into the restaurant, either. They seemed to have just given up.

After twenty minutes I was picked up by a young couple—another first for this journey—in a pickup with a cap. He was on his way back from a rodeo; his hobby was steer wrestling.

"Isn't that dangerous?" I asked. Naw, he said in his aw-shucks manner, while his silent girlfriend, sitting between us, leafed through a small horses-for-sale newspaper. "You got a bulldog-ging horse and a hazing horse, one each side of the steer, and you basically get off your horse onto the steer and pull him to the ground." It was his second year, and he was breaking even. In the daytime he worked construction. I had to work hard to get this much out of him, and now he lapsed into silence, a medium in which he was comfortable, and let his girlfriend rest her head on his shoulder. Every so often she would point out a horse, and he'd look at it and smile affectionately at her, and she at him.

They dropped me off shortly before four at a grassy rest area beside a small river, six or seven miles from Garrison. The sun was very hot indeed, and for the first time I was standing on a highway with no speed limit, so half the cars would have needed brake parachutes to stop—but as usual I needn't have been concerned, for within ten minutes I was setting off in a Toyota station wagon heading for Three Forks, at the headwaters of the Missouri. I never learned the driver's name. Each year he set out on his own to fol-low some of Lewis and Clark's route. He was planning to cycle over some of the mountain passes they crossed, to get some sense of the effort involved.

Around Butte, Montana, the land opened up and dried out into semi-desert. My benefactor had done his own share of hitch-hik-ing, he said, though not in this country: He was in the Peace Corps in Chile from 1968-1971, and anyone would pick you up as long as you didn't mind climbing in the back of the truck or pickup along with whatever or whoever else was in there. He wouldn't do it now. "Thirty years ago I didn't know what I had to lose."

He dropped me off at a little exit in the middle of a broad plain; if it had had corn on each side it could have stood in for Cary Grant's rendezvous with the crop-dusting plane in *North By Northwest*. Almost at once I was picked up by a early middle-aged guy who taught at the university in Bozeman, on his way back from a hiking and climbing trip in Canada. Bozeman was a great little town, he said, a wonderful place to raise children, with a great arts and music festival every summer. And it looked pleasant enough, set in a broad valley between mountain ranges, a leafy spot with a couple from the fire department getting married and running out to the honeymoon fire engine—but the festival had packed every room in town, and just when I was hoping to collapse into a bed, I was out on the highway again, being picked up by a calm, serious young man just out of college who was, I suppose, a traveler himself of a kind, living down by Yellowstone and teaching himself the demanding art of 4" x 5" photography, an Ansel Adams of the future.

I ended up, late in the evening, at Livingston. Outside the Harvey's, a deeply tanned woman wearing a tanktop and peasant skirt, who looked as if she might have been riding a Harley for a few weeks, sat on top of a picnic table with her knee drawn up to her chin, watching the sun set. As I passed her, she lit a cigar.

CHAPTER 25

Jeff Bridges Has a Ranch Up Here

August 9—Livingston, Montana

U p and on the ramp by 7 a.m., writing in my journal:

The watchword for the morning is patience. Move calmly. Be here now.

Two mule deer frisk around a junkyard below the interstate ramp, their long tails whisking from side to side.

The sun is in the drivers' eyes. They can barely see me and I can barely see them, with their visors down. I feel no exchange of cheerfulness, no dialogue. By this time yesterday I had already gone 50 miles....No, you can't allow yourself to think like that. Stay in the moment. Look out at the lumber yard below, filling the air with the smell of cut pine. Row upon row, maybe a hundred stacks of plywood sheeting, eight by four foot I expect, a faded cream pickup lurching between them, splashing through puddles as the work day begins. Stacks of weathered pallets, four gray-and-yellow boxcars on a railway siding. Behind them the first ridge of pine-covered mountains, and beyond that the jagged peaks of Yellowstone.

Hitchhiking is starting to look like a spiritual exercise. It fosters patience interspersed with gratitude. It demands faith, hope, and other people's charity, and demands the Buddhist virtues of selflessness and an acceptance of not-knowing. It enforces St. Benedict's principles of poverty, chastity (despite the sexual mythology of the thumb), and obedience—to the rules of the road, and the rules of chance.

I turn the full force of my attention on the cars, and a young guy waves at me with a piece of bread he's chewing.

Minutes later I was picked up by Mike, who was going to Big Timber, another of those vivid and almost hopelessly heroic western town names. He worked for the phone company, he said, but it turned out to be rather more than that. "I'm a farrier—I shoe horses—and I work for the phone company. And I'm a former Mormon bishop. I used to say 'I can shoe your horse, fix your phone, marry you, and bury you,' because I also own a cemetery." He was also a small farmer, with eight head of cattle. "We sell the calves for Christmas money."

I instinctively warmed to this guy. In Vermont, another rural state with almost no major employers, everyone practices this crazy fiscal quilting, patching together an income, no talent unexploited. "If you're making eight or nine dollars an hour in Livingston, you're making good money, and you've got to have a four-wheel-drive in this country."

We cruised on in the quiet, early morning sunlight, following the broad, flat plain of the Yellowstone River, mostly cattle land. "Those mountains over there," Mike said, pointing to a low, barren, angular range away to the left, "are called the Crazy Mountains. Most mountain ranges around here are glaciated, so their ridges and valleys run north to south. The Crazies are volcanic dikes, so their ridges run every which direction." Good hunting up there, he said—ptarmigan, mountain goat, elk, bear—but the fly-fishing was even better, the best in the country. "Tom Brokaw has a ranch on the Boulder River. Jeff Bridges has a ranch up here. Peter Fonda's lived here for 20 years."

We passed a handful of windmills. "This is the third windiest place in the United States. I can remember winds up to 60 miles an hour going across that flat."

He pointed out a sharply pointed mountain on the southern horizon, part of the Beartooth Range running along the top of the Yellowstone National Park. "Big Timber is going to be the home of one of the world's biggest plutonium mines. See the ridge there, with the snow still on it? It's going to be over there. Two hundred jobs. They're going to bring in a big boring machine that'll bore 50 miles through the mountains on a railroad track."

Well, that's what he told me. Afterward I started wondering about the things we tell each other in the confessionals of our own cars, and called the Stillwater Mining Company. Actually the mine is designed to extract palladium, platinum, and rodium; it has two boring machines, the ore is only 18,000 feet into the mountain, and it is expected to create 600 jobs. "Mining," said the mining company's spokesman, "tends to inflame people's imaginations."

But I didn't care whether it was platinum or plutonium or palladium; I liked hearing this man talk about his feeling for this barren, wild country, even if, like most of us, he didn't always get the details right. Like me, he was passionate about trains, and he gestured at the track running alongside the interstate. "Livingston had the biggest rail repair shop west of the Mississippi. Employed about a thousand people. That's what put the town on the map. They did work for the Union Pacific, the Burlington

Northern, the Montana Railroad—they can build a train there. The whole thing. Now they're down to about 200 people. They've got contracts from Germany, Brazil. All of my relatives were railroad people. See the line down there? All those signals are a microwave to Missoula so they can keep track of where the trains are."

Then he was turning off to Big Timber, though I never did find out if he had to fix a phone or shoe a horse. He dropped me off, crossed the interstate, and all traffic at my exit ceased.

It was five minutes before the next car pulled past me onto I-80, and the next was five minutes after that. And this on a day I had to cover nearly 500 miles. I went back to my journal.

Big Timber, maybe. Big traffic, no. Actually, no big timber either, only a few trees along the Yellowstone River, but otherwise grassland, and bare mountains in the distance.

Thinking back to the Flying J in Post Falls and this business of going up to drivers and asking for rides—there's an arm-twisting quality about it I don't like. It changes the emotional equation: the driver may be operating more out of guilt than out of spontaneous generosity, and that isn't always a sound basis for a driving companionship. You're lowering the kindness standard, so you may also be changing the nature of the driver who picks you up. The fact that they're going where you want to go is only one criterion for a good ride.

For me, hitchhiking is a conversation. If the car looks full up, for instance, I acknowledge it by a nod and a wave, they shrug and throw up their hands and grin ruefully and I wave cheerfully to show there are no hard feelings. I greet truckers with something between a wave and a salute, because more often than not, they can't stop: it takes a long time to halt 20,000 pounds, and a lot of diesel to get started again, going up through twenty gears. They give me a signal back, often a more restrained half-wave of the right hand, lifted just off the steering wheel. A salute to the bikers, who always salute back. If I were really cool, I'd give them that bikers' "Further" signal, the index finger pointing up and ahead as if over the horizon. Out here on the bare existential tarmac these are the basic elements of human intercourse.

Just realized it's Sunday. No single guys travelling on business. All families and vacationers.

Patience. In the paddock just south of the exit, three horses toss their tails. In the far distance rise the plutonium mountains, snowy even in August, looking calm and innocent from here.

Should I stay here, or go down onto the interstate itself? The last few yards of the ramp curve to the right. If I walk down it to the highway, neither set of vehicles will see me until the last minute, and both will be at almost full speed. If I stay here at the exit and get only the traffic coming from Big Timber, am I condemning myself to local rides? I can't imagine anyone on a Sunday morning pulling out of this little valley and deciding "Nice day. Reckon I'll make for South Dakota." At 9:30 I'll go down to the freeway.

9:30. Down to the freeway through the long grass, watching for snakes but disturbing only dozens of small grasshoppers.

A new problem: When the traffic's moving very fast, you have to have your arm up so early and so long your shoulder starts to ache. Speed destroys dialogue: we are both just images to each other....

Not a good spot at all. I'll stay here until 10:30, then go back up. You try this, then you try that. Mind you, I don't see any traffic at all coming on at the exit. This is starting to remind me of the Trans-Canada Highway. It's like a zen koan: should you stand beside the road where no traffic will stop, or the road with no traffic at all?

I had barely written this, put my book away in my book pocket, and clicked my pen, when a guy screeched to a stop from 75 mph and took me all the way to Sturgis. The answer to the koan, as to all koans, was to be patient and to trust.

I wasn't going to write anything about this ride—a seven-hour, four-hundred-mile ride—because at the time I thought of the driver as the only guy I met who wasn't interesting. He talked in an expressionless voice I could barely hear; he didn't initiate conversation; he pointed out every KOA (Kampgrounds of America) we passed and his favorite social activity, he said, was singing Neil Diamond songs in a karaoke bar. He told me his name, but I immediately forgot it and never wrote it down. When I described him to my wife, a clinical mental-health counselor, she said "He sounds like that woman, the surgeon with brain damage, we heard on NPR."

This was the clue I had missed. Around Billings he told me that he had served in the military (yet another blue-collar guy who had thumbed home on furlough) in Germany, first "riding at the back of a deuce-and-a-half with an M60," and then as a MP. "I always wanted to be a policeman," he said, which surprised me, coming from this slim, quiet bloke. One dark night a guy he'd previously arrested waited for him in an alley with a metal pipe. He was flown back to hospital in the U.S.; and even though he appeared to recover, he kept suffering from headaches and an inability to concentrate, and his vision was affected for a while. In any event, he couldn't serve as an MP and the Army tried to switch him to a menial desk job, but he hired a lawyer and got himself an honorary medical discharge.

After that, now I come to think of it, he seemed to have lost himself—not entirely, just a little. The pipe had knocked out some of his purpose and direction. He had lived at home in Michigan with his mother, spent several years doing undemanding construction work for a drunken boss, had been dumped by a girlfriend, or a wife, and sang karaoke, even cutting his own karaoke Neil Diamond CD. Then he abruptly decided to see America. I inwardly cheered this; it sounded like a radical act, even a revolutionary one. It was a curious adventure, though: he knew a guy who owned houses in various places all over the map, so he would periodically drive a couple of thousand miles and paint or roof somewhere else, staying in KOA's on the way. He wasn't a hippie: not only did he not have wild and crazy adventures, he didn't seem to want wild and crazy adventures. Yet he was out there on the road—and he had pulled over to pick me up, after all.

We cruised through southeastern Montana, the mild, beautiful grassland rising and falling between the bare hills. No wonder this land could support a hundred million bison. On the southern horizon, there were mountains like the threat of thunder. We drove through Crow lands, the few cheap houses looking dumped in the wilderness as if by government helicopter, as far from white civilization as possible. Before I left home, debate was swirling as to whether Clinton would apologize for slavery on behalf of the American government. Out here in the town lyrically called Crow Agency, it was clear that nobody would ever apologize to the American Indians. If a president accepted responsibility for slavery, he'd face billion-dollar lawsuits for reparation. If he accepted responsibility for the treatment of the Indians, he'd have to hand over the entire bloody country.

And this is bloody country, because this is the site of the Battle of the Little Bighorn. (Monuments to battles where the whites massacred the Indians are, of course, rather less well marked.) Yet it's also heartbreakingly beautiful. The river runs alongside the highway for a while, down on the right, in a valley between the bare hills. Who could have looked down at the grassy meadows and the lush trees clustering on both banks and not seen it as perfect ranching country, imagining a little wooden house down there by the treeline, sheltered from the wind and snow, water at the back door and cattle grazing at the front? And as if to make the point, we passed a large sign: "You're in cow country. EAT BEEF."

Across the line into Wyoming, we stopped for lunch at the tiny town of Ranchester, where the only people moving outside on this hot, hot day were the players in the big horseshoe tournament just down from the Silver Spur Bar and Lounge, and a small convoy of bikers coming back west from Sturgis. They were debating whether to turn south and head through the mountains. "There's bears up there, man," said one, shaking his head. "Step out in the road, knock you right off your bike."

We settled back onto the interstate, droning east through country that became progressively flatter and duller. Why did Gillette claim to be the "energy capital of the United States"? "We have, like, 17 coal mines," a lady from the Chamber of Commerce said when I called back later. "We have an awful lot of oil, coal, uranium, that kind of thing." If I had known that, I might not have been fooled by a cloud of smoke that at first, in the distance, I thought was a prairie fire, then a steam train, then a train on fire, but turned out to be a coal train of immense length, with plumes of coal dust blowing off each open wagon. I looked north for the Devil's Tower, but it was too far away, a tiny thumbprint on the horizon. Every few miles we passed a billboard for Wall Drug, the drugstore in Wall, South Dakota, that, in 1936, was the first eatery to serve that most American of drinks—free ice water. It now occupies an entire block.

I finally roused myself out of my stupor and asked him about the culture of karaoke, and whether his mouthing Neil Diamond really turned women on. Without changing his mild demeanor, he moved into a different gear. Sure, he said. He was propositioned all the time. Something about him made me decide he was incapable of lying, or even of boasting. This led to other stories, and then he was back in his youth, before the accident.

He got his first job, cleaning up a topless bar in Indianapolis, when he was 17, he said. He was too young to be in the place legally, so the manager would let him in at 3 a.m. when the place closed, lock him in to do his job and then let him out when the place opened at 7 a.m. He was in teenage heaven. Not only did he have access to unlimited booze, as long as he did a decent cleaning job, but after a while they started letting him in earlier and he'd hang out in the kitchen, which was en route between the stage and the girls' dressing (so to speak) rooms. As soon as they found out that he was a virgin, they were all over him, he said. "Come up to our room, we'll make a real man of you!" He declined; I think he was scared. The most solid evidence he had of the girls' extracurricular activities was that once he was promoted to (unofficial) janitor, he was constantly being asked to fix the sinks in the men's room, which were coming away from the walls, and he'd have to put in bigger and longer bolts to fix them back against the wall. Seems the girls had the guys sit in the sinks in order to give them the best professional attention. There he stopped, for we had reached Sturgis.

Yet even in telling this story he sounded a little distant, as if these events had swirled around him like vapor, leaving him mildly amused but untouched. He remembered and understood them perfectly well, he knew their value as a story, but there was an odd painting-by-numbers quality about his tone. Whatever the incidents had done for him at the time, he was no longer engaged in them—just as he seemed to be no longer engaged in America, taking work here and there that didn't commit him to anyone or anything, gliding back and forth across its freeways and pausing at its campgrounds, where nobody had to take root.

At first glance, the outskirts of Sturgis were as anonymous and dull as any other small plains town, but as I wandered down off the interstate exchange, I heard the first whispers of the heavy metal thunder. A pair of bikes cruised by, then another quartet, then some singles. The show was getting on the road; the circus was leaving town. A young guy slouched on the front porch of a small shanty by the road called out to ask me the time. "Hey, would you like a beer?" he asked.

He was short, stringy, roughly dressed, pasty-faced, and his eyes were still looking for the top line on the chart. He was English, he said, slurring his words slightly, but had been brought up in Ireland. He'd already traveled halfway round the world, had lived in Asia as a heroin addict, now he was hitchhiking mostly by rail across the U.S. "Amazing time. Amazing country." He'd already seen a moose swimming the Columbia River. He'd seen elk, deer, and golden eagles. He'd strolled into Sturgis ten days ago knowing nothing about the rally and someone at this house had offered him a basement to sleep in, beer, and sex. This was his version, at least.

So what was his impression of the rally? "It's funny," he said, after a moment's reflection. It was a bit like the Glastonbury Festival in England (a sort of perennial Woodstock), he said, except that Glastonbury is far more civilized, with theater and ballet, everything. "Here all you've got is hairy aging rockers and Harleys." He laughed.

I asked about the two fresh scars on his forehead. "Fell into a barbed-wire fence," he said casually. "Didn't feel a thing. Absolutely hammered. Booze and grass everywhere."

When the rally was over, he said, he planned to make for Minneapolis to get a job on the barges and make his way down to New Orleans. I saw no reason why he shouldn't make it. In college, I knew a fair number of people who traveled the world like him. The only drawback was that they tended not to remember it. I thanked him for the beer and followed his perfectly cogent directions downtown.

Sturgis was closing down—or rather, like some aging comic-book superhero, it was tugging off its leather costume, and turning back into a mild-mannered small South Dakota town. The tearing-down taking place in the streets and shops was the dark reflection of the setting-up I'd seen at the Indianola fairgrounds, one childlike and wholesome, the other aging and raunchy. A pole-and-awning city was being dismantled. The Road Kill Cafe was closed, but Main Street Tattoo, next door, was still doing business. Two guys were hosing down the sidewalk in front of Millinger's Saloon. A surveillance camera, set up to shoot down Main Street, bore a small sign letting everyone know that the whole shebang was being relayed live on STURGISRALLY.NET. According to the *Sturgis Ratty Rag*, the newspaper of record ("Read internationally by the Rat set"), I'd missed Black Oak Arkansas, Lynyrd Skynyrd, Steppenwolf, Jesse the Human Bomb, the Amature (sic) Short Track race, the Swine Pit's Ladies' World Championship Pickle Lickin' Contest, and possibly TV host Joan Lunden, though the photo caption identified her as "Joan Lundgren," and it wasn't clear if she was really coming to Sturgis or just posing (in leather jacket) with Biker Billy, who in turn may or may not be the same person as Billy Gordon of the Blue Rockers, famous for their CD "Helmet Laws Suck."

I wanted a copy of *The Holy Bible for Bikers*, but the shop had closed. Four enormously fat bikers drove by in a Lincoln Town Car. Across the street, a small, neat building that looked as if it might be a polling station elsewhere in the year had a sign over the door that read Pyramid Presents Venders Penthouse Hooters, and underneath it a smaller handwritten one saying "Lingerie models wanted. Apply within." Next door was the Meade County Law Enforcement Center, which also seemed to have closed. A cop was going in the side door with an armload of stuff, cleaning up.

"How do you cope?" I asked him.

"I was born and bred here," he said looking away over Sturgis, choosing his words carefully, "so I'm used to chaos and confusion. You just do the best you can with what you've got."

How many bikers had turned up this year? He shrugged. "We don't know. Three hundred thousand? Four hundred thousand?" Another cop, passing him toward the same doorway, overheard and laughed. "Three hundred and fifty-seven thousand, two hundred and twelve. There were two hundred and thirteen but one left."

For a week, Sturgis swelled to a population the size of Minneapolis, yet the local paper police reported only 182 arrests for DUI, 281 misdemeanor drug arrests, 39 felony drug arrests, and 10 other felonies. A Minneapolis week: 400 larcenies, 100 car thefts, 60 robberies, 10 arsons, 10 rapes, a murder and a half.

I dug out the sock phone and called Tomasz, who turned out to be two blocks away. I was glad to see him, and this time, for once, he had good news. He had shot trucks with fantastic designs down their paneled sides. He had shot the inventor of the Body Web, the least amount of clothing a woman can wear without being arrested. He had shot the Mayor of Sturgis marrying couples on bikes, and the World's Most Tattooed Man.

We took a break for Indian tacos and Black Hills Gold ice cream at a food stand that was in the process of being converted back to its usual role as a plumbing-supply business. I sat on the curb next to a young dude who had been working in one of the biker-gear tents, and now was taking a break from pushing his dolly around, clearing out. He was from California; it turned out that this was part of a franchise operation selling what he called "sports supplies." They'd had four tents in Sturgis, each with a million dollars of inventory. He figured that they had done $2 million worth of business that week. Then Tomasz was off again, bobbing and ducking along next to a girl carrying what appeared to be an extra head. It was a mannequin she called Electra; she designed hair wraps. She tolerated Tomasz to a degree I found astounding. "If you get tired of him, hit him with the head," I encouraged her. "Give 'im a hooter shot," two bikers suggested amiably.

Tomasz introduced me to a woman biker from Colorado he had met. A fair number of women bikers—the Asphalt Angels—had come here on their own, she said. They bedded down at the Hub Heaven Campground ("a lot of the campgrounds are like cesspools by midweek") and each day went off on their own Harley excursions around the area. Guys could go on these trips, too, but only at the back of the motorcade, "sniffing their exhaust."

We wandered around in a happy daze for a while, then adjourned to a bar, still fairly crowded in the waning of the afternoon, and of the festival. On the sound system was Neil Young singing "Country Girl." This was nothing like Biker-Gang-Takes-Over-Small-

Town; the bikers' vulgar, good-humored shamelessness was rather sweet. Tomasz and I were accepted despite his accent and my odd clothing because for this week, at Sturgis, these guys were inlaws rather than outlaws. At the next table, a dwarf biker and his girlfriend held each other and kissed.

We were on our way back to the car when Tomasz grabbed my arm, said "I must show you something," disappeared into one of the dozens of leather shops that were offering final bargains while being dismantled, and dragged out its resident spokesmodel. She was wearing black leather chaps, a black leather bustier and a sort of black leather fig leaf fore and aft, leaving most of her back and both buttocks naked. She gave us a huge smile involving several ounces of fire-engine-red lipstick. Her name, she said, was Dawna. Tomasz shot us both by one of the dozens of bikes still lining the curb.

"I am thinking she is cool," Tomasz said, looking after her as she ended work for the year and marched off up the street, buttocks winking.

Another guy, short-haired, clean-shaven, wearing the classic fifties midwestern short-sleeved shirt, stood next to us and stared after her, his mouth open. "So long, Sturgis!" he said, shaking his head.

Tomasz had a double room in a hotel a little way south, at the foot of Mount Rushmore, handy also for the Badlands and the Pine Ridge Reservation, both of which I wanted to see. I drove us there, as he was apparently near death from driving a couple of hundred miles each way every day to Buffalo, Wyoming, where he'd been shooting a parade. "I feel every single part of my body. I could take Ph.D. in anatomy right now."

We had a drink at the Red Garter, a mock-saloon where if we ordered a Red Garter Special—vanilla schnapps and cranberry juice—from the waitress in Victorian western gear, it came with a red garter around the glass.

~

CHAPTER 26

Where My Dead Lie Buried

August 10—Keystone, Montana

I got up early to have breakfast on my own—if Tomasz had had his way he would have slept until Christmas— down at the Red Garter. Honky-tonk piano was hammering away on the sound system. The place was thoroughly fake, but I appreciated its thoroughness. The walls were wood-paneled, or else papered with Victorian red velvet wallpaper, and covered with paintings—portraits and hunting scenes near the window; dogs and horses above the fireplace, beside the nine antique rifles. The woman at the table next to me was eating a cinnamon bun the size of a soup plate. The doorways were hung with red velvet curtains, the chairs with period red Naugahyde. The black-stocking-and-red-garter outfits the waitresses were wearing the previous evening had gone; it's hard to imagine them being worn first thing in the morning back in Victorian times, either. Next to me was a panel of photographs of the forever unfinished statue of Crazy Horse, the chief's arm pointing, accusing, giving the sad, defiant quote: "My lands are where my dead lie buried."

This morning was the high point of my trip. I had made it to Sturgis on schedule, I had more time than I needed to get back home, and yet I was in no hurry to do so. This scholar-gypsy life was agreeing with me. I was sleeping well. My asthma had vanished. I was eating less and digesting better; I had discovered that, like most Americans, I normally eat twice as much as I need. Above all, I felt lighter, more curious and less afraid, as if by plunging into America I had plunged into life.

I imagined that people who could heal by touch alone might feel this sense of calm, and of available energy. As I walked up to the front desk to pay my bill, the manager and hostess were conferring over some problem, their foreheads furrowed. I made some light remark, I smiled, I don't know what I did; they looked up, relaxed, joked back. We chatted for a moment, and I walked outside—and almost at once, events began to deflate my vanity.

For a start, Tomasz, who was pleased with Sturgis but terribly anxious about his photographs as a whole, told me that the NATIONAL GEOGRAPHIC insisted that I spend a couple of days with him so he'd have some photos of me in a truck, in the West, in the Midwest, in a major midwestern city, and so on. I was to become a passenger rather than a hitchhiker.

Subdued, I got in the Skylark.

Mount Rushmore, just up the road, was smaller than I'd expected, and I had my usual reaction against anything that 250 other people are trying to see at the same time. I really wanted to see Crazy Horse, but by now I was mountain-statued out, and couldn't face doing it again.

We plodded downhill into Rapid City, where Tomasz recovered his spirits over more coffee; we bought Bob Dylan tapes for the car and headed off to the Badlands. Tomasz was thinking of hiring a helicopter to fly over the Badlands to take aerial shots. "Great idea," I said, remembering his helicopter disaster in El Salvador. "I'll watch from the ground."

We sang along with the Dylan tapes at the tops of our lungs. "All those people we used to know/They're an illusion to me now...." One of the radio stations in Warsaw used to play Dylan, he said. The censors were so stupid, he explained, that as long as the DJ prefaced the song with "Here's another illustration of how decadent and worthless western rock-and-roll is," or words to that effect, the station could play anything, especially as almost nobody could understand the words.

The Badlands looked like a Bryce Canyon dripped in wet cement by the devil, a savage landscape under a blinding gray-white glare. A fringe of canyons carved in a thick, putty-colored layer of ash and mud left by a long-extinct volcano, it was the rim of a dry, desolate plain that ran southward into the heat haze. Why on earth did the settlers newly arrived from the East try to farm this awful country? Owning land, and a house, as opposed to feeling owned, must have been a revolutionary act, an act of escaping not only a city, but a social structure that systematically denied everything worthwhile, or parceled it out to favorites—those of the same origin, or color, or religion. Settlers created a new landscape, yes, but also a new political landscape—the West.

We pushed farther south and east into the abandoned volcanic plain, crossing a river white with ash, like the effluent from a cement factory. This was the Pine Ridge Reservation, where the Lakota Sioux were driven more than a century ago following the massacre at Massacre Canyon. If anyone ever doubted that the American government herded the Indians into land that nobody else wanted, this hot, exposed, infertile landscape was proof. Cute little arrowheads framed the route numbers on road signs.

Somewhere around here was Wanblee, South Dakota, which turned out to be a bend in Route 44, where at some point in the recent past a small amount of federal money had paid for a few dozen flimsy project houses. No semiconductor factories, corporate headquarters, or organic farms. No shingles by the road announcing lawyers, doctors, dentists, tax accountants, chiropractors, or homemade preserves for sale. Not even a McDonalds. Pine Ridge is one of the poorest and most isolated communities in the U.S. Unemployment runs at more than 80 percent, and to find work many Sioux have to drive a hundred miles to Rapid City. Per capita annual income averages under $4,000, the lowest in the country. Above-average rates of every kind of illness. The alcoholism-related mortality rate is nine times the national average.

We were looking for Jaylene Quick Bear. Tomasz had met her then-husband Charles Chipps in Nevada. Charles was a Lakota spiritual leader who claimed to be a descendant of Crazy Horse. He traveled the country conducting sun dances and sweat lodges, rituals of celebration and purification.

Jaylene lived in a project that showed the classic signs of struggle in the face of economic abandonment. The houses were cheap and ugly. Children climbed in and out of ground-floor windows;

a board was nailed across one open front door, apparently as a child gate. The yards were mud and stringy grass. A teenage neighbor stuck his head out and asked the kids around him if anyone wanted to go in on a bag of maryjane. I was stunned. Living on the reservation, I'd have fled or gone crazy in a week. It astounded me that people had the resilience to survive such brutal conditions.

Jaylene's house was better cared for than most. Someone had built a rectangular canopy out of pine boughs to shade the front yard. A convenience-store ice machine had been set up along the front wall. Everything was covered with flies.

With our accents and our uncertainty as to who exactly we were looking for or where she lived, several minutes passed with us standing uneasily around the car while several small Lakota children ran around or stared, apparently not understanding us.

After a while, Jaylene came out; she had been making bread, surrounded by children. She was of medium height with a slightly fleshy face; long black hair that might have been beautiful, or wild; jeans, T-shirt, black sneakers. A torrent of laughing, fighting children poured out with her. She was raising 14. The kids all had shaggy black hair and dark skin. They all wore ragged shorts. Everyone had skin blemishes on their arms, chests, and legs. One of the boys hit another, who cried, and then hit one of the girls. Jaylene distractedly reprimanded them, and offered us a snow cone or some water.

Standing in the driveway, talking quietly and without rancor, she sketched us a picture of life on the reservation. There were no jobs. "You've got to be someone's relative to get a job. They want us women to work, but there are no jobs and we don't know what kind of people will take care of our children." The white teachers at the school, from New York and New Jersey, she said, didn't understand Lakota traditions or how to handle Lakota kids, and ended up calling the police on them. The kids ended up embarrassed to be Indian and to talk their own language. There was federal money, but Pine Ridge, she said, was rife with fraud.

She brought out a cheap tape recorder, and a tape of Charles speaking before the most recent sweat lodge. She set it up on a picnic table under the canopy so that we could listen.

"The ceremony will give you a stronger heart, a stronger mind, stronger lungs, and stronger blood," he said.

One of the boys threw a small stone at the other, who burst into exaggerated crying; moments later, they were spitting at each other. A kitchen knife was lying on the table, an accident waiting to happen. Flies landed everywhere, scores of them.

"All we have is our self-esteem," Charles said.

A white girl, Michelle, appeared—a pale, washed-out blonde with peasant clothes and a rather vague look. She was from Kentucky; her husband was from the reservation. She was pregnant, and he had said that it would be easier for the child to be a card-carrier—that is, someone entitled to Indian benefits—if it was born on the reservation. She said, "We want her to know both worlds and both spiritualities." I couldn't imagine willingly bringing a child up on the reservation, with its incredible hardships; but perhaps spiritual strength flourishes in such conditions.

Two-year-old Rochelle was playing with the car doors. "Get away from their car," Jaylene called. "It's locked, anyway."

"The car isn't locked," I said.

"Oh, God," she laughed, "you'd better lock it. This is the reservation."

On the tape player, Charles was preaching forgiveness.

The kids wanted piggybacks; maybe they missed their father. Rochelle walked around on my feet, holding my hands, then asked me to chase her around the car. The boys decided to try a different, less strenuous kind of clowning: Godfrey, 13, climbed into the wheelbarrow on the driveway and Trevor, 14, began playing the hose on him, creating a kind of small-scale bath-cum-shower.

"The pain you will receive in the lodge is a good pain," Charles was saying in his deep, gentle voice, "and it will help you. It's the very next thing to mother's womb. It's going to be hotter than hell." He chuckled.

The older children had scars from the recent sweat lodge: self-wounding is another traditional way to accustom oneself to pain. The kids started piercing at around ten, Jaylene said. Girls pierce on their arms, boys on their chests. When the word got around the reservation school that they'd been doing the sweat lodges, she said, they were taunted for doing witchcraft.

Jaylene wanted to exchange addresses and phone numbers so she could send us information about forthcoming sun dances and sweat lodges. "You know," she said plaintively, "our ancestors used to..." She made a cutting motion across the top of her head.

"Scalp?"

"Yeah, scalp white people. We don't do that any more. I think whites still think we scalp people, and they stay away."

She was 38, and she had no teeth left.

"It's hard to walk on this earth with all these children," she said, "but I'm healthy. I do the sweat lodges. I'll survive."

I didn't feel scalped, I felt gutted. Tomasz wanted to shoot some more of the Badlands, but I was in a foul mood and didn't want to talk to anyone. As I wandered off through some scrub toward a view point, a woman tourist said "Watch out, there's a rattlesnake around. We saw it go over there." I felt like the rattlesnake, ready to bite anybody who came near me.

I was too angry to hitchhike. We drove along dead-straight road after dead-straight road until night fell and we hit Pierre. Throughout the West, I'd seen the destruction of history and the remythication of the past, the steady burning of cultural bridges. No wonder the architecture struck me as phoney: It was trying to fill the gap left by missing pueblos, encampments, and seminomadic seasonal settlements. I thought of wooden Indians outside trading posts, and of their silence.

~

CHAPTER 27

The Hitchhiker Remains at Large

August 11—Pierre, South Dakota

Next morning, the Sioux Falls *Argus Leader* carried an AP story announcing that although three Americans in ten live in poverty, for most of them it's a condition that doesn't last forever. "Most who are poor pass through poverty," the headline read. Phew. Imagine Jaylene's relief. Just a few more generations and it'll all seem like a bad dream. "Blacks, Hispanics and children are among the poorest groups." No mention of Native Americans.

The same newspaper carried a front-page story of a local five-year-old boy who had been abducted by a hitchhiker. My heart sank. That's all hitchhikers need: more bad publicity. The truth, of course, was far less sensational. The boy was visiting his noncustodial father in California for two weeks, as he did each year. The father, who had picked up a hitchhiker in Utah a couple of days previously, took his son and the hitchhiker to a bee farm in Fresno.

The father went off, leaving the two in the van, and the hitchhiker took the van. He drove it to the bus station in San Francisco and left the boy in the van, quite unharmed. Nobody would read this far in the story, though: Drivers all over South Dakota would load for bear, and anyone standing beside the road was in for a lynching. "The hitchhiker remains at large," the paper said, ominously.

The air seemed damper and thicker; the previous night, when we'd pulled into the motel forecourt, clouds of moths and gnats circled under the lights of the parking lot, the first insects I'd seen in three weeks. I already missed the brilliant clarity of the western weather, and its desert light, especially now we were under scowling skies on a landscape pressed by a steam iron and punctuated only by grain elevators, the cathedrals of the plains. I was gripped by a strange gloom that was somehow made worse by the monomania of straight roads in perfectly rectangular patterns and the torture of the steady *bump-bump-bump* of the tires on the concrete slabs, feeding the urge to drive as fast as hell to the horizon or into some heavy solid object, to go home or just go mad.

A storm was coming up behind us; Tomasz wanted to shoot me hitchhiking in that brilliant purple light called storm light. We stopped.

There are probably dozens of countries in the world where one might see a Buick pull over to the shoulder and disgorge two middle-aged men, one of whom would pretend to be hitchhiking while the other took photographs of him; but only in America would a lobbyist for the Concrete Pavement Association—his name was Bill Brinkmann—stop, ask the two men if they needed any help, recommend the five-cent cup of coffee at Al's Oasis in Chamberlin, South Dakota, and tell them that there was a Stradivarius in Vermilion that was once owned by an Indian.

"All you have to do is get out of the car," I said in wonder, as Tomasz restarted the Skylark. "All you have to do is get out of the car, and things come to you. It never fails. It's just a matter of getting out of the car."

"What do you mean?" Tomasz asked.

I took the plunge, and tried to explain how being "in the car" meant to want to be in control, to be insulated from the world not only physically but mentally. To be out of the car meant to be vulnerable, alert, and spontaneous.

Beyond that, I went on, I can't tell you how many people have told me, "I never pick up hitchhikers"—yet they had picked me up anyway. Something had changed their minds. Beyond that, though I'd begun noticing, how many people had picked me up when, if everything had gone according to plan, they wouldn't even have been on that road, at that time. The KOA camper who took me to Sturgis was supposed to have been traveling a day earlier, with another guy, who had dropped out at the last minute. The guy who took me to Bozeman had left a day later than planned, too. Hank had decided at the last minute to take the desert route through Nevada for no good reason—in fact, he kept wondering aloud why on earth he hadn't driven up the coast as usual. Jay had been as out of the car as anyone in a car can be, just meandering around with no fixed route in mind and no deadline.

I couldn't shake a very strong sense that giving up control exerts some kind of attraction that is, in the language of quantum physics, "non-local": It affects people and even objects in ways and at distances that it shouldn't. It doesn't seem to have much to do with the conscious mind; in fact, our conscious mind seems mostly to get in the way, by second-guessing and worrying too much. Every time I've started worrying about whether I'll get a ride, I told him, it has done me no good. I told him what had happened at Big Timber, the zen koan, and the immediate ride all the way to Sturgis.

I'd come to think of this as the weak force—though I don't mean it in the usual sense, where it describes one of the four elemental forces of the universe. For me the term refers to a paradox: Often what seem to be the weakest connections between people have the most surprising and beneficial results. Many of the people who bring about the greatest changes in our lives are strangers, and, by the same token, many of the most important events seem to arise by sheer coincidence.

The most startling example of the weak force at work had happened a few years previously, during the period right before my mother's death, a time that was full of odd happenstance. The last time I flew over to see her, my plane landed at Heathrow at 5 a.m. on a Sunday. The bus and Underground stations wouldn't be open for hours, so even though it was still dark I decided to walk the mile or so to the M4 motorway and hitchhike to Bath.

It was not an easy hitch: clouds moved in and drizzle began to fall. Cars seemed to have gotten newer and people ruder since my teenage hitchhiking days. By mid-afternoon I finally reached the Bath exit, where I hoped I might be picked up by a student for the last few miles into the city. After five or ten minutes, a small blue car, driven by an elderly woman, passed me and pulled over some 30 yards up the road. As I ran up to it, I realized the woman was my Aunt Barbara.

She was as surprised to see me as I was to see her. Normally she never stops for hitchhikers, she said; it was just that she was heading back to Bath from Cirencester, where she had been visiting friends, and idly listening to the radio, when someone said that we should always be kind to strangers, as any of them might be God in human guise. Almost at once, she crossed over the M4 and saw this hitchhiker, and thought, well....

Later, when I told this story to a grief therapist in Vermont, she took it in stride. "Those who work in hospice from a more spiritual perspective hear stories like that all the time," she said. "We're surprised when something like that doesn't happen."

By now we were in Sioux Falls, looking here and there for the Sioux Empire Fair. The fair turned out to have precious little to do with the Sioux, or their Empire; instead, it featured Spam. We would miss the Spam cook-off, sadly, but the Hormel Foods representative gave me a glossy pamphlet of Spam recipes, featuring Spam Quesadillas, Singapore Spam Salad, Maui Spam Muffins, Spam à la King, Elegant Potato Spam Casserole, Spam Strudels with Mushroom Sauce, Spam Carbonara.

The owner of Nordstrom's Auto Recycling was offering an unusual contest: guess the original make, model, and year of two cars that had been reduced to cubes of crushed metal. Beside them was a motor home that had been thrown, dumped, and crushed by the tornado that without warning had hit a small town nearby a couple of months back and virtually wiped it out. "First the electricity went out, which took out all the sirens, and about a minute later the tornado hit." The motor home was an especially sad story: It had been the property of the most recent owner's brother, who had just passed away out in California. The Dakotan went out to pick it up, drove it back, put $6,000 into it, and then the tornado came along. "Took out his home, his shop, his tools—everything." Only 11 houses were left standing, and they were all damaged.

Amazingly, only five people were killed, though a lot of people were injured by flying debris. "There was a fully loaded semi standing under a grain elevator," he said. "It was picked up, spun around, and dropped down about where that tent is," some 40 yards away.

Tomasz and I, too, seemed to be spinning, plotting routes back East that neither of us really wanted to travel. We wound up in Minneapolis, but we might as well have been anywhere. The only restaurant that seemed to be still open refused to serve me because I was wearing shorts. We'd have to sit at the bar. Quite right, too, Tomasz said unexpectedly. "If I were properly dressed for dinner, I would not want someone in shorts sitting at the table next to me. I would be insulted." We got into a polite but bitter argument in the bar, in which Tomasz was championing the importance of class and I found myself furiously defending the American ideal of classlessness, even though the evidence against me was fawning over wealthy patrons in the next room. On the way through the curiously deserted streets back to the hotel, we passed a beautiful young Asian girl sitting silently in a glass bus shelter, the yellow light from a street lamp falling on her headscarf.

CHAPTER 28

The Lord Said It Was All Right

August 12—Minneapolis, Minnesota

Hitching in a small town, you feel like part of its life. Tomasz drove me across the Mississippi and dropped me off in Prescott, Wisconsin, planning to wander on ahead looking for pictures while I hitched down 35, a slender thread of a road that might take me down the eastern bank of the Mississippi. We'd try to rendezvous in Madison, or far-off Milwaukee.

I settled down at the southern end of Prescott, able to see pretty much all of the old town center: up the broad, old-fashioned main street called Broad Street, with its small, neat brick buildings in the classic American square-top style with the arched Romanesque windows; up to the Steamboat Inn (its name painted in tall, thin, heavily serifed Victorian lettering in the riverboat style), where Route 35 joined Route 10 and the St. Croix joined the Mississippi. I felt like a part of the barge trains nosing bluntly up the river, part of the people crossing the road to the shops, part of the smell of newly mown grass. Who lived here? Who would rent the apartment available on the corner of Kinnikinnis Street?

This is an undervalued virtue of hitchhiking, or of waiting for a bus, or a train: that you spend a lot of time just standing still, looking around, not doing but being. At home, I rarely allow myself such silence: Every moment has to mean something. This enforced surrender, on a warm day with a light breeze, felt like the greatest luxury. Flags lifted and fell back against their poles. Grasshoppers chirped in the undergrowth. Even the little traffic heading south on 35 seemed determined to follow the same slow rhythm for the day, for half of it was dump trucks sauntering down the road to some sand or gravel pit, filling up and heading back; and the other half cruised slowly up to me, pulled a wide, lazy U-turn, and went back to park in a vacant slot in front of the shops.

After I'd been there an hour and a half, though, I started to get concerned that I'd be there all day, and Tomasz would have to turn round and drive a hundred miles back to find me. I pulled out the phone, hit Power, and before I could dial a car pulled over.

It was two retired guys from St. Paul, former employees of the city. As we cruised south through the woods and cornfields, between the river bluffs on our left and the Mississippi on our right, the driver looked around him with a childlike joy. "Diamond Bluff! What d'you think of that! We're from St. Paul. We're just out to kill the day and see the country. We're going to get sweet corn. Maybe ten dozen ears. We've got a friend who owns a farm down here someplace. He says 'I've got more than I can handle. Take some and give it to your friends.' Look, here's the railway!" He had hitchhiked way back when he was in the Army, he told me, from Indiana all the way to Nashville, Tennessee, to see the Grand Ole Opry.

They went five miles or more out of their way to cross back over the Mississippi and drop me on Route 61 in Red Wing, where the boots are made. I wasn't sure I wanted to be on a bigger road, but they were so determined to be kind, I didn't have the heart to say no.

Then, another first: A young couple with four children in an SUV, which I'd have put somewhere below a dyspeptic billionaire in a Rolls-Royce on the Hitchhiker's Scale of Unlikely Rides. They took me a few miles down to Lake City on Lake Pepin, a sort of artificial lagoon of water ballooning on the Mississippi, where they were going to work on their sailboat before the summer ended. They dropped me off at a drive-up hamburger-and-shake stand, because their kids thought it was cool that you could get served right at your window without getting out of the car. I left the car and went over to the counter and chatted amiably with the smiling waitresses, high school girls with healthy Midwest complexions. I asked if they ever wore roller skates, like the drive-in waitresses of the early 1960s. They said they'd like to, but some of the tables were beyond the parking lot, over on the grass, so they couldn't. Still, it'd be kinda cool.

I drank a milkshake, then strolled half a mile down the road through Lake City. Tomasz and I had agreed that small towns were our favorite parts of America. They haven't yet lost their core to office-block-and-parking-garage developers, and their suburbs don't yet straggle away like apathetic teenagers. I also wondered whether I was getting rides from unlikely candidates because these were small towns, and people were simply less afraid here.

I set up shop on the way out of the town center on the lakeside road, opposite the sailboats and the bluffs on the far shore of the Mississippi, and promptly a young girl, perhaps 18 but racy for Lake City with her small tattoo, pulled over in her subcompact and said, "I'm not going very far." That was fine, I said, getting in—I was enjoying this day of short rides between small towns. I settled in my seat, put on my seat belt, and she said. "This is where I turn off." She had taken me all of 400 yards.

It was wonderful. I thanked her and got out, laughing, as she turned into the leafy residential street where she lived. This, for her, was hitching: You did it to get home from the center of town, not to cross the continent. And this is the state of the art, I suppose. A number of my students hitch to the Green Mountains to hike or ski; hikers on the Appalachian Trail often hitch off the trail into a nearby town for supplies, and some people hitch when their cars break down. No, it's the long-distance art, the grand enterprise, that is dormant. Throwing oneself on the mercy of the continent.

A couple of minutes later, a battered van pulled over and an American Indian kid—long shiny black hair, broad shoulders, meaty body—leaped out, beckoning me as I hesitated. I climbed in the front and sat down, surrounded by an amazing collection of sacred trinkets: pipes, bracelets, sticks, stalks of sage twisted into circles to be worn as bracelets or crowns. The driver looked weathered but not exactly Indian. "I'm Bruce," he explained. The artifacts were from a sun dance he'd recently been to, held by Chief Leonard Crow Dog; the children in the back were David, Juddy, and Bo, Anashnase kids from Minneapolis, where there are some 25,000 Anashnase, he said, some in reasonable shape, some not doing so well. "I've sort of adopted them, or they've adopted me." One of them, he said, was the grandson of Dennis Banks, one of the founders of the American Indian Movement.

The kids, who seemed to range from about nine to twelve, sat in the back of the van happily drawing. Bruce was a genuine hippie, a veteran of the Rainbow Gatherings virtually every year since 1973— veteran too of the usual gauntlet of drink and drugs. Some of the time, Bruce told me, he did migrant farm work, some of the time he offered massage therapy. At the moment he was looking for land in Wisconsin, maybe a farm, to set up a kind of sanctuary, a place of respite from the city where the Native kids could learn to hunt and fish, where they could rest and pray and generally dry out from a society that was, at least to them, toxic. "I wanna show these kids that there's a way to live without using. We grow up in an addictive death culture in this capitalist society. Our own cultures have abandoned us. Even we Europeans have lost our tribes and their cultures. In a lot of ways the Native people are in better shape, because they know who they are. They've been genocided for hundreds of years and they turn round and share their most sacred ceremonies with the whole world.

"I'm 45," he continued, "and all my cousins are fuckin' rich. Jewish. Too middle class and materialistic. 'When are you going to get a job?' If I get a job I'll be so busy working I'll forget how to be with people. I'll forget how to be with the earth. Besides, I've got a job. I'm living.

"When I go to see them, the first thing they ask is, 'How's business?' When I see my Native friends, the first thing they ask is, 'How are you? Are you hungry?' It's going to pass. All that stuff about money will pass. I'm going to be patient."

His father, he said, was in an expensive nursing home, learning the dire horror of being alone and helpless in America.

He gave me one of the prayer bracelets from the dashboard. One of the kids in the back called out "Which picture do you like, Bruce, mine, or Dave's?"

"Let me see 'em," he called back over his shoulder. Bo handed Bruce two drawings. He glanced at them. "I like 'em all," he said, sticking them up on the dashboard. "I love 'em all."

Bruce dropped me off just beyond the Mississippi near La Crosse, at the on-ramp for I-90, but in the middle of the usual ugly guardrail architecture, among the dying roadside weeds, I could barely keep my feet on the ground for sheer joy. A good ride is a benediction: in the middle of nowhere, through no virtue of your own, you are blessed with kindness, as cleanly and abruptly as if you are a gong being struck by an unseen hand; and then you are back on your own again, your heart still ringing and astounded, left to recognize that, yes, these are the things that sustain us, even while we're breathing exhaust or being knocked back by the bow wave of a semi, picking up speed for the long haul.

The next person to pick me up, a bio-geneticist named John (in yet another pickup truck) told me two of his own hitchhiking stories, dating back more than 35 years to when he used to hitch regularly back and forth between college, in Utah, and home, in California, making sure he looked like a respectable college student by carrying a suitcase with a BYU sticker on one side and a USC sticker on the other.

On one trip west he got picked up by a wild-looking old character who seemed decent enough, but as they neared the Nevada border, this guy reached across to the glove compartment and took out a handgun. "I was terrified. I was sure he was going to shoot me. He opened his window, leaned out, shot into the air, and told me 'I shoot off whenever I cross a state line.'"

John also told me the story of the guy in Utah who passed John and his brother hitching, pulled up some way farther up the road and stayed there for about ten minutes before coming back for them. "I imagine you noticed I went up there aways and stopped there for some minutes," he told the two lads. "Well, I wasn't sure if it was safe to pick you up. So I stopped and prayed about you, and the Lord said it was all right."

He dropped me off in Baraboo, Wisconsin, birthplace in 1884 of the Ringling Brothers Circus and home of the Circus World Museum, where Tomasz met me and took pictures. I remembered that I really don't like circuses —their garish con games, their abuse of animals. "The exhibiting of trained animals I abhor," wrote Albert Schweitzer. "What an amount of suffering and cruel punishment the poor creatures have to endure in order to give pleasure to men devoid of thought." The tiny town center was a classic, though, with its leafy courthouse square, its field gun, its war memorial—the most perfect, in my day, of small towns.

We climbed back into the Skylark, and headed east. "When I get back to Warsaw," Tomasz said, "I will do several mantras, I will visit several psychotherapists to rebuild my mental condition, which is screwed up, and I will do lots of physical exercise to rebuild my physical condition."

"And you'll eat lots of vegetables, too," I said.

We made for Milwaukee, just because it was there. You'd think that I'd have learned from my day that small towns are more approachable and welcoming to the tired traveler than cities, but apparently not.

CHAPTER 29

Falling by the Wayside

August 13—Milwaukee, Wisconsin

Two consecutive nights of fitful sleep, and my allergies playing up—
I'm losing steam. Three weeks ago I couldn't wait to be up
and on the road; now I want to sleep, and to let Tomasz drive from one
designated photo spot to another. He professes to be utterly exhausted,
but this may be a Polishism: under the same circumstances my brother,
for example, would use classic English understatement: "I'm a bit knack-
ered, chief."

We slogged down I-94, a wreck of a road, driven to destruction. This was, in essence, the same pleasant Wisconsin landscape
I'd seen yesterday, but abused beyond recognition—beyond the
point of being a landscape. We might as well have been in a storm
drain. The real America seemed to be slipping out of my grasp.

Tomasz told me that Poland introduced a program to encourage
hitchhiking in the sxties and seventies, a curiously capitalist enterprise. A potential hitchhiker would buy a coupon book, and hitch

by the traditional thumb method or by holding out the book, just as truckers in England will hitch by holding out their log books. When he was picked up, he would give the driver a coupon, which could be redeemed for various goods and prizes. The book also had blank pages in which one could write dates, destinations, and perhaps the drivers' names—a traveler's journal.

I can't see any reason why something along these lines should-n't be perfectly workable today. In fact, given the GPS technology, the hitchhiker (really a sort of low-impact commuter) could have a credit card that he passes to the driver picking him up, who swipes it through his GPS machine, sending a signal via satellite informing Caltrans (or whomever) who has picked up whom and where, and automatically crediting the driver's gasoline credit card according to the distance he takes the hitchhiker. Safe and environmentally sound.

Tomasz also confided in me, in boyish embarrassment, that on his first trip to America, he had stolen a "Do Not Disturb" sign from every motel they'd stayed in. He had ended up with a collection of several hundred. This is why I like this guy, I thought.

We checked into a Holiday Inn around noon, planning to take the El into Chicago. As we waited for the train at Belmont, two very large guys wearing the black uniforms of National K-9 Security parked themselves beside us and ordered their Rottweilers to lie down. The guys were carrying handcuffs; the dogs were wearing steel muzzles. Tomasz, who has never met a dog he didn't like, tried to engage the humans and dogs in light conversation, and was severely rebuffed. In a whispered aside, he admitted that Rot-tweilers are the only dogs his wife won't accept in their animal shelter. When the train arrived, a very young couple, she with a nose ring, was sweetly entwined in each other's arms.

Tomasz, still in love with America's love of glitter, was determined to have lunch at Planet Hollywood. Charles, our maitre d', confessed that Planet Hollywood Chicago was smaller than other Planet Hollywoods (or should it be Planets Hollywood?), but claimed that it had more movie paraphernalia, pointing up at deck chairs and life jackets from *Titanic* hanging from the ceiling above us, like escapees from a late Magritte. My seat had a fine view of the Pink and Yellow Power Rangers' backsides, and one of the Teenage Mutant Ninja Turtles, who, on closer inspection, turned out to be Donatello. When my Los Angelean Lasagna arrived, it looked as if it had been designed by Werner von Braun for the 1938 New York World's Fair, all rocket shapes and space-age geometry. It was actually rather good, but it was hard to taste anything because my other senses were working overtime. If the lights and deafening music and constant video clips on the TV monitors, as Tomasz said, reduce a human being to a sort of vegetable, what do they do to vegetables?

We split up to explore the town. I liked Chicago: it has energy without insanity, style without pretense, and people throng the sidewalks without trampling each other. I liked the owl gargoyles on the public library, and the way the El train suddenly appeared between one pair of buildings and vanished between the next like a conjuror's trick. I liked the detail: the fleur-de-lis, the cornices, and mouldings on the old buildings that say that the human hand was there. The new skyscrapers—Tomasz, to my delight, pronounced the word "high-scrappers"—were impossible to take in, though: they seemed like science fiction. I couldn't imagine people inhabiting them; they were more like monuments, or weapons.

My knee has a long memory, however, and soon I needed a place to sit down. No benches. I would either have to find a park, buy a seat at a restaurant, or sit on the sidewalk with my back to a building like a bum—which I often do, out of defiance, but only when I'm wearing clothing dark and heavy enough to take the dirt. I was not equipped, so I limped on, thinking that this lack of benches was interesting: it meant that the sidewalk was not a public space, in the sense of a space actually intended and designed for the public. No public maps; no signposts to the Art Institute or the park. No bus shelters, even though this was the Windy City. Pay phones, yes, but no public emergency phones like we have in Burlington. No push-button crosswalk lights, either, which meant that the traffic was in control of the pedestrian rather than vice versa, and the narrow, dark garbage alleys made part of every block potentially dangerous. It was as if the city needed the public in order to do business, but given its druthers, it would do just fine without us.

When I got to the park, I found the public: a young couple taking photos of each other in front of a fountain, two women (one black, one white) jogging together; a mother pushing her daughter in a stroller, the daughter reaching out in glee at the scattering pigeons; a run-down black guy with his possessions in a plastic bag, reading a magazine; and an even more run-down white guy asleep on a stone bench, his head resting on another model in the perennially popular line of plastic grocery-bag suitcases.

The doorman of a hotel in the shadow of the El hailed a cab with the most spectacular display of whistling I'd ever seen, piercing but also remarkably musical, the Clifton Chenier or Sonny Boy Williamson of the finger whistle. How did you do that? I asked. "Oh, I just did this," he demonstrated with one hand, the fingers in a triangular two-over-one arrangement, the tongue rolled up. "When I was a kid, I couldn't whistle with just my lips," he said cheerfully, making useless blowing sounds to illustrate his point. "So I learned how to whistle with my fingers. Or you can do this," he said, using the index finger of each hand, waggling one to produce vibrato like a harp player, changing pitch with his tongue. "Take it easy." And he strolled back into the lobby.

CHAPTER 30

Between Order and Chaos

August 14—Evanston, Illinois

I stole Tomasz a "Do Not Disturb" sign. He seemed quite touched.

On the subway into Chicago I fell in love with the fantastic hair styles African-American women were wearing—the cornrows, the African braids, which I was told can take up to eight hours and cost several hundred dollars, and something I'd never seen called finger waves. A woman on the El had a finger wave that had been dyed to create a two-tone effect, black and a kind of toasted copper color—a stunning effect. In search of a work-in-progress, I went into one salon, and I nearly passed out from the humidity. The receptionist was not interested in my interest. Those fashions, she said, were to be found out in the neighborhoods. "Downtown, we go for the softer look," she said, which I took to mean less Afrocentric, less assertive.

More evidence of the sixties being downgraded to the butt of cool jokes: an ad in the Chicago Reader, which should know better, for Mac University, consisting of a black-and-white photo of a hippie girl with her face painted in stripes and the peace symbol, the stripes presumably red and white and the symbol blue. The caption read, "Back then, self-expression required very little training." No, but it took a certain amount of courage. Besides, what do you mean by self-expression? She may look like a child who has spent the morning face-painting, but she was trying to stop a war.

I went back to look for the whistler of the previous evening. The hotel was the Crown Plaza on Wabash. The morning doorman, Marzette King, identified the virtuoso as Andrew Thomas, but made no big deal of it. "We can all do that. Look, I'll show you." He led me out of the lobby, explaining, "We all did that as kids. We knew each other's code. We'd call each other out of the house—I thought everyone could do that. I thought it was a guy thing." He reached the curb, reached into his mouth, and blew a whistle a little less musical than Andrew's but so loud it set off a car alarm.

At the public library for a buck or two I bought half a dozen books-to-be-tossed, including *The Gentleman in America* (1949) by Edwin Harrison Cody, associate professor of English at Syracuse. "[T]here are still Americans trying to be gentlemen. But the years of the modern in America...have made code and class considerations irrelevant....What is a gentleman? A gentleman is a man whose inner balance of sensibility, good-will, and integrity issues in moral dependability (the instinct to act rightly in a crisis); in courtesy (the instinct to serve other people's physical and psychological needs); and in the excellent performance of some good social function. Or it is anyone who is sincerely trying to be a gentleman." After the trip was over I reminded Tomasz of our argument over gentlemanliness, and he laughed and told me the story of his grandfather, who traveled extensively around Europe and Russia, carrying in his luggage a collapsible rubber bath. At every hotel he had the staff erect it and fill it with hot water.

While I was at it, I bought Tomasz *Talk American: A Practical Guide for Eliminating a German Accent* by Lewis and Marguerite Shalett Herman, published in 1944, and presumably a hot seller among spies. "The American language is inconsistent (*inkonsequent*) in its spelling," said the introduction. "American is spoken with much less energy (*kraftaufwand*) than German.... American speech tends to run its words together in ordinary conversation....Most Americans do not move their mouths as much as Germans do."

By evening, I wanted to hit the town. Tomasz decided to stay at the hotel and work on restoring his lymphocyte count, but he insisted that I call him whatever time I got back. I wasn't sure whether to see Tarkovsky's movie *Andrei Rublev* or the Blue Man Group. Tomasz told me that when he saw the BMG he laughed so hard he fell sideways into the lap of the man next to him and didn't manage to sit back up for 20 minutes. "I had laugh attack, like this," he said, and made those sea gull-like wheezing noises you make when you laugh so hard you can't catch your breath.

The Blue Man Group turned out to be just your basic taiko-drumming mime cabaret satire, performed in blueface and featuring an endoscopy; a Rorschach test, to which the correct answer was "Charlie's Angels"; a vibraphone of illuminated intestines, on which the blue trio played something that reminded me of Tubular Bells, except that it made musical sense, and later "White

Rabbit" by Jefferson Airplane, reinterpreted for the information age. The performance also included some intellectually undeveloped stuff about Mandelbrot sets, in which the faceless announcer pointed out that fractals exist on the frontier between order and chaos. As if to illustrate what this frontier might be like, the show's climax was a sort of happening, a participatory experience involving black light, a strobe, and hundreds of yards of paper in rolls that we passed over our heads down to the stage. But if it was a happening, it was a happening for the nineties—safe and, at 45 dollars, expensive. The Blue Man Show was an electric kool-aid acid test without the acid. "I don't think people nowadays would know how to behave at a happening," Debbie Harry of Blondie recently told *Esquire.* "I think they'd need little instruction booklets."

By now it was dark, and the city night breathed heat and danger. What might I do with the rest of what was, in effect, my first evening off? The bars were stuffed torpid with stiffs drinking beer and watching baseball on TV. No. A sign caught my eye: "Tabou-Tabou. Whips and Paddles for All Occasions." Of course. Here I was, 45 years old and I'd never been in a sex shop.

My first impression was that the sex shop looked surprisingly like any mall store. The two largest signs were

> DO NOT CRACK OR SWING WHIPS IN SHOP
> YOU WILL BE ASKED TO LEAVE
> and
> WE NO LONGER TAKE AMEX

The chrome hangers and racks made most of it look like a lingerie shop, and as for the sex toys and devices…well, they were proof that if you objectify anything, you steal its heat and urgency, and these objects amounted to the ultimate objectification: after all, sex is one of the few human activities for which one needs no objects at all, just people, yet the shop was selling not people but objects. The malling of passion.

Still, I was beset with curiosity, so I put on my best interview manner and approached one of the two girls working the joint. She had short orange hair, shaved eyebrows, and a snake tattoo down her arm. She was wearing black stockings and a faux leopardskin microdress. I didn't ask her name because I assumed she wouldn't want people to know she worked in a sex shop. Afterward, I realized I had learned nothing from my trip: I might have been embarrassed, but she was probably perfectly cool about it.

Handcuffs and whips were the most popular items, she said casually, and bondage chokers, though these were just as likely to be fashion accessories as they were sex accessories. Bondage is chic.

The oddest items in the shop—to me, at least—were pairs of wings, black or white, in various sizes. Did people like to dress up as angels for sex? Oh, they're very popular, she said, especially at bars. Bars? Oh yes, there are some bars where wings are all the rage. Black or white? Both, but mostly black. I shook my head in amazement.

What were her customers' strangest requests? Oh, nothing too bizarre. Gags you can breathe through. Nothing much.

By now several couples, and a small knot of Japanese tourists, were looking at and touching the merchandise without apparent embarrassment; again, it all seemed curiously wholesome and slightly silly. All this stuff laid out so nicely, so well lit—it was hard to take the sign "torture devices" seriously. I left without buying anything, though I was oddly tempted by the wings. Outside, a woman of the streets walked by—but this was a homeless woman of the streets, ragged, talking to herself. Maybe it's because

I'm 45, but I was moved by her more than by the picture of the girl in the satin gag and handcuffs.

Yet as soon as I had my pen out, pad on knee, foot up on windowsill, writing down what I'd seen—"the girl in the satin gag and handcuffs"—the old familiar illicit excitement returned, the dark stirring. More erotic in the writing than the seeing.

In the end, sex remained a mystery to me. Fractals, the Blue Man Group pointed out, exist on the frontier between order and chaos—well, so does sex. Sex lives where mind and body meet, dancing like a flame that is neither the coal nor the air above it.

Back at the hotel, Tomasz insisted on meeting for a beer, which was how we wound up in the strange little hotel bar at nearly midnight, him with camera, me looking for a game of pool.

I put down our four quarters and we met Ezra Becker, who described himself as an MBA student who was doing something in computers. A short, cheerful, stocky guy in his late 20s, his palm full of muscles when I shook his hand, he took it on himself, as a conscientious host, to introduce Tomasz to drinking shots of tequila with the salt thing and the lime thing, then to pay for the games of pool, and finally to show us the only bar in Evanston that was open after hours, Evanston having been dry until 1984 and still being damp only in small spots.

Ezra drove us through the less affluent quarters of Evanston to the Mark II Lounge, where three IDs were required by the doorman, a moderate-size mountain of a guy called Zeno, apparently one of the owners. Zeno greeted Ezra cheerfully—both members of a secret society of zeds, perhaps—and we were in. At once Tomasz pulled off his lens cap and infiltrated himself in the crowd. As always, I expected someone to break a cue over his head, but he was everywhere, his eyes gleaming thoughtfully, shooting young guys playing foosball, saying, "I wonder if I could ask you to...," grinning and ducking toward his viewfinder, at home anywhere.

The television seemed connected to a different time. Some old football game in black and white, then Nixon appeared. Then he vanished. The bar sound system played the Beatles "I've Just Seen A Face." Ezra pretended to be immune to all this sixties debris. The eighties produced much that was just as great, he said scornfully, though he couldn't name it all just at the moment.

The men's room also seemed to be stuck in time past. A slot machine sold a "Love Kit," consisting of Swedish Massage Oil, an Oriental Exciter Ring, an Exotic Condom, and Male Climax Control Creme, all for 50 cents. The condoms themselves might be Bold Black, Mint Scented (Stimulate Her Senses), Ultra Thin (36% Thinner For A More Natural Feeling), or Rough Rider Studded.

When I came back, Sammy Davis, Jr., was on the screen. While Tomasz prowled, Ezra and I played pool (and got thrashed), foosball (and got soundly thrashed), and darts, where my misspent youth had ingrained just enough neural connections for me to be able to win a few games despite the fact that the board had the annoying habit of blurring, like a propeller starting up, just as I was focusing on it to throw. When I finally quit, the TV was showing Olivia Newton-John.

"I admit it," confessed Ezra, now at that intimate stage of drunkenness when you talk to someone by draping yourself on them so they can see how open and pure your heart is. "I was born too late." He promised to show us the sights of Chicago next morning and we sloped out to his car. Before we got in, struck by a thought, he asked "Got a quarter?"

I fumbled in my pocket, squinted at the coins, and held it out on my open palm as directed. "I'm going to grab that quarter out of your hand," he said. "You're going to try to stop me, but you won't. If I snatch it, I get to keep it. If I don't, you get to keep it. Okay?"

What the hell? It was only a quarter. I held my hand out, he poised his own hand about a foot above it, and Tomasz stood by snickering.

Ezra grabbed the quarter. Just like that. I barely had time to move. "Let me try," said Tomasz, like the Polish team in the Drunkards' Olympics. *Bam.* Ezra had his quarter, too. "I put myself through college on that trick," he said, and drove us back to the Holiday Inn.

CHAPTER 31

Bitumen in Their Veins

August 15—Evanston, Illinois

God, my head. Three Tylenol. Up every 45 minutes drinking water. Another three Tylenol. More water....Never again. Just can't metabolize alcohol these days. Worst of all, after Tomasz and I struggled out of our respective beds to meet Ezra at ten, he never turned up; we didn't seem to have his number, and there were about 18 columns of Beckers in the phone book. We gave him an extra 45 minutes and then, in a fit of pique, decided to give up on Chicago altogether and make for Detroit, where I'd cross into Canada and make for London, Ontario, my last scheduled port of call. I wanted to meet Larry van de Maele, the son of the tobacco farmer I worked for in 1973. I navigated Tomasz through the South Side, with its abandoned streets and shuttered stores, and here and there billboards looming over the wreckage, advertising cheap divorces and bankruptcy counseling. He seemed shaken—and he had seen the slums of the Philippines.

Morning fell into afternoon. The sky got more overcast and humid as we went east, as if the air itself were getting more crowded. By now I had actively become allergic to tobacco smoke. Three weeks previously it had merely been annoying; now my sinuses swelled and started watering copiously at the first hint of smoke, and I started sneezing. I think Tomasz was slightly shocked; certainly, he smoked less.

It rained. Tomasz told me about being sent on a shooting assignment to Romania, and seeing room after room full of babies with AIDS. "What can you do for him?" he asked a doctor. "What, this?" demanded the doctor contemptuously, lifting an inert leg. "I saw red," Tomasz said. "They had to drag me off him."

The first truck stop we found—in Dearborn, Michigan, birthplace of Ford Motors and the assembly line—was so primitive and so depressing, we barely recognized it as such. It was more of a truck graveyard. We circled the area as if in a film shot, moving silently from one abandoned building to the next, from one vacant area of cracked pavement to the next, passing a couple of down-at-heel men on a stoop as if they, too, had bitumen in their veins; the camera shot came around to where it started as if to show that there was no way out.

We made for Woodhaven where, we'd been told, there was a bigger truck stop, one of the biggest in the country. The sky was the color of asphalt. The setting sun stuck in it like a rotten orange. Climbing steadily up an overpass, seeing nothing in the smog and low cloud, we might have been driving off the planet. Then the road crested, and we could see around us again—and it was a sight from hell, from a Hieronymous Bosch painting, but a modern Bosch, with no hellish, contorted people, just hellish contorted objects: refinery piping, tanks, high-tension wires. The air was hot and fetid; it smelled like a fume hood.

"This is in a way worse than the south of Chicago," Tomasz said, appalled. The South Side of Chicago was an example of man's inhumanity to man. This was an example of man's inhumanity to everything. "People say that Poland is polluted," he went on. "The worst place in Poland is far better than this."

We found the other truck stop, where Tomasz shot pictures of me in front of a car transporter, its lights on against the gathering dark. While he was changing rolls of film I chatted to the driver, a skinny, cheerful, young southerner, and realized that I had finally found my Alabama truck driver. Even in this forsaken place, it seemed as if a curse had been lifted, as if the past had finally detached itself and was being left behind in the petrol-stained water.

Well, maybe. In the attached restaurant, a trucker was hissing abuses at his wife in a loud whisper, while she stared back at him with steady hatred. Someone had pissed all over the floor of the men's room. "Grab your things. I've got to get out of here," I told Tomasz. I had the sense that a fight was going to break out any moment, or a gas main would explode under the building. He wouldn't go: he had been collared by a broadly smiling clean-cut guy who turned out to be from Cross Road Ministries, a mission from the Metro Baptist Church in Belleville, who was planning to hold a service the following morning in the Drivers' Lounge, followed by a second service in Belleville and a free home cooked meal prepared by "the ladies of the church." I dragged him away.

Just off this ghastly highway under this ghastly sky, we found ourselves in Raymond Chandler country again. A sour desk clerk stared down a young, nervous Japanese man who had a confirmation number from the airport but no room. "That's not my fault," she said. He had nowhere to go, and just stood there. He looked as though he was about to cry. "I got one room left, and that's the Jacuzzi room," she said. He said nothing. "Well, I guess I could find something," she muttered angrily, and gave him a different room. He opened the envelope he had been holding, and gave her three new 20-dollar bills. She offered the next guy the Jacuzzi room for $125. He took it. "The motor's broken," she said. "Don't use it."

It was a shell game. She found us yet another nonexistent room. There were dead insects in the sink, and the room stank of—bizarrely—old apple pie. "It's like a Hitchcock movie," Tomasz said in disbelief. "There is something in the air."

"I need a drink," I said. We dragged ourselves next door for a beer—next door being the next hotel. It was karaoke night. People sat in a windowless room, drank beer, and at the urging of their friends stood up and sang to a television screen.

CHAPTER 32

You Aren't Going to Blow Us Up, Are You?

August 16—Detroit, Michigan

Tomasz and I separated early on Sunday morning as he headed off for the trucker's spiritual breakfast. Later he told me that at 8:30 the Drivers' Lounge was empty except for two bedraggled and startled-looking truckers who seemed to have no idea what the hell was going on, and even the free food wouldn't lure them out to Belleville.

We both loaded up. He made me promise to call him if anything went wrong.

"Watch out for yourself," I said in return. "Before you know it, they'll have made you give up photography and you'll be saving souls in Romania."

"At this point," he said with a weary smile, "anything would be better than continuing this trip."

I didn't take this personally. As always, I was glad to be heading off on my own again, but I knew I'd miss him. Just by appearing every four or five days, he and even the wretched Skylark had acquired a faint hint of the essence of home, and I was always glad to see them. He and I disagreed on almost everything, but he was never furtive or malicious. We had plans to meet in Vermont, but I fully expected them to misfire, like all the rest of our plans, and our friendship to expire in one last cell-phone call: "Tomasz! Where are you?" "Well, I am in this small town in Pencil-vannya, quite charming, I must say, but the light is terrible...."

As it turned out, he would make a second trip around the country to shoot all the photos he had missed. Left to his own devices and directions, he would nearly incinerate in South Dakota and nearly freeze to death in Montana; he would meet a coffin maker who made coffin furniture that you could use around the house and then convert and climb into when your time came; and would be invited to take part in devious and dangerous sexual practices by an obese dominatrix in New Hampshire. Everyone finds the America he is looking for.

The on-ramp to I-75 was one of the nastiest places I've hitched in my life. The roadside was littered with bits of fiberglass, a steel flotsam and jetsam of car parts, a syringe, and a plastic tampon applicator. People in huge American cars stared at me as if I were a hunchback. Worst of all were the mosquitoes, which were many and vicious. The veteran hitchhiker in me completely forgot I had been carrying expensive bug repellant for 8,000 miles and ran back across the highway to a Best Western to have breakfast, soothe my shattered nerves, scratch my bites, and take a cab to the border.

Which turned out to be far easier said than done. The cabbie's name was Pat. "Where are you from?" Vermont, I said. "Montpelier!"

she cried triumphantly. As a kid, she said, she wrote to every one of the state capitals—"That was my little hobby, you know"—and was sent maps and brochures. She was still showing such go-get-'em, still working her way up in the world. She now drove a cab one day a week, instead of seven. Most days she now worked for a courier service, making better money and having her health insurance paid for her. She wore braces on both wrists. "Carpel tunnel syndrome?" I asked. "Yes," she said in disgust. "From driving?" I went on, wrong as usual. "No, from the computer," she said. "Driving doesn't affect me a bit."

Neither she nor the dispatcher had ever heard of anyone walking across the bridge to Canada—or through the tunnel, come to think of it—and had no idea if it were possible. That's ridiculous, I said. How would people without cars cross the border? She couldn't say. People without cars are unknown in Detroit. We decided that she would drive me to the toll booths at the American side of the bridge and see if I could walk across. If so, she'd drop me off; if not, she'd take me over.

That settled, she relaxed into looking around her at the highway which, it turned out, had recently been resurfaced. "God, this is beautiful!" she sighed. I dreaded to think what it had looked like before. Parts of Detroit, she kept telling me, were very pretty. Yeah, I thought sourly, but I don't expect that the line workers, the people who made the cars that made America famous, live in those parts.

As we pulled through the tollbooths on the Detroit side of the bridge, I saw that there was a sidewalk, as common sense would expect, running over the bridge, and no signs prohibited crossing by foot, so I paid Pat for the ride and the bridge toll, thanked her, and she headed off to cross the bridge and return to Detroit. I threw on my pack and set off along the sidewalk, passing a large metal sign (lying down) that read "Handguns PROHIBITED in Canada."

Within seconds, I heard yelling behind me, and a shortish, middle-aged guy in uniform was bouncing after me. "No walking on the bridge!" he yelled. "You can't walk on the bridge!"

"Why not?" I asked. "There's a sidewalk."

"Yeah, but you can't use it."

"How am I supposed to get across, then?"

"If you haven't got a car, you'll have to call a cab."

I explained that I had just gotten out of a cab, and that Pat was by now crossing back on the other side of the bridge in search of more of Detroit's magnificent new roads. He was stumped, but adamant. They couldn't let me walk.

"Why not?"

"This is a private bridge. We're not allowed to let walkers on it."

"A private bridge? But this is an international border. You mean this is a privately owned border crossing?"

And so it was. The toll guard, whose name was Joe, took me into the bridge supervisor's office as the intercom was screeching "We got a walker on the bridge! We got a walker on the bridge!" The bridge supervisor, whose name was Ralph, explained that the bridge was the property of one Maddy Moroun, who owned not only a major share in the company that owned the bridge but a substantial share in the tunnel, the only other means of crossing between Detroit and Windsor, Ontario. In fact, he owned the American side of the bridge through an American company and the Canadian side through a Canadian company. His companies also owned duty-free stores on both sides of the border, and a number of trucking companies that regularly crossed over the bridge or through the tunnel. But as to why I couldn't walk across, they had no answer.

Joe and Ralph came up with a compromise: I could hitch on the American side, on the approach to the tollbooths, and, if I was still there when their shift ended, they'd give me a ride over. This was very kind of them, but it must be said that standing on the verge of eight lanes of traffic, all sorting itself out and searching its pockets for change, is not the easiest place to hitch. An enormous black Cadillac pulled up with a front vanity plate that read YES BLACK WOMAN. One of the female toll workers asked me warily if I'd been threatened or attacked, and when I told her that everyone who'd picked me up had been kind and friendly, she replied "Those are the ones I'm afraid of—the kind ones. They lure you."

No sooner had I started to worry that I'd be there until Ralph's shift ended when a big American car pulled over and I got a ride all the way to London. With a communist.

His name was John Foley. He was stocky, medium height, with dark hair swept across his forehead, making him look younger than his 55 years. He kept strong hands on the wheel of his big, American, union-built car. He worked at the GM Delphi plant in Rochester, working in a machining area, deburring fuel rails, a part that brings fuel to the combustion chambers in the engines.

He was on his way back to Rochester from a meeting in Detroit. "I'm with a group called New Directions [for the UAW]. Which is really Old Directions: there's still labor, there's still management." While I'd been on the road, I realized, I'd missed the outcome of the big GM strike over relocating jobs to Mexico, and asked him what the result had been. He shook his head, as if the outcome had been not only unsatisfactory but predictable and all too familiar. The union had sold out. Leadership had caved in, made concessions, made a big show of cooperation with management in their common interest, and the workers had ended up losing yet more ground, another small step backward.

Wait a moment. This condemnation of the union leadership—specifically of the United Auto Workers Union, sounded familiar. Wasn't that what Michael Moore had implied in his documentary *Roger and Me*, which showed General Motors stripping and abandoning his home town of Flint, Michigan? He chuckled. "Michael Moore is hated by the UAW. *Hated*."

He talked about the sad, bitter history of American labor, from its initial sell-out a hundred years ago when the American Federation of Labor became the first procapitalist national labor organization; through the brutalities of 1918-1938, when strikers were attacked by Pinkerton men, police, the Army and hired thugs; to the Cold War, when the more enlightened industrialists realized they could live with unions as long as they were guaranteed to be docile, and agreed to recognize unions' right to exist in return for the unions agreeing to throw out their radical members, not to criticize Cold War policy and to refrain from social analysis and comment—in short, to castrate themselves as a political force in order to become "business unions."

I was curious: How had he become politicized in a country that is so conservative that the Democrats are regarded as left of center? And how had he stayed radical when the rest of us were wimping out?

It was probably in his family roots, he said. One grandfather had worked on the docks in Boston, the other was a fireman, and his parents were in the restaurant business. He spent a year at Bard College, dropped out, went into the Army from 1963-66, then worked in construction, in a textile plant, and finally at GM.

"In college, I was a liberal Democrat. I dropped out after a year; went into the Army, then into construction. It was the trade union stuff that got me to the left. The fella I worked for had a fairly extensive library. He was close to being political. He'd gone to Cornell Labor Studies School after World War II. I started to read about the early CIO and began to realize, 'Huh. There were a lot of left people around in the trade union movement,' even though they never elected anybody.

"When I was an organizer for the Service Employees International in Syracuse and Rochester we were organizing, but we were going around in suits. This was service model unionism: The workers voted in the union, and then the union sent in the suits to talk to the boss suits. Somehow this didn't seem right. We were like the gas company: you hired the gas company to take care of running gas through your house. Hire the union to run the union through your plant. You didn't create anything in the workers. If they had a question about the boss, they'd say to me 'You're in the union,' because they knew I was on the Education Committee, or this or that. In the end I gave up saying 'No, we're all in the union...,' because by that time less than 2 percent of the people were coming to meetings.

"The first two UAW presidents, when I got there in the mid-seventies had somewhat of a socialist or social democratic background. They still talked about workers taking control of the plants, about the sit-down strikes of 1936, 1937. Social unionism was still around in the UAW: you had a women's committee, a civil rights committee...."

By "social unionism," I took him to mean a sense of universal sister-and-brotherhood, a concern for all working Americans and indeed workers of the world, rather than uniting merely to protect one's own job. As soon as he started talking in this vein I knew that this was the last, uncharted territory on my trip, the missing Left side of the country, as misunderstood and misdescribed as the Louisiana territory, left of the Mississippi, in 1799.

"The UAW still had summer schools. You'd still hear people saying 'These corporations don't care about jobs, cars, or people; they just care about profits.' You'd still hear that kind of statement from a course instructor at the UAW Cornell Summer School. They still had political economists in their research department, people who could use words like 'capitalism.' They didn't use the word 'socialism' very much, but many of them came from a socialist background."

And now? "Social unionism is dead. They've internalized the corporate agenda. Everything that comes down from management is a joint statement. A change in the hours—they're now going to butt the shifts instead of overlapping them, which means we effectively have to work an extra half hour—that will probably come down as a business decision that the shop committee has signed on to. I'm sure that the young [workers] can't tell you where the union begins and where the company ends."

Ironically, this sounds just like the way unions were co-opted in eastern European countries under Stalin: They chose power instead of principles. "So they're aiming for a frictionless relationship?" I asked.

"Right. Which is, of course, bullshit. There are strikes, sure, when work is outsourced or sent to a Mexican plant, but there's no social vision or trade union vision any more in the United Auto Workers leadership." One leader recently said "Well, even if they go to nonunion plants, we want them to be American non-union plants," which is straying dangerously close to right-wing nationalism.

Despite his opposition to the UAW, he was still prounion. "Unions do left things: They redistribute wealth and power at the point of production or service. You don't pass the overtime out to whoever you want; you pass it out on an equalized basis." I found myself thinking of Bob, the trucker who never got a load going to Texas because dispatch hated him. I was coming full circle. "There are objective reasons why someone gets a promotion, it's not subjective. And if the objective criteria are equal, then seniority prevails. Workers do still have some power through their union to control what happens to them, but that's slipping away. In 1982 the union started concessionary movements, saying that workers had to cooperate with management to fight off foreign competition—the Japs, as they called them. As soon as that stuff started, everything else went."

I asked John when he joined the Communist Party. "In the mid-eighties, I was working with an unemployment council in upstate New York. Some of the people who were doing the best work with agencies in the area were communists, and that's when I got recruited into the CP. And I enjoyed all the people I met—it was as much social as political. I was looking for some place on the left to hang my hat. Since I was an industrial worker, they were very happy to have me, since most of the party members were middle class—teachers, government employees.

"I was around for effectively five or six years, and then a group of us walked out. Angela Davis left. In spite of what they said, they were still Stalinists." At one big, successful meeting of a thousand labor people from the broad left, "this old party hack showed up" and starting talking about taking the conference over. "I looked across at this guy who was the vice-president from Local 1199, we were in the party together, I was on the state committee for New York, and it was like 'Jesus Christ!' But that's the way those old left people talk. It's hard enough talking about the left to workers who have had no exposure without Stalinists talking about 'We're going to take this over....' "

He continued to work as a rank-and-file activist, running the education committee, but it was an uphill struggle. "Most union workers' level of vision was 'Let's get Bill Clinton elected.' My God! The first thing he did was to push NAFTA!" John was always more committed and more radical than the majority of union men around him, even those on the education committee. "One guy would literally walk out of the room when I talked about this stuff, and now he's a lobbyist for the Professional Employees' Federation."

Hearing this story of the decay of radical sentiment, I asked him what happened to the so-called new left that arose with the Civil Rights marches, the free speech movement, and opposition to the Vietnam War—the youthful energy and commitment of my generation?

"The activism of the sixties was basically self-interest. There was nothing underneath the new left politics that required permanent change. Everyone could still go to college. Income was still going to be distributed the way it had always been. Power was still going to reside in the government, with a few adjustments. There was no class analysis in the new left. People going off to live in the hills weren't going to change anything."

In our defense, I couldn't help adding that thanks to McCarthy, when the radical generation finally arrived it had no exposure to left ideas and no left organizations to call on as allies. Everything had to start from scratch, from ignorance, among middle-class members of the new left who didn't feel personal, day-by-day class injustice.

"There were working-class people in the new left," he agreed, "but once it was over, it was over. The war was stopped, and that was good, but after that there was no reason why those people [from different backgrounds] would meet each other on a daily basis."

Meanwhile, the manufacturing economy began to dwindle just as minorities were beginning to get into steel, say, so they were pushed out into the growing service industry, the least unionized sector in the country. "There was an article in the paper yesterday about a messenger on Wall Street who carries piles of money—checks, obviously, nothing he could steal—around all day for $5.50 an hour and lives in a homeless shelter. And an African-American who had a job as a cook in a restaurant on Long Island who was living in a homeless shelter."

At the same time, the history and memory of the American left has fallen into a willful oblivion. "People [aren't] disloyal to capitalism because they [don't] know how to be disloyal to capitalism. The thousands of socialist newspapers that had been published by the foreign language societies [have] gone because the people were Americanized. I was carrying a copy of the *Monthly Review*, the Independent Socialists' magazine, and this electrician said, 'You aren't going to blow us up, are you?' The only time he'd ever heard of anyone being a socialist was some kind of radical bomb-thrower. The Italian syndicalists—even most Italian-Americans don't know about them. Wonderful tradition. Very important in the Lowell and Lawrence strikes. But what kid who lives in that town knows about them?"

Like Bruce, the hippie befriended by the Anashnase, John had had his battle with drink. It's hard to imagine anyone swimming against a current as broad and strong as mainstream American capitalism without suffering some damage. "How do you manage to sustain yourself?" I asked.

"Psychological profile. I'm an oppositional figure. This is how I get to be a pain in the ass. Maybe only certain people can do it because they're used to going right where everyone else goes left, and vice versa. It may be something you can't do if you want to get on with people. There may be people who could tell you the same things I've told you and have learned the same things I've learned, but they wouldn't want the alienation that came with it." He's used to a solitary life. He doesn't go deer hunting; he goes up into Canada to see movies and listen to jazz.

Did he see signs of hope anywhere? "The Saturn workers have just thrown out their UAW leadership for agreeing to take nonunion parts," he said. Mind you, the news from Saturn wasn't all good. "An African-American worker came and spoke to us who had gone down to Saturn headquarters near Spring Hill, and management said to him 'Don't you want to see the plantation?' They'd built a model plantation, with slave quarters and everything! He said, 'No, thank you. I'd just like to leave Tennessee.'"

He was the best-read, most thoughtful person who picked me up, and the first thing he did after dropping me off on the outskirts of London was to drive sixty yards down to the on-ramp and pick up a couple more hitchhikers.

Let's see, I thought, looking around the stores and businesses clustered around the interstate exit. How would I know I was now in

Canada? By the United Furniture Warehouse? Superstore Mall? Giant Carpet? Discovery Zone? McDonald's? Costco? Burger King? Arby's? Ah, yes, there was my evidence: the Amoco gas station. It proudly bore signs saying, "All Canadian Independent."

Yet the place was different, despite the superficial glaze of American commercial culture. As I was eating a fish sandwich in the McDonalds, a couple in late middle age came over to me and asked me if I was hitchhiking, and if so, would I like a ride to Toronto? When I declined, grateful and astonished, but said that I planned to head on in that direction in a day or two, they gave me a list of places to stay and things to see. A young couple with a child asked me the same question as I was leaving. This was the hitchhiking I remembered: ordinary, simply part of the landscape. I wondered if it had anything to do with the fact—well, the rumor, I suppose, as I haven't been able to find anyone in office with a memory long enough to verify it—that in the early 1970s the Canadian government, concerned about Quebec separatism and rumblings of dissent from the West, decided that it was vital for the future of the nation that young Canadians think of the nation as a whole, and came up with a brilliant and visionary plan. They would appropriate a small amount of money to beef up the country's youth hostel system and start a propaganda campaign to encourage hitchhiking, and to encourage people to pick up hitchhikers. If this is what actually happened, never in human history has a government so neatly caught and used the spirit of the age; and never has $6 million in federal money had such widespread and long-lasting effect that it was still being felt 25 years later in a fast-food joint.

When Larry and his wife Josie arrived in the family van, we didn't recognize each other. Of course, last time that I saw him, he had a full, stringy beard and long hair piled under a baseball cap, and

I'd forgotten his large, piercing eyes. But then I hadn't really known him at all: I had no idea he loved sailing, and had bummed his way down to and around the Caribbean for a year. I'd forgotten that his first child had already been born by that harvest summer; I didn't know he had divorced his first wife and remarried....All I remembered, really, was him showing me the opening to "Stairway to Heaven," the smell of exhaust as he backed his '55 Chevrolet out of the garage that was the other half of the bunkhouse where we pickers lived, and his passionate wish not to follow his father into the tobacco.

Oh, and one other thing: I remembered that he had a high school friend called John Bentley who appeared halfway through the season and asked for a job, becoming our sixth picker. John had long hair, loose, old clothes and spoke slowly, half to you and half to the middle distance. He had spent the previous three or four months riding up and down the Rockies on a horse. He declined a place in the bunkhouse and slept in his sleeping bag out on the grass, where I couldn't stand for a minute without being devoured by mosquitoes.

"John, how do you do it?" I asked him after a while.

"Well," he explained slowly, with his knowing grin, "you've heard that all living things give out vibrations?" All right, I thought, I'll take this and see where it leads, and I nodded. "Well," he said, his grin slowly growing wider, "if you're really, really in tune with Nature, you don't give out any vibrations. Then the mosquitoes can't find you."

Later that day, I ran this explanation by Larry. He snorted. "If I'd spent the last three months on a horse, would you want to bite me?"

We drove out to Larry and Josie's neat little suburban house. Since I'd last seen him, he had fulfilled his greatest ambition and got out of the tobacco. "Eighty was my last crop, or eighty-one." He retrained in electronics repair, putting himself through tech school by playing in a country band at night, and ended up owning his own repair business in London. A lot of people are following him out of the tobacco: The total yield is down 30 percent since 1973, and the number of farms in the area has halved.

Ben had died after two heart attacks. Larry visited him in hospital after one collapse and Ben said "I've been flying." Flying? asked Larry quizzically. Yes, said Ben, the most sensible and phlegmatic man you'd ever meet, and described the classic near-death experience of floating around the room, then the hospital, then out around a tree there in the grounds—and of course Larry realized that from the bed where Ben had been lying, he couldn't see that part of the grounds, or have known that there was a tree out there, just where he described it. By the time Ben died he had sold off portions of land, then the farms and one of the houses, leaving his financial fields in good order and his family well provided for.

When we got home, Josie's sons, Jordan and Brandon, were in the den watching...wait for it...*The Monkees*. "This is Tim," she said. "He's a traveler," and out of the blue, or the black, or whatever color we ascribe to forgetting, came a memory: when I came home after my trip to America in 1973 my little sister Jennie, then nine, had stuck a homemade sign on my bedroom door saying, "Welcome Home Traviller." I've still got it.

Tonight was a billiards night: Josie and two of the boys were in a local league: small prizes for weekly winners, and the one in each category with the most wins gets a trip for two to Las Vegas. She changed into her pool shark's-gear: lamé top that left her midriff bare, and denim shorts. "I'd always been competitive at baseball and volleyball," she said. "When I turned 40, I looked around for something else to be competitive at, and I found pool." She had won the local event once, Larry Ben three times, Jordan twice. The boys already had their own cues, and she had just ordered herself a custom cue, too, which would cost $350. We pulled back the cover, brushed off the baize, and played a few warm-up games. I played a couple of times and managed some good runs, but while I was fading, trying too hard, the others were moving up through the gears. She bought the table, she said, so the kids would have something to do at home, something that would keep the family together. Now the family was heading out into town like a trio of gunfighters.

Larry and I climbed into the van in search of the past. Many of my most vivid memories of that summer were from the tobacco: Ben leaning in the bunkhouse door, switching on what he called "the hydro" and calling "Time to empty a kil', boys." Mary's enormous breakfasts, huge plates domed high with scrambled eggs, pancakes, sausages, bacon. Struggling into waterproofs, as the plants were always wet with a vicious dew that had soaked up nicotine: One drop in your eye and you were blinded for two or three minutes until the stinging passed and you stopped cursing. The hard-edged metal framework of the picker that crawled the rows, and the boxes into which you slapped the leaves, and the fact that the slightest knock against that metal left a gouge or cut that wouldn't heal for weeks, the scab getting soaked and softened by each morning's dew. Then stripping off the waterproofs by 9 a.m. as the sun rose, and from then on every leaf you broke off at the stem threw a drop of sap onto your hands, or your forearm, or your hair, or anywhere nearby; and as it dried it formed a tiny speck of black tar. I've got a photo of myself in among the leaves, and there's a black smudge on the tip of my nose.

And after work, taking a shower in the greenhouse, where the water was cold on cold days and scalding on hot ones. There was nothing to do in the evening but drink beer, so every couple of nights we walked two or three miles along a dirt road into Vienna (population: 450) whose only hotel had not only a bar but a pool table. The sun had just gone down at the end of an other cloudless day, and for the first time I noticed that between the dusty orange at the horizon and the purple of the night the sky managed to be green, a color that was beyond my comprehension. This was not the breezy, nimble English evening sky I knew; it was the motionless, hermetic nightfall of the mid-continent, where the universe seems to have been painted on the inside of a vast glass ball in which the sounds of insects and of a footfall scuffing dirt might travel forever, and anything could be about to happen.

Larry drove me out to see his mother, and to look at the old farm after all these years. It was dusk. The old hotel had burned down; the new Vienna was just a half-lit crossroads scrawled on the evening landscape. Down the road, the tobacco plants were smaller than they seemed when I was bent double underneath them, picking the leaves from the ground up, and were now gray in the twilight, row on row vanishing into the darkness. The new owner must have consolidated farms, for the buildings were silent and empty, the wooden kilns stood open and the yard was full of nothing but moonshadow.

Mary lived in a small, well-kept house; she and Larry greeted each other with affectionate courtesy. She offered us boys a beer, and then she and Larry remembered all those pickers from years ago: a Barbadian, some Floridians, the kids from northern Ontario who worked alongside me. Mary couldn't picture Boots, the one who told me that he had been expelled from high school for sniffing gasoline;

she didn't like Weeds at all, and Lonnie was forever combing his long blond hair and wrapping it carefully in a T-shirt so that when the sap dried the tobacco tar wouldn't cake on it and ruin it. Ben was forever cursing Lonnie, she remembered, saying "Goddamn that boy, he's always the last in the trailer!"

Now she kept busy as best she could, took calls from her children, had just come back from a trip to Grand Bend "with four other widows," she added, a little caustically. She was dreading the coming winter. She had pulled her shoulder out bringing in firewood when Ben was sick and despite physiotherapy, chiropractic, and massage, she said, "I don't think it'll ever be completely better." She had a cabin in the woods, but out there she felt even more isolated; she often thought she might sell it, but then changed her mind.

Larry was the last of my revisits. It had been a curious experience, meeting figures from so far back in my life that I no longer knew them; and in any case my memory had played its card game on them, shuffling the facts and picking out only the details it wanted. Simply confirming that the experience had happened seemed to be a tonic. Even the odious Richard resurfaced: I discovered from one of his distant relatives in Canada that he was married and living in Norway, and to my amazement, I found myself feeling glad that he was still alive and doing well. The fact that a person had entered my life at all was apparently something to be grateful for. It was like Bell's theorem—that once two elementary particles have been in contact, it's impossible for them to remain unaffected by each other, no matter how far estranged by distance or time. As if love were simply the warmth created by brushing up against each other.

I came to believe that we are an aggregate of the personalities we have been in our lives (and, some would say, our previous lives), but instead of collecting selves we tend to abandon them, afraid that they will embarrass us in public, or get us in trouble. As any parent knows, having a child encourages us to be a child again, and a self that had been put away in the attic with the toys now rushes out to meet us with open arms, in all its rolling-on-the-floor impishness and delight. Finding these people also involved finding the part of myself that had set out to explore the world, and realizing that that self was still available, if I wanted him. Life is not just consumption and decay: We can blow on the embers of the past to rekindle the present.

≈

CHAPTER 33

Dowsing for Kindness

August 17—London, Ontario

Next morning found me looking for a bus stop, walking through a neat little development of bungalows and two-story houses in brick, in the English fashion, with neat lawns and flower beds. It seemed to be a sensible mid-Atlantic compromise, like so many things Canadian. In America, each house and its land would take up at least twice as much space; in England, slightly less. The bus was prompt and clean, the driver courteous. Downtown was in good repair; the population was ethnically diverse; nobody looked lost or broken. The buildings were modest in scale and ambition, and there was no sense of waste. I felt as if I'd just spent the previous four weeks in a Third World nation, or at least a post-apocalyptic First World one.

Life in America seemed plagued by both fears of crisis and unrealistic hopes. In America, teenagers might or might not be taking drugs, Christ was wrestling with Satan, the Stock Market might boom or bust, the President might shrug it all off or be impeached, the U.S. Cavalry might save the world or destroy it, and your local public radio station would go broke without your contribution, so call now.

On the other hand, the landscape of the United States, so scruffy by contrast—cheap slotted utility poles at every angle but the vertical, untrimmed hedgerows, cracked paving, traffic lights swinging on absurd little wires—gives me, at least, a perverse sense of value. We don't want America to grow up and be sensible; we want it to be forever risky, the place to live on the edge, to take chances, the place to sharpen our edge. In trim and tidy Canada, as in England, I feel as if everything has already been taken care of by someone else, things are going on very nicely without my help. In the U.S. there is work to be done, a country still to be built. Heroes needed: apply at the third window on the left.

I caught a second bus, which dropped me off by 401, dragged myself to the on-ramp, and put my thumb out. I wanted to go home, but I didn't want to give up this trip: I hadn't gotten enough out of it, yet, to let it go. I'd hitch to Toronto, I thought, then catch a train to Montreal—I love trains—and a bus down to Burlington, but it felt like giving up.

After 20 minutes, I was picked up by a young guy selling $2,000 vacuum cleaners, the kind that vacuum even the air.

"I hope you don't mind if I drive fast," he said.

"Just as long as we get there alive," I said, my usual answer, intended to perch in the back of his mind like a macaw speaking the voice of reason, but this time it didn't work. He hit 99 mph, in traffic, on 401 just west of Woodstock. At that speed, tires feel as if they're melting: The car starts to lose its grip on the road and you feel it starting to float from side to side over the tires. By the time

I got out I was shaking and my nerve had gone. *That's it,* I thought. *I've had enough. I'm too old for this kind of thing.* I couldn't even bring myself to stick my thumb out. From the rubble beside the shoulder, the cars and trucks looked not like opportunities but lethal weapons—a deer's-eye view.

Yet as I was standing there ten feet back from the highway, feeling small and beaten, not even hitching, I got picked up. A Volvo pulled over—another first—driven by Walter Bak, a roly-poly young Polish guy, the son of a machinist who had one day packed his suitcase and walked to Austria to escape communism. (He was a tool-and-die worker, but when he reached Canada the government sent him to Saskatchewan, where there's nothing but wheat. It's not only communism that produces daft bureaucracies.) After Walter dropped me off at Kitchener, I was wandering reluctantly through stringy grass toward the on-ramp, thinking, *I still don't want to do this,* when a car pulled over and another young guy called out, "Are you hitchhiking?"

"Uh...yeah," I said uncertainly.

"Where are you going?"

"Toronto."

"I'm going to....ah, what the hell, I'll take you to Toronto." His name was John Ouzas, he was just about to leave for a year at the University of Glasgow. Having nothing much to do he drove me 50 miles out of his way to Toronto, and I knew that somehow, I was being taken care of. If I wasn't going to the drivers, they would come to me.

Oddly, I had been half-expecting something like this to happen. Even before I set out from home, I wanted to know what would happen once I relaxed my usual vigilant, slightly anxious grip on my life, and allowed other forces to come into play—forces I couldn't name or explain, let alone control. Would things fall apart, or would I be, in some strange way, helped? And for me this led to a broader question, one that underlay everything: how does our life turn out the way it does? Luck? Hard work? Or is there sometimes an invisible hand on the wheel, whose light touch affects our course only if we're not gripping too tightly, too desperately?

I wanted to know because that's what seemed to have happened in 1973. After the tobacco season was over, I had three weeks of vacation left and, apart from the need to be in New York on October 3 to fly back to England, I had no particular place to go. I thought I might make for Boston, as I'd heard it was a cool city, but in the back of my mind I had a far more ambitious destination: I wanted to find a way to stay in America.

I was on the New York State Thruway east of Buffalo when a black Porsche stopped. I've never had a ride in a Porsche, before or since. The driver said he was going onto the Mass Pike, but then he'd have to let me off, as he was turning south and going to New Haven. All right, I thought, I'll go to New Haven. Mitzi was there— she had transferred to Yale—so I could crash with her. As we pulled into New Haven, though, I realized I didn't know her address, and I had no means of finding her. The driver dropped me off on a corner downtown, I put down my holdall and guitar, stretched, looked around, and there was Mitzi, standing right next to me.

So I slept on her couch for a few days, got to meet her housemates, and that Friday one of them told me he was going up to his parents' place in Vermont, and did I want to come? Sure, I said. Why not? I'd heard it was a pretty place. So we drove up, climbed one of the Green Mountains, ended up drinking beer in a bowling alley, went back down to New Haven, and the following day I got on the bus for New York, and the plane back home.

So when I applied for teaching jobs in the U.S., the University of Vermont was on my short, naive list; and even though my sooty letters of application were hand-typed on an old manual typewriter, and were so badly spaced that they either ran one line onto a second page or were squashed onto one page by typing in the top and bottom margins, UVM offered me a job.

Looking back down the forking path that left me in Vermont, it now seems an impossibly fragile twig. I never understood the choices I faced, never made informed decisions, and yet I ended up in a place that, although entirely unfamiliar, would come to feel more like home than anywhere else I'd lived.

So that was the lasting discovery of my journey, not so much a creed as a set of metaphysical possibilities to spell out and spend the rest of my life testing: that thoughts, when fed with passion or with energy, are also forces that may subtly affect others who are on a similar wavelength. That we are cared for, and can sometimes draw to ourselves the very people we need, or who need us. That living spontaneously can bypass the constricting effects of anxiety and give us access to astonishing inspiration and energy. That hitchhiking is, in effect, a sort of prayer, and the better part of me is the part that can let go, as if it were hitchhiking, thumb held out like a hazel twig, dowsing for kindness.

Downtown Toronto was full of miracles of steel and glass, but I'd had enough of miracles of steel and glass. I was tired. I just wanted to be home.

The VIA train left a slender footprint on the land, slipping quickly and quietly through the woods and fields of Ontario, spreading little exhaust and delaying almost nobody else. The car, by contrast, drags an entire paraphernalia of commuting out into the countryside, like a honeymoon car dragging a string of ever bigger tin cans: first the road, like string, then knotted onto it gas stations, quick-stops, fast-food joints, supermarkets, chunks of asphalt, Coke cans, cigarette packets, pieces of metal trim, drive-in ATMs, golden arches, cappuccino stands, car dealerships, Styrofoam coffee cups, parking lots, billboards, gasoline dregs in puddles, outlet centers, stop signs, and minute particles of pulverized rubber and brake linings— the entire nowhere landscape of the car that we had seen everywhere and had driven Tomasz insane.

On the train I met Gwendoline, a chic French-Canadian girl with oval glasses and her hair pulled back into four stainless-steel clips, the spray of hair over her eyes dyed blue. She was 15, though she looked four years older. She was returning from a stint as a live-in nanny for an American family, having hated it, but she was determined to keep practicing her English, even if it meant borrowing my English newspaper and reading about cricket. We started talking; she asked me searching questions about my trip, and after some time announced that she, too, was going to start hitchhiking. In fact, next summer she and a girlfriend were going to South America. What did I think of that idea?

Well, I thought, that's asking me to put my money where my mouth is, isn't it?

Plenty of women, I told her, have hitchhiked safely and successfully, and some still do. One of my UVM students whose car had broken down somewhere in Colorado wound up leaving it there and hitching to the West Coast and up through Oregon to Washington, climbing mountains, having wonderful experiences. (She carried a knife, though she never used it.) At the same time I was making my road trip, Jen Knops, the daughter of a friend of mine, set off across country with her boyfriend, slept in caves in the Black Hills, drove out to Seattle where she dumped him—another casualty of cross-country travel—then spent several months hitchhiking and riding freight trains up and down the West Coast with friends she'd met en route, picking up odd jobs. She was away six months in all.

"Did you ever feel at a disadvantage because you're a woman?" I asked.

She laughed and shook her head dismissively. "The only time was when I went into manpower agencies looking for work. 'Sorry,' they'd say, 'we've got nothing clerical.' I'd say, 'Give me a break. I've worked on trail crews; I've worked as a cook; I can handle hard work.' 'Okay,' they'd say, and they'd offer me some guy work, but say 'Sorry, we can only pay you $5.50 an hour because you're a girl....'"

All the same, going off to South America, where Gwendoline wouldn't speak the language, at 16, sounded a bit ambitious for anyone, boy or girl. I suggested she do as many small, safer trips as possible first, to learn how to cope: what to do if you fall ill, or run out of money, or the car breaks down, or there's nowhere to spend the night. How to get people to help you rather than take advantage of you; how to shrug off misfortune. The problem with imagined catastrophe is that it is absolute: In our nightmares we are helpless, our enemies superhuman—and we assume that, when confronted by the drunk or the thug there's nothing we'd be able to do. In fact, the outcome is in our own hands to a remarkable extent, but those may be untutored hands; making the best of a difficult situation is a learned skill, or a thousand learned skills. A *New York Times* columnist recently wrote about a 65-year-old Brooklyn woman who had driven through all 48 contiguous states. Almost all her encounters were not only safe but deeply affecting.

Once, though, she was harassed by a drunken man shouting obscenities at her while she used a pay phone at a campsite.

"I had been given mountain-lion training because a mountain lion had swiped a woman and her child," she reported. "We were told if we saw one, keep your ground, act big and make a lot of noise. I never saw a mountain lion, but that's what I gave this guy. I never shouted so loud in public."

Peggy Bradley, commenting in the *Los Angeles Times* in 1970 from the perspective of a woman who had been hitching for four years without ever being assaulted, said, "When you hitch it is important to feel relaxed and in control of your body. Once this feeling of confidence is mastered you will grow to love being on the road and constantly meeting new people." When she wrote "your body" she may have been thinking of the female body, with its supposed vulnerability, but it's true for all of us. Anyone can look like a target; anyone can look robust and self-reliant.

Gwendoline was clearly not your average 15-year-old. She had lived abroad, where she had to speak her second language, and she struck me as wary, yet curious, intelligent, well-read—she might go far. When I shook hands with her to say goodbye, her grip was surprisingly strong, and she looked me straight in the eye.

Meanwhile, another teenager had been chipping in on our conversation—Joe, a bright kid just about to start college at Vassar, coming back from Detroit where he and his mother had been helping relatives work on their house.

Joe, speaking with a slight lisp because of his pierced tongue, asked me if I wanted a ride—hitchhiking was determined not to let me give up. I was being offered rides even when I was on a train!—as his father would be meeting them at Cornwall, Ontario, and taking them home to the village where they lived in upstate

New York. Next morning they had to go into Plattsburgh; if I wanted, they could drive me to the ferry that ran across Lake Champlain to Vermont.

His father, Larry, who worked as a prison chaplain, picked us up at the train and drove us back to the tiny village of Churubusco, where over a late dinner he talked about the strange events following his father's death.

"We weren't doing that well financially," he began. "He died around Christmas, and I went down to be with my mother. She asked me to go through all his clothes and take anything I could use. I knew my dad: he was off and on, losing weight, gaining weight, losing weight, gaining weight. I knew there was nothing that was going to fit me. But something kept coming to me in the night: 'Your mom says, "Check the clothes."' Finally, about two days before I left, I went through his entire closet, and all ten different sizes, everything fit. Including shoes marked size seven and a half. I wear a size nine. I still have those seven-and-a-halfs.

"After that, I started feeling his presence a whole lot. I talked to a priest about it, because [in the Catholic religion] there is a warning: You don't speak to the dead. I told him, 'This is getting too strange.' He said, 'Wait a minute, Larry. Do you think your father went to heaven?' I said, 'Yeah, I think he went or he's on his way.' 'Then he is with the communion of saints?'

"Anyway. I'd be at work, and I'd get dizzy and disoriented. It was like I was floating through a channel. I would lose my train of thought. Finally, the revelation—and I feel it was a revelation—came to me. 'I've lived for 77 years in this physical presence. I'm in transition right now. I'm going from the known to the unknown. I need a link so I don't lose my way.' For whatever reason, my father chose me as that link."

His father "said" that he needed to resolve certain conflicts before he could let go and move on. "I remember feeling often that he was just drifting, and that he needed to feel, to hold on to what had become normal [to him] over 77 human years. I knew that he was reaching out to me. He and I weren't that close, but during that period I knew I was being used, willingly, by him to help with that transition from the physical life to the spiritual. It was incredibly powerful, to the point where if I was at work I'd have to sit down, and say, 'Okay, Dad, what are you spinning about right now?' "

Larry said he was the youngest of three brothers. "In theory it should fall to the oldest, but it came to me: 'Larry, you may be the youngest but now you are the patriarch of the family.' That was scary. I was given the care of my mother, for sure. Dad really had to talk to me. We talked about the fact that growing up he never said he loved me, or was proud of me. One night [during this transitional period] we had, oh, it must have been an hour-long conversation, and he made it quite plain that he did love me deeply, and was proud of me. "Apart from the personal matters, it was mainly 'I'm uncomfortable. This doesn't feel right. It's not what I'm used to!' It was confusing to him. Maybe he had a preconceived notion of what it was going to be after [death], and it wasn't the way he thought it was going to be!"

As time went on, the contact became less powerful and less frequent. "I remember saying 'How long is this supposed to last? This is really starting to affect my work, it's starting to affect everything.' And it came to me: 'How long did it take for the Master to go through his transition [in the wilderness]?' Well, 40 days. 'It will not be as long as the Master.' And that was it. On the 37th day the cloud lifted, the fog lifted. It was weird. It was really weird.

"Do I believe in the afterlife? After that, you bet I do."

For some reason, I lay awake that night thinking of my grandmother. Widowed in middle age, she moved to the south coast of England and lived in the same village for her last 30 years, but her life was seldom dull. Not only was she a great walker, like her daughter, my mother, but she kept a kind of global open house. Whenever my Aunt Ruth, who emigrated to New Zealand, heard of a student heading for England, or my Aunt Barbara set off on one of her vagabond trips to North Africa or the Middle East or China, they would pass out my grandmother's name, address, and phone number; and as a result, the doorbell of the little house in East Dean was rung day and night by an unpredictable cascade of visitors, some having barely arrived in the country and speaking almost no English, who signed her visitors' book and slept in her spare bedroom. They kept her on her toes; they may have kept her young, for she lived to be a spry 92. I found myself thinking of her as the inventor of stationary hitchhiking.

~

CHAPTER 34

We Should Do All Right

August 18—Churubusco, New York

In the morning it was drizzling. For the first time in a month I pulled on my jeans, borrowed an umbrella, and walked around the dripping maples, the three dozen fading, white wooden houses, and a stone Catholic church around a single hollow square that is the village of Churubusco.

Larry drove us down to Plattsburgh, a somber trip in the drizzle: The trees on both sides were bent or shattered from January's catastrophic ice storm; and those that were still upright now lacked most of their upper branches, so they looked as if they'd been given a buzz-cut. "I hadn't seen that kind of devastation since Vietnam," Larry said.

Joe pointed out Lyon Mountain, where they mined the iron that made the Golden Gate Bridge, though the mines are long closed. Both of them talked about the difficulties of living in a small impoverished town in upstate New York, especially, Joe said, if you're a teenager with long hair and a pierced tongue, or in fact any kind of independence of thought.

"A lot of kids in our class have never made it out of Clinton County," Joe said. Most of the students he graduated with would stay around town, and many of those who went away to college typically returned after a few weeks, finding the outside world too much for them. "We're so secluded that people lose the desire to do anything that involves leaving the town," Joe said. "It's very sad."

The drive was somber also because I was almost home. I wished I had been able to spend longer away; I wished I'd been able to spend more time on back roads—but then part of me might never have returned. At the end of *Trio's Trek*, the story of three women's hitchhiking trip from England via France, Spain, the North African Coast, Egypt, the Sudan, Uganda, and Belgian Congo to Kenya, Mary Jacques-Aldridge wrote: "Now the three of us would settle down to ordinary, mundane lives again; the freedom, the camaraderie, the novelty, the open road would become only memories...." I dreaded that fall back to earth, and with it the loss of my solitary certainty, my sense of direction.

On a bright day, the view from the Lake Champlain ferries is spectacular, with the wooded shorelines, the Green Mountains rippling down the eastern horizon and the younger, taller, and more rocky Adirondacks to the west. Today was was gray and cold. Nobody from the boat picked me up on the far shore, even though I was in my home state, even though I was passed by cars with University of Vermont stickers. I walked a mile, thumbing, thinking that for the first time, I could conceivably walk the 20 miles home if I didn't get a ride, though it would take me until dark and my knee would probably be wrecked. Then a well-ridden pickup—

God bless pickups!—being driven in the opposite direction by a typical old Vermont farmer, made a U-turn and stopped.

He wasn't a farmer, of course, and he wasn't from Vermont. This was my final reminder that reality would always be more complex and interesting than I expected. His name was Robert Stowell. He was born and brought up in small towns near Syracuse, New York. He used to hitchhike a lot when he was in high school, he said, never thought twice about it. Only time anything scary happened was when he and his friend Jimmy were hitching after dark and a friend of theirs came by on his motorbike and picked them both up. They had a close encounter with a tractor-trailer on a curve that straightened them right up as it passed, and halfway home there were headlights behind them, and the friend up front said, "Oh my God, it's the cops! If they catch me with three on a bike I'll lose my license!" So he went tearing around these little country roads at 80, 85 miles an hour. When they finally got into Clyde, New York, and Robert went to get off the bike, he found that Jimmy, behind him, was still clutching onto his jacket for dear life. "It's okay, Jimmy, we're home. You can let go now," he said, but poor Jimmy was so petrified it was several minutes before he could bring himself to unclench his fingers.

Robert had worked as an engineer for 26 years and was now retired, he said, living in Huntington, Vermont, just doing odd jobs here and there. He was pretty comfortable around fixing things; he only drew the line at jobs that would take two fellows. Then he said, "Well, you'll just have to find someone else to do that for you." He was supposed to paint someone's porch, but with the rain and the cold wind off the lake he thought, well, he might have to take it easy today, and I knew I was back in Vermont just by his dry wit. Only later did I notice that this was yet another instance of being picked up by someone whose plans had been changed for them, whom circumstance had diverted toward me.

"I'm a garden freak," he said. He and his dad used to have an acre garden, a couple of hundred tomato plants, three hundred peppers, lettuce, kohlrabi....The garden in Huntington hadn't done well, too much shade in the autumn; and he and his wife weren't so keen on winter, so they were thinking that they might move down to the western part of North Carolina some day.

"We're kind of reserved. She does her crocheting or her knitting. I'm independent. She lets me do what I like, cooking, baking, cleaning up around the house. I play around with the computer, or I work in this little wood shop I've set up."

Now I think about it, there was something very English about the life he described. Pottering around in the garden, tinkering in his shed—it's straight out of "When I'm 64." And that Englishness is increasingly important to me, as it is to many expatriates passing through middle age like the arch of the parabola. Wanting to spend less time and energy constantly remaking ourselves, keeping up with the adopted idiom, the second language.

Robert was 59, and when he turned 62 he'd have a couple—actually, three or four—pensions coming in, from the Navy, and the company he worked at for 26 years, and all that time he was doing work for the local school board. "My wife'll have her Post Office pension, too, so we should do all right. We don't smoke, we don't drink, we mostly eat in, though I like to go out for a buffet breakfast on Sundays now and then."

Maybe it was just because I was tired, but by now everything was starting to seem very simple. Journeys, like days and lives, are parabolic: We blaze away full of ambition, then slowly our energies dim and we fall back to earth. At the end of each journey, when ambition and vanity are burned away, we're left with the qualities that work for all times. Kindness. Gratitude. Everything beyond that is just a matter of working out the details.

As for how America has changed in the last quarter-century, I can barely even conceive of America as a single place, having seen so much of it, and its vast contradictions. Instead, it seems to be me who has changed. I think I once read that in the time of the Crusades a knight would go to the Holy Land twice, once as a young man, to conquer; once late in life, as a pilgrim, to ask forgiveness for the sins of his youth.

Robert drove 15 miles out of his way—"Heck, I didn't have anything better to do today anyway"—and dropped me off right at the top of my driveway, where the old Volvo had been sitting idle for too long, and everything needed a good weeding.

~

A Short History
of Hitchhiking

One of the great charms of hitchhiking is that it never sold out. Nobody ever got a grant from the Pentagon to study the tactics of hitchhiking, or from NASA to study sweat loss under zero traffic conditions in New Mexico. No hitchhiker ever made it onto the cover of *Time* or *Newsweek*. There was never a Hitchhiking Channel, nor a Hitchhiking Hall of Fame. No daily mileages were ever published in the *Wall Street Journal*, no rankings in *Sports Illustrated*. Nobody ever sold giant hitchhiking thumbs inscribed with "We're #1" at roadside stands. No specialist hitchhiking clothing in the L.L. Bean catalog, no websites, no *Hitchhiking for Dummies*, no OBE's or knighthoods for services to hitchhiking.

Not surprisingly, then, nobody has ever published an authoritative history of hitchhiking. People must have been begging rides ever since one person had transport and another didn't. Hitchhiking as we understand it, though, seems to have been born with, or shortly after, the automobile. John T. Schlebecker, writing in *The Historian* in 1958 said, "Hitchhiking probably began during the First World War [among soldiers], but the art apparently declined immediately thereafter. It was taken up again in the 1920's, with strong overtones of adventure. In 1921, J. K. Christian won membership in the Chicago Adventurer's Club by hitchhiking 3,023 miles in 27 days," an astonishing rate of progress considering the roads of the time, and the small number of cars.

In the twenties, Schlebecker suggests, a slight depression, the land boom in Florida, and the growing number of cars spurred a rapid increase in the number of hitchhikers, who were now being noticed by the police, the press and by self-appointed keepers of public morals. In 1925 the *New York Times* editorialized, "Most of these people...are not dangerous. They are simply immeasurably impudent." The *New Republic* estimated in 1931 that 300 miles a day in the West and 250 in the East were considered average—not a bad rate of progress even today. I've done 600 miles in a day, but it was a long, long day.

A remarkable number of these early references mention women. As early as 1927 the *New Masses* wrote, "Most young janes have their heads full of a trip to Paris, or a hitchhike through New England." In a series of short stories for *the Saturday Evening Post*, Booth Jameson chose as heroines a pair of girl hitchhikers who worked as waitresses up and down the coast between New York and Florida. Claudette Colbert and Clark Gable hitched in the 1934 movie *It Happened One Night*. The Baltimore *Sun* reported in 1933 that "New England...is filled with young men and young women who are continually thumbing their way from one camp to another," like early Grateful Dead fans.

The Great Depression forced hordes onto the roads. As part of the New Deal, a Transient Bureau between 1933 and 1936 established and ran some 300 centers for the care and shelter of transients—the infrastructure of hitchhiking. Still a mix, though: hobos, people looking for work or relatives, college students out for adventure, children hitching to places of recreation. "In fact, during this decade, college men seem to have considered any other form of travel as slightly reprehensible," suggests Schlebecker. By 1937 one writer estimated that at least one man in ten had hitchhiked once in his life.

As the popularity of hitchhiking rose, so did the number of stories of crimes by and against hitchhikers. "Every imaginable type of nastiness, cruelty and brutality was perpetrated by hikers," writes Schlebecker, adding perceptively that such crimes were thought particularly despicable—and therefore particularly newsworthy—because they had been committed by those who had been befriended. The new laws prohibiting hitchhiking were supposed to protect motorists, but were actually heavily supported by public-transport companies: one electric railway claimed to have lost more than $50,000 from hitchhikers in only one year.

Hitchhiking was officially prohibited by the Army and the Air Force in orders going as far back as 1936 for being "unmilitary" and "a discredit to the service." All the same, during and after WW II the Defense Victory Ride Program, organized under the auspices of the Good Neighbor Association, aimed to enlist "an army of civilian motorists engaged in giving the uniformed men a lift, to and from their destination, whenever possible," and if they couldn't offer a lift, giving the V for Victory sign to boost the GI's morale. By 1944, more hitchhikers were on the road than ever before, especially because of gasoline rationing. Even Emily Post, mistress of manners, approved of female defense plant workers hitching to and from work.

In the conservative fifties, hitching came under sustained public attack from newspapers, magazines, automobile clubs, and the FBI. In this climate, some hitchhikers may have abandoned their art but others, typically, simply took it farther. Andrew Tangelos, a retired diplomat, told me that when he graduated from high school in 1953 and went down to interview at Harvard, he hitched there and, following his usual practice, found a used car lot and slept in the backseat of a car. The same decade saw a boom in hitchhiking memoirs, such as Joseph Bormel's *Around the World on Fifty Dollars*, Donald Knies's *Walk the Wide World*, and *Harvard Interlude*, in which Charles Stone Borden writes about his travels with his friend Paul Southwick across the U.S. in 1941. "The most obvious conclusion to draw from our experiences on the road is that the proletariat is our friend, the Good Samaritan, while the bourgeoisie are implacable enemies. The latter fly by in their shiny cars and look at us, if at all, with curiosity, animosity, or at best, indifference."

In *Black Like Me* (1960), John Howard Griffin, a middle-class white sociologist who had his skin turned black in a series of surgical maneuvers, wrote about hitching through the South. "In a car at night visibility is reduced. A man will reveal himself in the dark, which gives an illusion of anonymity, more than he will in the bright light." (He went on: "Some were shamelessly open, some shamelessly subtle. All showed morbid curiosity about the sexual life of the Negro.")

I don't know when the hitchhiking boom of the sixties began, nor why, nor how many people were on the roads at any given moment. In 1970, the *New York Times* reported that each summer at least three to four million hitchhikers were on the European roads; but in 1970, I was on the roads, and nobody counted me or anyone else I know. Here's one thought, though. Hitchhiking has always offered a chance for young adults to prove ourselves. If at any given period the way to personhood and respect is to get a steady job or start a family, then working in a bank is a way of proving ourselves. Hitchhiking rose rapidly at a time, and in a constituency, when we needed to prove that we were *not* good citizens, capable wage earners, good parents, good team players, loyal employees, because those qualities seemed to lead to the problem, not the solution. We proved ourselves on the opposite scale—as travelers and individualists, paupers and outsiders.

Yet hitchhiking was always as pragmatic as it was romantic. In 1973 the city of Fort Collins, Colorado, adopted a legalized and controlled hitchhiking system, and after nine months the hitchhiking co-op had 2,600 members, with no reported complaints. Marin County, California devised a similar plan, and something along the same lines was included in a report produced by the University of Colorado-Denver for the U.S. Department of Commerce.

The Denver report, by the way, tried to assess just how dangerous hitchhiking was. The Los Angeles Police Department announced that 22.6 percent of rapes involved hitchhikers, even though no official statistics on violent crime include under what circumstances the crime was committed. The California Highway Patrol concluded that hitchhiking contributed to .6 percent of all crime in California. When researchers pinned down the District Attorney of Adams County, though, he had to admit that in ten years as a D. A. he had come across only two cases of violence involving hitchhikers, both of which involved a driver robbing someone he had picked up.

Countless novels and nonfiction works included hitchhiking in a glamorous or casual way. An anthology of poems about hitchhiking was published in 1969. There was even a comic for and about hitchhiking called *Hit The Road*, published in 1971 in—not surprisingly—Berkeley.

But a boom in hitchhiking always seems to be accompanied by a backlash of warnings. From the early 1970s on, an almost constant stream of anti-hitching propaganda appeared in newspapers and magazines and on television: "Hitchhiking: Road to Rape"; "Hitchhiking—Too Often the Last Ride"; "Hitchhiking: The Road to Rape and Murder"; "Thumbs Down." In 1977, the Los Angeles City Schools produced a pamphlet called "The free rider: hitchhiking, can you afford the risk?" The Walt Disney company seems to have been especially alarmed. In one of the most bizarre anthologies imaginable, Disney released the cautionary after-school special *Andrea's Story—A Hitchhiking Tragedy* on the same video-cassette as *20,000 Leagues Under the Sea,* the latter presumably intended as a warning not to hitchhike by submarine.

Most astonishing is the way hitchhiking was lumped together with a hair-raising list of social deviations. In 1973 the sociologists Greenley and Rice of the University of Wisconsin wrote that women hitchhiking constituted "quasi-deviant behavior," even though two-thirds of the female university students they surveyed had hitchhiked, which would seem to imply that *not* hitchhiking was the deviant form. None of the respondents reported ever having been raped, attacked, or kidnapped. In 1986, the McGruff drug-prevention and child-protection program (format: 2 sound cassettes, 1 hand puppet, 1 teacher's guide) lumped hitchhiking together with child molestation, child abuse, alcohol, drugs, vandalism, robbery and burglary, marijuana, gangs, shoplifting, inhalants, arson, cocaine, and crack.

I don't know why hitchhiking fell out of fashion. All the aforementioned propaganda can't have helped, but I suspect it's also because the eighties destroyed the solidarity of misfortune: no self-respecting student wanted to look poor, to be thought a loser. Nowadays, when we do hear of a hitchhiker, it's almost always in terms of disaster: nothing is more reassuring, in a twisted way, than something that confirms our opinions, even if what it reinforces is fear. Perhaps the most famous recent American hitchhiker is Chris McCandless, in Jon Krakauer's *Into The Wild* (1996), who had so imperfect a sense of danger and his own limits that he froze to death in Alaska.

~

Product Testing Notes

By the end of the trip, the equipment and clothing I was using regularly had been whittled down to the following items, indispensible for the next generation of hitchhikers:

Sandals: Teva Terradactyl. In Canada after a long wait on a hot day, I put my feet up on the dash and caught of whiff of the most nauseating rancid stench, which I thought was the Tevas decomposing. Turned out to be my feet. $65. Eastern Mountain Sports, South Burlington (EMS).

Pants: Ex Officio microfiber parachute pants. Light, cool, dry instantly, Velcro cargo pocket the right size for notebook. $59. EMS.

Pen: Dr. Grip by Pilot. People seem to either like chubby pens or hate them, but it felt companionable and never leaked. Only shortcoming: hard to keep it behind your ear. $5.99. Staples.

Notebook: *The Small Travel Journal* by Graphic Image, Inc. Best notebook I've ever owned—beautiful, light, well-bound, the perfect balance between suppleness and stiffness—but at $19.95 it should be. Barnes & Noble.

Tape recorder: Wretched, battered old Panasonic. Made everyone sound as if they're being interviewed while pacing about in a huge revolving drum of corn flakes, but good portable cassette recorders seem to be a thing of the past. Paid $80 or so for it. Can't remember where.

Shorts: for dry weather, Royal Robbins heavy cotton. Backside pocket (with Velcro) so deep it'll hold a road map. $48. EMS. For wet weather, Columbia nylon. Dry quickly, double as swim trunks. $15. Pre-season sale, Phil's Trading Post, Essex Junction, Vermont.

Belt: Patagonia nylon webbing. Never let me down in times of crisis. Light, washable. $10, plus or minus. EMS.

Backpack: EMS 3000LT. Worked remarkably well considering it was being used by someone (a) with a history of back problems and (b) who stuffed far too much into it. Imagine how amazing it would have been if I'd gone back and had all the straps tuned up. $99.50. EMS.

Rain jacket: EMS Gore-Tex. A wonderful piece of contemporary clothing technology, but I can't help thinking that if I'd needed to, I could have found something half as good for a tenth the price. $300. EMS.

Jeans: Wrangler. $13. 2-for-1 sale, Ames, Essex Junction.

Shirt: Gramicci microfiber. Took other shirts, but gave up wearing them. Of all my high-tech equipment, the most worthwhile. $54. EMS.

Sneakers: Nike Air. Light and comfortable. Survived the trip, then blew out both sides on the tennis court. $5. Tent sale at Mills & Greer, South Burlington.

Antihistamine: Allegra.

ACKNOWLEGMENTS

This trip and this book would not have been possible without the self-lessness of my wife, Barbara, who kept home and family running when I was away. There should be a Guild of Travel Writers' Wives, who are awarded royalties of their own. Thanks also to two editors, Gail Hudson, who asked tough questions, and Oliver Payne at NATIONAL GEOGRAPHIC, who was not just an honest, encouraging, and intelligent editor, but a partner in crime. Tomasz Tomaszewski suggested the title, Chris Pedler and Seth Martin contributed valuable research, and Andrew Hendrickson recovered the first five chapters after they'd vanished off my hard drive.

ABOUT THE AUTHOR

TIM BROOKES was born in London, but now lives on a dirt road in Vermont with his wife and daughters. He is the author of two previous books, *Catching My Breath: An Asthmatic Explores his Illness* and *Signs of Life: A Memoir of Dying and Discovery*. He is currently working on a subjective geography of Lake Champlain. He teaches at the University of Vermont, and if he had any sense he'd hitchhike to work.

Predicting
New Words

The Secrets of Their Success

Allan Metcalf

Houghton Mifflin Company
Boston New York

Visit our website: www.houghtonmifflinbooks.com

Library of Congress Cataloging-in-Publication Data

Metcalf, Allan A.
    Predicting new words : the secrets of their success / Allan Metcalf.
      p. cm.
    Includes index.
    ISBN 0-618-13006-3
    1. English language—New words. 2. Lexicology. I. Title.

PE1583.M48 2002
420′.014—dc21

2002068583

Manufactured in the United States of America

QUM 10 9 8 7 6 5 4 3 2 1

For Molly
Now it's your turn!

Contents

Introduction

I knew it was an outrageous idea. But it just might work.

If *Time* magazine could choose a Person of the Year for its year-end review, why couldn't the American Dialect Society choose a New Word of the Year? We didn't have the clout or circulation of *Time,* but our little group of people curious about the English language in North America did have the leading experts on new words — scholars who studied new words and dictionary editors who were on the lookout for new words.

We had, in particular, John Algeo, who with his wife Adele edited the column "Among the New Words" in the society's quarterly journal, *American Speech.* Each installment contained dozens of freshly gathered new words too recent to appear in any dictionary.

We also had David K. Barnhart, managing editor since 1982 of the *Barnhart Dictionary Companion,* the only periodical devoted to new words. It was founded and edited by his father, the eminent dictionary editor Clarence L. Barnhart. Each quarterly issue contained detailed evidence and definitions for hundreds of new words.

The idea to make use of their talents came to me in

midsummer 1990. As executive secretary of the American Dialect Society, I was arranging the details for our annual meeting in December. With the guidance of these experts, I thought, we could choose the new words that mattered most in the year gone by and proclaim them. I wrote to Algeo and Barnhart, and they agreed.

MAKING HISTORY

And so on December 29, 1990, at 7 p.m. in the St. Clair Room of the Barclay Hotel in Chicago, history of a sort was made. As I had anticipated, the nominations for New Word of the Year were intriguing and the debate was vigorous. As I had not anticipated, however, the results were anything but predictable. I had imagined that the experts would present us with a few candidates of obvious importance, words headed straight for our everyday vocabulary and secure places in the dictionaries. Instead, the experts presented us with many words, none of which seemed more important than any of the others.

So it was that after spirited discussion of words in various categories — Most Original, Most Outrageous, Most Useful, Most Amazing, Most Unnecessary, and Most Likely to Succeed — the assembled members and friends of the American Dialect Society voted the New Word of the Year 1990: *bushlips.*

What's that? Hardly anyone knew it, even then. *Bushlips,* we were told, meant "insincere political rhetoric." It referred to President George H. Bush's declaration, "Read my lips: no new taxes," a promise he had broken in approving a tax increase in 1990. The word caught members' attention because of its cleverness and the point it made about politicians. Even in 1990, though, it was not at all well known or widely used. Since then, instead of ending up in dictionaries, it has ended up on the ash heap of history.

RAISING QUESTIONS

From these obscure beginnings this book was born. I didn't know it at the time, but the questions raised by the choice of *bushlips* and by subsequent Words of the Year were challenging enough that they required a whole book to do them justice. This is that book.

The very first New Words of the Year vote raised puzzling questions. We know that hundreds of new words enter the vocabulary every year — words like *jazz* in 1913, *hijack* in 1923, *supermarket* in 1933, *acronym* in 1943, *UFO* in 1953, just to take a few examples from earlier in the twentieth century. So where were the words of 1990 that would become part of our vocabulary? Why hadn't the experts identified them?

One of the subcategories in that first New Words of the Year selection was Most Likely to Succeed. Maybe long-lived words could be found there. In 1990 there were two winners in that category: *notebook PC* and *rightsizing*. Neither has been especially stellar since. The former term, designating a lightweight portable computer, has had staying power, although nowadays it is usually referred to simply as a *notebook*. The latter was noted as a euphemism for firing employees to make a company the "right size." That term still has marginal use, but it is far lesser known than the more direct *downsizing*.

Even in 1990, incidentally, it was clear that *Word* in *New Word of the Year* would have to be interpreted in its broader sense as "vocabulary item" — not just words, but phrases (like *notebook PC*), acronyms (like *PC*), prefixes (like *e-* to indicate something in the world of the Internet), and suffixes (like *-gate* to indicate a scandal), because units of meaning do not always correspond to single words. That wasn't a problem. The problem was to find the right vocabulary items, the truly significant ones that would take root in the language and continue to be used for generations. It was apparent that we had no way of doing this, no guidelines to follow. We just guessed. And we were often wrong.

With the benefit of hindsight, we now know that a more significant 1990 entry in the vocabulary was the prefix *e-*, applied not just to *e-mail* (in use since 1982) but *e-text* and later *e-payment, e-commerce, e-currency,* and the like. According to a 2001 note in the *Oxford English Dictionary,* this *e-* was "perhaps the most productive element in word-formation of the late 1990s and early 2000s." But none of the experts proposed *e-* for the 1990 vote.

MOTHER OF ALL NEW WORDS

Still, we kept trying. For 1991 we chose a more popular item: *mother of all.* This was a translation of a phrase used by Saddam Hussein on January 16, 1991, in response to the attack by the international coalition at the start of the Gulf War: "The mother of all battles has begun." With Saddam's quick defeat in that war, the phrase just as quickly became ironic and was applied to matters of lesser as well as greater import. It still is today, for example, in *mother of all search engines, mother of all excuses, mother of all actuarial glossaries,* and *mother of all paellas* (Valencian paella), phrases I have found by searching the Internet. So *mother of all* was, and remains, fairly successful.

We now know that for 1991 we also could have chosen *carjacking, ethnic cleansing,* and *FAQ,* as well as *spam,* in the sense of junk e-mail. But *mother of all* wasn't too bad, and for Most Likely to Succeed in 1991, our choice was *rollerblade.* That too remains in today's vocabulary and marks a case in which a successful trademark has gained a generic use. Perhaps we had found the way to pinpoint significant words.

Not! That expression of dramatic negation, as in *That's a great idea. Not!,* was the Word of the Year for 1992. It was also an indication that we were back to our losing ways. *Not!* was indeed a popular expression that year, made famous by *Saturday Night Live* and the movie *Wayne's World,* but as we soon discovered, it was anything but new. Jesse Sheidlower, now head of the American office of the *Oxford English Dictionary,* and Jonathan Lighter, editor of the *Random House Historical Dictionary of American Slang,* soon found evidence of the same *Not!,* with slightly different punctuation, in a Princeton University student publication of 1893, and with the exact modern punctuation in 1905. F. Scott Fitzgerald and Rex Stout had used it, too, in the intervening years.

So another puzzle had emerged. A word we had crowned New Word of the Year was a century old. How could something so old have escaped the notice of the experts for so long?

Our 1992 choice for Most Likely to Succeed was fairly successful: *snail mail,* or *s-mail.* While the abbreviated *s-mail* (patterned after *e-mail)* is not widely used today, the rhyming *snail mail* for physically delivered mail remains common. As a supposed new word, though, it too had a problem with age, though compared with *Not!* it was a mere youth. *Snail mail* goes back at least as far as 1983 (and in the *New York Times* at that), nearly a decade before it was the society's choice as a New Word of the Year.

With the benefit of hindsight, we now know that 1992 made a more significant contribution to the vocabulary. That was apparently the year *cyber* became an adjective, able to stand by itself in referring to anything related to computers. The society did recognize it as Word of the Year — in 1994.

Questions about our judgment continued to be raised by our choices for 1993. The New Word (or Phrase) of that year was *information superhighway,* a term for the Internet popularized by newly elected Vice President Al

Gore. Even in 1993, however, *information superhighway* never posed a serious challenge to the name *Internet*, and it faded from use along with Gore's involvement in promoting the Internet. There was also the question of whether *information superhighway* was a new term. Gore claimed to have invented it some fifteen years earlier, and he was indeed an active promoter of Internet use and high-speed Internet connections from the time he became a member of the House of Representatives in 1976. The earliest evidence unearthed so far for *information super-highway* is from 1988, but even that is five years before it was chosen as our New Word (or Phrase) of the Year. Once again, the new-word experts were behind the curve.

Most Likely to Succeed presented the same problem that year. Our choice was none other than *like* used to introduce a thought or quotation, as in "I'm *like*, 'This is such a great idea!'" That *like* has indeed continued in widespread use. The only problem is that it had been in widespread use earlier than 1993 — since 1982, at least.

NO LONGER NEW

By the mid-nineties, in fact, the difficulty of finding truly new words led to a change in the policy for the annual vote. Now, instead of New Words of the Year, the vote was simply for Words of the Year, characterized as words that were new "or newly prominent" in the year just past. That change took care of the embarrassment of repeatedly discovering that "new" words weren't so new, but it only highlighted the question: Why was it so hard to recognize significant new words from the beginning?

Nobody ventured answers, and the society continued to make what might be called schizophrenic choices, exemplified by the 1995 voting that ended in a tie between *World Wide Web* and *newt*. The former was well known but not that new; the latter was brand new but not that well known. *World Wide Web* was also chosen, justifiably, as Most Likely to Succeed. That was a safe enough bet after it had been around and developing for a few years; the Web itself, as well as its name, was invented by Tim Berners-Lee (with help from Robert Cailliau) in 1990.

Newt, on the other hand, was new but so obscure, even at the time, that it required explanation. After the Republicans thrashed the Democrats in the elections of November 1994, Newt Gingrich, Republican from Georgia, became Speaker of the U.S. House of Representatives. He was an outspoken advocate of a Republican "Contract with America" that attempted to drastically curtail government expenses and operations. The verb *newt* appeared in 1995 and meant to make aggressive changes, especially reductions in government. But the Contract with America soon ran out of steam, and after the Republicans lost their majority in the House of Representatives in the 1998 elections, Gingrich's star faded, and *newting* faded with it.

The story has remained much the same with the Society's choices to the present day. (For a complete list of American Dialect Society Words of the Year through 2001, see the appendix.)

QUESTIONS AND ANSWERS

By this point, the Words of the Year experiences had evoked a whole cluster of questions:

> Why are prominent new words often just a flash in the pan?
> Why are not-so-prominent new words often the most successful?
> Why do successful new words often turn out to be older than we thought?
> And above all: How can one pick the winners? What are the qualities that make for success?

Enough information has accumulated over the years to make it conceivable that some answers can be found, that a crystal ball can be fashioned that will help predict which words will succeed. Perhaps some criteria can be crystallized for choosing the enduring words from the crowd of transient ones. Perhaps, indeed, some criteria can be identified that will help someone who wants to coin a new word and make a success of it.

This book is my attempt to answer these questions and determine these criteria. My method is to review the case histories of numerous words — not only those chosen by the American Dialect Society, but many others — to see if they have anything in common. As it turns out, they do.

A well-known linguist (but no one remembers who!) once said: Each word has its own history. A well-known author (Tolstoy) once said: All happy families are alike; each unhappy family is unhappy in its own way. Borrowing from both authors, I think it can be said: Each new word has its own history, but successful new words are alike in ways that promote their success, while unsuccessful new words are alike in ways that promote their failure.

The rest of this book will explain why this is so.

A Note on Sources

The sea of new words would quickly drown any investigator were it not for the life rafts, arks, and cruise ships provided by researchers past and present.

The ark that preserves more of the English language than any other is the *Oxford English Dictionary*. Its capacious volumes (originally ten, now twenty) hold three hundred thousand separate entries with two and a half million quotations to illustrate the origins and histories of words. Although some of the entries were written as long ago as 1884, the dictionary is now being completely revised to bring it up to date. As befits a twenty-first-century work, it has shed its paper form and become ethereal, available by subscription on the World Wide Web. This allows the revisions to be posted and available for inspection almost as soon as they are made.

Two current historical dictionaries of American English are modern cruise ships that hold words beyond the scope of the *Oxford English Dictionary*. There is the *Dictionary of American Regional English*, edited by Frederic G. Cassidy and Joan H. Hall (Harvard University Press, 1985–), now in four volumes from A through the middle of the letter S, and the *Random House Historical Dictionary of American Slang*, edited by Jonathan Lighter (1994–), in two volumes, A through O.

Books specifically about new words are abundant, but few have reliable historical information. The most useful are the Barnhart series, culminating in the *Third Barnhart Dictionary of New English* by Robert K. Barnhart, Sol Steinmetz, and Clarence L. Barnhart (Wilson, 1990), and the two editions of the *Oxford Dictionary of New Words* (Oxford University Press, 1992 and 1997), different in content though they have the same title.

Two periodicals, mentioned earlier, keep track of new words and their histories: the *Barnhart Dictionary Companion*, a quarterly journal edited by David K. Barnhart, and "Among the New Words," a column now edited by Wayne Glowka in the American Dialect Society's quarterly journal *American Speech*. A collection of those columns from their beginning has been published as *Fifty Years Among the New Words: A Dictionary of Neologisms, 1941–1991* (Cambridge University Press, 1991), edited by John Algeo, who also provides a valuable interpretive overview. Numerous other articles on new words and their origins have appeared in *American Speech*. The most notable are Allen Walker Read's five articles on the origins, history, and folklore of *OK*, published in 1963 and 1964.

The volume on my new-words bookshelf I turn to most often is an index to all the rest: *The Barnhart New-Words*

Concordance by David K. Barnhart (Lexik House, 1994, with a 2001 supplement).

Stories of older new words are found in *The Merriam-Webster New Book of Word Histories* (1991) and *Coined by Shakespeare: Words and Meanings First Used by the Bard* by Jeffrey McQuain and Stanley Malless (Merriam-Webster, 1998). New words of a century ago are brought to life in *Word-Coinage: Being an Inquiry into Recent Neologisms, Also a Brief Study of Literary Style, Slang, and Provincialisms* by Leon Mead (Crowell, 1902). The master storyteller about words of American English is H. L. Mencken. The final revision of his classic book *The American Language* is the one-volume abridgment by Raven I. McDavid, Jr. (Knopf, 1963).

The most important current publication on the origins and history of American slang is the monthly *Comments on Etymology,* edited and published by Gerald Cohen at the University of Missouri–Rolla. Amazingly, it has a subscriber list of less than a hundred.

Only a few scholars have ventured to propose factors that make for the success of new words. One is Göran Kjellmer, whose article "Potential Words" in the journal *Word* for August 2000 also reviews previous proposals. He and I reach different conclusions.

Along with books and periodicals, there is the Internet, my other major source of everything but the kitchen sink, and sometimes even that. In particular, the Internet makes possible extensive searches for examples of how words are actually used today. I have searched the two billion pages indexed by Google.com countless times to find current uses of words under discussion.

Acknowledgments

People as well as publications have helped make this book possible. First of all there are those who attended the 1999 meeting of the Dictionary Society of North America and gave me their reactions when I proposed the first version of what I now call the FUDGE scale.

Almost every day since, I have become further indebted to members of the American Dialect Society: those who join in the search for Words of the Year at the society's annual meeting and especially the members of the society's e-mail discussion list, ADS-L. Among those who dive deep for the origins of words and report their findings on ADS-L are Fred Shapiro of the law library at Yale University and the tireless researcher Barry Popik of New York City. I am particularly grateful for Barry's extensive postings on *scofflaw* and *OK*.

Then there are the indispensable people who helped directly with the making of this book. As usual, I thought it would be easy, and as usual, I learned better. Sustaining me through two years of effort was my editor at Houghton Mifflin, Joseph Pickett, who patiently insisted not only that I get it written, but that I get it right. He was indefatigable in asking for revision after revision and bringing me back to my point when I began to stray from it. At key moments his colleagues Steve Kleinedler and David Pritchard also provided important inspiration.

Others at Houghton Mifflin who helped bring this book into being were Margaret Anne Miles, senior art and production coordinator, and publicist Gracie Doyle. Diane Fredrick did a meticulous job copyediting the manuscript. I appreciate them all.

My thanks also go to Mary Ellen Blackston of Henry Pfeiffer Library at MacMurray College, who cheerfully obtained through interlibrary loan all manner of articles and books for me. I appreciate William DeSilva, who provided stimulating conversation almost every day of the week while keeping my office clean. I am grateful for my reliable and creative student assistant Erin Klee, who kept the office running, reformatted the manuscript at deadline, and told me about *skategate*. And as always I appreciate my wife, Donna, for her relentless insistence on readability and excellence.

And now it's time to meet the new words. They're a hard bunch to pin down. They come and go, and just when you think you have them in focus, they're likely to jump up and move around. But it's possible to gain an understanding of them in their native habitat all the same. Let's take a look.

1

The Mystery of Success

The history of new words is largely a tale of failure. New words are as numerous and evanescent as straws in the wind. They are like acorns, not many of which grow into oaks. Sometimes it seems as if a new word has about as much chance of developing into a permanent addition to our vocabulary as a single sperm has of fertilizing an egg and developing into a fully grown human. New words don't have it quite that bad, but the odds are strongly against them.

On the other hand, new words are not like new babies. Each day in the United States more than ten thousand babies are born. Nearly all of those, about 99 percent of each day's ten thousand, survive and thrive. Similarly, each day in the English language at least as many thousands of new words are born. Yet after a year's time, only a few hundred of these will remain as serious candidates for the dictionary and a place in our permanent vocabulary. Here is the mystery: Why so many and yet so few? And is it possible to predict which few will be successful? Thanks to vastly increased knowledge about words and their histories, it is now possible to answer both questions: the first with good reasons, the second with "Yes." That's what the rest of this book will do.

Words are not living things. Yet new words appear to undergo a Darwinian struggle of survival of the fittest. As with living creatures, the fittest often are not the biggest and flashiest, but rather those best able to camouflage themselves.

Each word has its own history. So this book will proceed case by case. But from these individual examples will emerge the general principles that not only explain the secrets of successful words but establish a five-item scale that enables precise predictions of the future success or failure of new words. This will provide the opportunity to evaluate some recent candidates for their probable staying power. After that, it will take just forty years to see if the predictions come true.

BACK TO THE FIFTIES

That's because it takes about two generations to know for sure whether a word will be a permanent addition to the vocabulary. The investigation of new word successes and failures, then, needs to begin at least forty years back.

New in 1957, *moonlighting* and *sputnik* both were inspired by lights in the nighttime sky, but only one prevailed in the lexicon. *Moonlighting* derived from a familiar word that underwent a metamorphosis of meaning that year, and this new meaning has become firmly established. *Sputnik,* on the other hand, was not at all familiar, and it proved to be just a brilliant flash in the pan, surviving only as a historical relic.

Time for Moonlighting

Moonlight, of course, was anything but new to the vocabulary, but it gained a brand new meaning in 1957 as the verb *to moonlight* and its related noun, *moonlighting.*

Time magazine, then as now a spotter of trends and showplace of smart vocabulary, beamed *moonlighting* at its readers in its issue of July 22, 1957. It probably was not the first appearance of this old word with its new meaning, but this seems to have been its debut with the general public. According to *Time*, it was in fact not just a new name, but a new trend and a new concern. "MOON-LIGHTING," proclaimed the headline: "A Problem Born of Prosperity." The editors evidently thought the word was unfamiliar enough to require a definition, so *Time* provided one in the first sentence of the story: "One of the paradoxes — and problems — of the U.S. full-employment prosperity is moonlighting, i.e., holding two jobs at once." The article continued with statements like these:

> "Now one in 18 U.S. workers is a moonlighter. . . ."
> "To Columnist Abigail Van Buren a wife complained about her moonlighting husband. . . ."
> "In some lower-salaried groups, or those with short hours, moonlighting is already traditional."
> "The amount a man makes on his regular job does not necessarily determine whether he moonlights."
> "Furthermore, moonlighting is a powerful argument in itself against the shorter week, and against short hours v. the acquisitive nature of man."

All told, the article used *moonlighting* or its relatives *moonlighters* and *moonlight* sixteen times. By the end of the article, the reader had been thoroughly moonstruck.

As a noun, *moonlight* goes back with the moon itself to the beginnings of the English language and even earlier to the Germanic and Indo-European ancestors of English. Presumably ever since humans could speak, they have talked about the light of the moon. As a verb, *to moonlight* is more recent, but it still goes back to the nineteenth century. From the start it has meant doing something by the light of the moon, but at first this was something that could get one arrested. In the nineteenth century, *moonlight* was a slang term for the activity of burglars, who benefited from moonlight at their work. In the twentieth century, it was also used for herding cattle and hunting deer by moonlight. Whether it was the illegal work that in 1957 caused the transmutation of *moonlight* into a standard term for legal work, or whether this new meaning was independently derived from the original *moonlight,* nobody knows. And it doesn't matter much. Either way, *moonlight* meaning "the light of the moon" easily took on its second meaning of "to work a second job," and Americans have been moonlighting ever since. This second meaning seems likely to stay in the vocabulary, as long as people continue to hold down second jobs.

The Traveler

In 1957 a momentous event in the night sky brought another change to our language. It came in a wake-up call from space, first heard at 8:07 p.m. Eastern Time on Friday, October 4, 1957. The NBC and CBS networks interrupted their television and radio programs to broadcast live the pinging signal received from the first artificial satellite in history as it passed over the United States for the first time. To a startled world, the Soviet Union announced that the signal came from a sphere 22 inches in diameter and weighing 184 pounds, which was circling the earth every hour and a half at an altitude of 500 miles.

What should this new creation be called? On its front page the next day, the *New York Times* used terms like *man-made earth satellite, artificial moon, artificial satellite,* and, quoting the Soviet news agency Tass, *artificial earth satellite.* Most often it was simply *satellite,* the term still used today.

But we also learned the Russian word for it. By the following day, the *Times* was explaining the word to its readers: "To a Russian, the earth satellite launched by the Soviet Union is 'something that is traveling with a traveler.'

That is the literal translation of *sputnik,* the Russian word for the satellite." And while the *Times* continued to use *satellite,* others quickly made *sputnik* at home in our language. In its first two articles on the event, *Time* magazine used the Russian word exclusively after introducing it with a brief translation. "Highly surprised scientists and military men drew some quick lessons from sputnik's success," wrote *Time,* and "U.S. intelligence had no warning of the firing of the sputnik," and "In choosing an orbit for the sputnik, the Russians were daring." The first example from *Time* uses *sputnik* like a proper name, without *the,* but the rest of *Time*'s discussion makes *sputnik* a generic word, with an article and no capital letter. It took just that long (in *Time*'s reckoning) for *sputnik* to make itself at home in our vocabulary.

In Russian, the *s* of *sputnik* means "together," *put* means "path or road," *nik* means "someone who." Together, therefore, they mean "one who travels along" (with the earth, in this case). As a professor at Clinton College explained in a letter to the *New York Times* in November, "*sputnik* is the technical term for an astronomical satellite; preferably one of second and not of first degree. That is — the moon is not, in the narrower sense, a *sputnik;* but asteroids flying about the earth would be." (*Sputnik* is also not to be confused with *popútchik,* another Russian word that translates as "fellow traveler" but means a non-Communist who sympathizes with Communism.)

In adopting *sputnik* we pronounced it our own way. The Clinton College professor admonished, in vain, that "the 'u' in *sputnik* is approximately as the 'oo' in 'hoot.' All those who are rendering it as the 'u' in 'but' are actually talking Bulgarian, not Russian." But at that point *sputnik* wasn't just a visitor from Russia; we were adopting it into our own language, and an adopted word has to play by our rules. So in English it kept the sound of *but* or *sputter.*

A Dog's Tale

The Russian *sputniks* inspired first awe, then humor. The humor came with the launch of the second *Sputnik* on November 4, 1957. This one orbited at more than 900 miles high, weighed more than a thousand pounds, and carried a dog.

That shaggy dog story was irresistible for the wags in the media. *Time* admiringly noted that newspapers nicknamed the satellite *muttnik, pupnik, poochnik, woofnik,* and *sputpup.* That creativity, in turn, inspired the addition of the suffix *-nik* to anything associated with satellites. In the journal *American Speech,* Louise M. Ackerman noted the use of *puffnik* for a flare rocket, *mousenik* for a rocket designed by schoolboys that carried a mouse, and *spooknik* for a "ghost" radio image of Sputnik I. Other inventive combinations with the Russian (and Yiddish) suffix *-nik* included *kaputnik, flopnik, stayputnik,* and *dudnik* when the first American attempt to send a satellite into space, a Vanguard rocket, fizzled on its launching pad on December 6, 1957.

So *sputnik* took on the extended meaning of any artificial satellite, even an American one. Although the word

sputnik

satellite was never entirely displaced, the Russian *sputniks* had a lead of nearly four months before the first American satellite went up on January 31, 1958, so the talk of the time increasingly used *sputnik* for all artificial satellites.

That it was an important word was immediately apparent to those who make dictionaries. One even stopped the presses for it. Upon hearing the news and the name *sputnik*, Clarence L. Barnhart, editor-in-chief of the *Thorndike-Barnhart Comprehensive Desk Dictionary*, pulled the page where *sputnik* would appear, consigned a lesser word to oblivion, and inserted a three-line definition of *sputnik* in its place. Only then would he allow the new printing of the *Thorndike-Barnhart* to proceed.

As the most talked-about phenomenon in the heavens, with a comfortable Englished pronunciation, and drawing further attention to itself with lots of wordplay, *sputnik* seemed a sure bet for permanent residence in the English vocabulary. To this day it is listed in every general dictionary. But where it used to be considered a synonym for *satellite*, as is still the case in *Merriam-Webster's Collegiate Dictionary*, nowadays most dictionaries limit its definition just to those early Soviet versions. The fourth edition of the *American Heritage Dictionary*, for example, defines *sputnik* simply as "Any of a series of Soviet satellites sent into Earth orbit, especially the first, launched October 4, 1957."

In 1997, forty years after the first *sputnik*, a replica built by Russian and French teenagers was launched into orbit from the Mir space station. By then *Sputnik* was always spelled with a capital letter in English and used only as a proper name for the first Russian satellites, never a general word meaning satellite. But back in late 1957, *sputnik* as well as *moonlight* seemed destined to become permanent additions to the English vocabulary. Indeed, at the time, *sputnik* was much more the talk of the country. Why then did *sputnik* fail as a general word while *moonlight* succeeded?

Perhaps it looked too strange. *Moonlight* was an old familiar word; *sputnik* was not only new but decidedly foreign-sounding. English is used to words of many shapes, but the ending *-nik* is not one of them. Only a handful of *-nik* words were already resident in English, all still foreign-looking. There was *nudnik*, Yiddish for a person who is a pest; *kolkhoznik*, a member of a collective farm in Russia; and *kibbutznik*, a member of a collective farm in the new state of Israel. All use *-nik* to indicate a person, not an object in space or elsewhere.

Strangely enough, the only lasting *-nik* coinage apparently inspired by *sputnik* was *beatnik*, invented by *San Francisco Chronicle* columnist Herb Caen for a column on April 2, 1958. Years later Caen explained: "*Beatnik* slipped out of my typewriter one day when I was writing about one or another of the Beat types — Kerouac, Ginsberg et al. — who flourished here at the time." This is what slipped out of his typewriter on that occasion:

> Look *magazine, preparing a picture spread on S.F.'s Beat Generation (oh, no, not AGAIN!), hosted a party in a No. Beach house for 50 Beatniks, and by the time word got around the sour grapevine, over 250 bearded cats and kits were on hand, slopping up Mike Cowles' free booze. They're only Beat, y'know, when it comes to work.*

Why did *beatnik* survive when *sputnik* didn't? Perhaps just because *beatnik* is an offbeat word, appropriate for describing an offbeat person.

In turn *beatnik* quickly produced an offspring, *neatnik*, a person who is extremely or obsessively neat. It appeared thus in a 1959 *New York Times* article: "The beatniks and the neatniks had at each other this week." But being just a clever twist on *beatnik*, *neatnik* is little used nowadays.

No More Skyjacking?

Another forty-year-old word referring to the sky is now falling from favor: *skyjacking.*

Is it because the hijacking of airplanes has come to an end? Of course not. The most horrible skyjackings of all time occurred on September 11, 2001, and despite all precautions instituted since that date, there is no way to be sure of preventing future skyjackings.

But the word *skyjacking* itself seems on the way out. It has been around since the first hijackings of American airplanes in 1961 (for flights to Cuba), so it was on the verge of making a permanent place for itself. Recently, however, it seems to be used less and less. Why? Apparently it's too clever, too much of a joke. Even four decades after it was coined, it still is an obvious play on words. The rhyme of *hi* and *sky* makes light of a serious situation. Given its decreasing use, *skyjacking* may well be dropped from future editions of dictionaries, just as *ecofreak, masscult,* and *data diddling* (manipulating or falsifying data) were dropped from the fourth edition of the *American Heritage Dictionary*.

In contrast, *skyjacking*'s cousin, *carjacking,* first used in 1991, does not suffer from over-cleverness (*car* doesn't rhyme with *hi*). Furthermore, it has developed its own distinct meaning: taking a car from its owner rather than stealing an unoccupied car. So *carjacking* may well survive into a long life, if that unfortunate practice continues.

NINETIES WORDS

The puzzle of prediction is further exemplified by two splendiferous words introduced in the early 1990s: *digerati* and *sylvanshine.*

digerati: Experts in computers and the Internet.
sylvanshine: The reflected glow of some forest trees at night.

There is an unusual opportunity to examine these particular words closely, because it is known exactly how they each originated. A decade is not enough time to tell whether a new word will be a success, but an out-and-out failure would be apparent by now. To date, one of these words has held on to its tenuous place in present-day use, while the other has sunk utterly from sight.

The two words had equally glittering and reputable beginnings. *Digerati* came first. Like many successful new words, it made its initial appearance without announcement or explication. It was lucky, however, to be born in an upscale neighborhood, the business section of the *New York Times*. On Wednesday, January 29, 1992, in a story about a design for a "radically different supercomputer," it appeared in a somewhat prominent place as the last word of a long paragraph:

> *Igniting the Kendall Square controversy was an article by the economist George Gilder, published this month in a narrowly circulated but closely read Silicon Valley magazine called* Upside. *Mr. Gilder, perhaps best known as the supply-sider whose book* Wealth and Poverty *provided the intellectual underpinnings of the so-called Reagan revolution, has no experience in computer design. But he has written widely on the subject in recent years and his opinions, though often controversial, are taken seriously among the computer digerati.*

Even though the word had never appeared before, its meaning was clear from the context. "Digerati" must refer to people like the knowledgeable readers of *Upside*. That they are experts on computers is clear not only from the identification with the *Upside* readership and from the article's earlier reference to a "community of elite scientists and engineers," but also from placing the word *computer* in front of *digerati*.

And the word itself has elements that associate it with both computers and experts. The first syllable of *digerati* is the same as the first syllable of *digital*, the all-purpose word used to refer to computer technology. (How *digital* developed from fingers to numbers to computers is another story, but the article had already mentioned "a computer designer at Digital Equipment.") The last part of *digerati* is a play on *literati,* a dignified Latin word used in English since 1621 to mean "scholars" or more exactly, "persons of letters" — that is, people really good at reading and writing. Helping the popularity of *literati* was a related coinage, circa 1940, *glitterati,* referring to those that we might nowadays label *celebrities.*

But there was no need to be aware of the sources of *digerati* in order to catch its meaning. The context made it clear.

The Birthing of *Digerati*

Thanks to a later report, we know the exact circumstances of its birth. An editor, Tim Race, introduced the word into the story by John Markoff. Perhaps Markoff had originally written something like "computer literati," a playful substitution of *literati* in the phrase "computer literate." Whatever Markoff wrote, Race took it a step further and ended up with *digerati.* Still, buried deep in a continuation of a story on page B7, *digerati* might have faded from sight after its creation. Such is the usual fate of invented words; the word sparkles and then vanishes from sight, all the more sparkling because of its evanescence.

But in this particular case, the word made friends in high places. Markoff's story happened to be read by the editor-in-chief of Time Warner, Jason McManus, who in turn notified William Safire, language columnist for the *New York Times.* Safire hadn't noticed the new word, but upon learning of it from McManus he inserted a birth announcement in his "On Language" column in the *New York Times Magazine* of March 1, 1992. "It did make me smile with appreciation," McManus wrote to Safire, "in the trust it was Mr. Markoff's invention to lighten up a highly technical story."

Safire investigated and discovered that Markoff had merely provided a foster home for the word; Race was the actual birth parent. So Safire courteously permitted Race to define his creation. *Digerati,* according to Race, are "people highly skilled in the processing and manipulation of digital information; wealthy or scholarly techno-nerds."

Once a word is born it takes on a life of its own, sometimes defying the wishes of its creator, but *digerati* has managed to stick close to its original meaning. The mock elitism of the word, so suited to its meaning, may have encouraged its use. Safire reflects this mockery in his heading: "Dig Those Digerati." Its cleverness, on the other hand, like the punning in *skyjacking,* may keep it so conspicuous that it can't slip into the permanent vocabulary. Whatever the ultimate outcome, *digerati,* with a serious definition now, is ensconced in discussions of the computing world, and in the *American Heritage Dictionary* and other leading dictionaries of the early twenty-first century.

Night Light

Just two years after *digerati,* an even more glittering word was coined. It was based not on computers, but on a natural phenomenon anyone can observe — only in the summertime, to be sure, only at night, only in a forest of blue spruce, and only with a flashlight or automobile headlights. Maybe those special conditions are why nobody had written about this phenomenon before Alistair B. Fraser came along. Fraser, a professor of meteorology at Pennsylvania State University, was driving through the woods of British Columbia one summer night when he noticed the varied effects of his headlights. In the same light, some trees shone brightly, while others remained dark. The headlights weren't flickering. If this wasn't an enchanted forest, what was it?

Fascinated by this mystery that seemed to defy common sense, Fraser returned to spend night after night in the woods, shining a powerful flashlight at different trees and shrubs and measuring their reflection. He discovered that when you shine a light at certain trees and shrubs — blue spruces, yews, and rhododendrons — they don't merely become visible; they light up like Christmas trees, or like snow-covered trees in winter moonlight.

It's a remarkable sight on a warm summer night: a tree that seems to be blanketed in snow. And Fraser arrived at the explanation. It has to do with drops of dew on the leaves acting as mirrors to reflect and diffuse the light. Why just certain trees? Because the reflection depends on the shape of the leaves. When the angle of reflection increases above 140 degrees, as is the case with those particular trees and shrubs, the reflection is spectacular.

All this Professor Fraser explained in the July 1994 edition of the scientific journal *Applied Optics*. And as the first to describe this reflection, Fraser was entitled to name it. He chose a name that, like the glow itself, was strangely beautiful: *sylvanshine*.

Like most new words, *sylvanshine* was based on others that were already well established. *Sylvan*, a poetic word referring to the woods and its inhabitants, dates back more than four hundred years in the English language alone. It traces its origins to ancient Rome; Sylvanus was a Roman god of fields and forests. *Shine* can be both precise and poetic, and goes back even farther in our language, more than a thousand years. Put them together and you have a beautiful word for a beautiful phenomenon.

But there was more to it than that. Fraser had scientific reasons for calling his phenomenon *sylvanshine*. He modeled his word on *Heiligenschein*, the technical term for another optical illusion of the outdoors, namely the bright daylight halo that appears on dewy grass at the edges of a person's shadow. *Heiligenschein* is a German word, *Heiligen* meaning "saint" and *schein* meaning "shine," that is, the shine around a saint's head — in English simply a *halo*. Fraser substituted the woods (*sylvan*) for the saint (*Heiligen*) and changed the spelling of *schein* to its English equivalent, thereby transforming a plain German term to an enchanting English one.

Applied Optics has a limited circle of readers, but Fraser's discovery was spectacular enough to warrant a news report in the June 9, 1994, issue of the widely circulated British journal *Nature*, which made prominent mention of the new name. That in turn earned it special mention in the American Dialect Society's annual search for Words of the Year. A new category, Most Beautiful Word of the Year, was created for it and has never been used since. A dazzling name for a dazzling phenomenon, it would seem.

But those brief mentions were all the publicity it got, and that turned out not to be enough. With all its potential, *sylvanshine* didn't succeed. You will look in vain for it in any dictionary, even the compendious *Oxford English Dictionary* or the *Barnhart Dictionary Companion*, which specializes in new words. If you hear of *sylvanshine* at all nowadays, it's because a few people liked the sound of the word and applied it to other things. It is the title of a song for the album *Natural Language 0098* on the now-defunct em:t label. It's the name of a white iris developed in 1997 that, according to an iris website, "blooms with the tall beardeds and Siberians" and has an "attractive rounded form with a slight violet tinge at its base." And among the sixteen horses owned by the novelist Jane Smiley is a broodmare called Sylvanshine, a.k.a. Jackie.

Aside from these odd names and occasional references to Professor Fraser's studies, *sylvanshine* never became visible in our language. And though the woods still shine any time you drive at night through a forest of blue spruce, *sylvanshine* is nowhere in sight. There is no guaranteeing that even the brightest of words will catch on.

So neither beauty, nor ingenuity, nor the need for a name for a new object or phenomenon can guarantee the success of a word. Even auspiciously inaugurated ones like *sputnik* and *sylvanshine* have fallen by the wayside. But maybe there is a knack for creating successful words; there certainly are people renowned for the words they have created. The next chapter will look at the creations of famous wordsmiths to see what their inventions can tell us.

2

How to Be a Loser

> As advice for the aspiring coiner, I can offer only this: Culti-
> vate your dark side and listen for the potential fragments of
> innovation scattered in commonplace speech. . . . keep at
> it, but don't be **pittwitted.** If the word you invent turns out
> to be unnecessary or inelegant, let it go and accept the fact
> that at times **swakkle** simply will **denuggify** your **whoop-
> dujour.**
>
> — *Paul Lewis, "A Week in the Life of a Neologist"*

Most new words are born in obscurity. If their parentage ever was known, they soon become orphans, to be
adopted or ignored by others according to standards to be
explained later. In some cases, to be sure, like those of
digerati and *sylvanshine,* we do happen to know the exact
circumstances of their birth. But there is one other class
of new words that had a privileged start: those created by
experts, people for whom creating words is not just an
occasional byproduct, but a focus of their work. They tend
to be playful, but they devote considerable effort to the
making of their words. Indeed, several have made entire
books of their creations.

This chapter will look at the bountiful work of some of
these creators, ranging from the great humorists Edward
Lear and Lewis Carroll of the mid-nineteenth century to
Adam Hanft and Faith Popcorn of the present day. The
creations of the latter pair are too new to know what will
become of them, but the rest have taken the test of history.
Most have failed.

Frankenfood
parody of Kellogg's Tony the Tiger character on a breakfast cereal box

THE FRANKENFOOD MONSTER

A new word's success or failure does not seem to rest on how clever or ambitious its creator is. Take the case of *Frankenfood,* a scary word for genetically modified foods. It's a fairly successful new word, and we know exactly how it came into being. It was a deliberate coinage by Paul Lewis, humorist and English professor at Boston College. In a 1992 letter to the editor of the *New York Times,* he presented his newborn word to the world:

> *Ever since Mary Shelley's baron rolled his improved human out of the lab, scientists have been bringing just such good things to life. If they want to sell us Frankenfood, perhaps it's time to gather the villagers, light some torches and head to the castle.*

Lewis's breezy humor provides a context that makes the meaning of *Frankenfood* perfectly clear. With a twist on the General Electric slogan "We bring good things to life," Lewis reminds us of the monster artificially created from human spare parts by Victor Frankenstein in Mary Shelley's novel of that name. Remembering the evil obsession of that scientist-creator as well as the deadly horror he created, we recognize that *Frankenfood* means artificially created food, viewed as the evil product of an evil scheme.

This shot in the dark was heard round the world. It was first noticed at the *Times* itself, where a writer following the developments in genetically modified foods used it in a front-page article twelve days later. Finding *Frankenfood* ideal for scare headlines, an environmental news service picked it up, and before the summer was over it was in newspapers and magazines from London to Los Angeles and was discussed on National Public Radio.

In short, the word was an instant success. Professor Lewis was delighted, and he thought he knew why it was such a hit. In October he explained its virtues to a *Boston Globe* reporter: "It has a phonetic rhythm, it's pithy, and you can use the 'Franken-' prefix on anything: 'Frankenfruit,' say. You can say, 'We're breathing Frankenair.' 'We're drinking Frankenwater.' 'It's a Frankenworld.' "

SCHMOOZING NEW WORDS

Lewis's success with *Frankenfood* inspired him to try another, which he revealed to the *Globe* in that interview: *schmoozeoisie,* a combination of *schmooze* and *bourgeoisie.* "This is that class of people who earn their living by talk. It includes such traditional groups as teachers and therapists, but it's expanding. Oprah's a member of the schmoozeoisie elite. Government is all schmoozeoicrats taking trillions and giving back words."

This word too seemed destined to become a success when it caught the attention of two eminent authorities on language. One was the author of the "Word Watch" column in the *Atlantic Monthly,* dictionary editor Anne H. Soukhanov. She included *schmooseoisie* (with a change of the *Globe* reporter's spelling) in her 1995 book *Word*

Watch: The Stories Behind the Words of Our Lives. Her listing, in turn, caught the attention of *New York Times* language columnist William Safire, who reported Lewis's new brainchild later that year.

With these accomplishments, the professor decided he had found a new calling. His second success inspired Lewis so much that he spent a whole week in the fall of 1995 inventing new words. It is rare to be able to watch a coiner of words in action, but happily he gave an account of this experience, "A Week in the Life of a Neologist," in a column in the *Boston Globe* a month later. His tone is tongue-in-cheek, as befits a humorist, but his coinages seem sincere. And his method is one that previously led him to success: "I sew words up (like puns) out of existing linguistic units."

In that article he put into circulation ten new words involving politics, the media, and teen culture. His political words were *Republicants,* Republicans who wanted to limit government spending; *Republicuts,* budget cuts resulting from the Republicants' views; and *Democrits,* "aging progressives deep in denial of their past record as supporters of the programs now subject to Republicuts." All this he considered a *Newtmare,* named after Republican leader Newt Gingrich.

He had just one media coinage, *celebfatigue,* "induced by excessive exposure to the mundane details of the lives of the undeservedly famous," like O.J. Simpson.

His teen culture words were inspired by a visit from his fifteen-year-old Californian niece. He wondered whether she would be *MPeedout* by excessive viewing of the television show *Melrose Place.* He observed her shopping habits and wondered whether she risked "becoming mall-minded, succumbing to mallitis, or just being malled." And he also wondered if she would become *pittwitted,* trapped in "a bubble-headed frame of mind that results from constant consumption of stories about Brad Pitt's favorite hairstyles, T-shirts or lipsticks."

Lewis also lists a few words he wouldn't create: happy words like *whoopdujour* or obscure ones like *denuggify* and *swakkle.*

CATCHING THE CULTURAL WAVE

His enterprise attracted attention. To a reporter for the *Boston College Chronicle* he explained in 1996: "There are those who do this sort of thing seriously, but for me it's just fun. I stumbled into it with *Frankenfood,* and it got me thinking about how new words are created. In working towards words like *mall-minded* or *Newtmare,* I am trying to catch a cultural wave." He told the reporter about his latest creation: *likespeak,* "teen dialect based on the assumption that objects and concepts only approximate what they pretend to represent."

Lewis was on a roll. Or was he? As it has turned out, all of his later coinages never made it to first base. With *Frankenfood,* Lewis had beginner's luck. Everything else vanished from sight.

That includes even *schmooseoisie,* despite its auspicious launching. Despite significant help from Soukhanov and Safire, it was picked up by only a few other writers about words (one chose it as a "Word of the Day") rather than actually put to use. Among the more than two billion pages archived by Google in early 2002, for example, there is only one actual use of *schmooseoisie.* That comes in a 1996 speech to the Society for Information Management, Atlanta chapter: "The digital future has fallen into the clutches of the schmooseoisie — pseudo-experts engaged in content-free opinionizing." The schmooseoisie themselves have failed to use it. And despite Soukhanov's earlier championing of the word, *schmooseoisie* is not among the 100,000 entries of the 1999 *Encarta World English Dictionary* for which she served as American editor.

Why would *schmooseoisie* be such a failure when *Frankenfood* was such a success? Maybe because *schmooseoisie* is more funny-looking. Yes, the images evoked by the two words make *Frankenfood* the odd one; monsters created of human spare parts are certainly more grotesque than people who earn their living by talk. But when the words themselves are considered, *schmooseoisie* sounds sillier. Its first part comes from the down-to-earth slang *schmooze* (from the Yiddish); its second from the genteel *bourgeoisie* (from the French). It's a blatantly mixed marriage.

Frankenfood, on the other hand, has two straightforward parts that simply combine to reflect the concept it expresses. *Frankenstein*, of course, is the creator of the monster in Mary Shelley's legend. And *food* is just food. Put them together and you have food created by a modern-day Dr. Frankenstein.

Lewis's other coinages disappeared even faster than *schmooseoisie*. You'll look in vain for any instance of *celebfatigue* or *pittwitted*. As for *Newtmare* or *mall-minded*, the cultural wave Lewis tried to catch seems to have gone flat before those words could surf it. The *Newtmare* of the mid-1990s came and went without any employment of that word. The occasional sightings of *mall-minded* are surely independent spontaneous coinages rather than references to Lewis's invention: "star jock Zack gets dumped by his mall-minded girlfriend" in a 1999 review of the movie *She's All That*, for example, and "Beyond the valley of parking lots/and Mall minded credit seeking/Card carrying members/of Neon Society" in a 1998 poem by Bedros B. Afeyan.

Similarly, a search of the World Wide Web using the Google search engine turns up only one instance of *LikeSpeak*, and it seems unlikely to be Lewis's doing. Michigan diarist Erica M. Mercer seems to have reinvented the word in 1999 as she considered the way girls talk on the phone: "They talk around these parts in like language. Like is? . . . like are, . . . like I think, like I do not know, like . . . Really! . . . oh my god. . . . They speak extremely fast running all and any words in between the likes together." The next day her diary records, "Moo left a message on the machine last night that was totally unintelligible. I had to play it back 20 times before I had the brilliant idea of simply turning the volume down, which allowed me; the worry mother [to] decipher this phrase in LikeSpeak *smgnimgingtotpoftheparkhomemidnit,kay* click." (She doesn't provide a translation.)

There are also very few instances of *Democrits,* none of them with Lewis's definition. The word is evidently a spontaneous coinage in a political website comment just before the close presidential election in November 2000: ". . . I wholeheartedly disagree with your thesis (shared by many, I'll grant) [that] the Democrits and the Repulsivecans are identical. . . ." Other seemingly spontaneous pairings of that time include "Damnocrats and Repulsivecans" and "Desperationcrats and the Repulsivecans."

FRANKENFAILURES

And *Frankenfood* did not develop the variants Lewis predicted. His *Frankenair, Frankenwater,* and *Frankenworld* are not to be found. They might have rhythm, as Lewis said, but they didn't have resonance. Apparently Lewis did not realize the monstrous significance of the *Franken-* prefix he brought to life: it doesn't mean something "polluted" or "damaged," but focuses on an unnatural creation, possibly by someone with sinister motives. That's why *Frankenfood* caught on among those who oppose genetically modified food. Like *pro-life* and *pro-choice* in the abortion debate, it was a loaded word. *Frankenfood* has been more widely used in Britain than in the United States, because concern about genetically modified food has been greater there. British writers also began using the expanded version *Frankenstein food,* to make the allusion even more obvious.

Frankenfruit got a small breath of life in 1999, seven

years after Lewis coined it, when a "WTO Welcome Committee" announced that it had destroyed genetically modified *frankenfruit* trees in Summerland, British Columbia, in advance of the World Trade Organization meeting in nearby Seattle. But this *frankenfruit* may well have been an independent coinage based on *Frankenfood* rather than a recollection of Lewis's earlier invention.

A number of *Franken-* variants Lewis hadn't foreseen have enjoyed limited but occasional use. *Frankenchickens* has been used in connection with an urban legend about KFC switching from real chickens to "genetically manipulated organisms" when it changed its name from Kentucky Fried Chicken to KFC. Genetically modified salmon have raised concerns about *Frankenfish,* and there is a rock group *Frankenscience.* All these are natural outgrowths of the original *Frankenfood,* rhythm or no.

In short, Lewis succeeded only with the one coinage that adapted itself naturally to our language. It was an instant hit, although he apparently did not notice why. And it seems quite possible that *Frankenfood* itself will eventually vanish into the frozen wastes, much as Shelley's monster does. Any serious discussion about the perils of genetically modified foods will not refer to them as *Frankenfoods* more than once or twice, by way of acknowledging the attitude that the word epitomizes. *Frankenfood* is and always will be a joke, and it's hard for a joke to find a permanent place in our vocabulary.

HALL OF FAME

In his avocation as humorist–word creator, Lewis was following an illustrious (or at least illustrated, by Arnie Ten) predecessor who made the creation of new words a popular sport in the 1980s. From 1984 to 1989, comedian Rich Hall ("& Friends") produced a series of books full of *sniglets,* which he defined as "Any Word That Doesn't Appear in the Dictionary but Should." The success of the first book inspired a daily comic panel that in turn led to several more compilations. After *Sniglets* and *More Sniglets,* Hall continued with *Angry Young Sniglets, When Sniglets Ruled the Earth,* and *Unexplained Sniglets of the Universe.*

Here are some of the original sniglets:

> flirr: A photograph that features the camera operator's finger in the corner.
> mustgo: Any item of food that has been sitting in the refrigerator so long it has become a science project.
> orosuctuous: Being able to hold a glass to one's face by sheer lung power.
> tacangle: The position of one's head while biting into a taco.

Hall is long since retired from the enterprise, but others have continued the sniglets tradition into the twenty-first century. Practitioners in different fields have customized them. Various authors offer hairstyling sniglets:

> crudzia: Random foreign objects stuck in your hair.
> cruffle: The action of pulling your fingers through the ends of curls to get them to separate.
> meno-dreads: The hair around your ears that gets soaked during hot flashes.
> snaglet: A tiny hair snarl that occurs in the wispy tendrils around the face.

There are emergency medical service sniglets:

> blurrections: Unintelligible directions to the scene of a call; usually utilizing landmarks with names like "Jed's tractor graveyard" and "Where the big wreck was in '69."
> breathanol: The still potent form of gaseous alcohol wafting from the mouths of drunk patients.
> dashtritus: The assortment of hamburger wrappers, run report code sheets, billing forms, and other detritus that accumulates on the dashboard of the ambulance.

There are quilting sniglets:

> fabflipate: Sewing one piece of fabric inside-out.
>
> smeld: Sewing your project to your clothes.
>
> erratiseams: Seams that don't match.

There are computer sniglets:

> covlexia: When, after something has been installed, the cover on the computer just won't go back on as easily as it came off.
>
> micro-inch: The amount of extra length needed on the keyboard cord to allow you to sit somewhere besides right in front of the monitor.
>
> ttyyppeelexia: When typing one character somehow yields two.

And there are Jewish sniglets:

> drashush: Sounds made by the congregation to request that people be quiet for the rav's drasha.
>
> shaboss: The mother who gives her children strict rules about cleaning up before Shabbat.
>
> yarmulcult: The practice among those who are not Jewish of wearing colorful yarmulkes on their heads because it's fashionable.

SNIGLETS ™ by Rich Hall

TACANGLE 12-23

(tak' ang ul)

n. The position of one's head while biting into a taco.

tacangle

These and many more examples show that *sniglet* itself has become a word. As one writer observes, "The linguaphiles call new words neologisms, but the rest of us call them Sniglets." True, you still won't find *sniglet* in most dictionaries, but that may be because the makers of dictionaries are behind the times; they may not have noticed that *sniglet* is used freely by others besides Rich Hall.

But even more striking is that the sniglets themselves — the words that are sniglets, that is, not the name *sniglet* — remain outside the language. Hall's books present hundreds of them, and there probably have been thousands more since. Yet apparently not a single sniglet has had any appreciable use outside of the books and articles that introduce it.

It's not because sniglets have no usefulness. After all, there truly is no word for "Possessing the ability to turn the bathtub faucet on and off with your toes" (sniglet: aquadextrous) or "The act, when vacuuming, of running over a string at least a dozen times, reaching over and picking it up, examining it, then putting it back down to give the vacuum one more chance" (sniglet: carperpetuation) or "Manhandling the 'open here' spout on a milk carton so badly that one has to resort to using the 'illegal' side" (sniglet: lactomangulation). When we talk about these matters, or others like "The slime that accumulates on the underside of a soap bar when it sits in the dish too long" (sniglet: slurm), we have to resort to more than one word. It would seem more efficient to have one word for one thought, yet we still resist the sniglet opportunities.

Why have all the sniglets failed? One reason may be that the proposed words are too odd, as was the case with *schmooseoisie.* You might well get a laugh if you admitted to *carperpetuation* or said you were going to get rid of the *slurm.* Or you might get a blank look. Your listeners would not know what you meant; the words have a familiar sound, but they are clever jokes, and the definitions turn out to be surprising punchlines instead of self-evident combinations. Take this test: Can you guess the meanings of these original sniglets?

genderplex
krogt
snacktrek
cinemuck

Here are the official sniglets definitions:

genderplex: The predicament of a person in a restaurant who is unable to determine his or her designated restroom (e.g., turtles and tortoises).

krogt (chemical symbol, Kr): The metallic silver coating found on fast-food game cards.

snacktrek: The peculiar habit, when searching for a snack, of constantly returning to the refrigerator in hopes that something new will have materialized.

cinemuck: The combination of popcorn, soda, and melted chocolate that covers the floors of movie theaters.

Of these four, only *cinemuck* is straightforward enough to allow a reasonable guess. Perhaps you figured out that it was used to mean "muck in a cinema." Because of its relative transparency, one may actually find a stray use of that word with that meaning, as in this 1995 article: "The complete movie experience requires rickety seats, concessions with absolutely no nutritive value whatsoever, four to six inches of cinemuck on the floor. . . ." But in actual use it also can refer to the content of the movie itself, as in this reviewer's complaint about *Me, Myself, & Irene:* "I would've walked out of the theater in the first 20 minutes except I get paid to sit through even the worst cinemuck." This different usage indicates that this instance of *cinemuck* was an independent creation owing nothing to the original sniglet.

One or two such instances, of course, don't get a word into any dictionary. Rich Hall & Friends introduced hundreds of new words. All he wanted was to get laughs with

them, and that was all they yielded, except for the word
sniglets itself. His sniglets are useful models for humorists,
but not for those serious about coining words.

RUNCIBLE SPOONS AND CHIMPS

Or maybe those examples are just not foolish enough.
Could the secret to success be utter nonsense? To find out,
let's go back a century before Lewis and Hall to those ultimate practitioners of nonsense, Edward Lear and Lewis
Carroll.

The year 1871 was a great one for nonsense verse. In
that year Edward Lear, the Englishman who had cleaned
up the limerick (it didn't stay clean long) and introduced
it into polite society, published *Nonsense Songs, Stories,
Botany, and Alphabets.* Among the poems in that book
was "The Owl and the Pussy-cat," which included these
memorable lines:

> *They sailed away, for a year and a day,*
> *To the land where the Bong-tree grows. . . .*
>
> *They dined on mince, and slices of quince,*
> *Which they ate with a runcible spoon;*
> *And hand in hand, on the edge of the sand,*
> *They danced by the light of the moon.*

A *Bong-tree!* What's that? And a *runcible spoon?* Lear
provided no explanation of either in his deadpan verses.
Children (and adults) throughout the English-speaking
world would recite his poems and learn those words. But
repeating a word whose meaning is unknown won't make
it part of one's vocabulary, and words like *Bong-tree* bore
no fruit. It was not till the next century that *bong* became
a word in the English language, and none of its twentieth-
century meanings (the sound of a bell, a mountaineer's
piton, a water pipe for marijuana) appears to have anything to do with Lear's 1871 tree.

Dolomphious Duck

Runcible might have had the same fate, except that Lear continued to use it as if it were a perfectly ordinary word. In an illustrated alphabet in his 1872 *More Nonsense, Pictures, Rhymes, Botany, etc.,* he presented "The Dolomphious Duck, who caught Spotted Frogs for her dinner with a Runcible Spoon" as well as "The Rural Runcible Raven, who wore a White Wig and flew away with the Carpet Broom." (About *Dolomphious,* don't ask; it went the way of the *Bong-tree.*) His *Laughable Lyrics* of 1877 tell of "Aunt Jobiska's Runcible Cat with crimson whiskers," and the 1888 edition of his *Nonsense Songs and Stories* introduces Mr. Lear himself with his "runcible hat." That year, unfortunately, Mr. Lear himself died, but his lyrics continued to be published, and the 1895 edition of *Nonsense Songs and Stories* has "What a runcible goose you are!" and "We shall presently all be dead,/On this ancient runcible wall."

Evidently these uses were enough to establish the word. In the early twentieth century a consideration of its possible meanings led one scholar to the conclusion that "A runcible spoon is a kind of fork with three broad prongs or tines, one having a sharp edge, curved like a spoon. . . . Its origin is in jocose allusion to the slaughter at the Battle of Roncevaux [in Spain in 778], because it has a cutting edge." Lear's own illustration of the Dolomphious Duck with her Runcible Spoon suggests otherwise, but never mind. With this 1926 interpretation, later writers on etiquette calmly mentioned the *runcible spoon* as if it were a centuries-old term.

Still, *runcible* is marginal at best. Forget Mr. Lear's hat, raven, cat, goose, or wall; only the phrase *runcible spoon* maintains a precarious existence in our language and in our dictionaries. The rest of Lear's copious coinages remain confined to the pages of his nonsense books.

They were copious, to be sure. Let us sample just one year's output. His 1872 alphabet depicts the *Fizzgiggious Fish* and the *Scroobious Snake,* not to mention the "The Yonghy-Bonghy-Bo, whose head was ever so much bigger than his Body, and whose Hat was rather small." The "Nonsense Botany" in his 1872 book includes sketches of such plants as *Stunnia Dinnerbellia* (shaped like a dinnerbell), *Washtubbia Circularis* (with a washtub as a flower), *Shoebootia Utilis* (with shoes and boots as its fruits), and *Barkia Howlaloudia* (with barking dogs' heads for flowers). "Nonsense Cookery" has recipes for an *Amblongus pie, crumbobblious cutlets,* and *gosky patties.* Everywhere one turns, other freshly minted words show up: "On the top of the Crumpetty Tree/ The Quangle Wangle sat," begins one poem, and another ends with a sparrow remarking, "Witchy witchy witchy wee, Twikky mikky bikky bee, Zikky sikky tee."

Surprisingly, aside from *runcible,* the only other established word for which Lear might possibly deserve credit is *chimp.* This is just a possibility, not a certainty, because when Lear mentions *chimp* in "The Dong [don't ask!] with a Luminous Nose" in his 1877 *Laughable Lyrics,* the word is not explained:

> Over those plains still roams the Dong;
> And above the wall of the Chimp and Snipe
> You may hear the squeak of his plaintive pipe

If that *chimp* is in fact an abbreviation for *chimpanzee,* Lear gets credit for first use. But it's hardly likely that this glancing mention influenced any writers or speakers of the twentieth century who shortened *chimpanzee* to its first syllable (the first example in the *Oxford English Dictionary* is from 1928). No, even the great popularity of Lear's poems did not make his inventions into household words.

WHAT ALICE FOUND

For all the appeal of "The Owl and the Pussy-cat" when it appeared in Lear's *Nonsense Songs* in 1871, it would be eclipsed at the end of that year by an even greater (or at least more famous) nonsense poem also making its first public appearance. It was in the middle of the first chapter of *Through the Looking-Glass and What Alice Found There*, a children's story by a mild-mannered Oxford mathematician using the pseudonym Lewis Carroll, that readers first encountered "Jabberwocky," probably now the best-known and most often memorized nonsense poem in the English language. On the other side of the mirror in her parlor, while trying to help the White Queen and White King, Alice notices a book with mirror-image writing. Holding it up to a mirror, she reads a short epic that begins:

JABBERWOCKY

'Twas brillig, and the slithy toves
Did gyre and gimble in the wabe
All mimsy were the borogroves
And the mome raths outgrabe.

Alice finds herself awash in strange words: " 'It seems very pretty,' she said when she had finished it, 'but it's *rather* hard to understand!' (You see she didn't like to confess, even to herself, that she couldn't make it out at all.) 'Somehow it seems to fill my head with ideas — only I don't exactly know what they are! However, *somebody* killed *something:* that's clear, at any rate —' "

Humpty Dumpty

If she had left it at that, the poem might have receded into obscurity while Alice continued on her adventures. But it comes back with renewed interest in chapter 6, where Alice meets Humpty Dumpty, linguist par excellence. "I can explain all the poems that were ever invented — and a good many that haven't been invented just yet," he declares. So Alice asks him about "Jabberwocky," with the results as indicated on the next page.

Brillig, slithy, toves, gyre, gimble, wabe, mimsy, borogroves, mome, raths, outgrabe: You too very likely have heard, possibly even memorized this poem with all the odd words in it. The question is, can you remember Humpty Dumpty's definitions? Have you ever used, or heard, any of these words outside of "Jabberwocky"?

Probably not. Despite Humpty's more or less logical explanations, placing the words within the usual word creation practices of English, there is little evidence of any independent uses of these words either in Carroll's time or today. *Gyre* might be an exception, but it turns out that *gyre* is also the one word that wasn't new. It had been in the English language with the meaning "revolve, gyrate" since at least 1593.

As it happens, this first stanza of "Jabberwocky" was originally created by Carroll in 1855 as a fake "Stanza of Anglo-Saxon Poetry," with slightly different interpretations

. . . .

Humpty Dumpty's Explanation of "Jabberwocky" Words

" '*Brillig*' means four o'clock in the afternoon — the time when you begin *broiling* things for dinner."

"That'll do very well," said Alice: and '*slithy*'?"

"Well, '*slithy*' means 'lithe and slimy.' 'Lithe' is the same as 'active.' You see it's like a portmanteau — there are two meanings packed up into one word."

"I see it now," Alice remarked thoughtfully: "and what are '*toves*'?"

"Well, '*toves*' are something like badgers — they're something like lizards — and they're something like corkscrews."

"They must be very curious looking creatures."

"They are that," said Humpty Dumpty: "also they make their nests under sun-dials — also they live on cheese."

"And what's to '*gyre*' and to '*gimble*'?"

"To '*gyre*' is to go round and round like a gyroscope. To '*gimble*' is to make holes like a gimlet."

"And '*the wabe*' is the grass-plot round a sun-dial, I suppose?" said Alice, surprised at her own ingenuity.

"Of course it is. It's called '*wabe*,' you know, because it goes a long way before it, and a long way behind it — "

"And a long way beyond it on each side," Alice added.

"Exactly so. Well, then, '*mimsy*' is 'flimsy and miserable' (there's another portmanteau for you). And a '*borogove*' is a thin shabby-looking bird with its feathers sticking out all round — something like a live mop."

"And then '*mome raths*'?" said Alice. "I'm afraid I'm giving you a great deal of trouble."

"Well, a '*rath*' is a sort of green pig: but '*mome*' I'm not certain about. I think it's short for 'from home' — meaning that they'd lost their way, you know."

"And what does '*outgrabe*' mean?"

"Well, '*outgribing*' is something between bellowing and whistling, with a kind of sneeze in the middle: however, you'll hear it done, maybe — down in the wood yonder — and when you've once heard it you'll be *quite* content."

. . . .

of the words than Humpty Dumpty gives. Carroll's 1855 translation is: "It was evening, and the smooth active badgers were scratching and boring holes in the hill-side; all unhappy were the parrots; and the grave turtles squeaked out." The six stanzas he added for *Through the Looking-Glass* were more sparing in the use of obscure words and therefore more successful: one can deduce the meanings of the strange words from the context of familiar ones. "He went galumphing back" declares one line of the poem, and "He chortled in his joy" says another. *Chortle* and *galumph* — both of them what Humpty Dumpty calls *portmanteau words* — are both in use today. *Chortle* comes from "chuckle" and "snort"; *galumph* comes from "gallop" and "triumph."

MR. CARROLL'S PORTMANTEAU

Still, in view of the large number of nonsense words Carroll created, these few mark only a small success. Carroll had greater success with a word that is not nonsense at all. In the conversation with Humpty Dumpty about the words of "Jabberwocky," the most successful of Carroll's innovations is not any word of the poem, but *portmanteau* in Humpty's explanation.

In fact, Humpty's remark has kept *portmanteau* in the English vocabulary even after the portmanteau itself has disappeared. In Carroll's time, a portmanteau was a small piece of luggage, a stiff leather bag that opened like a book. We have long since traded portmanteaus for briefcases, overnight bags, and backpacks. But linguists have used Humpty's explanation, "two meanings packed up in one word," to create the technical term *portmanteau* to describe new words or forms made by combining others. So *portmanteau word* is firmly established.

Even that term, though, is likely to draw blank stares from most of the English-speaking population; only those few who study and write about words will know and use it. The *Oxford English Dictionary,* whose editors were busy collecting examples of contemporary usage during Carroll's day, quotes him dozens of times and gives him credit for the first examples of *bandersnatch, curiouser and curiouser, frabjous, frumious, jabberwock, jubjub, manxome, mimsy, mome, outgrabe, phlizz, portmanteau (word), rath, slithy, snicker-snack, thingum-a-jig, tove, tulgey, uffish, unbirthday, vorpal,* and *wabe,* as well as *chortle* and *galumph.* But their acceptance in that dictionary of dictionaries was no guarantee of success. Most of those words appear only in Carroll's poems and stories or in allusions to them.

Perhaps it is more than coincidence that Charles L. Dodgson, a.k.a. Lewis Carroll, was a professor at the very institution that sponsored the *Oxford English Dictionary.* Lear, who wasn't a professor anywhere, got no such royal treatment from that dictionary for his creations.

CURIOUSER AND CURIOUSER

So well known are Carroll's works that when his created words do appear elsewhere, they are usually in a context recalling what Carroll wrote. Take the phrase *curiouser and curiouser,* for example. It occurs for the first time in the 1865 *Alice's Adventures in Wonderland,* at the start of chapter 2: " 'Curiouser and curiouser!' cried Alice (she was so much surprised, that for the moment she quite forgot how to speak good English); 'now I'm opening out like the largest telescope that ever was!' " It's not "good English" because of the rule that *-er* may to be added only to words of one or two syllables; a three-syllable word like *curious* requires the use of *more* instead, so Alice would properly have said "More and more curious!" But, recalling Alice and her truly curious adventures, *curiouser and curiouser* has passed into general use as a phrase to evoke any situation so curious as to cause one to forget "good English."

In short, Carroll's writings are more famous than his words, so any use of his words recalls his writings, and his words therefore do not have much of an independent life in the vocabulary of English. However, there is one apparent innovation of Carroll's that has entirely escaped the confines of the Alice books to enter the general vocabulary. It is a different sort of innovation than any of his made-up words, and it fits so naturally into present-day English that its originality is hard to detect. It occurs in this passage from chapter 1 of *Through the Looking-Glass:*

> *"Kitty, dear, let's pretend — " And here I wish I could tell you half the things Alice used to say, beginning with her favourite phrase "Let's pretend." She had had quite a long argument with her sister only the day before — all because Alice had begun with "Let's pretend we're kings and queens;" and her sister, who liked being very exact, had argued that they couldn't, because there were only two of them, and Alice had been reduced at last to say, "Well, you can be one of them then, and I'll be all the rest."*

What's so modern about this passage? It's the use of *pretend* in the sense "To feign in play; to make believe," as the *Oxford English Dictionary* puts it. According to the evidence of that dictionary, Carroll may well have been the first to use *pretend* in that way, as opposed to the earlier (and still current) adult sense of making a false claim.

This emergence of a highly successful new meaning of a familiar word is very different from the creation of novelties of vocabulary in "Jabberwocky." Imagine for a moment how you might interpret the passage containing *pretend* if you lived when it was first published. You would be well acquainted with *pretend* in uses like "She pretended she was my friend," but back then you might never before have heard or seen the phrase "Let's pretend." Still, in the context of child's play, and with full explanation by the author, "Let's pretend" would seem a natural extension of the older meaning. You might even use it yourself the next time you played with a child, and children would learn "Let's pretend" as they read the book or had it read to them. In that way, the word in its new sense may have spread as easily as *like* or *way* in today's teen talk.

The success of this new meaning comes from its *not* calling attention to itself. And that may be the lesson to learn from the humorists and would-be coiners of new words: If you want a new word to succeed, don't use it to make a joke. Don't brag about it; better yet, don't even mention it. Just slip it in where it will seem natural and pass unnoticed. Maybe it's best if you don't even notice it yourself. It's quite possible that Carroll wasn't aware he was offering a new meaning for *pretend.*

BROMIDES AND BLURBS

After Lear and Carroll, the next great coiner of nonsense words was an American, Gelett Burgess. At first he seemed destined for unparalleled success. A century after he coined them, two of his words are firmly established in our vocabulary. Well, maybe one. . . .

To succeed in coining new words is so rare an accomplishment that even one success is worth celebrating. Success with two words is rare indeed, and worthy of extreme hype. It is appropriate, then, that one of the most successful coiners of the twentieth century, the father of two (well, maybe one) well-established words, is known especially for his own shameless and amusing promotion of those words. He is the humorist-writer and illustrator Gelett Burgess (1866–1951), and his words are *bromide* and *blurb.* His invention of both the name and the function of the blurb helped him take the art of self-promotion to new heights.

The success of the first word, *bromide,* led to the invention and success of the second. Burgess presented to the world, or at least to readers of the magazine *Smart Set,* a new meaning of *bromide* in a 1906 article entitled "The Sulphitic Theory." According to the mock psychology of this theory, some people are *Bromides:* boring and utterly predictable. Their opposites, the much rarer people who think for themselves, are *Sulphites.*

Bromide wasn't a new word. It is a chemical term from the early nineteenth century meaning a compound made with the element bromine. One such compound, potassium bromide, was and still is used as a sedative, and in this use it is often simply referred to as *bromide.* So Burgess seized on the name of a sedative to label the type of person who puts you to sleep.

Not content with expounding his theory in *Smart Set,* later that year Burgess found a publisher for a whole little book on the subject, grandly titled *Are You a Bromide? Or, The Sulphitic Theory Expounded and Exemplified According to the Most Recent Researches into the Psychology of Boredom, Including Many Well-Known Bromidioms Now in Use.*

Here are a few of his *bromidioms,* as hackneyed now as they were a century ago:

—I don't know much about Art, but I know what I like.

—My mother is seventy years old, but she doesn't look a day over fifty.

—I thought I loved him at the time, but of course it wasn't really love.

—Why, I know you better than you know yourself!

—Now, this thing really happened!

—It isn't so much the heat (or the cold), as the humidity in the air.

—You can live twenty years in New York and never know who your next-door neighbor is.

—He's told that lie so often that he believes it himself, now.

—Don't worry; that won't help matters any.

The opposite personality was *Sulphitic:*

> *Sulphites are agreed upon most of the basic facts of life, and this common understanding makes it possible for them to eliminate the obvious from their conversation.*

Burgess's article and book made both *bromide* and *sulphite* the talk of the town. Frank O'Malley of the *New York Sun* joined in the fun; Burgess credits him with coining *bromidiom* and being "one of the most ardent and discriminating collectors of Bromidioms." But the fad soon faded. *Sulphite* never caught on as the designation of a personality and reverted to its purely scientific use. *Bromide,* on the other hand, gradually drifted from Burgess's definition and acquired the related meaning of a remark uttered by a person who is a *bromide,* that is, a platitude such as the bromidioms listed above. In that sense, it has stayed with the language ever since.

Now here is how *bromide* happened to lead to *blurb.* Burgess was a popular writer, so his publisher gave the 1906 book version of *Are You a Bromide?* a special sendoff at the 1907 convention of the American Booksellers Association. This is how *blurb* was coined, as publisher B. W. Huebsch later explained:

> *It is the custom of publishers to present copies of a conspicuous current book to booksellers attending the annual dinner of their trade association, and as this little book was in its heyday when the meeting took place I gave it to 500 guests. These copies were differentiated from the regular edition by the addition of a comic bookplate drawn by the author and by a special jacket which he devised. It was the common practise to print the picture of a damsel — languishing, heroic, or coquettish — anyhow, a damsel, on the jacket of every novel, so Burgess lifted from a Lydia Pinkham or tooth-powder advertisement the portrait of a sickly sweet young woman, painted in some gleaming teeth, and otherwise enhanced her pulchritude, and placed her in the center of the jacket. His accompanying text was some nonsense about "Miss*

Blinda Blurb," and thus the term supplied a real need and became a fixture in our language.

Burgess's special book jacket not only introduced "Miss Blurb," but with its effusive language set an example that other publishers soon followed. Every hardcover book jacket nowadays has its *blurb* on the inside front flap, foreshadowing the book's contents in glowing terms.

So Burgess now had two successful new words. And the second one was a total surprise; it swept into general use without Burgess even trying. Granted, neither word had the particular meaning originally intended by Burgess, but both had meanings that derived from his intentions. Not surprisingly, these successes inspired him to numerous other coinages. He proudly presented exactly one hundred of them in *Burgess Unabridged: A New Dictionary of Words You Have Always Needed,* published in 1914. Proudly among the hundred was a full page on *blurb.* Burgess had invented the word, not the definition, but he contentedly went along with the meaning that had developed:

blurb *n.* 1. A flamboyant advertisement; an inspired testimonial. 2. Fulsome praise; a sound like a publisher.
blurb *v.* To flatter from interested motives; to compliment oneself.

In the front of the book he defines *blurb* more briefly as "Praise from one's self, inspired laudation." These definitions make no reference to the key element of *blurb* as we know it today, its location on a book jacket. But Burgess's discussion of the word includes that as well:

> On the "jacket" of the "latest" fiction, we find the blurb; abounding in agile adjectives and adverbs, attesting that this book is the "sensation of the year;" the blurb tells of "thrills" and "heart-throbs," of "vital importance" and "soul satisfying revelation." The blurb speaks of the novel's "grip" and "excitement."

So Burgess can be crowned as one of the champion coiners of modern times. Yet even he was far from automatically successful. *Bromide* made it, but it was such a natural extension of the medicinal meaning that it might have been coined anyhow. According to the *Oxford English Dictionary,* around the time of Burgess's *Smart Set* article another publication called the *Daily Chronicle* included the comment, "Literature is resentful at being mistaken for bromide."

Blurb was unquestionably original as well as successful. In this case, however, Burgess did not set out to coin a word. He drew a cartoon of an attractive woman, named her "Blinda Blurb," and added some hype about his book. It must have been a bookseller or publisher — or perhaps Burgess himself, later — who transferred the meaning from the woman to the words of praise.

And what was the fate of the other ninety-nine words he invented for *Burgess Unabridged?* Failures, all of them. They are charming failures, to be sure, with ingenious definitions. In fact, it is tempting to quote them all. Here are some:

agowilt: Sickening terror, unnecessary fear, sudden shock.
alibosh: A glaringly obvious falsehood or exaggeration.
bleesh: An unpleasant picture, vulgar or obscene.
cowcat: An unimportant guest, an insignificant personality.
critch: To array one's self in uncomfortable splendor.
diabob: An object of amateur art, adorned without taste.
edicle: One who is educated beyond his intellect, a pedant.
eegot: A selfishly interested friend, a lover of success.
fidgeltick: Food that it is a bore to eat; a taciturn person.
flooijab: An apparent compliment with a concealed sting.
gowyop: A perplexity wherein familiar things seem strange.
gubble: Society talk, the hum of foolish conversation.
hyprijimp: A man who does woman's work; one alone amid women.
impkin: A superhuman pet, a baby in beast form.
jirriwig: A traveller who does not see the country.
jujasm: An expansion of sudden joy after suspense.

kipe: To inspect appraisingly, as women do one another.

meem: An artificial half-light that women love; gloom.

nink: An "antique" resurrected for decorative effect.

oofle: A person whose name one cannot remember; to forget.

pawdle: One vicariously famous, or with undeserved prominence.

rawp: A reliably unreliable person, one always late.

spigg: A decoration of overt vanity; to attract notice, paint.

tashivation: The art of answering without listening to questions.

tintiddle: An imaginary conversation; wit coming too late.

udney: A beloved bore; one who loves but does not understand.

vorge: Voluntary suffering, unnecessary effort or exercise.

wijjicle: A perverse household article, always out of order.

wog: Food on the face; unconscious adornment of the person.

wumgush: Women's insincere flattery of each other.

yamnoy: A bulky, unmanageable object to be carried.

To each of these and the rest of his hundred words, Burgess devotes a full page of definition and commentary, along with an eight-line poem. Even a century later, the humor is not stale. Here is part of what he has to say about *wog*, for example:

> *Have you ever seen the gentleman with the Niagara-Falls moustache? Pretty woggy, what? When beautiful Bessie drinks buttermilk and forgets her napkin, what can you say? . . .*
>
> *But facial stalactites are not the only wogs, alas! Millicent's hair is wogged — prithee catch the hairpin before it falls. As you pick a thread that wogs your wife's grey gown, she discovers a blonde hair on your coat-collar, the most embarrassing of all wogs. . . .*

Burgess Unabridged is perhaps the most entertaining dictionary since Ambrose Bierce's *Devil's Dictionary*, but it didn't contribute even one new word to our language, except for *blurb*, which was already there. Perhaps the failure of the words in *Burgess Unabridged* comes from Burgess's impish way of inventing words. In his introduction, he shows that he knows how words usually come into being, derived in familiar ways from existing words. "But to invent a new word right out of the air or the cigarette smoke is another thing," he notes, and then declares, "And that's what I determined to do."

3

Winning Creations

After the examples of the previous chapter, it's time for a note of encouragement. If you're reading this book in hopes of creating a word of your own, don't let the failures of the experts dissuade you. There are successes too (but not by self-appointed experts in word coinage) and lessons to be learned from both successes and failures. And there's still plenty of room at the top. An amateur may actually have a better chance for success, because many of those who try more seriously for vocabulary fame go about it the wrong way.

Furthermore, it's an innocent hobby. No animals are harmed in the making of a word, and you can splice all the word-genes you want without creating a genetically modified *Frankenfood.*

To be sure, if you want to contribute to the vocabulary, you must have a nonprofit attitude. You can't collect a toll every time someone uses your word, because speech is free and words can't be copyrighted or trademarked. (Brand names are different, but they too can be used freely as long as the user is not trying to profit from them.) Dictionary makers don't pay for the words they use, either, and (to add insult to injury) they won't accept a new word unless they can find independent evidence that the word is widely used.

But none of this has stopped people from trying, and this chapter will reveal the secrets of some ringing successes.

ALL WORDS WERE ONCE NEW

When even the experts are near-perfect failures at creating successful new words, amateurs might be discouraged. But though most new words fail, some obviously succeed. Depending on how one counts them, there are many thousands of words in each person's vocabulary, more than a hundred thousand words in a standard desk dictionary, and nearly half a million words in the biggest dictionary of all, the *Oxford English Dictionary*. Even that great dictionary misses many of the words we use. Of all these hundreds of thousands of words, only a few thousand at most have survived from the Old English of a thousand years ago. These are mostly basic words like *hand, fish, swim,* and *love.* All the rest were once newcomers.

And new words continue to find places for themselves. The English language as a whole often seems like Teflon, so smooth that no new additions can cling to it, but sometimes it turns to Velcro and snags them. From the exceptional words that have succeeded, it will be possible to find clues to assist in the success of words yet to be born.

THE SUCCESSFUL SCOFFLAW

First prize for Successful Word Coinage (Twentieth Century) goes to a term whose success as a word is proportional to its failure to eradicate the thing it describes. It was invented to serve the noble cause of preventing people from drinking alcoholic beverages. That "great experiment" failed, but the word created to shame those who flout the law lives on.

The place was Boston, home also of America's most successful coinage of the nineteenth century, *OK* (in 1839). The year was 1923. The need arose like this: In 1919, the Eighteenth Amendment to the U.S. Constitution had been approved, prohibiting "the manufacture, sale, or transportation of intoxicating liquors" in the United States. That same year Congress passed the Volstead Act to enforce this prohibition. That should have ended America's problem with alcohol. And yet . . . to the chagrin of the triumphant prohibitionists, people ignored the new law and went right on drinking.

A prominent member of the Anti-Saloon League and graduate of the Harvard Class of 1895, Mr. Delcevare King of the Boston suburb of Quincy (the "City of Presidents," home to John Adams and John Quincy Adams), viewed the situation with concern. In October 1923 he wrote to the Harvard Glee Club to protest their singing of "Johnny Harvard," a song he called "the most drinking of drinking songs" and one that "comes pretty near to scoffing at the prohibition law."

He had a point. The song goes like this:

> *Oh, here's to Johnny Harvard! fill him up a full glass,*
> *Fill him up a glass, to his name and fame,*
> *And at the same time don't forget his true love;*
> *Fill her up a bumper to the brim.*
> *Then drink, drink, drink, drink,*
> *Pass the wine cup free,*
> *Drink, drink, drink, drink,*
> *Jolly boys are we. . . .*

An attitude change clearly was needed. King decided that this might be accomplished by a word, a word that would sting and shame the drinker. A man of means, he offered a prize of $200 for a word "which best expresses the idea of lawless drinker, menace, scoffer, bad citizen, or whatnot, with the biting power of 'scab' or 'slacker.'" The cause was noble and the sum significant, so by the contest deadline of January 1, 1924, he had received

25,000 suggestions. Among them, according to a report in the *Boston Herald*, were:

Vatt, still, scut, sluf, curd, canker, scrub, scuttler, dreg, drag, dipsic, boozlaac, alcolog, barnacle, slime-slopper, ell-shiner, still-whacker, sluch-licker, sink, smooth, lawless-ite, bottle-yegger, crimer, alcoloom, hooch-sniper, cellar-sifter, rum-rough, high-boozer, and *law-loose-liquor-lover.*

It is Mr. King's hope [the *Herald* continued] that the word that he selects will be so opprobrious and soul stirring that the liquor law violators will hang their heads in shame, promise themselves not to drink any more and, perhaps, even persuade their lawless friends to do likewise. He admits that if he finds a word that will accomplish a reformation of the steady drinkers, it will indeed be a powerful word. But he says it is worth many times $200 to him to arouse the public to serious thought regarding violations of the prohibition law.

'SCOFFLAW' WINS WORD CONTEST

Chosen as Best to Describe "Lawless Drinker" from 25,000 Submitted

SENT IN BY TWO; $200 PRIZE SPLIT

Delcevare King of Quincy last night announced that "scofflaw" is the winning word in the contest for the $200 he offered for a word, to characterize the "lawless drinker" of illegally made or illegally obtained liquor.

"Scofflaw" was chosen from more than 25,000 words submitted from all the states and from several foreign countries. The word was sent by two contestants, so the prize will be equally divided between Henry Irving Dale of Shawsheen Village, Andover, and Miss Kate L. Butler, Dorchester House, Dorchester.

scofflaw
excerpt from the January 16, 1924 issue of the Boston Herald

On Wednesday, January 16, 1924, the *Herald* announced the winner: *scofflaw,* proposed separately by both Henry Irving Dale of Andover and Miss Kate L. Butler of Dorchester. Entries had come from every state and a few foreign countries, but the winners were in the *Herald* circulation area.

The newborn word wasn't left to sink or swim on its own. King immediately sought to nurture it, and thereby fight the foes of Prohibition, by announcing another contest with prizes totaling $200. This contest solicited essays of 100 words or less on why those who drink illegal liquor should be called *scofflaws.* And he had evidently nurtured it privately, too; by the time of the *Herald* announcement he had already persuaded the organizers of a conference on law enforcement to adopt the word as a slogan for their meeting in the coming week.

Other newspapers reported the choice of *scofflaw,* some with amusement, some with approbation. The *New York Times* opined on January 17:

> *Perhaps it will serve, though it lacks the merit of coming trippingly from the tongue, and, at least when first heard, is a sound with little or no meaning.*
>
> *Carefully considered, the term becomes significant enough, and, as intended, it may turn the more or most sensitive sinners from their evil ways. Its weakness lies in the fact that said sinners will not be startled nor abashed at being told that they do what they never have tried to conceal, and they will ask to have it proved that they who scoff at one law necessarily and inevitably are scoffers at all law.*

And the *New York Tribune* dismissed its chances:

> *It is much easier to manufacture synthetic rubies than synthetic slang. The prize contest for a word "to stab awake the conscience of the lawless drinker" has enriched the language with* scofflaw! *This grotesque compound is not likely to leave a trail of bleeding consciences.*
>
> *To feel its feebleness put it alongside specimens of the real thing that just grew —* roughneck, highbrow, boob,

> jazz, hootch, hoodlum, *and so on. Words like these were not produced by competition and couldn't be. If George Ade, Finley Peter Dunne, Mark Twain and Artemus Ward were to collaborate they might be able to invent a pricklier noun than* scofflaw, *but the chances would be against it. Slang and poets are born, not made, and the unknown geniuses who coin catchwords do so in inspired moments, never by malice aforethought.*

Scofflaw was taken up by others outside the Prohibition movement, but with different results than anticipated. The scofflaws themselves evidently relished the term rather than flinching from it. On January 18, in his column "The Conning Tower" in the *New York World*, Franklin P. Adams offered this poem by "C.W.":

> *I want to be a scofflaw*
> *And with the scofflaws stand;*
> *A brand upon my forehead*
> *A handcuff on my hand.*
> *I want to be a scofflaw,*
> *For since I went to school,*
> *I hate to mind an order,*
> *I* hate *to keep a rule.*

Three days later, Adams foresaw the quick demise of the word:

> *An announcement comes from Preferred Pictures Corp. to the effect that that organization is about to begin work on a production to be called "The Adorable Scofflaw." The picture, the announcement concludes, will be released in the spring. We don't believe it. We don't believe, that is, that it will be released under that title. For unless we are wrong — and nothing in the past leads us to suspect we ever could be — by St. Valentine's Day only a few antiquarians will recall the word.*

But it would prove to have staying power, despite or perhaps because of the mockery. On January 27, for example, just eleven days after the first public announcement of the word, the *Chicago Tribune* reported this reaction from Paris:

> *Hardly has Boston added to the gaiety of nations by add-ing to Webster's Dictionary the opprobrious term of "scoff-law," when Jock, the genial manager of Harry's Bar in Paris, yesterday invented the Scoff-Law Cocktail, and it has already become exceedingly popular among American Prohibition dodgers.*

A cocktail website yields the ingredients in Harry's Scofflaw Cocktail: one ounce Canadian whiskey, one ounce dry vermouth, a quarter ounce lemon juice, "and a hearty dash of both grenadine and orange bitters." This drink was popular until Prohibition itself came to an end with the repeal of the Eighteenth Amendment in 1933.

Within a few months after its introduction, *scofflaw* was well ensconced in the vernacular. In June 1924, for example, sportswriter and storyteller Ring Lardner wrote a humorous column proposing "Sane Olympics": "contests which will show if a man or woman will make a good or a bad husband or wife." The first event of his "new pentathlon" was:

> *1. Patience. Each contestant is required to set a table in a scofflaw cabaret with her pretended husband. The win-ner is the one that don't say let's go home.*

Scofflaw is significant not only for its success when launched, but for the criteria used to choose it from among the 25,000 entries. According to the *Herald,* the judges (the secretary of the Massachusetts Federation of Churches, the regional superintendent of the Anti-Saloon League, and King) had five specific "principles" in mind. In its form, the judges wanted a word of just one or two syllables. They wanted it to begin with *s,* to give it a "sting." In its meaning, they wanted it to refer not to all drinkers but just the illegal ones. They wanted to emphasize the law, rather than liquor, so they looked for a word with *law,* not *liquor,* as its basis and one that would apply to all lawbreakers, not just liquor violators. Their last "principle" was to find a word that could "be linked to the statement of President Harding, 'Lawless drinking is a menace to the republic itself.'"

These principles seem level-headed compared to the ones apparently followed by others who made a point of coining words. Instead of looking for the most clever and innovative creations, they wanted a short plain word. Instead of a limited specialized meaning like "a photograph that features the camera operator's finger in the corner" (Rich Hall's sniglet *flirr*), they wanted a word widely applicable beyond the specific act of illegal drinking.

And they judged wisely in wanting their word to be based on something as familiar as *law*. That word had been at home in English for nearly a thousand years. The contest winners joined it to *scoff*, a word that had been in English both as a noun and as a verb since the 1300s. Both *scoff* and *law* are from the Old Norse language, a close cousin of English that also gave us familiar words like *scare, scrap,* and *scold,* all of like antiquity. In fact, the two words *scoff* and *law* are of such similar background and age that they could have been combined seven hundred years earlier. They might have been, if the sheriff of Nottingham had thought to offer a reward for a word to characterize the insolent lawbreaker Robin Hood. As it was, the sheriff could only call Robin an *outlaw.*

It may have helped that the new word had a distinguished sponsor and was to be used for the most worthy of purposes. Its association with high society prevented any possible objections to it on the grounds of unknown or vulgar origins. Paradoxically, it may also have helped that the contest and the word received so much scorn and mockery from the scofflaws themselves.

But perhaps the most important reason for the success of *scofflaw* was that it didn't seem new. Even though we know better, it fits so well in the crowd of *law* words that it seems as if it has been around a long time. Our usual defenses against newcomers are disarmed.

ANOTHER SUCCESS: SKYCAP

Not all words are coined for such solemn purposes as was *scofflaw*. In a lighter vein, a prize of $100 was offered in 1940 to find a suitable name for the porters (at the time, always African-American men) who carried luggage for airline passengers at New York City's airlines terminal on 42nd Street at Park Avenue. According to a *New York Herald Tribune* article of December 24, 1940, found by researcher Barry Popik, there were 2,780 entries in the contest. The winner was Willie Wainwright of New Orleans with the term *skycap*. His term was another instant success, or at least an enduring one, because airline porters across the nation are still called *skycaps* to this day.

What made *skycap* so successful? Once again, it was because it seemed so natural that it hardly seemed new. In 1940, everyone in America knew that railroad porters were *redcaps*, so called since the early days of the century because of the red caps they wore. Wainwright substituted another three-letter word for the first syllable of that word, and the *redcap*'s cousin the *skycap* was born.

Today there are so few railroad passengers and so few redcaps that that word is almost obsolete, but skycaps keep busy with curbside check-ins.

NINE-YEAR-OLD WONDER: GOOGOL

The youngest successful word coiner on record is Milton Sirotta, responding to a request by his uncle, the mathematician Edward Kasner. Milton was nine at the time, or maybe eight, depending on which story you follow; the year was perhaps 1938. In other words, the exact details are uncertain, but there is no doubt that the name *googol* arose in a conversation between nephew and uncle, and apparently so did the name for a much larger number based on the googol, the *googolplex*. Here is the story of their origins, as related by Kasner and James Newman in their 1940 book, *Mathematics and the Imagination:*

> *Words of wisdom are spoken by children at least as often as by scientists. The name 'googol' was invented by a child (Dr Kasner's nine-year-old nephew) who was asked to think up a name for a very big number, namely, 1 with a hundred zeros after it. He was very certain that this number was not infinite, and therefore equally certain that it had to have a name. At the same time that he suggested 'googol' he gave a name for a still larger number: 'Googolplex'. A googolplex is much larger than a googol, but is still finite, as the inventor of the name was quick to point out. It was first suggested that a googolplex should be 1, followed by writing zeros until you got tired. This is a description of what would happen if one actually tried to write a googolplex, but different people get tired at different times and it would never do to have Carnera [Primo Carnera, an Italian boxing champion] a better mathematician than Dr Einstein, simply because he had more endurance. The googolplex then, is a specific finite number, with so many zeros after the 1 that the number of zeros is a googol. . . . You will get some idea of the size of this very large but finite number from the fact that there would not be enough room to write it, if you went to the farthest star, touring all the nebulae and putting down zeros every inch of the way.*

The *googol* and the *googolplex* were presented as specific examples of a very big number and a very much bigger number. In the standard terminology, the googol is equivalent to 10 *duotrigintillion*, but that is too exotic a name to remember, and even a little hard to say. *Googol*, in contrast, was simple yet also properly scientific-looking with its *-ol* ending, as in familiar words like *aerosol* and *alcohol* and more exotic ones like *dinitrophenol* and *pentylenetetrazol*.

Most nine-year-olds — indeed, most children and people of all ages — are quick to invent new words. Most of these get no use beyond their own families, if that. The difference in Milton Sirotta's case is that his uncle was the expert, the first to write about the properties of *googols* and *googolplexes*. The scientist who invents a new idea usually gets to name it.

TURN ON, TUNE IN, DROP OUT

To fathom hell or soar angelic
Just take a pinch of psychedelic.

What do you call those drugs that alter your state of consciousness? Hallucinatory? Psychotic? Those terms seemed too negative to a certain scientist and his writer friend who were experimenting with them in the mid-twentieth century. In the 1950s, Dr. Humphry Osmond, clinical director of a hospital in Saskatchewan, Canada, had been studying the benefits of mescaline and LSD for treating alcoholics. In 1953 when Aldous Huxley, author of *Brave New World,* inquired about his work, Osmond responded by bringing him a vial of mescaline. By 1955 Huxley had tried LSD, too. Seeking a term to affirm the value of mind-altering drugs, Huxley in a 1956 letter to Osmond coined the word *phanerothyme,* meaning something like "revealing the soul." He presented it in a poem:

To make this trivial world sublime,
Take a half a Gramme of phanerothyme.

Osmond thought he had a better idea and replied with the couplet at the start of this section, introducing the word *psychedelic.* Like *phanerothyme*, it used a combination of classical Greek words to mean "mind-revealing." In 1957 Osmond began using *psychedelic* at conferences and in scientific papers. When the counterculture of the 1960s began to "tune in, turn on, and drop out," they followed Osmond's lead and turned on with *psychedelics.*

Ever since Aristotle, of course, serious science has displayed its seriousness with words derived from Greek. Both *psychedelic* and *phanerothyme* are suitably based on

Greek, but *phanerothyme* is less diaphanous to English speakers. We are familiar with words about the mind that begin with *psych-*, including the name *psychology* itself, but there is no such easy recognition of *phan-*. If we recognized it from the word *phantom*, it might suggest a ghost rather than a soul or the mind.

Once Osmond the scientist began using *psychedelic*, others followed. The word seemed to legitimize and dignify the experience of tripping out.

SPEAKING WITH FORKED TONGUE

No book has called as much attention to the political possibilities of language as George Orwell's *1984*, published in 1949. In that book, under Big Brother's rule, not even one's thoughts are permitted to deviate from the party line; it is *crimethink* to do so. The party is busy reducing the English language to a simplified version, *Newspeak*, designed to make *crimethink* impossible by making it unthinkable. The words *crimethink* and *Newspeak* reflect the simplification of form and vocabulary achieved by Newspeak: they use *think* and *speak* instead of *thought* and *speech* in order to keep variety in the vocabulary at a minimum and fend off impolitic thoughts. "All words grouping themselves round the concepts of liberty and equality, for instance, were contained in the single word *crimethink*," Orwell wrote in an appendix on Newspeak, "while all words grouping themselves round the concepts of objectivity and rationalism were contained in the single word *oldthink*. Greater precision would have been dangerous." Although *1984* is written in *Oldspeak* (the English we know) — not just because it's the language of Orwell's readers, but also because, according to the story, Newspeak was just being developed in 1984 — the novel gives a number of examples from the new language: *goodthink*, for example, which means "political orthodoxy," and *duckspeak,* "to quack like a duck" in repeating the party line without thinking — a good thing.

Four of the Newspeak words of *1984* have made their way into the *Oxford English Dictionary: unperson, double-think, Newspeak,* and *Oldspeak.* In *1984,* an *unperson* is one who, having "incurred the displeasure of the Party," vanishes completely, not just from present notice but also from the rewritten records of the past. It is as if the person never existed. The bluntness of *unperson* has brought it into general use for those who are treated as if they don't exist by various authorities.

Doublethink is the logic, or illogic, that allows a loyal party member to believe everything the party says, even if it is contradictory or contrary to the evidence of the senses. Winston Smith, the protagonist of Orwell's novel, learns that 2 + 2 = 4 or 5 or whatever the party wants it to.

But the most successful of the words generated by *1984* is one Orwell did not use in the book: *doublespeak.* It's a combination of the first part of *doublethink* with the last part of *Newspeak* or *Oldspeak,* and it means the speaking of nonsense, or replacing unpleasant truths with euphemism. It is a twist on *doubletalk,* but while doubletalk can be innocent, doublespeak is malicious.

In turn, *Newspeak, Oldspeak,* and *doublespeak* have made *-speak* into a productive suffix referring to jargon, often insincere or meaningless. For example, a recent essay by Louis Menand, a professor at the Graduate Center of the City University of New York, uses *deanspeak:*

> Talk about "values" and "civic education" is still mostly deanspeak; it's the philosophical padding for certain intellectual changes for which no one has yet devised a very coherent public-relations-tested rationale.

The many other varieties of *-speak* include *business-speak, childspeak, computerspeak, cop-speak, doctorspeak* or *medspeak, sciencespeak, sportspeak,* and of course

Bushspeak and *Clintonspeak.* The use of *-speak* where *-speech* or *-talk* would be expected is a reminder that the language so characterized is facile rather than thoughtful.

YAHOO!

Long before Yahoo.com existed as a search engine on the Internet, there was a *yahoo.* No, it wasn't a cheer either. Those who have read Lemuel Gulliver's account of his voyages to exotic places nearly three centuries ago recognize the *yahoo* as — us.

Jonathan Swift, of course, is the satiric author behind the four volumes of Gulliver's *Travels into Several Remote Nations of the World,* published in 1726. The fourth volume is "A Voyage to the Country of the Houyhnhnms," where Gulliver encounters civilized horses, the Houyhnhnms, leading peaceful, rational lives in harmony with nature. He also encounters filthy brutish creatures, servants to the Houyhnhnms, who turn out to be biologically human, as he is reminded to his disgust and embarrassment when one of the females jumps his bones. These *yahoos,* he observes, "appear to be the most unteachable of all animals. . . . Yet I am of opinion this defect ariseth chiefly from a perverse, restive disposition. For they are cunning, malicious, treacherous and revengeful. They are strong and hardy, but of a cowardly spirit, and by consequence insolent, abject, and cruel." For page after page Gulliver horrifies his Houyhnhnm masters by explaining the vile practices of the European yahoos. When he is forced to leave the land of the Houyhnhnms and returns home, he can't stand the company of humans and spends much of his day conversing with his horses.

Yahoo, then, is humanity in its most disgusting aspect. Ever since, the label *yahoo* has been used for humans who behave in an uncivilized manner. The word itself has the form of a shout, which reinforces its meaning of boorishness. The shout and the prominence of Yahoo.com

Lilliputian

have nudged the word's modern meaning more towards exuberance rather than crudeness.

One other contribution to the English vocabulary from *Gulliver's Travels* is *Lilliputian,* meaning miniature. Many who have never made it to Book IV still have enjoyed Book I, where Gulliver finds himself shipwrecked on an island where everyone and everything is one-twelfth his size. Thus the ordinary human Gulliver becomes *Quinbus Flestrin,* "the Great Man-Mountain." That Lilliputian term and most of the other words from the languages Gulliver encounters — like *splacknuck* from his visit to Brobdingnag, where he is the one who is one-twelfth the size of everyone else (and where he is the size of a *splacknuck*) — remain within the covers of the book. But because Gulliver's story of Lilliput is so well known, *Lilliputian* has entered our vocabulary; and *yahoo* is so successful that it is known even among those who have no knowledge of Swift's book.

THE AGNOSTIC

In the early days of the Christian era, the apostle Paul came to Athens, where he debated with Epicurean and Stoic philosophers and then gave a sermon. Looking for common ground, he said, "Athenians, I see how extremely religious you are in every way. For as I went through the city and looked carefully at the objects of your worship, I found among them an altar with the inscription, 'To an unknown god.' What therefore you worship as unknown, this I proclaim to you. . . ." In the original Greek, "To an unknown god" is *agnostōi theōi.*

Nineteen centuries later, at a meeting in 1869 of the Metaphysical Society in London, the scientist Thomas Henry Huxley, grandfather of Aldous Huxley, took the first word of that inscription and added *-ic* to form a new word of English, *agnostic.* It meant someone who does not know whether God exists, in contrast to the much older word *atheist* (first used in the 1500s), referring to one who denies the existence of God. For those who know Greek, Huxley's was a logical choice; *gnostic* refers to a "knowing" person, in particular one who has spiritual knowledge, and *a-* is a prefix meaning "not."

The word was immediately accepted because of Huxley's prominence in public discussion of the debate between science and religion. And even though it doesn't look like an everyday English word, it had the advantage that our language has made ample room for words of Greek origin that have to do with *philosophy* and *theology* — both of these words, indeed, being from the Greek.

THE QUIRK OF THE QUARK

Greek and Latin are the usual sources for scientific and psychological terminology in English, as in the cases of *psychedelic* and *agnostic.* But in science the inventor or discoverer has considerable authority over nomenclature, so a quirky departure from the solemn ancient languages is also possible. That was the case with *quark,* the name chosen in 1963 for a hypothetical subatomic particle by the theorist who postulated it, Murray Gell-Mann. Instead of looking in a Greek dictionary for something meaning "small," he simply used a word that suggested smallness to him, *quork.* Shortly after he had labeled his particles *quorks,* he was reading James Joyce's obscure and punning novel *Finnegan's Wake* and came upon a line from Joyce's poem about legendary King Mark: "Three quarks for Muster Mark!" At the time, Gell-Mann had posited three kinds of quarks (there are now six), so Joyce's word seemed suited to his new concept. Accordingly, Gell-Mann changed the spelling to match Joyce's *quark.* Joyce himself apparently got the word from German, where it means "curds" and "nonsense." If Gell-Mann happened to be aware of those meanings, they would have reinforced his whimsical choice.

The existence of *quarks* has since been confirmed by experiments. Since Gell-Mann initiated the discussion of *quarks* and was respected by other physicists who followed up and confirmed his hypothesis, there was no doubt about *quark* being the word they all would use. In 1969 Gell-Mann was awarded the Nobel Prize in physics for his discovery.

BRUSH UP YOUR SHAKESPEARE

All the creations in this chapter, impressive as they are, pale when set next to the accomplishments of William Shakespeare. In addition to being the unquestioned champion of English literature, he is also the champion coiner of new words in English. In fact, the two championships go together. Shakespeare's writing is so memorable that the words he created remain in our collective memory. And of course they are repeated every time his plays are performed, which is often.

Shakespeare's plays and poems have a vocabulary of

more than 20,000 words, greater than that of most other writers. His creative use of language and wordplay are apparent. Not surprisingly, then, he has been credited with coining not just one or two but hundreds, perhaps even more than a thousand new words.

Unfortunately, there are no notes from Shakespeare's desk or commentaries from Shakespeare's time about any of his coinages, so it's not possible to learn his techniques from looking over the great wordsmith's shoulder. We can only judge from the results.

The list of words for which he has been given first credit is amazing. Here are just a few:

amazement	fashionable	noiseless
assassination	frugal	obscene
auspicious	generous	pedant
bandit	gloomy	premeditated
birthplace	gust	puke (verb)
circumstantial	hint (noun)	quarrelsome
cold-blooded	hurry (verb)	seamy side
courtship	jaded	shooting star
critic	Judgment Day	swagger (verb)
deafening	lackluster	tranquil
downstairs	laughable	undress (verb)
dwindle	lonely	unreal
employer	misquote	watchdog
eventful	monumental	well-behaved
excitement	mountaineer	wild goose chase
farmhouse	negotiate	worthless

In addition, Shakespeare has many coinages that involve switching verbs to nouns or vice versa. He apparently was the first to use the nouns *design, dialogue, scuffle,* and *shudder,* for example, made from older verbs, and the first to use the verbs *drug, elbow, gossip,* and *lapse,* made from older nouns.

Until just recently, there had been no doubt that Shakespeare holds the all-time record for bringing new words into the English language. According to the *Oxford English Dictionary,* the authority on such matters, Shakespeare's use is the earliest evidence for more than a thousand words that we use today. But there is growing evidence that Shakespeare was not the inventor of quite so many words, just the popularizer of them. The editors of the *Oxford English Dictionary* are discovering this new evidence as they revise that work for the twenty-first century. They are scrutinizing many lesser known texts of Shakespeare's time, texts that were passed over in making the first edition of the dictionary. In this process, time and again they have found other authors using words before Shakespeare did.

Work on the current revision of the *Oxford English Dictionary* has begun with the letter *M.* In just the first section of entries for that letter, there are half a dozen words formerly credited to Shakespeare that now have earlier attributions: *madcap* (adjective), *majestic* and *majestically, manager, marketable, marriage-bed,* and *metamorphize.*

These discoveries, however, do not detract from Shakespeare's importance in the creation of new words. As later chapters will show, the most successful new words are those so close to the edge of the vocabulary that they are invented over and over again till they finally catch on. By virtue of his matchless use of language, Shakespeare's lines and words were given unparalleled opportunity for success. Words that otherwise might have flickered and faded have become permanent presences in our vocabulary through his works.

Consider *marketable,* for example, a word originally credited to Shakespeare. The current editors of the *Oxford English Dictionary* have discovered that in 1577, when Shakespeare was just thirteen years old, one John Dee used *marketable* in a book called *General and Rare Memorials Pertayning to the Perfecte Arte of Navigation:* "At the time of their being marketable . . . they would evidently appear, so, to be rated." It was a quarter of a century later when Shakespeare used it in *As You Like It:*

> Rosalind: *Then shall we be news-crammed.*
> Celia: *All the better: we shall be the more marketable.*

Shakespeare's turn of phrase makes *marketable* memorable. The word may not have needed that boost, but it certainly didn't hurt.

When the editors have finished revising the *Oxford English Dictionary,* Shakespeare may be seen as one who made brilliant use of the words of others rather than inventing so many himself, just as he made brilliant use of the stories of others rather than inventing them himself. But his importance in popularizing them will remain. And this development is further evidence of an important principle: New words don't come just from a few geniuses; they come from everyone. John Dee was just as likely, or almost as likely, to come up with a successful new word as was Shakespeare.

4

The Myth of Gaps

Yes, my modest "Unabridged" will "fill a long felt want." It
will solidify the chinks of conversation, express the inex-
pressible, make our English language ornamental, elegant,
distinguished, accurate.

— *Gelett Burgess,* Burgess Unabridged

What's the best way to ensure the success of a
new word? Some say it's this: find a gap in our language
and fill it.

It's easy to see why so many people follow this principle. After all, the vocabulary of a language is not just a
haphazard heap of words (a great heap, in the case of English), but an organized whole. It's a network, a great web,
with one word tied to another. If there were no connections, word associations would be impossible. But there
are connections. Say *cheese,* for example, and a listener
will think of mozzarella or mice or photographs; say
cheesecake, and the listener will think of dessert and perhaps even pinups. Psychologists use word associations to
test our preoccupations and also our intelligence, because
our knowledge and our thinking depend on the connections we make among words.

Everyone has firsthand experience of these connections
in language. From searching among several related words
to find the right one, or trying to retrieve a word on the
tip of the tongue, we know that words are indeed related
in our minds. And it's in our minds that we create new
words. They are born there, not on the pages of dictionaries.

Now if words form a mental network, mightn't that network have some missing nodes? Mightn't there be gaps in our language just waiting to be filled? If this were so, the surest way to succeed in coining a word would be to find such a gap and fill it. It would be like finding a missing piece of a jigsaw puzzle. Or like filling a pothole in the road that everyone has had to swerve around, thus providing a public service.

Some of the coiners in the previous chapters have sought to fill gaps, but they haven't succeeded very often. Could it be that they didn't recognize the right gaps? Or is the gap theory fatally flawed? To test the theory, let's identify some prominent gaps and see what fits.

A NEW CENTURY, A NEW DECADE

In the late 1990s, an obvious gap in the language began to open. As the turn of the century approached, the gap got wider and wider and the need to fill it grew more urgent. Everyone assumed it would be filled, but it wasn't. It just gapes at us as we step around it in our present-day conversation.

What is that gap? A name for the first decade of the twenty-first century.

We needed a time-specific label to apply to the trends, fads, and characteristics of this decade, just as we had for most of the decades of the twentieth century. Especially after World War II, our culture seemed to divide itself into decades: the prosperous and complacent *fifties,* the rebellious *sixties,* the Me Decade of the *seventies,* the Greed Decade of the *eighties,* the booming *nineties.* Those decades gained their names readily enough, so naming the new one shouldn't have been too difficult. It was just the matter of finding the right word for the new decade so the pundits and prognosticators could go to work labeling its themes, predilections, and styles.

So after the *fifties, sixties, seventies, eighties,* and *nine-*

ties would come the — whats? As the nineties came to a close, the experts made their predictions. We would call the new decade the *aughts* or the *naughts* or the *zeros* or the *ohs* or maybe even the *oh-ohs*. Then everyone settled back to see which term would prevail. January 1, 2000, came and went . . . and January 1, 2001, . . . and January 1, 2002. Now, several years into it and against all expectations, the question still remains: What should the decade be called?

It turns out we have found no way to name this decade that would fit the pattern of the *twenties, thirties, forties, fifties, sixties, seventies, eighties,* and *nineties.* All attempts to come up with an alternative have failed because they were too obtrusive, too noticeably different from the established pattern. The gap remains.

The lesson of the Decade That Wouldn't Be Named is plain: Just because a word seems needed doesn't mean we will find one. Instead, we may resort to circumlocution rather than adopt a word that doesn't fit. So the first decade of the twenty-first century is just that: *the first decade of the twenty-first century* and nothing more.

One other lesson of the Decade That Wouldn't Be Named is the answer to the follow-up question: What will we call the decade 2010 through 2019? It doesn't take a linguist to figure out that the name will have to be *the second decade of the twenty-first century* or *the decade of the tens and teens* or another phrase, rather than a single word.

But just wait till we approach the year 2020! Headline writers, pundits, and prognosticators will welcome the *twenties* with open arms. Gentlemen and ladies, start your books now, with your title *The Twenties: Decade of . . . .*

THE EVENTS OF SEPTEMBER 11, 2001

On September 11, 2001, the peace of a sunny late-summer morning was shattered by the impact of four hijacked airplanes on the World Trade Center towers, the Pentagon, and a field in Pennsylvania. There were more direct casualties in these disasters than on any previous day in American history, and soon the entire country felt the impact in damaged or destroyed lives, businesses, and sense of security. Out of the ashes came patriotism, resolve, unity. And out of the ashes came new words, too, to describe new situations never before imagined.

Or did they? Here would seem to be a gap in the language as big as that where the World Trade Center towers had stood. But the day and its events are so far beyond our imagining that we cannot come up with a word for it.

A place name won't do as a designation for those events. The events stir memories of *Pearl Harbor* and *Oklahoma City,* and we refer to other memorable occasions by their locations — *Lexington and Concord, Gettysburg, Little Big Horn,* and *Wounded Knee* — but in this case that won't work. It's not just because several places were involved, but also because the places are too famous. *New York City* and *Washington, DC,* have too many other connotations; so do the *World Trade Center* and the *Pentagon.*

For lack of a suitable designation deriving from place, we have used the date as a reference point: *September 11.* That does have a well-known precedent. One other event in American history is referred to by its date: *July 4* or *the Fourth of July,* the date in 1776 when the Declaration of Independence was proclaimed in Philadelphia.

In addition to the spelled-out month and day, the numerals *9/11* or *9-11* have been used. Never before has such a historic event been so labeled (we don't write *7/4* for the Fourth of July), but because of the striking coincidence that *911* is the telephone number to call for help in an emergency, that numerical designation has been a success. Headline writers like the concision of this expression, just three numerals to take in all the events of that day. Further, there is a precedent in using paired numbers as a word in *24/7,* the recent slang term for 24 hours a day, 7 days a week. Still, the use of numbers in this way has no precedent in our vocabulary for commemorating a date, and the casualness of *9/11* seems not in keeping with the devastating personal loss and serious political consequences associated with the events. So as time goes on, we are more likely to use a phrase in referring to what happened on that day instead of filling the gap with a single expression. We will say *the events of September 11, 2001,* or *the terrorist attacks of September 11, 2001,* or some other phrase that appropriately encompasses the day's events.

So far, the events of that day have resulted in just one new term: *ground zero,* for the place of impact, the center of destruction in New York City where the World Trade Towers once stood. That phrase has succeeded because it is not really new; it's an old term for the location on the ground directly under a vast atomic explosion, corresponding to *air zero,* the location in the air above the ground where the bomb goes off. *Ground zero* had been gathering dust on the shelf in recent years because of a fortunate lack of atomic explosions. No one knows who first said *ground zero* in reference to the site where the World Trade Towers were attacked and collapsed, but the term immediately caught on because of its familiarity and emotional power.

A CORNUCOPIA OF GAPS

But back to the gaps. If you look closely enough, there seem to be gaps everywhere. For example, there seems to be no word for the "Tom Sawyer syndrome — using false joy to try to talk someone into sharing an undesirable task," or "hoping to debauch someone through false joy." Diana Welch of Woodland Hills, California, noticed that gap. She proposed in a 1992 letter to the *American Heritage Dictionary* that someone who does this could be called a *toyeur,* and the act *toyeurism.* "I think it's an excellent new word for our society," she explained, "as toyeurism is a common problem and there doesn't seem to be an appropriate word." She said she derived her terms "by somewhat condensing the words Tom Sawyer, knowing that most words in our English are simply condensed statements." *Toyeur* remains unused, however, and those who want to discuss this condition still have to say *Tom Sawyer syndrome.*

Specialists sometimes see gaps that would not be noticed by the rest of us. For example, who is aware that we have no word to describe the distinctive form of rhyming phrases exemplified by *fat cat, funny money,* and *night flight?* For most of us, it would probably do to say that these are *two-word rhyming phrases,* but apparently that's awkward when you're a specialist trying to construct a puzzle. Charles A. Mueller of Maryland, a creator of puzzles and word games, is another who sent a suggestion to the *American Heritage Dictionary* in 1992: "I've devoted an enormous amount of time researching the precise term, but without success. Several of my puzzles require extensive use of this phrase, and being unable to find a proper one, I was inspired to coin one to meet these needs." His proposal was *birhymagram,* from *bi* meaning "two," *rhym* meaning "rhyme," and *gram* meaning "message." A perfectly reasonable proposal, but it hasn't caught on at all in the decade since he proposed it, so it's still necessary to say "two-word rhyming phrase."

FOREIGN AID

One way we can confirm that there are gaps in our own language is to observe other languages. Anyone who has tried to translate from a foreign language into English knows the frustration of finding gap after gap where a single foreign word has to be patched with a whole phrase of English.

Take German, for example, our close kin as a language because we share a common ancestor. Someone translating German *Mann* or *Buch* will have no problem rendering those as the single English words *man* and *book*. But suppose a *Mann* with a *Buch* visits a *Konditorei*. What then? A *Konditorei* is a kind of café where you can indeed get coffee, but it's also much more of a bakery than we think of with the word *café*. And it gets harder. What about German *Gemütlichkeit*, for example? That word refers to a pleasant state of mind, but *pleasantness* hardly begins to cover the ground of *Gemütlichkeit*, which includes everything from friendliness to approachability to good nature. Or there is *Sprachgefühl*, to take another example. Its literal translation is "feeling for language," but more precisely it means having a sense of the nuances of expression in a language. And Volkswagen recently made a point of advertising the *Fahrvergnügen* of its cars, seemingly so much more than just the English "driving pleasure."

If a foreign term is important enough, a translator may want to bring it into English rather than having to resort to paraphrase time and again. That has happened with some German words that are now somewhat at home in English even as they keep a bit of a foreign look. In English-language dictionaries you'll find *Wanderlust*, the strong desire to travel. And you'll find that great aesthetic term *Kitsch*.

Kitsch is best defined as art that aims high and falls low. It is monumental, but in the sense that artwork so labeled stands as a monument to bad taste. It is earnestly banal. It is portraits of Elvis on velvet, lava lamps, paintings of dogs playing poker, pink flamingoes on the lawn — when these are taken seriously, that is. If you laugh at kitsch, its spell is broken.

FRENCH GAPS

When we borrow words from French, they look more at home. That is because speakers of French ruled England for nearly four hundred years, starting with William the

Conqueror's victory in 1066, and their domination of England resulted in deep influences on the English language. As a result, French is the language that has been the most generous in bequeathing words to English. Nearly half of our present-day vocabulary (including the words *language, generous, present,* and of course *vocabulary*) comes from French. Down to the present day, English speakers have continued to borrow words from French, everything from *prairie* (1773) to *entrepreneur* (1852), *elan* (1880), *decoupage* (1960), and *bustier* (1979). But even with a hundred thousand or so words from French already in English, there are still many French concepts we haven't borrowed.

Here's one. Have you ever heard of a *psychoéducateur?* No, it's not a teacher gone mad, but an occupation in French-speaking Canada. The word designates a professional who applies the insights of both psychology and education to the treatment of troubled children and adults. "The originality of this profession lies in the conviction that the daily life of these people offers privileged occasions for intervention," explains one source, "and, consequently, intervention in shared life situations becomes the cornerstone of the later developments." For such a person we might use a phrase — *educational psychologist* or *developmental psychologist* — rather than the single word *psychoéducateur.*

Another French word knocking at the door of English, so far unsuccessfully, is *terroir.* It means something like "territory," but with a human touch. That is, *terroir* is the land that nature provides, together with the way humans cultivate it. Because of this combination, every region has a unique *terroir.* It is argued that no matter how one might try, one can't produce the same wine, or for that matter the same potatoes, in two different places. *Terroir* is thus a matter of grave consideration (and contention) for winemakers, and is also the underpinning for the European

Community notion of "protected designation of origin"; no place can substitute for another. Although we could use *terroir* in English, we don't, except for a few wine lovers discussing French conditions. Instead, we use a phrase when that topic comes up.

How about *volupté?* That French word is related to the more ponderous English *voluptuousness,* but it has a *je ne sais quoi* that resists simple translation. It means taking pleasure in the senses.

Turning from the senses to the mind, we find the terms introduced into philosophical discourse by the anthropologist Claude Levi-Strauss: *bricoleur* and *bricolage.* As Levi-Strauss explains it in *The Savage Mind* (1962), a *bricoleur* is someone adept at performing a great number of diversified tasks. In contrast to an engineer, however, the *bricoleur* doesn't look for materials and tools specifically suited to each project; the *bricoleur* makes do with whatever is at hand.

There is a potential English equivalent for *bricoleur* in the name *MacGyver,* the eponymous hero of a television show who for seven seasons (1985–1992) saved the day by improvising solutions via kitchen science. In one episode, for instance, MacGyver used the case of a ballpoint pen to fix a fuel line and then fashioned a cannon out of a muffler, seat stuffing, gasoline, and a steering wheel knob — don't try this at home! But the words *MacGyver* and *MacGyverism,* used to refer to any of the hero's extemporaneous inventions, remain limited mainly to their old fan base. *Bricoleur* and *MacGyver* reveal a gap in the vocabulary of English, all right, but we are evidently comfortable leaving that gap unfilled.

AROUND THE WORLD IN EIGHT GAPS

Now that it's possible to circle the globe on the World Wide Web, it's easy to find translators struggling with gaps in the English language wherever you look. Here are eight examples of words for which translators have found no equivalent in English:

Spanish: desengaño. According to Wooil M. Moon, translator of the works of Baltasar Gracian (1601–1658), a Spanish Jesuit priest, in *desengaño* lies the beginning of wisdom. "*Desengaño* is more than 'disillusionment'; it implies the dispelling of deceit (*engaño*) and an awakening to truth. It is the moral straightedness, tempered with skepticism; a putting aside of naive and sentimental illusion."

Greek: kairos. In 1990 Carol Goss recorded her month-long travel in Turkey on videotape, 35 millimeter slides, black and white film, and a journal. These were the basis of the video art program she calls *Kairos,* explaining that "*kairos* is the Greek word for 'epochal time' or a 'changing of the gods,' for which there is no equivalent in English, because the cultural memory of that language group is too brief."

Hebrew: hesed. According to the Gospel of Luke, Mary's response to being chosen the mother of Jesus is the "Magnificat," a song or poem praising God, based on an original in the Hebrew Bible. One verse translates "And His mercy reaches from age to age for those who fear Him," but a translator offers this note: "*hesed* is the Hebrew term used for 'mercy'—there is no equivalent in English, but it involves God's mercy, tenderness, and His love for His people."

Arabic: Rabb. Here is a passage from an English translation of the Qur'an: "And thy Rabb has decreed that you obey none but Him, and do good to parents." Commentator Naseer Ahmad Faruqui Sahib explains: "I have not tried to translate the word *Rabb* in the above text as there is no equivalent in English language. The nearest rendering of the connotation of the Arabic word *Rabb* is One Who creates and then evolves and fosters through gradual stage to perfection or the goal of creation. This is an illustration of the excellence of Arabic over other languages. One simple word contains a whole world of meaning."

Sanskrit: shraddha. Shri Sai Baba was "a personification of spiritual perfection and an epitome of compassion" who lived in Shirdi, India, in the late nineteenth and early twentieth centuries. One of the cardinal principles of the "Sai Path" is *shradda*. A follower of Shri Sai Baba explains: "At best it can be understood as faith with love and reverence. Such faith or trust is generated out of conviction, which may not be the result of any rational belief or intellectual wisdom, but a spiritual inspiration."

Japanese: shakaijin. If you're a respectable working person holding a suitable job, you're a *shakaijin* in Japanese. Dori Digenti, Director of Training of the MIT Japan Program, explains how the *shakaijin* is molded: "From early childhood, the priority of the Japanese child-rearing and education system is to create the *shakaijin* (a responsible member of society). Through imparting Confucianist values of merit and achievement, combined with societal values of perseverance and competition/cooperation, the educational and training systems serve as a vetting mechanism for the large Japanese company. When the young recruit enters the company, he is further trained in the company culture, resulting in a malleable, effective, and highly competitive human resource base."

Tagalog: takal. Even as concrete and simple a concept as *takal,* in the Tagalog language of the Philippines, has no equivalent in English. A translator comments, "It basically means the number of 'scoops,' 'cups,' 'liters,' etc., the volume of grain using any measuring instrument — it could be a cup, a glass, etc."

Wolof: jom. In 1982 Ababacar Samb of Senegal in West Africa made an 80-minute feature film entitled *Jom, The Story of a People.* He explained, "*Jom* is a Wolof word which has no equivalent in English or French. Jom means courage, dignity, respect. It is the origin of all virtues." A critic, Roy Armes, commented that "the film travels exuberantly through time to capture situations linked only by their common concern with the concepts of honor and dignity, the importance of keeping one's word and not being bought or corrupted."

GAPS LEFT AND RIGHT

Almost everywhere the mind turns, it seems, a gap presents itself. In the *Vocabula Review* for August 2001, for example, Julian Burnside points out a foreign gap and some domestic ones:

> —An equivalent for Italian *ma gare,* meaning something like "Ah, but that it were so."
> —A word for the sensation of disaster narrowly averted and later remembered from the vantage point of safety, and for the opposite, a moment when you feel guilt despite knowing you are innocent.
> —A word to take the place of *yes,* when it is used in conversation to signify that the hearer is understanding, but not agreeing with, the argument being developed by the speaker.
> —A word for the sensation when sleepiness swerves briefly back into alertness at the moment your head drops forward during a dull lecture.
> —A noun corresponding to the verb *ignore,* but different from *ignorance,* one that could be used in a statement like "She treated him with contempt and ignore."

Needless to say, none of these gaps shows signs of being filled. The English language continues to discuss such matters in more roundabout phrasing.

THE NEEDIEST CASES

Even the most visible gaps can remain gaping long after they are exposed. In 1955, for example, in the *New York Times Magazine,* the editor of the bridge column pointed out seven major gaps in the English vocabulary that were far from trivial. The author, Albert H. Morehead, wasn't an uninformed crank; he was in the midst of a second career as an editor and publisher of dictionaries, thesauri, and encyclopedias. The gaps he noted weren't obscure matters like labels for two-word rhyming phrases. They weren't sniglet situations like the sound an empty aluminum can makes when it's crushed or the position of one's head while eating a taco. Instead, they dealt with situations in everyday life. These are Morehead's seven neediest cases:

1. A dignified substitute for *boyfriend*, suitable for women who are no longer teenagers but have a committed relationship with a member of the opposite sex.
2. A similar substitute for *girlfriend*.
3. A replacement for *am not* in questions that would avoid the stuffiness of *am I not*, the stigma of *ain't I*, and the supposed ungrammaticality of *aren't I*.
4. A word meaning brothers and sisters that does not specify gender. In other words, *siblings*, but that's too scientific a term.
5. A word meaning "to state an opinion." You can say *opine*, but people are likely to laugh.
6. A word to indicate that you're listening to someone: not *yes*, which implies agreement with what the person has to say, or *Indeed!* which sounds stuffy, and not just a nod or grunt. (Nearly fifty years later, Burnside expressed a similar wish in his *Vocabula Review* article.)
7. A word to mean *he or she*. (Yes, even back in 1955, before the women's movement and its demand for pronoun equality, it didn't seem right to have a non-gender-specific *they* for more than one person but to be forced to choose between *him* or *her* for just one.)

Morehead saw these as gaps to be filled and was optimistic that they would be. "Usually when there is a serious gap in a language someone invents a word to fill it," he concluded. "At first the new word may be called slang, but if it pleases the public it will eventually become respectable."

More than two generations have passed since he wrote that plea, time enough for words to be invented to fill those gaps and become established in our language. At the start of the twenty-first century, do we still recognize these as gaps, or have they been filled?

The answer is apparent: Every one of those seven gaps still remains.

These examples — and there could be countless more — demonstrate that there are indeed abundant gaps in our vocabulary. Some are trivial, but some are serious. Though we have half a million words at our disposal, we could easily use half a million more.

But a gap in the vocabulary does not mean a gap in the language. Our language, like all human languages, can express anything. Sometimes we use a single word; sometimes we use a phrase. The evidence of this chapter shows that we are often quite satisfied with the phrases. Gaps there are, but they resist filling. Calling attention to a gap in the language is largely a waste of breath.

In fact, as we will see later, multitudes of new words are created day after day, month after month. They are in the air all around us, like snowflakes falling from the sky of human creativity. Some, like *jukebox* (1939) and *fast food* (1951), fall in newly opened gaps, giving us a term for something that was just invented. Some, like *teenager* (1941) and *24/7* (1985), land on solid ground, where we already had a perfectly good word or set phrase (*adolescent, round the clock*). These words do not fill a gap at all but give an additional perspective to something familiar.

Since there are many more concepts than there are pre-existing words, there will always be gaps in the vocabulary of any language. Many of these gaps will go unfilled, despite being called to our attention and despite any number of ingenious and utilitarian proposals to fill them. Whether a new word survives thus does not depend on whether it fills a perceived gap in our vocabulary, and not even on whether it is useful, since the landfill of discarded new coinages has an ample supply of useful terms. It depends rather on whether the word resonates with the speakers of a language, and that depends on a number of factors that we will investigate a little further on.

5

Exceptions That Test the Rule

As we have seen, the notion that gaps in a language must be filled doesn't hold up under scrutiny. Gaps there may be, but it's possible to talk around them. A language doesn't need a word for everything as long as it has sentences.

But what about new things: new products, new discoveries, new ideas, new causes? Don't they need new words? In these cases, wouldn't the things help the words succeed? Well, yes and no.

BRAND NAMES

If there's anything a new product needs, it's a brand name. To the extent that the product succeeds, the name will too. It's a sure thing, the one way to guarantee that a new term will be a success: spend mighty amounts of money on marketing, persuade people to buy and keep on buying a product, and they will call it by the name you give it. *Cadillac* or *Coffeemate, Vaseline* or *Viagra* — if it sells, they'll talk about it.

Of course, a name is a special kind of word. Most brand names, like other kinds of names, aren't included in dictionaries, because they aren't part of the general vocabulary of a language. They designate one particular thing, while words in the general vocabulary accommodate whatever thing of a certain type comes along. For example, *Big Mac* designates only a particular kind of hamburger sold by McDonald's (in this case consisting of two beef patties, sesame seed bun, American cheese slice, sauce, lettuce, pickles, onions, salt, and pepper), while *hamburger* or *cheeseburger* can apply to any such item of food regardless of who makes it.

When you want a product, a company would like you to think of its brand name rather than a generic term. Think *Listerine* instead of *mouthwash, Jell-O* instead of *gelatin dessert, Clorox* instead of *bleach, Band-Aid* instead of *adhesive bandage, Ben & Jerry's* instead of *ice cream.* It is a measure of their success that these brands need no further explanation. One needn't say *Listerine mouthwash, Clorox bleach, Ben & Jerry's ice cream;* the brand name alone will do. Lesser-known brands do require the generic term for clarification: *Mentadent mouthwash, Friendly's ice cream.*

Sometimes successful product names cross over and become generic terms. It's a kind of success that companies hate, because a word in the general vocabulary is no longer private property. As long as a company can keep its brand name out of the general vocabulary and restricted to its product, it can prevent anyone else from using that name for a rival product. But the company does want people to talk about the product. There's the dilemma.

The Coca-Cola Company wants people to think of a *Coke* when they want a soft drink. But if the marketing is successful enough and the name *Coke* is embedded in people's vocabulary, people will ask for a *Coke* and be satisfied if they get a Pepsi. In fact, in the southeastern United States, home of Coca-Cola, *Coke* is such a successful brand that many people there (and in the rest of the country) refer to any soft drink as a *coke.*

Nevertheless, Coca-Cola is able to maintain the distinctiveness of its brand by aggressive marketing and vigilant lawyering. The two go together. To the extent that marketing buys success for a brand name, it is also likely to foster use of the name as a generic word. The company's lawyers try to keep the name on a leash, warning rivals as well as innocent bystanders not to play with it so freely.

Despite such efforts, however, some brand names have slipped the leash, run wild, and joined the pack of the general vocabulary. Here are some of them:

aspirin: A name for acetylsalicylic acid, trademarked by the Bayer Company of Germany at the start of the twentieth century.

elevator and escalator: Both originally trademarks of the Otis Elevator Company.

zipper: A name given to a "separable fastener" by the B.F. Goodrich Company many years after it was invented. The new name helped the zipper attain popularity in the 1930s.

loafer: For a moccasin-like shoe.

cellophane: For a transparent wrap made of cellulose.

granola: A trademark registered in 1886 by W.K. Kellogg, now used for a "natural" kind of breakfast cereal.

ping-pong: For table tennis, a trademark registered by Parker Brothers in 1901.

Still on the edge nowadays, although straining at the leash, are:

Xerox: For photocopier.

Kleenex: For facial tissue.

Band-Aid: For adhesive bandage.

Tupperware: For storage container.

Scotch tape: For transparent adhesive tape.

Jacuzzi: For whirlpool bath.

Jazzercise: For exercise to jazz music.

Unlike most brand names, these words on the edge do show up in dictionaries. That makes the companies uneasy, because the presence of a word in a dictionary is an indication that the word is being used as a generic term. Lawyers for the companies scrutinize new editions of dictionaries and send letters to their publishers asking them to make sure that the names of their products are listed as trademarks.

CREATING BRAND NEW BRAND NAMES

Most brand new words arise naturally, as the next chapter will explain. But most brand new brand names are different. They are consciously created, like the words discussed in chapters 2 and 3. While most of those deliberately coined words fail, brand names have something to cling to. They stay around as long as the product itself— unless someone decides to rename the product.

To be sure, some brand names arise by natural processes. It's natural to give a product the name of its originator. So our cars are *Fords* and *Chryslers,* our soup is *Campbell's,* our chocolate is *Hershey's,* our fast food is *McDonald's,* our department stores are *Sears* and *Macy's* and *Marshall Field's.* The possessive *'s* shows that the sense of proprietorship remains strong, even if (as with McDonald's, for example) the original proprietor is long gone. It's considered such a positive influence that some products are given made-up names like *Aunt Jemima* and *Betty Crocker.*

It's also natural to use a place name: *Old Milwaukee* beer, *California Pizza Kitchen, Kentucky Fried Chicken.* Or to use a self-explanatory name: *Payless Drugs, Save-On-Foods, Thrifty Car Rental.*

Today, however, trendy companies want something more than a handle for a product. They want a name that will sell it. So they go to experts in creating brand names.

And what do the creators of brand names look for? Strangely enough, the same things that creators of new words look for. You can hire Yourdictionary.com, for example, to design a brand name for you that will have all these qualities:

—Clear meaning.
—Creative structure, a combination of elements that suggest the desired qualities of the product.
—Appealing sound.
—Recognition value.
—Prestige value, conveyed for example by a French or Italian name.
—Catchy rhythm: "A roller coaster named 'Super Duper Looper' may sound silly, but people remember the name."
—Emotive value of words such as *American, mother,* or *family.*

Lexicon, a California company that designs brand names, waxes poetic:

> *Conventional wisdom suggests that a good name is distinctive, memorable and easy to pronounce. We agree. But a great name is a different story. A great name speaks for you. It leads the way, breaking down old perceptions and creating new ones.*
>
> *A good name gets your attention. A great name changes your thinking. Like a well-written poem, a great brand name has a purpose; it provokes, inspires, uplifts. Don't settle for less.*

What poems has Lexicon written? Here are a few of the brands they have named:

Pentium, Celeron, Itanium, and Xeon (for Intel)
Slates (dress pants for men by Levi Strauss & Co.)
Forester and Outback (for Subaru)
VUE (for Saturn's SUV)
Embassy Suites
Optima (for American Express)

As well known as these brand names are, most consumers probably would not classify them as provoking, inspiring, or uplifting. They just seem reasonably familiar and comfortable, qualities that help any word succeed. The Intel names sound properly scientific; the Subaru names sound properly outdoorsy (with a whiff of Australia in *Outback*); *VUE* is nearly an anagram of SUV; *Embassy Suites* is descriptive with an air of prestige; and *Optima,* so close to "optimum," conveys "the best."

Lexicon was more provocative when it invented the name *Dasani* for Coca-Cola's bottled water. The Dasani website gives this answer to a question about the name:

> *People are having a lot of fun guessing the origin of the name* Dasani. *One Coca-Cola executive jokingly said it sounded like a "Roman god of water." Actually, the name* Dasani *is an original creation. Consumer testing showed that the name is —*

Wait just a minute. Before you find out what qualities consumer testing showed, take just a moment and consider what the name *Dasani* suggests to you. Don't read ahead!

OK, ready? According to the website, the name *Dasani* "is relaxing and suggests pureness and replenishment."

That seems a heavy and unlikely load for a word that doesn't have any close relatives in the English vocabulary. If any associations are possible, the *-ani* ending might suggest something Italian like *frangipani* (a flower) or *timpani* (kettledrums), or perhaps something altogether different, like *Pakistani.* This is not to say *Dasani* is a failure as a name, just that it's hard to imagine the name *Dasani* by itself generating sales. The tail rarely wags the dog, and a brand name is the tail.

Lexicon also invented *Swiffer,* the name of Procter & Gamble's disposable mop. It competes with SC Johnson's *Grab-It.* Is either product going to grab the greater share of sales because of its name?

And finally, Lexicon came up with the name *Nexcare Active Strips.* What might they be? They are 3M's counterpart to *Band-Aids* and *Curad Adhesive Bandages.* Compared to these names, *Nexcare* is more creative, but it doesn't convey what the product does.

Consumer testing can determine whether people like a name. But consumers are curious about the product, not its name. A company that specializes in brand name creation can be helpful in warning against names that will cause a negative reaction, but even an ugly name need not prevent a brand from succeeding: "With a name like Smucker's, it has to be good!"

The "meaning" of a brand name can be manipulated. Consider *Marlboro.* After *Coca-Cola, Marlboro* is the most recognized brand name in the world, and it is far and away the best-selling American cigarette. Thanks to "the Marlboro man," the brand now conveys an image of the rugged outdoors. But it began as quite the opposite: a dainty ladies' cigarette, introduced in 1924 with the slogan "Mild as May." In 1955 it was abruptly repositioned as the cigarette of "the Tattooed man" who was utterly manly even as he accepted a filter in his cigarette. Pictured as a cowboy, the Marlboro man and his Marlboro cigarette became icons of ruggedness. No matter, either, that the name migrated to the United States in 1902 from *Marlborough* Street in London, England, where the British Phillip Morris company had its main factory.

With all those changes, *Marlboro* is doing fine as a brand name, in part because it isn't clever. Cleverness is a problem facing Segway, the name of the personal transporter unveiled in 2001 as the urban answer to the automobile. It's a witty respelling of *segue.*

A good brand name, like a good new word, won't be too obtrusive, and this may present the biggest problem for a company in hiring a professional firm to create a brand name. Like the creators of new words, creators of brand names often want recognition, and recognition comes from doing something conspicuous. That will not succeed with words or with brands.

OPERATION SMART NAME

We have come to expect a lot from a certain kind of brand name, the name for a military operation. Assigning code names for such operations began in the twentieth century, and namers quickly realized that the designations shouldn't be arbitrary. A name had to serve three purposes: safety, to avoid revealing the strategy or goal of an operation; dignity, so soldiers would not appear to be sacrificing their lives for trivial or comic purposes; and inspiration. To these ends Winston Churchill issued these instructions to his commanders during World War II:

> *Operations in which large numbers of men may lose their lives ought not to be described by code words which imply a boastful or overconfident sentiment, . . . or, conversely, which are calculated to invest the plan with an air of despondency. . . . They ought not to be names of a frivolous character. . . . They should not be ordinary words often used in other connections. . . . Names of living people — Ministers and Commanders — should be avoided.*

Following these principles, the originally proposed name *Roundhammer* for the invasion of Normandy was recognized as too frivolous and was changed to *Overlord*.

With varying degrees of success, U.S. namers of operations have followed these principles in recent years. For the 1983 invasion of Grenada, the U.S. Atlantic Command chose the somewhat overblown designation *Urgent Fury*. The invasion of Panama in 1989 was named *Just Cause*, soon to be followed by *Desert Shield* and *Desert Storm* of the Persian Gulf War.

After the terrorist attacks of September 11, 2001, the United States embarked on an unprecedented war against terrorism. The uncertain nature of the war was reflected in the code name for the operation, which underwent two changes within the first two weeks after September 11. At first it was *Noble Eagle*, then *Infinite Justice*. But on September 20 a reporter raised a question about this in a press conference with Secretary of Defense Donald Rumsfeld:

> Q: Speaking of vocabulary, is Infinite Justice the name of this operation? And I ask that for a very specific reason.
>
> A: I have heard those words. I do not know that they've been adopted, and I think they're probably under review.
>
> Q: Because in talking to several Islamic scholars, they find that name offensive. The only person or thing that can grant infinite justice, according to their religion, is Allah.
>
> A: I understand. I understand. And obviously the United States does not want to do or say things that create an impression on the part of the listener that would be a misunderstanding, and clearly that would be.

The name was soon changed to *Enduring Freedom*.

Such experiences have taught military namers to avoid exaggeration as well as frivolity. If a name is not carefully vetted, it can lead to trouble. A website that randomly generates names for military operations shows the potential trouble thoughtless coining could bring. Here is a recent list generated by the American Military Operation Name Generating Device:

1. Operation Expansive Hellhound
2. Operation Nervous Daisy
3. Operation Shining Bull
4. Operation Beaming Wolverine
5. Operation Ireful Knife Blade
6. Operation Overpriced Sucker Punch
7. Operation Fabled Turban
8. Operation Bisexual Explosion
9. Operation Red Demon
10. Operation Bloodthirsty Hydra

To overhear discussion of *Operation Nervous Daisy* or *Operation Bisexual Explosion* would certainly confuse an enemy, but those names would confuse our own soldiers, too. Churchill's rules still apply.

SCIENTIFIC TERMS

Suppose you're advancing the cause of science rather than pitching a product, and you have something new to report — a new element, a new compound, a new species. How does it get a name?

Paradoxically, if instead of creating a new word you aim to create new understanding of the physical world, any word you create has a much better chance of succeeding than does a new word in the general vocabulary. Scientific terminology is different from everyday vocabulary. There is no official register for the ordinary words of English, no dictionary that has the force of law, no Academy of the English Language to set standards for admission. There are no judges. It's the law of the jungle, survival of the fittest.

But it's different with scientific terms. Just as scientists take animals and plants from the wild and protect them in sheltered environments to study them, so they take words they have coined for new discoveries and give them special protection. In science, there are national and international associations that set policy and give approval for the names of new things.

If you discover a new element, for example, you must get approval for its name from the International Union of Pure and Applied Chemistry. There can be a fierce argument, but it will be settled by the international union rather than the law of the jungle. Sometimes there is indeed considerable disagreement about the names of elements. In the 1990s Americans, Russians, and Germans had created new elements 104 through 109 in their laboratories, and all wanted their roles in the creations properly honored by the names. For element 106, for example, the

Lawrence Berkeley Laboratory in California wanted *seaborgium*, in honor of one of their chemists, Glenn T. Seaborg. Others wanted to call element 106 *rutherfordium*, in honor of physicist Ernest Rutherford, a New Zealander. After long negotiations, the union finally ruled that element 106 would be called *seaborgium*, while element 104 would have the name *rutherfordium*. That was it; everyone abides by that decision.

All aspects of chemistry have strict rules for terminology, governed by the International Union of Pure and Applied Chemistry. Organic compounds, for example, use the "Hantzsch-Widman suffixes" in their names. If they have three rings containing nitrogen and are unsaturated, the suffix must be *-irine;* three rings containing nitrogen but saturated, *-iridine;* three rings without nitrogen and unsaturated, *-irene;* three rings without nitrogen but saturated, *-irane.* Numbers also must be stated according to a specified pattern. For example, if a compound consists of 486 of something, its name must begin with the prefix *hexaoctacontatetracta-*, which breaks down as: *hexa-,* "six"; *octaconta-,* "eighty"; and *tetracta-,* "four hundred."

In biology, the method of naming organisms is well known. Following the system established by Carl von Linné (Linnaeus) in 1758, the name of the genus or family comes first, then the species name. Both names come from Latin or are made to look like Latin: *Homo sapiens* (that's us), for example, or *Raphus cucullatus* (that's the extinct dodo). Each species also belongs to larger named categories that can include kingdom, phylum, class, order, suborder, infraorder, superfamily, family, subfamily, and tribe before getting to genus and species.

Common names of plants and animals are quite different. As part of the general vocabulary, most of them were in existence long before Linnaeus. They operate by the conventions of everyday language, not the logic of scientific analysis. As a result, while the scientific names are orderly and agreed upon, the common names show wide variety and disagreement. One creature may have many common names, like the fish called *alewife, big-eyed herring, blueback herring, branch herring, gaspereau, kyack, river herring, sawbelly, skipjack,* and *spring herring.* To biologists those are all simply *Alosa pseudoharengus.* Conversely, one common name may cover a multitude of different species. The plant name *Jacob's ladder* can refer to *Polemonium caeruleum* and other species of the genus *Polemonium,* as well as *Smilax herbacea, Celastrus scandens, Linaria vulgaris, Streptopus roseus, Chelidonium majus, Diodia virginia,* and several others. It is only the scientific names, not the common names, that respect the authority of the scientists.

Who gets to bestow the scientific name on an animal or plant? That honor goes to the author of the first publication using a valid name. There is an International Commission on Zoological Nomenclature that determines standards for names of animals and an International Association for Plant Taxonomy that does the same for plants.

Although scientific names are decided by higher authority rather than by the open competition of the general vocabulary, there is one principle that applies to both: a successful new term needs to fit in. Rules established by the governing bodies see to that in the case of scientific words, while the law of the jungle that puts a premium on camouflage sees to it in the case of ordinary vocabulary.

IDEAS AS BRAND NAMES

What about those who have nothing so tangible as an element or a new species to tell about, but instead have a new idea to offer? This too needs a name. Some people who have become famous because of their ideas find that the ideas take on their names: *Darwinism* or *Freudian psychology,* for example. Others may use their names in hopes of making both themselves and their ideas famous, as with *The Peter Principle: Why Things Always Go Wrong* by Dr.

Laurence J. Peter and Raymond Hull (1969). (This principle can be stated in a single sentence: "In a hierarchy every employee tends to rise to his or her level of incompetence.")

Most authors, however, aren't celebrated or brash enough to use their own names as new words, especially when they are just beginning to advance an idea. Instead, they invent a word or phrase that gives an inkling of the idea. They then wrap it in a book and add a subtitle that explains what the word means. For example:

Your Erroneous Zones: Step-by-Step Advice for Escaping the Trap of Negative Thinking and Taking Control of Your Life by Wayne Dyer (1976).

The Cinderella Complex: Women's Hidden Fear of Independence by Colette Dowling (1981).

Selfishians, Otherishites and Fairishers: A Guide to Harmonious Relationships by Costas Hercules (1982).

Cultural Literacy: What Every American Needs to Know by E. D. Hirsch, Jr. (1987).

Innumeracy: Mathematical Illiteracy and Its Consequences by John Paulos (1989).

Flow: The Psychology of Optimal Experience by Mihaly Csikszentmihalyi (1990).

Edge City: Life on the New Frontier by Joel Garreau (1991). An "edge city" is defined as a new city springing up around freeway interchanges on the outskirts of an established city.

The Pinball Effect: How Renaissance Water Gardens Made the Carburetor Possible, and Other Journeys through Knowledge by James Burke (1996).

GoodStress: How Rational Emotive Behavior Therapy Can Help You Change Unwanted Emotions and Behaviours by Wayne Froggatt (1997).

Interface Culture: How New Technology Transforms the Way We Create and Communicate by Steven Johnson (1997).

Friendshifts: The Power of Friendship and How It Shapes Our Lives by Jan Yager (1999).

Bobos in Paradise: The New Upper Class and How They Got There by David Brooks (2000).

Sometimes two thinkers hit upon the same word to characterize their ideas, as in the case of two recent books for bereaved women:

Widowing, Surviving the First Year by Jane Krimbill and Nancy Brown (1995).

Widowing, A Guide to Another Life by Nancy H. Payne (1997).

Sometimes, too, the new word is sufficiently clear from its constituent parts not to need a subtitle. *Barkitecture* by Fred Albert (1999), a book about the architecture of doghouses, is an example.

For all the publicity that the marketing of a book provides, however, most words invented as brand names for ideas fail to become adopted. They are usually too clever for their own good.

barkitecture

Futurologists and predictors of trends have been especially active in coining new words for the new circumstances they foresee. The titles of Alvin and Heidi Toffler are examples, starting with *Future Shock* (1970), referring to the fear of rapid technological change and telling how to cope with it. Then came *The Eco-Spasm Report* (1975), warning of economic and social collapse. *The Third Wave: The Classic Study of Tomorrow* (1980) informed us that we live in a *third wave,* an information age which has replaced the earlier agrarian and industrial cultures. Next came *Powershift: Knowledge, Wealth, and Violence at the Edge of the 21st Century* (1990). And recently the Tofflers wrote a foreword to promote *Cyberschools: An Education Renaissance* by Glenn R. Jones (1997).

FAITH IN THE FUTURE: 99 TRENDS

Today nobody works the future as assiduously as Faith Popcorn. Back in 1986, she foresaw that Americans would be going out less and staying home more. Expressed that way, the prediction might not have been recognized as brilliant insight. But Popcorn invented a word for it — *cocooning* — and with that one word, she made staying at home a fashionable trend. The once-despised *couch potato* suddenly had a front-row seat at the cutting edge.

Popcorn's *cocooning* was a successful coinage that now has a place in most dictionaries. It established her reputation as a predictor and apparently whetted her appetite for coining words. She has made many predictions and coined many words since.

In 1996 she wrote a book with Lys Marigold titled *Clicking: 16 Trends to FutureFit Your Life, Your Work, and Your Business.* Not only the title, but the 17 trends (she increased the number by one for a later edition) have names of her own invention: *99 Lives, Anchoring, AtmosFear, Being Alive, Cashing Out, Clanning, Cocooning, Down-Aging, Egonomics, EVEolution, Fantasy Adventure, Icon Toppling,*

Mancipation, Pleasure Revenge, Small Indulgences, Save Our Society, and *Vigilante Consumer.*

In 2000, again with Lys Marigold, she expanded one of the 17 trends into a book of its own: *EVEolution: The Eight Truths of Marketing to Women.* The paperback version in 2001 had a double subtitle: *EVEolution: Understanding Women: Eight Essential Truths That Work in Your Business and Your Life.* The book's premise is that women are different from men not just biologically, but *shopologically.*

Also in 2001, this time with Adam Hanft, she produced a *Dictionary of the Future: The Words, Terms, and Trends That Define the Way We'll Live,* in which new coinages are the center of attention. The book presents future words in thirty-five areas ranging from Aging to New Behaviors, Technology and Transportation. Each chapter includes ten or twelve brand-new words created by the authors (they "found voids in the language that needed to be filled") as well as numerous additional words recently invented by others. The chapter on Biology and Biotechnology, for example, is full of words like *Anti-IgE* (a new kind of asthma treatment) and *pharmacogenomics* (creating drugs customized to an individual patient's genes), plus eleven words of the authors' own, including:

> *bio-freedom:* Freedom to indulge oneself after gene testing has determined one is not at risk for a certain factor like high cholesterol.
>
> *GENEology:* The study of one's genetic history.
>
> *womb service:* Fertilizing and growing a fetus to maturity outside of a woman's body.

It should be mentioned that, however successful she has been in predicting trends, Popcorn has generally failed to add words to our vocabulary. Only the first of her coinages, *cocooning,* has become part of the language. The conspicuous cleverness of her coinages, not to mention the occasional bizarre use of capital letters, makes them ill-adapted to everyday communication. That may be the way she wants it; they are bait to hook readers for her books.

IN THE NAME OF . . .

One other source of new words is new causes. Causes will naturally acquire descriptive labels, but those who advocate a cause often seek language that promotes their cause in addition to describing it, words that have the right connotations as well as denotations. For example, we are familiar these days with the clashing language about abortion from *pro-life* and *pro-choice* advocates. The former speak of the *right to life* of *unborn children,* while the latter uphold a woman's *right to choose* to abort a *fetus.*

In the late twentieth century, the women's movement perceived pervasive patriarchalism in the English language and made considerable efforts to change it. Publishers, professional organizations, and teachers have responded sympathetically to the numerous guidelines for nonsexist language that have been promulgated as a result of the movement. We now know not to say *man* when we mean *person,* not to say *he* when we mean *someone,* not to automatically refer to a doctor as *he* and a nurse as *she.* Usage has changed to the point that writing *they* for an unspecified individual, instead of *he,* has become the norm (*he or she* is a rarer choice, to the chagrin of those who would preserve the separateness of singular and plural). We have learned to say *flight attendant* rather than *stewardess, firefighter* rather than *fireman, letter carrier* rather than *mailman, server* rather than *waiter* or *waitress* (the odd ending of *waitron* has pushed that alternative into the background).

But certain new words advanced by some in the women's movement have been less successful. *Herstory* as an alternative to *history* and *womyn* as an alternative to *women* make their point by erasing *his* and *men* but are too clever and conspicuous to have received general acceptance. And the problem posed by the need to choose between *he/him* and *she/her* in the singular has proved utterly incorrigible. Over the centuries suggestions for a gender-neutral singular pronoun have been plentiful, including *shey, heshe, herm, em, en,* and *et;* but it is a gap that remains resistant to filling. English hasn't had a new pronoun for about a thousand years, and there is no sign it will acquire one any time soon.

In other words, the changes in the language achieved by the women's movement are relatively natural and inconspicuous ones. They are none the less significant, however, for being unobtrusive.

Names of different ethnic groups have shifted over the years to reflect the perspectives of those who belong to the group rather than that of outsiders. Finding a term that conveys the proper connotations can remain a problem, however, even after a name change. Also, since not all members of the groups share the same perspective, the terms continue to evolve.

American *Indians,* so named first by Columbus in the mistaken belief that he had reached India, have been renamed *Native Americans.* Yet there is a problem with this term, too, in its not being as distinctive or traditional as *Indian;* so some American Indians—perhaps the majority—prefer the older term.

Americans of African ancestry have been treated so badly by white persons that they have shifted several times from the names given them by whites. *Negro* was once the polite term, as was *colored,* but both words acquired negative associations as Americans of African ancestry continued to be the subject of pervasive discrimination. In the 1960s came the assertive, proud, plain, direct *black.* Today, with a shift of focus from color to ancestry, *African American* is the preferred term.

The kinds of new words discussed in this chapter represent special cases. Words for brands, science, ideas, and political causes operate under different rules than the ordinary words in our vocabulary. All involve people deliberately choosing terms they want adopted as standard in a certain forum, whether it is a market or a scientific field or a political cause. They all have institutional machinery, from publicity departments to political organizations, to promote the words they propose. To the extent that the things they stand for succeed, the words will too. This is very different from the conditions surrounding the birth of most new words. The next chapter turns to that natural process that governs the way most words come into being.

6

Natural Birth and Rebirth

> Don't make up your own language. If a word doesn't exist in a dictionary, how can other people understand its meaning?
>
> — *Nick Wright,* Plain English Network: The Business of Government in the Language of the People

Sorry, Nick. It can't be helped. Despite Wright's admonition, countless new words are born every day. They are part of a perpetual process of birth and rebirth natural to all living languages. As you mostly unconsciously search your memory for words to express yourself, you use not only the words that are already there but also new combinations of familiar elements. The process is so normal that it often goes without notice, even by yourself. Even if you are as cautious as Wright, you can hardly spend a day without coining a new word or two.

Not only are words easily born, they are also easily reborn. The majority of new words that endure are coined not just once, but many times before they become established. The circumstances that tempt one inventor are also there for another. Just as the calculus was independently invented by both Newton and Leibnitz when mathematics was ready for it, so new words appear again and again when the language is ready.

Most words come into being naturally. They need no high-tech lab, no fertility drug, no artificial insemination.

People just naturally give birth to words every day. These naturally born words are the healthiest and most likely to survive. Here are some true stories of natural word-birth:

> *In a department store, a mother became frustrated with her eight-year-old son. "Stop asking me to buy everything you see," she ordered. When that didn't work: "You'd better stop before I childabuse you!"*
>
> *Another mother to child: "You must behave." Child to mother: "I'm being have."*

In such cases, multiple independent births are common. That is, if a word is ripe for being born, it's likely to be born again and again. Here's one more true story to illustrate that point, with yet another mother to a child: "You won't get any treats at grandma's if you don't start *being have.*"

THE MAYOR "SCRUTINED"

It happens in high places, too. At a press conference in August 2001, Mayor Richard M. Daley of Chicago was asked about the increased scrutiny he would have faced if his brother Bill had decided to run for governor. The mayor replied:

> *Scrutiny? . . . Go scrutinize yourself! I get* scrutined *every day, don't worry, from each and every one of you. It doesn't bother me.*

It was a newborn word: *scrutined* instead of *scrutinized.* But the mayor wasn't the first to give birth to this new form. Here are a few other examples from the Internet:

> *But as surely as Ephesian Artemis represents the edibility of the pine nut, so too should other plants such as her Artemisia specie, named for her, be scrutined as possible sources of sustenance. Praise the Old Ways!*
> — World Seed Fund

The enduring appeal of community as 'being in common' needs to be scrutined as well. More specifically, how are communities brought together?
— Sociology department, Lancaster University, England

The Williams family has done and are doing so much for professional tennis and the thanks they get is harassment and their every move is analyzed, scrutined, and ostracized.
— Message board for the "Fabulous Williams Sisters," March 2001

In an ASCII form, a trace can be easily scrutined or generated using any text editor.
— Paper at International Symposium on Memory Management, October 2000

The means and ends of organizational activities must be scrutined and a way must be found to routinize the ethical analysis involved in their creation.
— Course outline, New Jersey Institute of Technology, Fall 1999

Despite this evidence of use, *scrutined* is unlikely to make its way to acceptability any time soon as long as *scrutinized* is established and well known. But it will continue to be born and reborn, and if enough mayors and tennis fans say it, one day it might become the norm.

REGARDS

Consider the well-known phrase *in regard to.* Unnoticed even by experts on language, in recent years a variant, *in regards to,* has not only been born again and again, but is nearly as widely used as *in regard to.* In early 2002 a Google search found 850,000 instances of *in regard to,* but also nearly 500,000 of *in regards to.*

In fact, there are those who regard *in regard to* as wrong. After all, we say *Give my regards to* and *as regards,* so why not *in regards to?* Traditionalists would reply that *regard* in *in regard to* means "look," and there would be one look, not many. In fact, one could construct a logical argument either way. *In regard to* has an advantage as the older phrase, but more and more modern writers find *regards* more natural, so it has a good chance for success.

LINNER TIME

When you give birth to a word, it seems entirely your creation. But often it turns out that others came independently to the same thought.

In the summer of 2001 Elaine A. Rauser of Hudson, New Hampshire, asked: "Could you please tell me if there is such a thing as 'word registration'? I have thought of a new word and would like to preserve its origin." Her word, she explained, is *linner* — "the meal which is eaten between lunch and dinner. . . . I told someone here at work and he said that he and his friend were just talking about that this weekend — the fact that there isn't a word to describe this event."

Something does seem to be missing from our present-day language: *brunch* is in the dictionary (and in our vocabulary), but *linner* isn't. As the previous chapter has shown, a gap in the language won't necessarily be filled, but here is a filler ready-made. Surely others will see how useful it is?

Yes indeed, and that turns out to be the surprise: *linner,* a straightforward combination of *lunch* and *dinner,* has been invented again and again. Here are a few examples from the Internet:

> *I had a cheeseburger for lunch/dinner. Linner. Dunch. It was yummy.*
>
> *— The Reject's Journal*
> on LiveJournal.com, March 3, 2001

> *you know, brunch is the most important meal of the day. not quite breakfast, not quite lunch. um, i dunno why*

they do not have lupper (lunch/supper) or linner (lunch/dinner).

— "dan the kitti man" on
LiveJournal.com, March 4, 2001

Basically a bunch of us [Turbo Toyota] mr2 freaks get together and chat for about an hour, then go for a short drive. After the short drive we eat linner (lunch/dinner).
— Alexius M. Ludeman Own Little Page, January 2001

We actually went out to linner (lunch/dinner) on Sunday, at one of my favorite Mexican restaurants, Rio Grande (great chips and salsa, good veggie fajitas, everything else is mediocre).

— Kerry in Virginia, February 2000

Due to an unexpected setback, we had a late lunch that day. It started a new tradition we liked to call "linner"— part lunch, part dinner—usually observed around 3–6 PM.

— Utah State University student trip
to Washington, DC, March 2000

. . . my dog barked upstairs. From that, I logically deduced that someone had broken into the house and was just waiting to kill me. So I went up to see what was wrong, and ended up hand-feeding her her lunch/dinner (linner? dunch?). It's now 4:43. . . .

— "Hazard Lights" at Diaryland.com,
January 2001

Spivak invented linner as the seventh important meal of the day after breakfast, brunch, lunch, linner, dinner, dipper and supper. Spivak couldn't hold down a job because he was always coming in late but he was never late for any of his meals.

— *The Shining,* version by
"Mauve Guest," October 2000

If brunch is a cross between BR-eakfast and l-UNCH, then is there a word for a cross between lunch and dinner? Luner? Dunch? Linner? Luer? Lun-Din?

— "contours provocations" journal,
February 1999

And finally, from David Letterman's Top Ten list for December 14, 1998, Things That Have Crossed President Clinton's Mind: No. 9, "How about a new meal between lunch and dinner called 'linner.'"

The examples could go on and on, but these are typical. By giving definitions, putting *linner* in quotation marks, speculating on other possible words for combinations of meals, asking if there is a word for it, or saying there should be a word for it, the various authors make it clear that each of them is inventing the word anew.

As "contours provocations" says, *linner* follows naturally on the pattern of *brunch.* Inspired by *brunch,* there have undoubtedly been thousands who have invented *linner* in the century since *brunch* was coined (in 1895 by an Englishman, Mr. Guy Beringer, according to the *Oxford English Dictionary).* As long as people hunger for a meal between lunch and dinner, there will probably be thousands more who coin *linner.*

But though *linner* is naturally and easily coined, it remains an open question whether it will ever make its way into the established vocabulary of English. There are some strikes against it, as can be seen in comparison with *brunch,* the word that inspired it. In *brunch,* the two words that make up its elements are more visible, including distinctive combinations of consonants, *br* and *nch.* In contrast, in *linner* the thin *l* is all that remains of *lunch,* and the isolated consonants *n* and *r* are the meager remains of *dinner.* And unfortunately, *inner* is a word by itself, unrelated to meals, so when someone uses *linner* to mean "a meal between lunch and dinner," an explanation always seems necessary.

Then too, the meal *linner* refers to is not nearly as firmly established as *brunch.* Many restaurants as well as homes serve *brunch,* but *linners* are rare. In fact, you may have to go as far as Moscow for an example. There the luxurious Hotel Baltschlug Kempinski advertises its *linner,* explaining it as "a Sunday feast between lunch and dinner." But this *linner* appears to be little more than an advertising gimmick. Baltschlug *linner* is evidently just a late brunch, served from 12:30 to 7 p.m. The *Moscow Times* restaurant guide explains *linner:* "The hotel's Sunday brunch includes unlimited amounts of sparkling wine, red and white wine, beer, juices, tea, coffee and fresh fruit, plus buffet brunch."

Nevertheless, *linner* remains readily available, frequently re-created in case of need or desire. If our eating habits shift significantly to later in the day, *linner* may be ready to establish itself.

MEALER INSTEAD?

Elaine Rauser still wanted credit for originating a word, so she came up with a truly original one. Abandoning *linner,* she proposed *mealer* as a name for a meal between lunch and dinner.

With *mealer,* there's no worry that someone else thought of it first. Rather, the problem is persuading anyone else to use it. Although it is composed of the familiar word *meal* and the familiar suffix -*er,* the combination of the two does not achieve a natural name for a meal. The -*er* suffix generally means "one who," so *mealer* naturally suggests "one who eats a meal" (and in fact there are instances of this use, as in *half-mealer,* one who eats just half a meal).This is the dilemma of any coiner who wants credit for a new word: If it's a natural creation, chances are someone else already has thought of it; if it's not natural, others are not likely to use it.

GOING TO PLERK

Plerk? That's *play* plus *work,* of course. It was coined by . . . Barry Stevens, a Gestalt therapist, author of *Don't Push the River.* No, it was coined by . . . Hans Ostrom, a professor of English at the University of Puget Sound. But when *plerk* is mentioned in a report on future jobs in the Brisbane region, commissioned by the city council of Brisbane, Australia, it's unlikely that the author relied on either Stevens or Ostrom. It's just another new word being born and born again.

MULTIPLE SOFTWARE

Well-established words as well as marginal ones have been born more than once. Take *software,* for example. That computer term was invented by John W. Tukey, a statistician at Princeton University. As long ago as 1958 he used the word in the *American Mathematical Monthly:*

> Today the "software" comprising the carefully planned interpretive routines, compilers, and other aspects of automative programming are at least as important to the modern electronic calculator as its "hardware" of tubes, transistors, wires, tapes and the like.

Tukey was already known for inventing another now-famous computer term. In 1946 he used the little word *bit* as the designation for a unit of information, a "binary digit" with value 0 or 1. That led a decade later to *bytes* (groups of bits, now always eight, a term invented by Werner Buchholz at IBM) and to today's *kilo-, mega-,* and *terabytes* of computer storage and information.

No wonder his inventions succeeded. They are natural developments of existing vocabulary, so natural that they hardly seem coined. A *bit* is indeed a "bit" of information, as well as a binary digit, and *software* perfectly contrasts with the physical *hardware* of a computer. The word is so natural it's surprising no one else thought of it.

Well, perhaps someone did. Here is the story of the birth of *software* as told by Paul Niquette, a California electrical engineer:

Until 1953, like most people at that time, I had never seen a stored-program digital computer—a von Neumann Machine. Then, while in my junior year at UCLA, I was actually paid to program the SWAC. It was in October of that year, that I coined the word "software" more or less as a prank. I never expected the term to be taken seriously. Although I uttered it in dozens of speeches and lectures, followed invariably by its definition, the consequent shrugs and smirks hardly provided an incentive to accept—let alone seek—any kind of credit for the word "software."

In other words, *software* too most likely had multiple parentage. There is no reason to doubt that, indeed, each person independently invented that word that was ready to be born.

PRO AND CON

Multiple births are most often natural and unobtrusive, but they can be conspicuous too. An example is *prosultant*. It's not natural, because it requires a clever reanalysis of the components of *consultant*. The prefix *con-*, a variant of *com-*, means "together," as in *conduct* (lead together), *conform* (shape together), *contract* (draw together). That's what it means in *consult* (take counsel together). By itself, however, *con* can be a negative, the opposite of *pro*. Interpreting it this way, two different enterprises have recently chosen to emphasize the positive in their consulting business by using *prosultant*. One is Prosulting Solutions, Inc., an information technology company in Ohio. President Michael D. Ochocki of Prosulting Solutions explains:

We are defining a new level of service above and beyond the level of "consultant" that you may have experienced in the past. This new level combines professionalism, leadership and expertise and may best be identified as "Prosultant."

Another is run by David S. Isenberg, author of "The Rise of the Stupid Network," who calls himself *Principal Prosultant^sm* and explains:

> PRO and CON are opposites. So a Prosultant^sm is everything that a CONsultant isn't. A Prosultant^sm is PROvocative, PROductive, PROactive. A Prosultant^sm has an attitude that's different from yours. A Prosultant^sm doesn't bring you fish, but goes fishing with you (and brings a big hook). A Prosultant^sm wants results, not employment. . . .

As the *sm* indicates, Isenberg has even registered *prosultant* as a "service mark," so if you want to advertise yourself as a prosultant, you need his license. Whether *prosultant* will ever enter the general vocabulary of English is another matter. It seems too clever by far to displace *consultant.*

AN INVENTIVE TRILEMMA

Another tempting coinage, more logical than *prosultant,* has emerged repeatedly over the centuries. In 1860 it was proclaimed by James Robinson Graves, a Southern Baptist preacher, to introduce his book *The Trilemma; or, Death by Three Horns:*

> TRI-LEMMA! Tri-lemma! It is not in the Dictionaries. Pray, what is a tri-lemma asks the Reader.
> When one is pinned between two difficulties, we say he is in a Di-lemma.
> When he is pinned between two difficulties, and pierced through by a third, may we not say he is in a TRI-LEMMA?
> Read and decide if Protestantism is not in just such a situation.

Graves thought he had invented *trilemma,* and for his purposes he had; but he was far from the first to do so. The *Oxford English Dictionary* offers this example of *trilemma*

from the diaries and letters of English preacher Philip
Henry in 1672:

> *Wee are put hereby to a Trilemma either to turn flat Inde-*
> *pendents, or to strike in with the conformists, or to sit*
> *down in former silence.*

And, in a 1725 book titled *Logick: or the Right Use of Reason in the Enquiry After Truth,* Isaac Watts, preacher and
composer of hymns, wrote:

> *This sort of argument may be . . . composed of three . . .*
> *members, and may be called a Trilemma.*

So the seventeenth, eighteenth, and nineteenth centuries had inventors of *trilemma,* and the twentieth did too.
Josh McDowell invented it for his 1972 book, *Evidence
Which Demands a Verdict,* which uses historical evidence
to argue for the truth of Christianity. His trilemma derives
from the choices presented by Christian apologist, scholar,
and fantasy writer C.S. Lewis, who posited that Jesus had
to be one of these three: liar, lunatic, or Lord.

In 1998, *trilemma* was invented yet again by Gwen
Morgan for her book *A Hitchhiker's Guide to the Child Care
Universe.* Her trilemma lay in the relationship among ra-
tios, wages, and price: in other words, quality for children,
compensation for staff, and affordability for parents.

It doesn't matter that *trilemma* is in the dictionary
now — at least in the *Oxford English Dictionary,* though
not in less comprehensive ones. It is still not in most people's vocabulary, but it lurks at the edge ready to be born
again. If people know *dilemma* and are faced with three
choices, they will be able to invent *trilemma* on the spot,
for the nth time.

AN OBJECTION

"If a word doesn't exist in a dictionary," Nick Wright reminds us in the statement at the start of this chapter, "how

can other people understand its meaning?" That's an important obstacle faced by new words: being understood. But the dictionary isn't the problem; a dictionary is a recorder of new words, not their source. Even if the writers of dictionaries chose to introduce new words, no one would know how to find them there, since you need to know a word before you can look it up. The few dictionaries of made-up words, like *Sniglets* and *Burgess Unabridged,* are amusing but utterly unsuccessful in persuading anyone to adopt their words. No, it works the other way around: people invent new words and, if these succeed, the makers of dictionaries then include them.

Of course, we do learn new words from dictionaries, but they are words we have already heard or read, words that are already established in our language. They are new to us, but not to English as a whole.

Alas for the publishers of dictionaries, we learn most of our vocabulary without their help. A typical adult vocabulary has been estimated to consist of sixty thousand words; even a six-year-old knows more than ten thousand. How many of these does anyone learn from a dictionary? Most of us learn most of our words instead from their shape and their context.

THE SHAPE OF NEW WORDS

The shapes of words we know lead us to shape new words. John Algeo, a leading scholar of new words, has demonstrated that almost all new words have familiar origins. They are extensions of our established vocabulary rather than completely new creations. In a study of some three thousand new words introduced between 1941 and 1991, Algeo noted six types of sources:

1. *Combining.* More than half of all new words result from making compounds, adding suffixes, or adding prefixes. *Moonlighting* is a compound, as is *scofflaw* and *doublespeak.* Some compounds may be spelled with hyphens,

like *also-ran* and *user-friendly*, or with spaces, like *dark matter* and *mad cow disease*, but these count as compounds because they are different than the sum of their parts. Familiar suffixes like *-ism*, *-ed*, and *-aholic* have helped create new words like *ableism*, *gendered*, and *shopaholic*. Prefixes like *pro-* and *docu-* have been used to create words like *prosultant* and *docudrama*.

2. *Shifting of meaning*. About 15 percent of new words are simply old words with new meanings. In recent times, we have seen *spin* take on a new political meaning, while *web* and *dot* have new uses in computer contexts.

3. *Shortening*. Somewhat less than 10 percent of new words result from either cutting back on existing words — like *bus*, from *omnibus*, or *fax*, from *facsimile* — or using acronyms — *radar*, from *r*adio *d*etecting *a*nd *r*anging; *scuba*, from *s*elf-contained *u*nderwater *b*reathing *a*pparatus; or *dink*, from *d*ual *i*ncome, *n*o *k*ids.

4. *Blending*. Compared with the other ways of forming new words, blends that use just parts of words rarely succeed, accounting for only about 5 percent of new words. That may be another reason why *linner* or *plerk* is unlikely

scuba

to attain a place in the established vocabulary. But *digerati* and *Frankenfood* have been moderate successes, and an all-time winner from the late nineteenth century is *smog.*

5. *Borrowing.* English is famous for swallowing words whole from other languages. In the Middle Ages, when England was ruled by speakers of French, English took in so many French words that French now accounts for perhaps half of our total vocabulary. We still borrow, but today only about 5 percent of our new words are taken from other languages. They are especially prevalent in the names of foods: *focaccia, salsa, vindaloo, ramen.*

6. *Creating.* The previous five categories provide for adaptation or adoption of words that already exist; this one involves making up words that have no connections to any others. At first glance this might seem the most likely kind of creation, but in fact, as Algeo says, "To make something out of nothing does not seem to be a human talent." None of the three thousand new words Algeo studied were without some foundation in existing words.

Created words may fail because of lack of clues to their meaning from the established vocabulary. Burgess's method of inventing new words for *Burgess Unabridged* helped ensure their failure; he knew that most new words came from old ones, but he preferred pure invention.

A few words (less than half of one percent of all successful new words) seem to have been invented solely because of the way they sound. *Burp, bebop,* and *gobbledygook* are among Algeo's examples.

ACTIVE *-ATE*

The lure of creation with familiar elements is almost irresistible. Consider the suffix *-ate,* for example. It means action! The *-ate* changes a noun or adjective to a verb, thus making a new word (and often requiring minor changes to the end of the original word in the process). Put it at the end of a quiet word, and it springs into action. Add it to the noun *origin,* and you *originate* something; to the adjective *valid,* and you can *validate* what you originated. If it's *active,* you can *activate* it; if it's *alien,* you can *alienate* it; if it's *equivocal,* you can *equivocate.* And so on. Even when you can't *separate* (ahem!) the suffix from the rest of the word, a word ending in *-ate* usually means action. *Celebrate, illuminate, differentiate, fascinate, annihilate, appreciate, associate, automate, bloviate, congratulate* — the pattern is clear. (There are other uses for *-ate,* as in *acetate* and *conglomerate,* but those need not concern us here.)

The suffix *-ate* is such a powerful goad to action that we sometimes add it to words that already are verbs. We sometimes say *orientate,* for *orient; administrate,* for *administer; commentate,* for *comment.* We have done so for a long time, incidentally: *orientate* goes back to at least 1849, *administrate* to 1639, *commentate* to 1794. There are those who object to these *-ate* words as unnecessary, but the ease of creating them (*create* is another *-ate* word) makes them too strong to resist. If they were banished from dictionaries and eliminated (*eliminate* is another!) completely from our present-day language, they would immediately sprout anew from many voices and hands.

But *-ate* is so natural that it spreads far beyond the bounds of any dictionaries. Had a conversation recently? That is, did you *conversate?* You won't find that word in dictionaries, but it's all over everyday conversation, in person and on the Web. For example, there's the club Hawaii 808, a website that provides an electronic place for Hawaiians to meet:

> *This Club was created to allow individuals from Hawaii, and others throughout the world, full access to this club. It's a place to make new friends, conversate about topics, and simply have fun at the same time.*

Gospel musicians "Chris and Chubby" of Oakland, California, have a religious song called "Conversate" that begins:

If you want to talk then let's conversate
I got spiritual food to fill your whole plate
I pray that you find fear in the Lord's name
and hope that you leave here not like you came. . . .

Sandy Close, executive editor of the *Pacific News Service* and founder of the teen magazine *Youth Outlook,* says it's a youth phenomenon:

> *Most young people I meet today have never had a conversation with a teacher outside the classroom. Yet, as members of a generation raised in empty households, they are so hungry for conversation they have turned it into a verb: they want to "conversate." . . .*

Maybe it's youth, or maybe it's Kansas. "Olivia," a young woman from Kansas, has a story of a flirtation on her website:

> *Last Monday while I was closing up at the mall, a guy dressed in a Papa John's Pizza uniform came over to shoot the breeze. He got around to asking if I was looking for a boyfriend, but just from the way he acted and from the things he said, I could tell he didn't have a chance in the world with me. After I was done closing up, he was still following me and yapping away in his rural Kansas accent.*
>
> *"Are you going to walk me to my car?" I said, making sure to keep my cool so he wouldn't be able to detect how nervous I was that he was possibly a psycho child molester.*
>
> *"No, I was hoping you'd hook me up with your number so we can get together and conversate."*
>
> *"Conversate," I repeated with a giggle.*
>
> *"Yeah, conversate."*
>
> *"Well, I'm a busy girl."*

Maybe it's the movies. Counting Down, "the ultimate fan site," posted this photo caption in April 2001:

> *This picture showcases actors Julia Roberts, Matt Damon (as seen from the back) and George Clooney conversating on the set of upcoming Ocean's Eleven.*

Or it could be African-American. Here's the refrain of a song called "Conversate" by the African-American singer Case:

> *Tell me can we conversate*
> *So we can get to learn each other*
> *I don't think that we should wait*
> *If this is a forever thing*
> *I know we made a few mistakes*
> *And in return we hurt each other*
> *We really need to conversate*
> *If this is a forever thing*

"Caramelly" (born 1978, raised on the South Side of Chicago) on the "Words and Ruminations" page of her website recognizes *conversate* as a black phenomenon:

> *Whassup my people. Let's talk for a minute. I mean can we rap about this word* conversate. *This word is not in the dictionary people. It is nowhere to be found yet my black people love to use it while thinking they sound so intelligent. The word to be used when you insert conversate in a sentence is actually* converse. *Converse is the word people, but if you can't remember that just say talk. Don't use a word unless you are sure it belongs. It doesn't take but a minute to look a word up in the dictionary. If you want your own proof that* conversate *is not a word look it up for yourself when you don't find it then you'll be feeling my words.*

Caramelly's comment is revealing in a number of ways. She hears the word used by black people and assumes it is used by them, just as Sandy Close listens to young people and assumes it's their word. (They're both right.) Caramelly resists the word because it's not in the dictionary, but even if it were, she probably still wouldn't like it and would accuse the dictionary of being too permissive. In doing so she recognizes that *conversate* conveys a different attitude than *converse.* The attitude may be described as the hunger or eagerness for conversation that Close mentions. To *conversate* is to be more actively conversational (there's that "active" connotation of *-ate*) than is the case with to *converse*.

Caramelly's argument is not likely to win many converts; those who like to *conversate* are not likely to rein themselves in because of a dictionary. But those opposed to *conversate* will resist just as vigorously, so we shouldn't expect to see *conversate* in standard dictionaries any day soon.

The *-ate*s just keep on extending themselves. Has anyone ever heard of *lamentate, temptate, provocate,* or *obituate*? Probably not. No dictionary carries these words. A teacher or editor would tell you to use *lament* for *lamentate, tempt* for *temptate, provoke* for *provocate,* and maybe something like *write an obituary* for *obituate*. Yet we don't always have teachers or editors in our heads, and so we just might, at suitable occasions, surprise ourselves and others by "activating" words like these. It's not just hypothetical. Here are some actual examples from the World Wide Web:

> *Man this 'revolution' is straight up to date*
> *Comin' through the headphones so tight it makes me*
>   *lamentate*
> > — lyrics to "Revolution: Revolution"
> > by Shadow of the Locust

> *Banality or kitsch doesn't temptate you?*
> > — Czech interview with
> > musician Bob Ostertag

> *Satani — Seduce me!*
> *Satani — Awake me!*
> *Satani — Temptate me!*
> > — "Fallen Angel's Symphony" by C. Anderle

HOW DOES IT FEEL

> *How does it feel to provocate the agonizing pain.*
> *How does it feel to be captured in this world of hate.*
> > — Praga Khan, "Tattoo of Pain"

> *educate . . . don't obituate!!!*
> > — "Graffiti" website

There are -*ate* words that knock on the door and are relentlessly rejected, only to be born again and again. Some invented by nonnative speakers of English follow natural processes of word formation but evoke only our laughter and criticism. For example, a tour guide in Iceland says *abandonated,* admitting that he's not sure it's a word. In Italy, a Cross-Country International Equestrian Vacation describes in its itinerary: "The landscape loses its wildness to more charming agricultural developments typical of centuries of occupation — picture-book Tuscany. We pass by abandonated farm houses. . . ." *A History of the Maya* explains that "many of these [Mayan] centers were mysteriously abandonated by the end of the Classic period." And a German expert discussing rebreather apparatus for divers says on his website, "I heard about diving experiments in 1994 that were abandonated due to problems with CO_2 and with eyesight."

When a native speaker of English uses *abandonated,* it's an occasion for laughter or poetry. As an example, consider this exchange in the Poet's Corner of a "Seniority Forum" on the Internet: when she learns that Lottie is going on holiday, Idris from Niagara, Canada, comments, "Oh oh, abandonated! Now i am in big trouble." To this, Bill from Ontario replies, "Good morning, poets. No, you have not been 'abandonated,' Idris. . . ."

With such resistance, it is unlikely that *abandonated* will be adopted into the vocabulary of English any time soon. It will no doubt continue to be reborn, however, and in some future situation — perhaps if a president of the United States utters it in all seriousness — it might just begin to gain a foothold.

MISUNDERESTIMATING THE PRESIDENT

"The folks who conducted to act on our country on September eleventh made a big mistake," said President George W. Bush on September 26, 2001. "They underestimated America. They underestimated our resolve, our determination, our love for freedom. They misunderestimated the fact that we love a neighbor in need. They misunderestimated the compassion of our country. I think they misunderestimated the will and determination of the commander in chief, too."

You won't find *misunderestimate* in any dictionary — yet. But it's lurking in the language of President Bush, who had used it before. "They misunderestimated me," he told an audience in Bentonville, Arkansas, on November 6, 2000, the day before the election.

And he used it unabashedly on April 12, 2001, in a ceremony celebrating Thomas Jefferson's birthday:

> *Most people don't realize this, but Thomas Jefferson and I share a hobby. We both like to make up words. (Laughter.) According to the* Oxford English Dictionary, *Mr. Jefferson contributed more new words to the language than any other U.S. President. I especially like his term for barbaric pirates:* barbaresques. *(Laughter.) I'm also impressed by his words* debarrass *and* graffage.

Thomas Jefferson

The other day I tried a new word for our press corps: misunderestimate. *(Laughter.) It's not quite in Jefferson's league, but I am giving it my best shot.*

Debarrass, incidentally, means to dis-embarrass — to distance oneself from anything embarrassing. And *graffage*, according to Jefferson, is "a wooden frame somewhat like a Stile, placed in a bank, where there is a water-course." Both words are indeed in the *Oxford English Dictionary*, but neither has much currency now.

Misunderestimate's chances might be all the better for not being in Jefferson's league. It's made up of a familiar prefix followed by a familiar word. The intent of the prefix evidently is to intensify the word, and *mis-* clearly intensifies the negative effect of *under*. Furthermore, we are already familiar with the combination of *mis-* and *under* in the word *misunderstand*. So although it is in no dictionary, there is no misunderstanding *misunderestimate*.

Talking with *USA Today* reporter Judy Keen about his ranch in August 2001, Bush rose to new creative heights. According to Keen:

> An expert in Texas trees, described by Bush as "an arbolist," is coming soon to identify all the varieties at the ranch. "Look up the word," he said. "I don't know, maybe I made it up. Anyway, it's an arbo-tree-ist, somebody who knows about trees."

President Bush may seem to be especially gifted in coining natural new words, but in fact he is only doing what most of us do. The difference is that he doesn't censor himself.

Here are a few more of his coinages, from the collection of *Bushisms* by Jacob Weisberg and Bryan Curtis on the *Slate* website:

> *subsidation:* Governor Bush will not stand for the subsidation of failure.
>
> — *Larry King Live,* December 16, 1999

mential: This is still a dangerous world. It's a world of madmen and uncertainty and potential mential losses.
— At a South Carolina oyster roast, as quoted in the *Financial Times,* January 14, 2000

analyzation: This case has had full analyzation and has been looked at a lot. I understand the emotionality of death penalty cases.
— *Seattle Post-Intelligencer,* June 23, 2000

subliminable: I don't think we need to be subliminable about the differences between our views on prescription drugs.
— Orlando, Florida, September 12, 2000

All of these inventions involve familiar suffixes applied in unexpected places, although not entirely unexpected; Bush was not the first to use *subsidation, mential,* and *analyzation* (a widely used substitute for *analysis*). Of the four preceding examples, only *subliminable* may be truly original.

President Bush gives new meanings to old words, too. Here are a few examples:

vile for *viable:* It's going to require a president who understands it's in our strategic interests to have a peaceful and economically vile hemisphere.
— March 2000

hostile for *hostage:* We cannot let terrorists and rogue nations hold this nation hostile or hold our allies hostile.
— Bartlett, Tennessee, August 18, 2000

pacemakers for *peacemakers:* We'll let our friends be the peacekeepers and the great country called America will be the pacemakers.
— Houston, Texas, September 6, 2000

reliant for *reliable:* I support current efforts to make Amtrak more efficient and competitive. I believe these efforts will result in better, more extensive and more reliant rail service for the millions of Americans who travel by train.
— Associated Press, September 17, 2000

anecdote for *antidote:* A tax cut is really one of the anec-
dotes to coming out of an economic illness.
— *The Edge With Paula Zahn,* September 18, 2000

resignates for *resonates:* They said, "You know, this issue doesn't seem to resignate with the people." And I
said, you know something? Whether it resignates or not
doesn't matter to me, because I stand for doing what's
the right thing, and what the right thing is is hearing
the voices of people who work.
— Portland, Oregon, October 31, 2000

gracious for *grateful:* Anyway, I'm so thankful, and so
gracious — I'm gracious that my brother Jeb is concerned about the hemisphere as well.
— Miami, June 4, 2001

The president's example emboldens others. In the Web
magazine *Slate* in July 2001, one writer declared, "Listen
don't misrepresentify (Thanks George now I can construct
the words I want to hear too) what I'm implying here."
And in the September 6, 2001, issue of *Atlantic Unbound*
a reviewer of the *Bush Dyslexicon* makes this point:

> *Bush's ascent is a sign to intelligent people with poor
> educations that they can overcome the social stigma
> attached to bad grammar. The fact that we almost always
> know what Bush means — an even-handed foreign policy,
> an education message that will resonate — bears out
> common experience. People with Bush-like problems get
> their point across all the time.*

From time to time, most of us have Bush-like problems
with language even as we are getting our point across. The
right word is not always at the tip of our tongue. When
we inadvertently create a new word, the response we get
is the normal one — laughter.

And laughter has been underrated as a conservative
force in language. When we back off from an accidentally
invented word, it's usually not because of teachers or editors but because we know our friends will laugh. George
W. Bush just happens to have a national audience for his
creations, and he doesn't back off.

George W. Bush

Laughter will stop the president's innovations, too, unless people misunderstand and mistake the mistake for the right word. Despite the efforts of purists, that has often happened in the long history of English. Some famous examples: both *nice* and *dizzy* originally meant "foolish." *Boy* was once the name for a servant, of either gender. And of course in the middle of the twentieth century *gay* and *queer* took on new meanings.

STRATEGERY

One of the best-known Bushisms was in fact not used by Bush at all. It began as a joke on *Saturday Night Live* a month before the election of 2000, at the end of a parody of the first presidential debate in which cast members portrayed moderator Jim Lehrer and candidates Al Gore and George W. Bush.

> *Jim Lehrer:* Well, that brings us to the close of tonight's debate. Each candidate will now give a brief closing statement.

....

Make the Pie Higher

(For George W. Bush's inauguration in January, 2001, Richard Thompson, cartoonist for the *Washington Post,* composed this poem entirely from the President's own statements.)

I think we all agree
The past is over.

This is still a dangerous world.
It's a world of madmen
And uncertainty
And potential mental losses.

Rarely is the question asked
Is our children learning?
Will the highways of the Internet
Become more few?

How many hands
Have I shaked?

They misunderestimate me.
I am a pitbull on the pant leg
Of opportunity.
I know that the human being
And the fish
Can coexist.

Families is where our nation
Finds hope
Where our wings take dream.

Put food on your family!

Knock down the tollbooth!
Vulcanize Society!
Make the pie higher!
Make the pie higher!
Major league.

....

Al Gore: Jim, may I make two closing statements?

Jim Lehrer: I'm afraid not. In fact, we are almost out of time, so I will instead ask each candidate to sum up, in a single word, the best argument for his candidacy. Governor Bush?

George W. Bush: Strategery.

Jim Lehrer: [stunned] Vice-President Gore.

Al Gore: Lock-box.

Jim Lehrer: This concludes the first debate. Thank you, and "Live, from New York, it's Saturday Night!"

Strategery was never uttered by the real George W. Bush. It was invented by *Saturday Night Live* writers to satirize Bush's propensity for inventing words — and unabashedly uttering them.

Yet even *strategery* is natural enough not to be entirely original. A year before it was dreamed up for *Saturday Night Live*, *strategery* appeared on the World Wide Web in the description of a computer game:

> *Warhammer 40,000 is a wargame involving many differing rules, races, vehicles, and miniatures. The main aim of the game is to over come your opponent with superior strength, be this strategery, cunning or power.*

But it was essentially a new creation, and it captured the imagination of Bush friends and foes alike. After the third presidential debate, Bush's communications director, Karen Hughes, jokingly explained why she and Bush felt "upbeat" with a Top Ten list that concluded: "And the No. 1 reason why George W. Bush won the debate: Strategery."

There were harsh responses to Bush's success with his *strategery*. A columnist for the short-lived website "Association" wrote in February 2001:

> *I'm apart of the dumbing down of society, for it is my strategery, to lower your brain cells, then as i adjust on my throne of skulls, calmly push the random red button that swallows you all whole, into a deep dark murky void. . . .*

And a political website supporting Democrats and ("when they occasionally do something right") Republicans made this request:

> *We are also looking to implement a 'strategery' (sic) of cataloging and indexing a lexicon of Bushisms, which the best we can tell is a hybrid between Ebonics, Southern, and potentially Texas smog asphyxiated brain damage.*

But *strategery* also gained aficionados as Bush gained the presidency. A writer for the *Gay Advocate* mused:

> *I have a new favorite word: strategery. . . .*
> *Strategery. It has a nice ring to it, tripping lightly off the tongue — and guaranteed to stop people in their tracks when dropped unexpectedly into an otherwise serious conversation. For example, Brian Bond, executive director of the Gay and Lesbian Victory Fund, has begun to use it in meetings focused on the future of gay, lesbian, bisexual, and transgender politics. He uses the word as a means to an end: It helps the participants think outside the self-imposed traditional approach to activism.*

And then Bush's advisors adopted the term themselves. On April 22, 2001, the *Washington Post* reported:

> *They call it the Strategery Group.*
> *Once a week, the dozen most senior White House staffers walk over to Room 208 of the Eisenhower Executive Office Building for a brainstorming session. Seeking inspiration in that storied room — the place where Secretary of State Cordell Hull confronted the Japanese in 1941 with evidence of the Pearl Harbor bombing — they think big thoughts about what should happen months, even years, from now.*
> *"We tried to come up with a nice sounding name," said Karl Rove, President Bush's chief political adviser. "We meet in the Cordell Hull Room, but nobody's buying off on the 'Hull Group.' I think we're going to be stuck with Strategery. . . ."*

A few days later Karen Hughes, now officially Counselor to the President, explained in a CNN interview:

> *I think the tone that you're hearing from this administration is different, and I think there's been a little bit of, you know, I think a mischaracterization of what we jokingly call the "strategery group." It's an office of strategic initiatives. And it really is not so much political as it is long-term planning. . . .*

Using *strategery* for this new purpose evoked both admiration and suspicion. Both were expressed by Bob Greene in a column in the *Chicago Tribune:*

> *It says one of two things:*
> *These people have a wonderful sense of humor — and are confident enough of their own skills, and their own intellect, that they can refer to themselves as the Strategery Group. The phrase says: Hey, we know what some of you think of us. Doesn't matter. We're good enough that we can laugh at it.*
> *The other thing it might say is that they are merely Machiavellian — they know that telling the world that they are the Strategery Group will make them appear to have fine senses of humor, will make them seem to be willing to laugh at themselves.*

As long as *strategery* remained humorous, it was unlikely to wedge its way into the general vocabulary of English. With the naming of the *Strategery Group,* however, there was at least a slight chance that the humor might recede into the background as the serious work of the group attracted public notice. Just possibly it could go the way of *gerrymander,* originally a cartoonist's response to Governor Elbridge Gerry's redistricting of Massachusetts in 1812, and now a serious political term. But the terrorist attacks of September 11, 2001, changed the mood of the country and of Washington politics. Planning for global and governmental matters was not to be joked about, and *strategery* dropped out of sight.

THE REAL THING: OK-NESS

As we have seen, the majority of our everyday inventions come from new combinations of old words. It's what the

Coca-Cola Company tried a decade ago when it introduced a new drink.

Ask yourself: Do you have a feeling of *OK-ness*?

Think about it for a minute.

OK. Whether you have that *OK-ness* feeling or not, you've just witnessed the birth of a word: *OK-ness*.

Chances are you've never heard *OK-ness* before, or if you have it's so rare you've forgotten it. You won't find it in your desk dictionary, yet it seems natural enough that you don't need to look it up to understand it. Ask others if they are feeling *OK-ness* and they may wonder at the question, but probably not at the word.

You understand *OK-ness* because it's made up of two familiar parts put together in a familiar way. Take (almost) any adjective — *happy, sad, strange, nervous* — and add *-ness* to it, and you have a noun, a thing: *happiness, sadness, strangeness, nervousness*. So even though you probably haven't encountered *OK-ness* before, you know that it means a thing, the state of being OK.

The procedure is so natural that it's likely *OK-ness* has been coined before. Actually, it's certain. On the World Wide Web we can find evidence of *OK-ness* being born and born again. For example:

> *On a website titled "I'm O.K., You're O.K.: Oh, Really!?" Tim Knappenberger writes, "For most of my life, my sense of well being ('OK-ness') has been based on how this list totals up. If there are more O.K.'s than Not O.K.'s, life is, well, a–O.K.!"*
>
> *On the* ParentNews *Magazine website, Michael K. Tonjum, PhD, offers this Behavior Tip: "When we turn to our family and friends to tell us we are ok, rather then validate ourselves, we may find ourselves doing and saying things to others that we wish we could take back. By holding your own OK-ness you remain in control of yourself and not needing to control others as much."*
>
> *In a discussion of archery in the Society for Creative Anachronism, Siegfried Sebastian Faust asks, "What if some Kingdom has (or soon after makes) an award*

not for 'excellence' in archery, but for 'ok-ness' in archery."

In a discussion of the After-Holidays Blues, Dan King writes, "Did you make it through the holidays without becoming an emotional casualty? In some families there was considerable pain. Oh, there was a lot of energy used to keep it stuffed down inside. But it was there, and after the holidays, B-A-H-R-O-O-O-F! The pain pushed its way up against the layers of external 'I'm O.K.-ness' that were stacked on it."

On Buddha's Village Forum, "Tim" posted this message: "The major change Buddhism has brought to me is a sense of 'ok-ness,' of confidence that what's uncomfortable for me isn't necessarily a bad thing. I don't automatically judge a situation as bad or good at its inception."

A website advertising David Leifeste's workshop "I'm Not OK, You're Not OK, But That's OK" explains: "David will equip participants to face the more vulnerable areas of pain and dysfunction and facilitate the discovery process that starts with admitting, 'I'm not OK.' From this self discovery comes not only 'OK-ness,' but also true self-acceptance."

The list could go on, but this is enough to show the frequent birth and rebirth of *OK-ness*.

Or does it? Do these quotations instead demonstrate that *OK-ness* is an established word that should be listed in dictionaries? Is there any reason to suppose that these instances of *OK-ness* are separate creations?

Yes, there is. In most of these examples, *OK-ness* is enclosed in quotation marks. That's the way writers call attention to words as words. To put *OK-ness* in quotation marks is to acknowledge, or proclaim, that it is not an everyday word. Furthermore, in some of the cases, the coiner has felt the need to provide a definition: "sense of well being" or "confidence that what's uncomfortable for me isn't necessarily a bad thing."

It's not just individuals who give birth to words. In 1994 the Coca-Cola Company tried its hand at *OK-ness*. That summer Coca-Cola began test marketing OK Soda, a beverage combining the flavors of fruit drinks and cola and aimed at teenagers, especially teenage boys, who at that time were said to be disillusioned and cynical. The marketing campaign for the drink included references to *OK-ness:* "The true nature of OK-ness is elusive. OK-ness embraces mistakes and contradictions. It is optimistic, yet ironic."

A word so contradictory in meaning would not seem likely to succeed. This *OK-ness* of Coca-Cola didn't catch on, nor did its drink. But the company didn't give up. In January 1995, a Coca-Cola project manager wrote to Houghton Mifflin, publishers of the *American Heritage Dictionary,* offering the word for inclusion in the dictionary with this definition: "An optimistic feeling that in spite of the complications of day-to-day life, things always work themselves out." Why should it be included? "Over the past year, this word has become a well-known slang term among youth, particularly teenagers," the Coca-Cola official wrote. "In addition, it has been frequently referred to by business and consumer press."

Well, hardly. "Well-known" and "frequently referred to" were wishful thinking, and in the summer of 1995 Coca-Cola ended its test of OK Soda, having sold only a million cases in eight markets over the course of a year. So you'll look in vain for the entry *OK-ness* in the *American Heritage Dictionary,* or for that particular definition of *OK-ness* anywhere else. When others use it, as in our previous examples, they don't agree that it stands for "an optimistic feeling."

What is surprising about Coca-Cola's effort is that, evidently unknown to them, *OK-ness* is in fact already in the dictionary — at least in the *Oxford English Dictionary.* There it is defined as "The fact or quality of being O.K.; acceptability" and attested as early as 1935 ("orthodoxy, decency and general o.k.ness of the . . . article"), 1950 ("O.K.-ness of French literature"), and 1962 ("theatrical

OK-ness"). But the examples of current usage show that, dictionary or no, *OK-ness* has not achieved widespread use; on each occasion it is coined anew. Like so many other words that lurk at the edge of the established vocabulary, *OK-ness* maintains its presence by being born and born again, reinvented as the opportunity arises.

7

Forget the Joke and Fly Under the Radar

Humor makes us notice a new word or phrase, but it also makes us resist adding that item to our vocabulary. Therefore, if a new term is introduced as a joke, it faces an especially high hurdle. To have a better chance of success, it should hide its origins and lose its sense of humor.

Here's an example: *Couch potato.* Get the joke?

Nowadays most of us don't. And because we don't, *couch potato* has become an everyday term for even the most serious discussions of our way of life.

Indeed, at the dawn of the twenty-first century, the *couch potato* is often a cause for serious concern. As the National Association for Sport and Physical Education solemnly warns, "a childhood spent as a couch potato produces an adult who is more open than others to chronic ailments such as heart disease." More succinctly, the BBC declares: "Couch potato women risk heart disease."

"In the past, exercise would have reduced the sugar circulating in the blood," wrote Mitzi Perdue for the Scripps Howard News Service in 2001. "But today we're in an era of the couch potato, of TV, Nintendo, Game Boy and the Net, and more of it is stored as fat."

Even when the focus is not on the problems it presents, *couch potato* seems pretty solemn. With a straight face, people promote "couch potato investing" (indexing as opposed to active management), "couch potato marketing," (marketing on the Web), and "couch potato dad gifts" (a CD of TV commercials, for example).

No self-respecting dictionary would go to press or website today without *couch potato:*

> "A person who spends much time sitting or lying down, usually watching television" — *American Heritage Dictionary*
>
> "A lazy and inactive person; especially one who spends a great deal of time watching television" — *Merriam-Webster's Collegiate Dictionary*
>
> "A chronic television viewer" — *Webster's New World College Dictionary*
>
> "One who spends too much time watching TV" — *User's Webster Dictionary*
>
> "A person who spends leisure time passively or idly sitting around, esp. watching television or videotapes" — *Oxford English Dictionary*

At first, it was just a joke. As long as the joke was recognized, *couch potato* remained at the edge of the vocabulary. As the joke was forgotten, however, the image of the potato on a couch remained, and the *couch potato* now is a fixture of our language.

True, there's residual humor in the term. *Couch potato* conjures images of a big potato on a couch, all eyes on the television. The image fits so perfectly that it's easy to imagine it was coined spontaneously by someone thinking of potatoes — dumpy, heavy, unmoving — on soft couches. But as *couch potato* settles more and more into its comfortable seat in today's authoritative dictionaries (some of which label it "slang"), its laughable origins become dimmer and dimmer. Not many English speakers

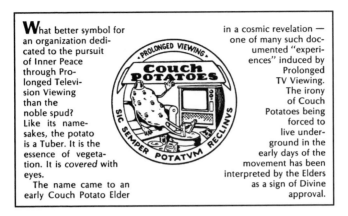

What better symbol for an organization dedicated to the pursuit of Inner Peace through Prolonged Television Viewing than the noble spud? Like its namesakes, the potato is a Tuber. It is the essence of vegetation. It is *covered* with eyes.

The name came to an early Couch Potato Elder in a cosmic revelation — one of many such documented "experiences" induced by Prolonged TV Viewing. The irony of Couch Potatoes being forced to live underground in the early days of the movement has been interpreted by the Elders as a sign of Divine approval.

couch potato

today remember that in its first heyday in the 1980s, *couch potato* was a joke, and a well-marketed joke at that.

According to an illustrated history, *The Official Couch Potato Handbook* (1983), written by two of the perpetrators themselves—"Elders" Jack Mingo and Robert Armstrong—the saga began in the 1960s with nine Southern Californians who got together on Thursday nights to watch *Lost in Space*. Calling themselves the "Lost in Space Club," they soon began meeting to watch other television shows as well. "One of them," the story continues, "known only as 'The Hallidonian,' soon made the discovery that any day, any time was all right for prolonged, indiscriminate TV viewing."

Then, reportedly on July 15, 1976, another of the nine "Elders," Tom Iacino, uttered the term *couch potato* in making a phone call to The Hallidonian. The illustrated history depicts the moment: "Hi, Annie Jo — Can I speak to the 'couch potato'?" asks Iacino's telephone voice, to which Annie Jo responds, "The wha——?" while across the room The Hallidonian relaxes on his couch, watching *The Flintstones*.

Why *couch potato?* Well, the members of the Lost in Space Club were *tubers,* that is, devotees of the *tube* (or *boob tube*), as television had come to be known in the land of slang. Here is how the *Official Couch Potato Handbook* explains it:

> What better symbol for an organization dedicated to the pursuit of Inner Peace through Prolonged Television Viewing than the noble spud? Like its namesakes, the potato is a Tuber. It is the essence of vegetation. It is covered with eyes.
>
> The name came to an early Couch Potato Elder in a cosmic revelation, one of many such documented "experiences" induced by Prolonged TV Viewing. The irony of Couch Potatoes being forced to live underground in the early days of the movement has been interpreted by the Elders as a sign of Divine approval.

The potato as tuber, the potato with eyes, the potato as vegetating, the potato as existing underground — these evidently were the qualities that inspired Iacino's "cosmic revelation." But as the historians explain, for years the term *couch potato* spread no further. "The only outlet these Tubers had for their ideas at first was the Underground Comics. In them they began placing obscure references to their organization . . . not yet daring to hint at the secrets they'd discovered." It was still "The wha—?" for several more years.

Indeed, *couch potato* might have remained in permanent obscurity but for the Doo Dah Parade in Pasadena, California, a spoof on the Tournament of Roses Parade held there on New Year's Day. For the second annual Doo Dah, in 1979, the Couch Potatoes entered a float that carried members sitting on couches and watching television. That was their only year in the parade; the next year motorized floats were outlawed, and no Couch Potato wanted to make the effort to pull the "Ceremonial Couch." But the 1979 appearance caught the attention of the public, and *couch potato* soon sprouted prodigious progeny.

Knowing a good thing when they saw it, Couch Potato Elders trademarked the name and began to market Couch Potato books, newsletters, bumper stickers, rabbit-ear pennants (to attach to the "rabbit ear" antennas of television sets in those pre-cable, pre-satellite-dish days), and "viewing tunics" (T-shirts with the Couch Potato emblem). There were caps, hats, and fezzes; dolls, parlor games, pillows, and soft stuffed Couch Potato dolls.

From Couch Potato World Headquarters in Dixon, California, the Elders issued *The Tuber's Voice: The Couch Potato Newsletter.* There were books, too, to explain it all. The first was *Dr. Spudd's Etiquette for the Couch Potato* (1982), followed by *The Official Couch Potato Handbook* and *The Couch Potato Guide to Life* (1985).

During the 1980s the World Headquarters also offered membership cards and certificates and encouraged local clubs. The appendix of the *Couch Potato Guide to Life* lists 128 "Couch Potato viewing lodges worldwide." Many of them had names recalling the humorous connection between "potato" and "tuber," including "The All-Seeing Tubers" (New Mexico) and "The Tubular Belles" (New Hampshire).

But it was not in the nature of Couch Potatoes to exert themselves, and by the 1990s the commercial Couch Potato fad had faded. Perhaps the Elders were just too tired to pursue profits when they could be watching television instead. In 1991, Armstrong let the trademark on *Couch Potato* expire, and the term went into the public domain.

It proved to be a turning point. The humor, the capital letters, and ™ fell away, and the modern *couch potato* was born. A new generation learned it as a descriptive (and negative) term for one who watches (too) much television. In recognition of this widespread use, it was entered in dictionaries. It had become a real word (or term).

In the twenty-first century, only historians and elders (the non-capital-letter variety) readily recall the punning origin of *couch potato.* Others are clueless. "Hey Guys!"

gerrymander

writes "Laura" on the *Filters Magazine* ("pop/sub/fringe culture") website. "I was wondering if anyone could tell me the origin of the slang term 'couch potato' or at least give me a somewhat reasonable lie. It's a school project and I can't find anything." A website for the public television station at Pennsylvania State University includes *mouse potato* ("a person who spends large amounts of leisure or working time operating a computer") in a list of new words and explains that it is "a take-off on another 1990's word, couch potato" — thereby obliterating the first two decades of *couch potato*. A website of 1980s slang misses the humorous beginning of *couch potato* entirely, giving this explanation for its origin: "With the boom of cable, MTV and home video, more people parked their butts on their couches."

To the historian of words, it's a sad falling-away from the truth, but to the champion of a new word, it's cause for rejoicing. A word needs to stop kidding around and get serious if it wants to enter the general vocabulary.

GERRYMANDER

One of the most celebrated words in American politics also owes its origin to a joke. The word is *gerrymander,* and the story is well known to historians. Back in 1812 Elbridge Gerry, governor of Massachusetts (and a signer of the Declaration of Independence), crowned his political career by causing the election districts of the state to be rearranged to the maximum advantage of his Democratic party. The partitioning in Essex County was particularly blatant, with one district running along the west and top edges of the county in a sinuous pattern. Gerry's opponents, the Federalists, were outraged when they saw the map of the redistricted county. It may have been the great painter Gilbert Stuart himself who added a head, wings, and claws to the outline of the reptilian-appearing district. Someone said, "That will do for a salamander," and someone else improved on the joke, calling it a *Gerrymander.*

There are conflicting stories about whether the drawing was made at a political meeting or in a newspaper office. Whether Stuart made the drawing and who coined the word are also in dispute. There is no doubt, however, that the term was applied to the image derived from the map of Essex County, and that *gerrymander* quickly spread into general use, at first for Governor Gerry's redistricting and then for any deformation of electoral boundaries designed to give one party an advantage.

Historians have kept knowledge of the word's origins alive even as they have disagreed on the details. But of those who use *gerrymander*, probably few know or remember the story. The two parts of the word no longer are clear reminders of its origins, either. The connection to Governor Gerry is less obvious: for one thing, the word is no longer capitalized; for another, Governor Gerry pronounced his name with a "hard *g*," as in *guest*, and the word today begins with a "soft *g*," as in *gem*. Few nowadays remember Governor Gerry, so even if the spelling and pronunciation were faithful to the original, most people wouldn't make the connection. The second half of the word is also obscure. What the original coiner characterized as a salamander, we would be more likely to identify as a dragon.

So *gerrymander* lost its topical humor, allowing it to become a serious technical term, fully accepted in our capacious language.

THE AFTERNOON SOAPS

It was another joke, more than a century after *gerrymander:* the *soap opera.*

In the late 1930s some clever person bestowed that name on the serial dramas aired on the radio. They were *operas* because they were so melodramatic. They were *soap* operas because they were sponsored by makers of detergents and soaps (like Procter & Gamble, Lever Brothers, and Colgate-Palmolive-Peet). *Soap opera* must have been funny the first few times.

In the course of time the daytime dramas moved from radio to television, and their original soap sponsors gradually yielded to those who promoted other products. But the popularity of the genre continued into the twenty-first century, and so did the term designating them, now usually reduced to *soaps*. These changes eliminated the humor; nowadays the joke is detectable only by a historian or a linguistic archaeologist. It is easy to find serious discussion of the *soap opera* today:

The defining quality of the soap opera form is its seriality. A serial narrative is a story told through a series of individual, narratively linked installments. Unlike episodic television programs, in which there is no narrative linkage between episodes and each episode tells a more or less self-contained story, the viewer's understanding of and pleasure in any given serial installment is predicated, to some degree, upon his or her knowledge of what has happened in previous episodes. . . . (Museum of Broadcast Communications)

The term lives on, entirely free of its funny beginnings.

BIG BANG

In 1950, the astronomer Fred Hoyle held to the generally accepted belief that the universe was in a more or less steady state. Speaking on BBC radio in a series entitled "The Nature of the Universe," he criticized the rival theory advanced by George Gamow that the whole universe had originated from a single dense spot and dismissed it as "big bang cosmology." It was a joke, Hoyle thought.

In the decades to come, more and more evidence appeared that made an initial *big bang* seem more likely. Today physicists and astronomers generally accept the theory that billions of years ago the universe did indeed get its start from a single small point. It's no longer a joke, so the term is used freely and seriously by all concerned. In fact, it's such a natural and self-explanatory combination of familiar words that nothing has been able to dislodge it, despite attempts to coin a more scientific term.

Some forty years later *Sky & Telescope* magazine held a contest to determine a better name for the *big bang*. They got a big response: The March 1994 issue announced that they had received nearly 14,000 entries, including *Big TOE* (Theory Of Everything), *Super Seed, The Grand Expansion, Space-Time Zero, Bertha D. Universe,* and *Jurassic Quark.* Needless to say, none of them displaced the *big bang.*

HOT DOG

The archetype of American food, the *hot dog* — so much in demand at the 2002 Winter Olympics in Utah that the original 500,000 from Usinger's in Wisconsin were consumed in the first five days, necessitating an emergency resupply of 200,000 more — began as a joke. And not a pleasant joke, either. Not until the joke had been firmly forgotten could Americans begin to swallow *hot dogs* with enthusiasm.

A *hot dog*, of course, is a sausage in a bun. During the nineteenth century, it was a running joke that sausages were often made not from beef or pork, as claimed by those who made them, but from whatever stray animals were at hand, especially stray dogs. Students at Yale University in the 1890s referred to sausages as *dogs*, and the lunch wagon where they were sold as a *dog wagon*. Served hot, in a bun, the sausages were thus *hot dogs*.

College students could stomach such a joke, perhaps, but others might be squeamish. As *hot dogs* became the fad food of the twentieth century, a legend arose that a famous cartoonist (T. A. "Tad" Dorgan) had invented the name by drawing a cartoon of a sausage that looked like a dachshund, in a bun, for sale at a baseball game. He didn't, but that kinder legend served to legitimate the *hot dog* for the rest of that century and into the twenty-first.

hot dog

YOUNG AND URBAN AND PROFESSIONAL

Yep, one of the great successes of the 1980s was the *yuppie*. It began as a joke but soon became as serious as the people it described, who were, on the whole, quite serious about their upwardly mobile status.

The word made its first known appearance in print in 1982. Two years later, after publication of *The Yuppie Handbook,* with tongue-in-cheek instructions on how to recognize and be one, *yuppie* was a major story in *Time* and *Newsweek,* the latter declaring 1984 "the Year of the Yuppie."

Yuppie came into being as a clever twist on several words and phrases. Its prehistory can be traced to the abbreviation *YUP* for *Young Urban Professional,* a term used at least since the late 1970s by public opinion analysts. This abbreviation fit the pattern of the first syllable of two other lifestyle words that had been around since the 1960s, *hippie* and *preppie,* so it was natural to add the *-pie* suffix to *yup* as well. A similar combination had been made in 1968 when the radical Youth International Party was founded; modeling the name on *hippie* and *preppie,* the members of that party ironically called themselves *yippies.* This was the connection explained in a March 1983 column by *Chicago Tribune* columnist Bob Greene that spread the word on *yuppie:*

> While [Jerry Rubin] and Abbie Hoffman once led the Yippies — the Youth International Party — one social commentator has ventured that Rubin is now attempting to become the leader of the Yuppies — Young Urban Professionals.

The conscious play on words is apparent in the early appearances of *yuppie.* Interviewed for *People* magazine, the authors of *The Yuppie Handbook,* Marissa Piesman and Marilee Hartley, said they had heard *Y.P.* and *Yo-Pro* but "picked Yuppie because it sounded like *preppy* and *hippie* and had the right ring."

Yuppie has become the model for other coinages. After *yuppie*, there have been *yumpies,* young upwardly mobile professionals; *suppies,* Southern yuppies; *buppies,* black urban professionals; *guppies,* geriatric urban poor persons; *dinks,* those with dual income and no kids; and *skippies,* school kids with income and purchasing power. These tend to fall by the wayside because they are too clever. *Yuppie* now stands firmly as the norm.

OK, OK

No better example of forgotten humor can be found than the most famous expression ever invented in America, or perhaps the whole world: *OK.* This expression has an amazing rags-to-riches story. It began as an obscure joke, the least likely of new words to succeed. A twist of fate, though, brought it seriousness and myths of noble origins, and today it is used every day by almost everyone, not only in English but in many other languages around the globe.

Thanks to the research of Allen Walker Read, the great historian of American English, and to further research by Barry Popik and others, we know the story of *OK* in detail. We know, then, that it had its beginnings in a craze for humorous abbreviations that filled Boston newspapers in the late 1830s. Here is the world's first *OK*, as published in the Boston *Morning Post* of March 23, 1839:

> *The "Chairman of the Committee on Charity Lecture Bells" is one of the deputation, and perhaps if he should return to Boston, via Providence, he of the [Providence] Journal, and his* train-band, *would have the "contribution box," et ceteras,* o.k. — all correct — *and cause the corks to fly, like* sparks, *upward.*

And another, in the Morning Post three days later:

> *Many of O.F.M. and several* futcheons *had the pleasure of taking these "interesting strangers" by the hand, and*

wishing them a speedy passage to the Commercial Emporium. They were o.k.

It would take a whole chapter to explain what this writer is talking about. Suffice it to say that he is trying to be funny, and in so doing he is using an abbreviation for "all correct" that is entirely not correct, since the initials of both words are misspelled. (*O.F.M.*, incidentally, is *our first men.* The *Commerical Emporium* is the Boston editors' epithet for New York City, in contrast with the *Literary Emporium,* their hometown. No one knows who the *futcheons* are.)

The misspelling of *o.k.* put it in a class with its predecessor *O.W.* (all right) and with a number of equally short-lived misspelled abbreviations that appeared later in 1839, when the fad had spread to New York: *K.G.* (no go), *K.Y.* (no use), *K.K.K.* (commit no nuisance, in those innocent times before the founding of the Ku Klux Klan), and *N.S.M.J.* ('nough said 'mong gentlemen). But only *OK* survived the quick fading of the fad for misspelled initials.

The case of *O.W.* in particular presents a striking contrast. It got its start nearly a year ahead of *O.K.* and was used for much the same purposes. Here it is in the Boston *Morning Post* for June 18, 1838: "We jumped in, and were not disappointed either with the carriage, distance, or price. It was O.W. — (all right)." The phrase that it stands for, *all right,* was then and is now an expression of approval — better known and more widely used than *all correct.* So why shouldn't *O.W.*, the humorous abbreviation of the more popular phrase, be the one used today?

Actually, that's the wrong question. It's unlikely that any abbreviation so obscure that it requires explanation would survive beyond a brief season in the sun. Even the most astute language prognosticator would not have given either *O.K.* or *O.W.* much of a future in 1839. In the whole history of English, no such misspelled abbreviation had become part of the general vocabulary.

The question, then, is not why *O.W.* didn't survive, but

why *O.K.* did. The answer lies in the presidential election that took place the following year. The election sobered it up and gave it respect. In that 1840 election, William Henry Harrison, a Whig, challenged incumbent Martin Van Buren, a Democrat. Whigs jeered at Van Buren as a "Kinderhook cabbage planter," in reference to his birthplace, Kinderhook, New York. The Democrats turned this into a positive epithet: *Old Kinderhook. O.K.?*

Yes, that was it. By March 1840, a *Democratic O.K. Club* in support of *Old Kinderhook* had been formed in New York City, and *O.K.* became a militant slogan. According to the Whiggish *New York American* of March 28, 1840,

> *The* war cry *of the [Democratic] locofocos was O.K., the two letters paraded at the head of an inflammatory article in the New Era of the morning. "Down with the whigs, boys, O.K." was the shout of these poor, deluded men.*

Thanks to the accident of Martin Van Buren's birthplace beginning with the letter K, then, *OK* extended its range from light humor into serious politics. By the end of the nineteenth century its laughable origin had been totally forgotten, so there was nothing to hinder *OK* from attaining the utmost respectability. Numerous stories were invented about its origin, all of them more plausible to the twentieth-century mind than a comic misspelling. Allen Walker Read devoted a twenty-page article to the folklore of *OK*, documenting these theories:

— It began as a telegraphers' abbreviation for *open key,* indicating that "all is right" for receiving a message;
— No, it came from the Choctaw Indian *okeh* or *oke* (with a strong stress on the second syllable);
— No, it came from the Mobile or Chickasaw trade language;
— No, it was an abbreviation for *Old Keokuk,* an early nineteenth-century leader of the Sauk Indians;
— No, it was an abbreviation for the Haitian port city of *Aux Cayes,* supposedly known for its excellent rum;

— No, it came from *OK* stamped on biscuits made for the army during the Civil War by *Orrin Kendall* & Sons of Chicago;

— No, it was Greek, from *ola kala* meaning "all good," supposedly used by the Spartans in 600 BC;

— No, it was German, from the letters *OK* standing for *Ober-Kommando* on documents signed by Baron von Steuben, who served with the U.S. Army in the war of independence;

— No, it was French, from *au quai,* approving a bale of cotton to be taken to the dock in New Orleans for export;

— No, it was Provençal, a misspelling of the word *oc* meaning "yes";

— No, it was Finnish, from *oikea* meaning "correct";

— No, it was Scottish, from *och aye* meaning "oh yes."

Its shameful origins thus disguised, *OK* won acceptance in the highest office in the land. President Woodrow Wilson, our only chief executive with a PhD, accepted the Choctaw explanation and somewhat pedantically wrote the Choctaw spelling *okeh* on government documents to signify his approval. From there it was a short distance to the ubiquitous *OK* or *okay* of the present day.

What can we learn about the acceptance of new words from the story of *OK?* It had peculiar success by managing not to seem peculiar. It entered the language with a crowd of other humorous abbreviations, moved quickly to the more serious crowd of political expressions, assumed distinguished myths about its ancestry, and thus became what it is now, the most ordinary of everyday expressions. All of its odd fellows — *O.F.M., O.W., K.Y.* (no use), and the like — were long ago left in the dust, eliciting only a few chuckles before vanishing.

FLYING UNDER THE RADAR

When a new word applies for entrance into the vocabulary of a language, it has an advantage if it meets certain qualifications. One, as we have seen, is seriousness. People use words to make jokes but don't want the words themselves to be jokes; a language is a serious matter.

The more general principle is that a word shouldn't call attention to itself, by humor or by any other means — its looks or origin, for example. If it does attract notice, chances are it will be rejected. If, however, it is unobtrusive and sounds familiar even if it is not, those who hear or see it are more likely to think it's something they have missed rather than something missing from the language. In that case, listeners or readers are inclined to give it a welcome rather than the boot.

There are professionals who are on the lookout for new words, either to capture them for their dictionaries or to shoot them down so they will not enter their cultivated language preserves. If a new word can sneak past these experts, it has a good chance of making a home for itself.

Here are a few that have made it: "stealth words," they could be called, ones that evaded the new-word-detection radar. Because they were so successful, their stories are short; we don't know who introduced them, how, or where.

New Words 101

One of the great stealth successes of recent times is this inconspicuous designation for a beginning college course. It slipped past the watchdogs of words, so there's no telling when *101* first extended its meaning to cover any introductory treatment, although there is evidence that it had done so at least as far back as the 1970s.

Nowadays on the Web you can find Romance 101, Breakups 101, Roman Numerals 101, Blackjack 101, Golf 101, Pumpkin Carving 101, Chops 101 (guitar playing), Aromatherapy 101, Toiletology 101 (the repair of toilets), Satanism 101, Cults 101, Free Stuff 101, College 101 (what they won't tell you in the official college handbook), Grammy Fashion 101 (what the stars were wearing at the

Grammy Awards ceremony), and countless others. Magazines, newspapers, and books will introduce any subject with *101*.

In the *Illinois Legal Times,* a 1998 article titled "Try Adding Civility, Kindness to Law School Curriculum" begins like this:

> *Here's a course for any lawyer who wants to originate business: Friendship 101. The syllabus might read: "How to make friends and deepen friendships, listen well, support others and help them feel comfortable in your presence."*

The tag *101* seems to be a favorite with headline writers. It will often appear in the headline but not in the body of the story, indicating that it was added by the person who wrote the headline. In February 2002 the *New York Times* carried this headline: "Campuses Across America Are Adding 'Sept. 11 101' to Curriculums," but the story itself had no *101*.

Plan B

What happens if things don't work out as intended? Go to *Plan B.*

It has entered our language under the radar. It's such a natural term that the experts have no idea where or when it began. But we all know what it means.

There's something impressive about *Plan B.* It means you actually have an alternate strategy in case your first attempt fails. It means you aren't giving up, and you aren't just trying the same thing over again. You're smart.

That's why the smart lawyers on the television show *The Practice* regularly talk about *Plan B:*

Bobby: What about Plan B?

Eugene: Do you think we should?

Bobby: Well, nothing else is working, is it? Can you think of an alternative?

Eugene: It could backfire. You know the risks involved. . . .

Not surprisingly, *Plan A* is not nearly as widely used. It's often not a plan at all, just the thing you first do. Only when that won't work do you implement a carefully thought out *Plan B.*

Heads-up

In ancient times, back in the mid-twentieth century, when someone called out *heads up!* listeners knew to lift up their heads and watch out for something dangerous. Nowadays *heads-ups* are plentiful, but they are nothing to worry about, just announcements or news. The National Aeronautics and Space Administration science news website is titled *Heads Up!* but warns of no danger. You can find *heads-ups* about seminars, auditions, special offers, headaches, ringworm, a new album, new search technology, quality products that prevent snoring, and this year's fall flight of ducks, just to name a few.

Some *heads-ups* are still in the nature of warnings. You can get a *heads-up* about recognizing college scholarship scams, handling a chemical accident, accepting all those credit card offers you get in the mail every day, or being aware of crabmeat fiber stuck in your teeth. Still, these are not warnings of imminent danger, and instead of the original exclamation, the two words have merged to become a plain noun. Most often today *heads-up* is used the way the UrbanStyle website has it:

> *In addition to fantastic shopping, our localScene features keep you up-to-date with the latest fashion trends and give you the heads-up about the hot talent, boutiques, and shows in the city.*

Hopefully

In the 1960s and 1970s, the most hated word in American English was *hopefully.* Guardians of the purity of the language were shocked to discover its widespread use as the equivalent of *I hope* in statements like "Hopefully, the rain will stop" or "Hopefully, I'll find a job soon" or "Hopefully, the crime rate will go down." A book on usage published in 1975 recorded these reactions to *hopefully* from its panel of "distinguished consultants":

— The most horrible usage of our time.
— Chalk squeaking on a blackboard is to be preferred to this usage.
— Strike me dead if you ever hear me using it in this way.
— This is one that makes me physically ill.
— Its adherents should be lynched.

Why did they oppose it? They gave logical technical reasons: You can't have an adverb modifying a sentence, they said, ignoring similar acceptable adverbs like *thankfully*. Their real reason, consciously or subconsciously, was probably that suddenly everyone was using *hopefully* as a weasel word. *Hopefully* is a way to express optimism and imply that one should get credit for a favorable result, without making promises and without taking responsibility in case what is hoped for doesn't happen. No wonder politicians, business executives, and workers of all kinds brighten their reports and build in an escape hatch with *hopefully*. We could hardly do without it nowadays.

Thankfully or regrettably, depending on your point of view, by the twenty-first century the controversy about *hopefully* had died down. It's still a point of contention in dictionaries and books of usage, but those who warn against its use are preaching to a small choir.

If *hopefully* caused such a stir, how can it be considered a stealth word? Because it was not in fact a new word at all in the 1960s. A thorough computer-aided search by researcher Fred Shapiro recently demonstrated, in his words, that "*hopefully* was in common use as a sentence adverb in both formal and informal speech by the 1930s. Its origins may go back a century or more before that." His many examples include this one from the *New York Times Book Review* in 1932:

> *He would create an expert commission . . . to consist of ex-Presidents and a selected list of ex-Governors, hopefully not including Pa and Ma Ferguson.*

And this from the *American Political Science Review* in 1934:

> *The breakdown of existing forms of industrial organization may hopefully direct attention to adequate measures of security for the worker.*

He found it, in fact, in the writings of New England Puritan minister Cotton Mather in 1702:

> *Although a Pastor should be willing to encounter many Difficulties and Infirmities with his People; yet, in case that Chronical Diseases, which evidently threaten his Life, might hopefully be relieved by his removal, it should then, on all hands, be allowed and advised.*

These uses of *hopefully* would raise no eyebrows today. *Hopefully*, then, in its widespread modern sense was around for more than two and a half centuries before the experts took notice. Hopefully that qualifies it as a stealth word.

8

The FUDGE Factors

As previous chapters have shown, the success or failure of new words is not entirely random. Some factors evidently make for success, while others hinder it. It appears, for example, that a word has a better chance for success if it is modest and inconspicuous than if it is showy and clever. It also appears that some factors expected to be influential don't matter; for example, a word that fills a gap in the vocabulary seems to have no particular advantage over one that doesn't. A language isn't a brick wall; it seems comfortable with gaps.

There will never be a purely objective way of determining which words will succeed and which won't. Generalizing from the examples in the preceding chapters, though, it is possible to construct a scale that will focus attention on key factors and allow accurate prediction of a word's future success — at least, a more accurate prediction than one based on a vague premonition or a wild guess. The factors that make for success can't be measured by instruments or calculated objectively, so a scale to predict the success of new words will need to be one that employs human judgment rather than one that circumvents it. It

Dr. Virginia Apgar
creator of the Apgar scale

has to delineate factors clearly, but it can't be too complicated.

THE APGAR SCALE

Fortunately, there is a model for such a scale, one developed by Dr. Virginia Apgar in 1952 to predict the future success of — you. It's not a scale that has a spring or a balance beam, but is a judgment scale that estimates the health of a newborn baby.

Thanks to Dr. Apgar, if you were born later than the mid-twentieth century, you probably took your first test one minute after emerging into the world. Four minutes later, you were given a second chance. You probably passed, too, or you wouldn't be reading this chapter.

The test is an instant physical examination for newborns, designed to tell medical attendants immediately if the baby needs help in staying alive. It requires no invasive procedures or laboratory analysis, just observation of five signs: heart rate, respiratory effort, muscle tone, reflex irritability, and skin color. Nowadays, for convenience in remembering them, the signs are labeled to correspond with the letters of Dr. Apgar's name: Appearance, Pulse, Grimace (reflexes), Activity, and Respiration. Each of these gets 0, 1, or 2 points, the higher the better. A score of 6 or lower usually calls for intervention; 7 or higher means the infant should be doing fine on its own. If you earn an Apgar 10, you have a great start on life.

Before Dr. Apgar's invention, medical attendants at birth had only inexact terminology to express the overall viability of a baby: "The baby looks healthy" or "It's in trouble." With the Apgar scale, the details of a complex situation could be precisely communicated to everyone present for appropriate action.

Although babies are one thing, and words quite another, both are complex human creations seemingly impervious to easy evaluation. Dr. Apgar's system, permitting simple and reliable assessment of something as complicated as human life, can be an inspiration for a scale that predicts the viability of new words. Her brilliant inspiration was to direct attention to five distinct and readily observed vital signs and to allow just three possible scores for each. That is precise, yet easy enough to remember and apply. More categories or more degrees would make judgments more difficult and would distract from the purpose of the scale, which is not to focus on itself but to reach an overall determination of an individual's likelihood of success.

Although it is designed for use by doctors and nurses, the Apgar scale does not require years of medical training to understand or to apply. A layperson can use it too, at least to get an approximate sense of whether a baby is in trouble. In fact, it teaches the lay observer as well as the medical professional what to look for.

Dr. Apgar's ingenious model can be applied to a rating system for new words. That is what the rest of this chapter will attempt.

THE FUDGE FACTORS

Dr. Apgar's invention is especially pertinent as a model for new-words prediction because here, just as in the Apgar scale, there appear to be five significant factors. They can be expressed in a scale like Dr. Apgar's that allows a grade of 0, 1, or 2 for each factor. And the initial letters of the factors spell a word, too. In this case it's FUDGE:

Frequency of use
Unobtrusiveness
Diversity of users and situations
Generation of other forms and meanings
Endurance of the concept

Exactly how to apply and judge a word by these factors will require some explanation and examples. The examples are not brand-new words but words from at least several decades ago whose success or failure we already know. They will thus serve as benchmarks for testing newer words whose fate remains to be determined.

Factor 1: Frequency of Use

This factor can also be expressed as popularity, plain and simple. Or perhaps not so plain and simple, because popularity can be defined in several ways. The kind of popularity a new word needs is attention: "Attention, attention must be paid," as Linda Loman says in *Death of a Salesman*. Attention brings a word from the fringes of language toward the center.

And so it is with Frequency. When first coined, a word or phrase has a frequency of 0, and 0 it remains as long as only one person uses it. Even a handful of friends, family, or coworkers won't be enough to raise the rating for Frequency above 0. Examples of words with frequency 0 are numerous, but by definition you won't have heard of most of them. Occasionally, though, there will be words that capture a bit of attention without inspiring anyone else to use them. These include many of the deliberate creations of serious (or not so serious) word coiners, like Gelett Burgess's *bleesh, critch, cowcat,* and *hyprijimp* and Paul Lewis's *pittwitted, denuggify,* and *whoopdujour.*

Level 1 of Frequency, the next step up, reflects spreading usage. Words at Level 1 are recognized by more people than you can count and used by more people than you know; we're talking thousands here, maybe hundreds of thousands. Perhaps you remember the story of *heaven-o?* It's the polite alternative to *hello* officially adopted by the county commissioners in a Texas town in 1997. News of the new word spread far and wide, though few seem to have adopted it. That year *heaven-o* was at Frequency Level 1; since then it apparently has slipped back to Level 0.

If Level 0 of Frequency is like a struck match, a flame ready to flicker and go out, Level 1 is like applying that match to a fuse, where a word can smolder, waiting for an opportunity to explode to Level 2. Or think of the fringe vocabulary of a language (Level 1) as a field sown with seeds ready to sprout. The seeds are the words invented and reinvented by individuals. There are some small sprouts, the words used by members of a family, neighbors, workers in a particular trade, hobbyists with a particular devotion. When the larger public showers attention on a particular part of the field, the seeds sprout, the sprouts shoot up.

A perfect example of Frequency Level 1 rising to Level 2 is *chad.* Until the presidential election of November 2000, it was an obscure word, known to those few who had occasion to work with punch cards. But when the hotly contested Florida vote for president attracted intense political and media attention to punch cards, *chad* became a front-page word. It sprouted varieties like *hanging chad* (chad hanging by a corner) and *pregnant chad* or *dimpled chad* (punched but not dislodged).

....

Texas County Votes the 'Hell' out of Hello

(The following article, written by Kelley Shannon, appeared on January 16, 1997 in various newspapers.)

KINGSVILLE, Texas — In this friendly little ranching town, "Hello" is wearing out its welcome.

And Leonso Canales Jr. is happy as heck.

At his urging, the Kleberg County commissioners on Monday unanimously designated "heaven-o" as the county's official greeting.

The reason: "Hello" contains the word "hell."

"When you go to school and church, they tell you 'hell' is negative and 'heaven' is positive," said the 56-year-old Canales, who owns the Kingsville Flea Market.

"I think it's time that we set a new precedent, to tell our kids that we are positive adults."

The new salutation, according to the county resolution, is a "symbol of peace, friendship and welcome" in this "age of anxiety."

On Thursday, courthouse employees were answering the phones, "Heaven-o."

"People seem to think that it might catch on," said county judge Pete De La Garza.

Canales, a Catholic but not a regular churchgoer, has been as serious as heck about "hello" since 1988, when he told his brother he might start greeting people with "God-o." His brother suggested "heaven-o" instead.

....

Reprinted with permission of The Associated Press.

Etymological experts burned the midnight oil to discover ancestral remains of present-day *chad*, tracing it as far back as 1939 to a patent application for a "chadless" telegraph tape. That application defines *chad* as "pieces of waste" (from a perforated tape). From 1939 to 2000 *chad* remained at Level 1, a specialized word confined to the communications of people who had to deal with it. In November 2000, suddenly everyone had to deal with it, and *chad* soared to Frequency Level 2. By 2002, especially in the aftermath of the events of September 11, 2001, *chad* had drifted down to Frequency Level 1 again.

New words that have attained Frequency Level 2 are, almost by definition, those that are the most familiar. Computer technology in the 1990s contributed a number of Level 2 words: *dot* (for "period" in an address, as in *dot-com*) and the prefix *e-* (as in *e-mail),* for example. In other examples, the terrorist attacks of September 11, 2001, raised *jihad* and *ground zero* to Level 2. *Ground zero* had been at Level 2 some decades earlier, when attention was focused on atom and hydrogen bombs, but the end of the Cold War had lowered it to Frequency Level 1. After the terrorist attacks, someone thought of *ground zero* as an appropriate analogy for the devastation at the World Trade Center site, and the term quickly attached itself to discussions of that location.

From these examples it is clear that a word or phrase can change levels of Frequency with changes in national attention. It is clear also that no one could have predicted the need for *chad* before November 7, 2000, or *ground zero* before September 11, 2001. But there remains a sharp divide between Frequency Levels 0 and 1. It's unlikely that *chad* would have risen to Level 2 if it had not already been in circulation. And now that it has been at Level 2, it's unlikely it will ever fall to Level 0; it is too firmly embedded in the historical record.

So the most important leap in Frequency a new word faces is from Level 0 to Level 1. How does this happen? Deliberate coiners of words rely on whatever bully pulpit they have available, their publications or their own celebrity, to get the word out. That by itself, though, is not enough. There are four other factors to consider.

Factor 2: Unobtrusiveness

Unobtrusiveness. In plain English, you don't notice it. A successful new word flies under the radar. It camouflages itself to give the appearance of something we've known all along. We might imagine a moat around our language, and high walls to keep out strange terms. Only a few are admitted through the gates: scientific terms, mostly, which have established procedures for nomenclature, and names of new inventions, where for the most part we allow the inventors to give names to their brainchildren. As for the rest of the infiltrators, if we detect them, we usually reject them.

There are professional critics who lead the charge against new words, defending the supposed purity of older vocabulary against incursions of new. But we really don't need the professionals. They lead the charge against words and phrases that have already attained wide acceptance — *hopefully, I'm like,* even (a long time ago) *OK.* If we had to wait for the judgment of the professionals, all the new words already would have crowded in.

But we don't wait. Each of us has our own wall around the words we use, a wall that turns away suspicious-looking strangers. Our minds are inclined to reject a conspicuous new word; it has to blend into the familiar landscape (or wordscape) before we can let it in.

Unobtrusiveness Level 0 applies to those words that are very obtrusive, very conspicuous. At this level are words that stand out because they are extremely foreign sounding: *sputnik,* for example, or *Infobahn.* As mentioned in chapter 1, the first is that Russian word for an artificial satellite, still looking Russian long after it was introduced to English in 1957, and still limited in English to a designation for certain of the earliest Russian satellites. As for *Infobahn,* it was a German rendition of *information superhighway,* with *superhighway* translated as *bahn* (from *Autobahn*). It crashed and burned a number of years ago. Both terms remained at Unobtrusiveness Level 0 because they were the opposite of unobtrusive; they remained strongly noticeable throughout their flirtation with English.

Also at Unobtrusiveness Level 0 are the many of the coinages of those who attempt their own inventions. Some are too bizarre, some are too clever. Remember these sniglets from chapter 2: *flirr, mustgo, orosuctuous, tacangle?* Or Gelett Burgess's *oofle,* a person whose name one cannot remember? Too bizarre, too clever.

Level 1 of Unobtrusiveness applies to words that are noticeable but not outrageous. Level 0 words are like guests who come to a wedding dressed in Halloween costumes; Level 1 words are like those who dress casually for a formal wedding, or formally for a casual one — they stand out a little but don't look that strange. At Level 1 we have Burgess's Miss Blinda Blurb naming a self-promotion on a book jacket after herself; we have mildly humorous *couch potato,* shaking off the terrible pun that kept it at Level 0 when it was born; we have consciously coined words like *acronym* and *Ebonics.*

Other words that were introduced at Unobtrusiveness Level 1 include Edmund Yates's *smog,* Aldous Huxley's *agnostic,* and Henry Irving Dale and Kate L. Butler's *scofflaw.* They all attracted notice but didn't shock. At Level 2 are such unobtrusive coinages as *moonlighting, boondoggle* (in the tradition of words like *bunkum, hornswoggle,* and *skedaddle*), and *server* (nonsexist for *waiter* or *waitress*). Level 2 also includes words and phrases so inconspicuous they escape the notice even of the experts, like *101, Plan B,* and the *heads-up* of *Give me a heads-up on that, will you?*

This crucial factor can determine the fate of competing words. *Waitron* has lost out to *server* as a neutral designation for *waiter* or *waitress.* The ending -*on* rarely is used for humans and thus puts *waitron* at Unobtrusiveness Level 1, while -*er* is natural and thus puts *server* at Unobtrusiveness Level 2.

Factor 3: Diversity of Users and Situations

It's not enough to have a lot of people using a new word. It also needs to be used by a variety of people in a variety of situations, or to make the point more emphatic, a Diversity of users in a Diversity of situations.

Here's a word that gets Level 0 for Diversity: *amuse-bouche.* Heard of it? Well, if you are a chef in the French tradition or a patron of French restaurants, you probably have; otherwise, not. *Wine Spectator* magazine explains: "The best restaurants offer a tiny serving of something interesting soon after you sit down, which ideally previews the cooking style of the restaurant. Most use the French term amuse-bouche (literally 'mouth amusement'). In some restaurants, it's also a way to present something luxurious to favored customers."

How about *fusin?* Biologists studying viruses know that it's a protein, discovered and named in 1996, that makes it possible for the AIDS virus to attack white blood cells. There aren't many others with *fusin* in their vocabulary.

Or take *usageaster,* invented in 1980 by linguist Tom Clark as analogous to *poetaster.* A *poetaster* pretends to write poetry; a *usageaster* pretends to know about questions of usage in language. If you happen to be one of the handful of researchers who write about the people who write about American English usage, you'll know the word. Otherwise you've probably never heard of it.

When technical terms run amok, when they begin to break out of the confines of their specialty and enter into general conversation, they rise to higher levels on the Diversity scale. At Level 1 are words that still cling to their technical reference but are known to outsiders. Politics, for example, gives us the Level 1 word *gerrymander;* psychology gives us *transference.* From computer technology we have such Level 1 words as *spam, spooler,* and *newsgroup.*

Another restricted category is slang. As long as a word is used just in the inner city or in the suburbs by those of a certain gender, race, and age, it is at Level 0. But since marketers and the media are on the lookout for the latest "in" language, slang often is quickly elevated to Level 1. That's the fate of everything from *homey* to *grody* to *dude*. If terms cross over from slang into general conversation, they reach Level 2. One that crossed over in the twentieth century is *guy*.

Level 2 words on the Diversity scale are used by anyone anywhere. A notable twentieth-century invention at Level 2 is *teenager;* there were *adolescents* in previous centuries, but that word has remained a Level 1 technical term while *teenager* has captured the better part of present-day culture. Another twentieth-century success story is *jazz*, referring not just to a kind of music developed by African Americans that came into its own during the century, but also to a historical era (the *jazz age*) and the spirit of energy and enthusiasm associated with the music.

Level 0 words are found only in specialized publications. Level 1 words will appear occasionally in general circulation newspapers and magazines, but often with a brief explanation. Level 2 words make themselves so much at home in general publications that they need no introduction.

Factor 4: Generation of Other Forms and Meanings

A new word that generates others also generates a greater chance for its own success. Like a plant that is watered and fertilized and gets plenty of sunshine, a successful new word grows. Branching out, it generates new forms and meanings.

Blockbuster is a simple example of a word at Generation Level 2 because of its variety of meanings. It was introduced during World War II as a term for an aerial bomb that could destroy a whole block of buildings. Even by war's end, though, the word was being applied to anything big and brilliant: a *blockbuster* idea, a *blockbuster* movie or book (one with spectacular sales). Taking *block* literally, *blockbuster* also was used in the late twentieth century for the unscrupulous real estate tactic of frightening homeowners into selling at low prices.

Or take *Watergate,* for example. Before 1972 it was simply the name of a posh residential and office building on the banks of the Potomac River in Washington, DC. But after an office burglary there that eventually led to the resignation of the president of the United States, *Watergate* took on a new meaning as the name for that scandal. If that had been the end of it, it would have remained at Generation Level 0, but *Watergate* took on water wings, as it were. Pundits, politicians, the public, and the media began talking about *Watergaters, Watergatology,* and *Watergatese* (the language used by those involved in the scandal), among other variations.

Even more flourishing was the second part of the name. Detaching itself from *Watergate, -gate* then attached itself to other political scandals, like *Winegate* (1973, the substitution of cheap wine for expensive Bordeaux in France), *Motorgate* (1975, fraudulent warranty claims submitted to General Motors), *Cattlegate* (1976, contaminated cattle feed), the Reagan administration's involvement in *Iran-*

Watergate
the Watergate complex

gate or *Contragate* (selling arms to Iran to support anti-Communist Contras in Nicaragua), all the way to *travelgate* and *Whitewatergate* during the Clinton administration of the 1990s, and *Shawinigate* in 2001, a conflict of interest scandal involving the Canadian prime minister. At the 2002 Winter Olympics in Utah, the scandal over judging in the pairs figure skating competition was immediately dubbed *skategate*. As long as *-gate* remains so productive, it will be at Generation Level 2.

Also generating new forms at Level 2 is *cam*, referring to a video camera aimed at a particular place or event. It developed from *minicam* and *action-cam* to *webcam* and its derivatives on the Web, including *traffic cams, news cams, scenic cams,* and countless individual *cams* beginning with *Jennicam* in 1996.

Some successful new words sprout new meanings as well as new forms. That great invention of the 1890s, the *hot dog,* not only is a staple of the American diet, but is also a flashy guy. *Hot-dogging* is showing off, and *hot dog!* is an exclamation of enthusiasm.

To the consternation of purists, nouns sprout verbs and verbs sprout nouns at the higher levels of the Generation factor. At Generation Level 1, for example, is *uptalk,* the practice of raising the pitch of the voice at the end of a sentence to make it sound like a question? *Uptalk* is a noun, but it quickly generated the verb *uptalk,* which in turn generated the noun *uptalking,* which generated the category of people known as *uptalkers.*

A similar sequence happened with *baby-sit* when it was introduced in the mid-twentieth century. Which came first, *babysitter* or *baby-sitting*? There is earlier evidence for *babysitter,* but the two are so closely linked that one probably generated the other soon after it was introduced.

At the low end of the scale, Generation Level 0 is related to Diversity Level 0. A term that is used in only a single technical sense in a single context, like *amuse-bouche* or *fusin,* is not likely to generate other forms. Other Generation Level 0 examples include *tower,* referring to a computer with a vertical profile, and *gustnado,* a name for a gust of wind that has the effect of a small tornado.

Factor 5: Endurance of the Concept

Factor 5 addresses the Endurance, or durability, not of the word itself, but of what it stands for. The relationship between a word and what it stands for is like the relationship between a flea and a dog. If the dog is healthy, so is the flea. If the dog dies, so does the flea — unless it's able to find another dog. *Icebox* is like the flea that finds another dog; when boxes holding blocks of ice to keep food cool were becoming extinct, *icebox* jumped over as an alternate name for the electric device that replaced it. Perhaps the reason *icebox* has remained alive as a synonym for *refrigerator* is that *icebox* could be reinterpreted as a box that holds or makes ice. Since refrigerators that make ice seem likely to endure for the foreseeable future, *icebox* would rate as Level 2 in Endurance.

Typewriter is another word whose dog died around the end of the twentieth century after a century of prominence. All was not lost, however. From *typewriter* came the verb *to type,* which has survived the obsolescence of the mechanical typewriter to apply itself to keyboards of electronic devices. So *type* continues at Endurance Level 2.

Many other words weren't so lucky and perished with the things they stood for. Here are some of the fleas on dead dogs of the twentieth century: *jalopy, phonograph, caboose, whistle-stop, streamliner.* Also gone are events (or situations) like the *space race* and the *Cold War.* All of these were enduring enough in their time that we still talk of them today; memories, revivals, and historical accounts keep these words on life support at Endurance Level 1. At Level 1 for the same historical reason we find certain kinds of clothing: *bustles, bloomers, zoot suits,* and *leisure suits,* for example, though the clothes themselves have been consigned to the dustbin of history. Level 1 also holds the hairstyle known as the *D.A.* and such fads as *flappers, kewpie dolls, pet rocks,* and the *Macarena.*

If these names for obsolete things are Level 1, is there anything so ephemeral that it merits Endurance Level 0? Yes, that level is for things that have been too brief in the spotlight to have left any enduring memories. There was the zany *Benigni moment,* referring to Roberto Benigni's exuberant behavior at the 1999 Oscars when he received the Best Actor award: climbing over chairs, leaping on stage, proclaiming his happiness so fast that he would start a new sentence before finishing the previous one. That moment is over. Another Level 0 example is the *Milly,* the dance commissioned by the city of Chicago to welcome the arrival of the new millennium on January 1, 2000. These might be called "firefly words," those that designate fads, fashions, and obsessions that come and go so quickly as to barely leave a mark. Slightly more endur-ing, but still at Level 0, is *Y2K,* the designation widely used during 1999 for the year 2000. It was associated with the phrase *Y2K problem* or *Y2K bug* — worries about whether computers would properly recognize dates in the 2000s. By early in the year 2000 those worries were gone, and *Y2K* faded away too. Another term unfortunately too short-lived to have left behind anything but a few regrets is *peace dividend,* a 1990 term anticipating reduced mili-tary spending because of the collapse of the Soviet Union and the end of the Cold War.

But the highest Endurance rating goes to new words that express intangible qualities that never will disappear: *hopefully,* for example, and the all-time success story, *OK.* There was no "need" for *OK* in our language; George Washington wasn't able to send his troops into battle with "OK, guys, let's go!" but he evidently found an alternative, as did everyone else until 1839 when *OK* was invented.

Actually, few people bothered to use *OK,* even in slang, until about 1900, managing to make do with *all right* and *certainly* and *correct* and the many other synonyms we still use today. But *OK* evidently stands for an enduring human attitude and response, because not only is it firmly embedded in American English, it has made its way into languages around the world. Endurance Level 2.

WHAT DOESN'T MATTER

Those five are the factors that seem to be the key ones for determining (or at least predicting) the success of a new word or phrase. There are other qualities that might matter but don't seem to.

For example, it doesn't seem to matter whether a word is brand-new or not. Many successful words — like *chad* and *hopefully,* to take two quite different examples — lurked in the language for a long time before attaining general notice. Others like *role model* (from 1957), *yuppie* (a 1982 coinage), and the phrase *mother of all* (meaning "greatest," a 1991 term inspired by the rhetoric of Saddam Hussein) seem to have caught on at once.

It also doesn't seem to matter if a word is already used for something else. *Dot,* for example, had its own meaning for centuries before encroaching on *period* in computer usage. *Media* was used by painters for a quite different purpose before advertisers began addressing themselves to particular *media* in 1921. Or consider *pork barrel,* a term that survived the demise of its literal meaning to become the conventional phrase for self-indulgent legislation early in the twentieth century.

In a larger sense, the elements from which a new word is constructed don't matter, as long as they don't make it look odd. Whether a prefix or a suffix is added to a familiar word, or two familiar words are combined to make a new one, or a familiar word simply gets a new meaning, doesn't affect its chances for success, as long as the result is un-obtrusive. That's why relatively few foreign words are directly imported into our language with success: they look too foreign.

The novelty of a word's meaning also doesn't seem to be a crucial factor. Brand-new things and situations often get new names, like *software* and *affirmative action* from the mid-twentieth century, but newness isn't necessary. There was no compelling reason to introduce *go postal* in the 1990s when English already had *run amok* and *go berserk,* for example. And as we have seen, a new concept doesn't always produce a new word, as evidenced by the missing name for the first decade of the twenty-first century.

It might seem that the obviousness of a word's meaning would be a deciding factor in its acceptance and that obscure meanings would prevent acceptance. But think of *couch potato,* for example. The association with "humans watching television" would be difficult to deduce from the combination of those two words, but that didn't slow it down. Or consider these other examples of new vocabulary from the late twentieth century: *rocket scientist, yuppie,* and *aerobics* — none of them is self-explanatory, but they were as widely accepted as *wannabe* and *rip-off,* two words whose meanings can be deduced from their components.

Surprisingly, even inclusion in a dictionary doesn't guarantee success for a new word. Being chosen for a dictionary is like being called up to the major leagues of baseball: that's where you belong if you're good, but if you don't perform well, you can soon be sent back to the minors. Some terms that were dropped from the 2000 fourth edition of the *American Heritage Dictionary* just six years after appearing in the third edition are *ecofreak* (a zealous environmentalist), *masscult* (short for culture popularized by the mass media), *microfloppy* (now called a *floppy disk*), *China syndrome* (nuclear reactor meltdown, a name taken from a 1979 movie), *scent strip* (a strip of paper dipped in perfume to provide a sample for consumers), and *binge-purge syndrome* (now *bulimia*).

But the FUDGE factors do seem to matter. The next chapter will apply the FUDGE test to current new words to estimate their chances for success.

9

The Crystal Ball

The evidence presented in the previous chapters is overwhelming: most newly coined words fail. They encounter resistance or indifference. And the more clever and conspicuous they are, the more likely they are to crash and burn. They are tourists who do not become residents. They are "firefly words" that may have a lively life in our short-term memory but do not make the transfer to our permanent language memory bank.

Yet every year some new words and phrases do succeed. As the previous chapters also have shown, there are five factors that seem to determine a word's chances for success: Frequency of use, Unobtrusiveness, Diversity of users and sources, Generation of additional forms and meanings, and Endurance of the thing or concept that the word refers to.

Of the five factors, Unobtrusiveness seems especially important. If a word seems familiar rather than new, it will insinuate itself into our vocabulary, as a cowbird insinuates its look-alike eggs into the nests of other birds, who then raise the chicks as their own.

Applied to known successes and failures of the past, the five factors seem to work, as illustrated in the preceding chapter. But that could be considered fudging; it's always possible to adjust predictions to fit already known results. This chapter will boldly go where many have unsuccessfully gone before to look at current candidates for permanent residence and predict which few will succeed.

THE FORTY-YEAR RULE: WORDS OF 1960

Admittedly, it will not be known right away which predictions for present-day new words are correct. Even if a new word or phrase seems spectacularly successful, past experience indicates that it will take about two generations, or forty years, to determine whether that word will embed itself in the permanent vocabulary. It's not enough for a word to have wide use at a given moment, or even for a decade; it needs to be adopted by succeeding generations rather than seen as the peculiar property of just one era. *Flapper,* for example, was very much in fashion in the 1920s as a designation for what we would nowadays call a cool young woman. But when the Roaring Twenties became the depressed thirties, the flappers vanished like Cinderella at the stroke of midnight.

Going by the forty-year rule, we can be reasonably confident about the long-term success or failure of new words introduced as recently as 1960. Here, for example, are some words of around 1960 that have stayed with us: *biorhythm* and *laser* in science; *neonatology, open-heart,* and *house call* in medicine (before then, it went without saying that doctors made house calls; by 1960, this had become such a rare event that it needed a label); *minivan, valet parking, health spa, dreadlocks, crudités, no-frills,* and *theme park* in contemporary culture; *dullsville, rap sheet, screwup* in slang; and *global village, big picture,* and *square one* in fashionable jargon.

Other momentarily successful words of 1960 failed to take root. *Castroism* and *Fidelista* were coined to refer to

flapper

the Communist regime Fidel Castro imposed on Cuba after his successful revolution of 1959. They gradually faded from conversation as his brand of Communism became less threatening to the rest of the hemisphere, even while Castro himself continued to rule in Cuba.

Another phenomenon of the 1960s, the *sit-in* to end racial segregation, was short-lived because it was so successful. The word *sit-in* itself, which dates from the 1930s, has remained because it is an enduring form of protest against all sorts of authority. Its spinoffs, though, have not had much staying power: the *kneel-in* to racially integrate churches in the South, the *wade-in* to integrate beaches, the *read-in* to do the same for libraries, the *play-in* likewise for parks.

Other momentarily successful words of the 1960s may have failed because they were too conspicuous. The *discomfort index* begun by the U.S. Weather Bureau in 1959

sit-in
Marlon Brando speaking with members of the Congress of Racial Equality at a sit-in at the California State Capitol in 1963

was so uncomfortable for the public that it was discontinued the next year; forecasters now tell us about the *heat index* and the *wind chill index.* And we no longer use *exosociety* to refer to intelligent life in other parts of the universe, nor do we refer to a nubile young actress nowadays as a *sex kitten.*

WORDS OF THE EARLY 2000s

But back to the future. What can we expect of words that have been newly coined or are newly prominent in the first few years of the twenty-first century? Here are some educated guesses. To find out if they're correct, you'll need to set this book in a safe place with the notation "Open in 2042." Before you do, you might write in some predictions of your own. Forty years from now, you or your descendants can let me or my descendants know how they turned out, and the 2042 edition of this book can be adjusted accordingly.

Here is a potpourri of words floating at the fringes of the English language in 2002. Will they sink or swim? Let the FUDGE scale help us predict.

AtmosFear

Faith Popcorn, diviner of future trends, named this major trend accelerated by the September 11, 2001, attacks: nervousness about pollution and possible attacks on our air, water, and food.

Frequency 1: actively promoted by a highly visible seer.

Unobtrusiveness 0: a conspicuously clever misspelling and mid-word capitalization.

Diversity of users 0: so far used only in her own publications and pronouncements. Maybe she likes it that way, keeping it proprietary.

Generation of meanings and forms 0: no derivatives.

Endurance of the concept 1: Acute fears may subside, but we'll never be perfectly safe.

Total score 2: very likely failure.

boomeritis

Yes, the baby boomers have their very own disease. And it's not just the whimsical creation of a boomer columnist, but a bona fide condition announced in 2000 by the American Academy of Orthopaedic Surgeons. They have even trademarked the word, so to get treatment you'll have to go to a certified orthopaedic surgeon. What exactly does it mean? The academy defines it simply as sports injuries— among people born between 1946 and 1964.

Frequency 1: The Academy endorsement gives it some publicity.

Unobtrusiveness 1: noticeably clever, but constructed by its inventor, Dr. Nicholas DiNubile, along the lines of *arthritis, tendinitis,* and *bursitis.*

Diversity of users 1: has appeared in a variety of popular media concerned about health.

Generation of forms and meanings 0: just the original form and meaning so far.

Endurance of the concept 1: The Academy endorsement gives it some durability, but boomers themselves will be history in a couple of generations. As time marches on, the Academy may be tempted to rename the condition *Generation Xitis.*

Total score 4: a boomlet, perhaps, but it won't live forever.

chad

Who could forget the dimpled and pregnant chads of the Florida ballots in the 2000 presidential election? We could, that's who, now that those usually insignificant bits of paper have returned to insignificance.

Frequency 2 (in late 2000), 1 (after the inauguration of George W. Bush in January 2001): central to American discourse, but only while the presidential election depended on it.

chad
inspecting a ballot in Florida in an effort to determine the outcome of the Gore/Bush presidential election of 2000

Unobtrusiveness 1: not a familiar word, but not an odd one either.

Diversity of users 1: till the election, only a specialists' word, afterwards becoming widely known.

Generation of forms and meanings 2: generated compounds like *hanging chad, pregnant chad,* and *dimpled chad.*

Endurance of the concept 1: short attention span for the election and its indecisive aftermath, but the thing itself will last as long as punch cards do.

Total score 6: hanging on by a thread.

clue stick

Virtual rather than actual, this is a stick whose impact is used to get the attention of someone who doesn't have a clue. In the old joke, a stick is needed to get the attention of a mule, hence the *clue stick.* The term has been around for a while.

Frequency 1: used on the Internet and in youth slang.

Unobtrusiveness 1: ordinary words, but the humor is obvious every time you use it.

Diversity 0: has yet to spread in the mainstream media; still used mostly in humorous contexts.

Generation of forms and meanings 1: generated the related term *clue-by-four,* alluding to the two-by-four used to get the attention of the mule.

Endurance of the concept 2: There will always be clueless people.

Total score 5, for now. If it should get more attention, it could stick.

cosmeceutical

Albert Kligman, a controversial doctor at the University of Pennsylvania, not only discovered that Retin-A fights wrinkles, but came up with this name for the combination of cosmetic and pharmaceutical products about twenty years ago. It's not just a cosmetic term for consumer consumption but is seriously used by medical practitioners. In 1998 *Cosmetics and Toiletries* magazine published a book

entitled *Cosmeceuticals: Active Skin Treatment* to bring together serious studies by Kligman and other authorities. It
includes articles like "Melanogenesis Inhibitor from Paper
Mulberry," written by eight coauthors. So what's keeping
it from a place in our dictionaries?

Frequency 1: Thanks to articles in magazines and newspapers, many patients as well as medical practitioners
know this word.

Unobtrusiveness 1: noticeably clever, but a familiar kind of
combination.

Diversity of users 0: limited to dermatologists and their patients, and the cosmetics industry.

Generations of forms and meanings 0: both an adjective and
a noun, but not extended beyond its literal meaning.

Endurance of the concept 2: As long as people grow old,
there will be a market for cosmeceuticals.

Total score 4: perhaps too conspicuously clever to use beyond its original specialized meaning.

desk rage

This one is one of the thousand-and-one varieties of anger
that seem to be sprouting in every nook and cranny and on
every occasion in American life. According to its second
annual survey of office workers to determine the extent of
desk rage, Integra Realty Resources reported in 2001 that
"stress leads to physical violence in one in 10 work environments. And almost half of those surveyed said yelling
and verbal abuse is common in their workplaces."

This particular phrase, coined in 1999, is too clever to
expect a permanent place in our vocabulary, although *rage*
itself in all its combinations is likely to become as established for anger as the suffix *-gate* has for the name of a
scandal. As far back as 1988 there was mention of *road
rage,* the phenomenon of drivers losing their tempers. In
the late 1990s, that *rage* began to diversify. Commentators
began to worry about such matters as *air rage* (1996),
airline passengers losing their tempers and endangering

everyone on a flight; *Web rage,* users of the World Wide Web losing their tempers at delays and unwanted ads; and *trade rage* (1999), day traders losing their tempers at the losses they encounter. As for *desk rage:*

Frequency 1: The survey got good publicity.

Unobtrusiveness 2: fits so perfectly into the *rage* pattern that it's hard to know whether it's new or old.

Diversity of users 1: The survey gives the casual term extra respectability, but the term is limited to discussions of work.

Generation of forms and meanings 1: part of the fertile *rage* complex, but has not generated new meanings of its own.

Endurance of the concept 2: As long as human beings work, there will be opportunities for rage.

Total score 7: likely to be reinvented if it ever drops out.

ground zero

This is the spontaneously generated name for the site of the World Trade Towers after they collapsed on September 11, 2001. In general use the term was as old as, and was associated with, the atomic bomb, designating the ground directly below the explosion. Its application to the World Trade Center site recalls not only the place but also the magnitude of the destruction.

Frequency 2: very widely used in the still frequent discussions of the site.

Unobtrusiveness 2: natural extension of the meaning of a familiar term.

Diversity of users 2: used in solemn declarations as well as ordinary conversations.

Generation of forms and meanings 0: refers to just one place in the aftermath of one event.

Endurance of the concept: 2: depends on the use to which the site will be put. If a prominent memorial is built, *ground zero* is likely to remain the unofficial name for the site. If buildings are put in place so that little is left as a reminder of the tragedy, the Endurance of the term could drop to 0.

Total score 8, very likely to succeed if the site remains a memorial; 6, not so likely if it does not.

homeland

In contrast to citizens of other nations, Americans have referred to their country as "my home, sweet home" but rarely as their *homeland.* The word gained new prominence in America with the appointment of a Director of Homeland Security in the aftermath of the September 11, 2001, attacks. Its new popularity still lies mostly in the phrase *homeland security.*

Frequency 1: not a household word, but the new concern has been widely reported and discussed.

Unobtrusiveness 2: What could be more homey?

Diversity of users 1: throughout the government as well as in discussion of government response to the September 11 attacks.

Generation of forms and meanings 0: not only not generating new forms, but mostly limited to the phrase *homeland security.*

Endurance of the concept 1: As long as there is an Office of Homeland Security with a big budget ($38 billion for 2002–2003), there will be talk. To give *homeland* a rating of 2 on the Endurance scale would be too pessimistic.

Total score 5: needs government support to endure.

nasdaq

In January 1992 the *Wall Street Journal* front-paged its sighting of a new use for the name of the NASDAQ stock market: "a synonym for loser." The noun had generated a related verb, *to nasdaq,* the equivalent of *collapse* or *fail.* Sightings began a year earlier, coinciding with the steep fall in values in that market.

Frequency 1: The *Journal,* at least, put it on the front page.

Unobtrusiveness 1: a well-established name, but making a proper name into a verb is a little out of the ordinary.

Diversity of users 1: not just specialist jargon, but still restricted to the context of the stock market.

Generation of forms and meanings 1: a verb generated from a noun.

Endurance of the concept 0: the Achilles heel. NASDAQ can't tank forever or even for very long. When it bounces back up, any noun or verb derived from its name will have the opposite meaning.

Total score 4: Failure seems certain because of lack of endurance.

paradessence

Alex Shakar invented this word for his first novel, *The Savage Girl,* a satire on trendiness and trend spotting published in late 2001. He defines *paradessence* as: "The paradoxical essence of a product. Two opposing desires that promise to satisfy simultaneously." As examples he cites the simultaneously stimulating and relaxing effects of coffee, and the eroticism and innocence of ice cream.

Frequency 0: So far just the author and his reviewers and readers have used the word.

Unobtrusiveness 0: a clever combination of two highfalutin words.

Diversity of users 0: just that one book so far, and one poem and one comment on advertising inspired by the book.

Generation of forms and meanings 0: potential for new forms if more widely used.

Endurance of the concept 2: an enduring idea.

Total score 2: probably too conspicuous a word to enter the vocabulary of others.

plaino

Not your plain old *plain old,* but a shortened version of it, as in "plaino text file," "plaino white (Elmer's type) glue," or even "a plaino-jaino database table." It means *plain* with emphasis on simplicity. Why would anyone bother to use it instead of plain *plain*? That's its problem.

Frequency 0: just a few widely scattered uses.

Unobtrusiveness 1: based on a well-known word but with an odd ending.

Diversity of users 0: only in a few Internet communications.

Generation of forms and meanings 0: nothing else.

Endurance of the concept 2: We will always have plain vanilla.

Total score 3: no chance unless pundits and presidents start yearning for the *plaino* life.

quarterlife crisis

Why wait till middle age? Now you can go through soul-searching and behavior changes while still in your twenties. Give the experience a name and you can write an article in *Mademoiselle* and turn it into a best-selling book: *Quarterlife Crisis: The Unique Challenges of Life in Your Twenties,* by Alexandra Robbins and Abby Wilner. Both the article and the book were published in 2001.

Frequency 1: a major magazine, a major publisher, major reviews; a good start.

Unobtrusiveness 1: noticeably clever but a logical twist on an established term, *midlife crisis.*

Diversity of users 1: used in media aimed at a particular demographic.

Generation of forms and meanings 0: just the term so far.

Endurance of the concept 1: as long as we believe in life crises.

Total score 4: good for a flirtation, but not for a lasting relationship.

secondhand speech

Another Popcornism, this term is from the *Dictionary of the Future* by Faith Popcorn and Adam Hanft (2001). If you are forced to overhear someone talking on a cell phone in a public place, you're suffering from *secondhand speech.*

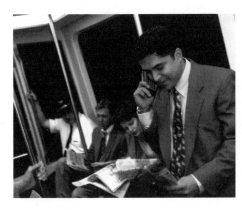

second-hand speech

It's a natural takeoff on equally irritating (if perhaps more harmful) *secondhand smoke*. If you have heard of it, it makes good sense, but most people haven't.

Frequency 0: one entry in one book.

Unobtrusiveness 1: natural, but conspicuously clever.

Diversity of users 0: one entry in one book.

Generation of forms and meanings 0: nice association with *secondhand smoke*, but no derivatives of its own.

Endurance of the concept 1: Cell phones may be just one stage of evolution.

Total score 2: needs to be talked up if it is to succeed.

she-eo

Referring to a woman CEO, this is an irresistible play on words for headline writers, contest organizers, and singers. It has various spellings: *she-e-o, she e o, she-eo,* sometimes with capital letters. In the year 2000, a Canadian company sponsored a *She-EO* contest for women only, awarding $250,000 Canadian for the best dot-com business plan. And then there is the women's a capella singing group at Harvard Business School that calls itself the *She E O's.*

Frequency 1: some headlines.

Unobtrusiveness 0: blatantly clever.

Diversity of users 0: strictly business, and not in other forms of writing.

Generation of forms and meanings 2: lots of spellings, and meaning stretched beyond simple CEO.

Endurance of the concept 2: Surely more women will break through the glass ceiling.

Total score 5: too clever for its own good.

shoshkele

A high-tech ad erupts onto a webpage that you've been looking at. Maddeningly enough, it can be programmed for particular times, locations, and service providers. That's a *shoshkele.* Why isn't it called by a more familiar name that involves *cyber, e-, web,* or *advertise?* Because it's not just a method, it's proprietary software belonging to United Virtualities, and *shoshkele* is said to be the middle name of the company founder's daughter. The term is trademarked.

Frequency 1: beginning to be talked up in the media.

Unobtrusiveness 0: This one stands out, not just as an unusual combination of vowels and consonants, but also for uncertainty about the ending; some mistakenly consider *shoskeles* singular as well as plural.

Diversity of users 0: just in the field of computer advertising so far.

Generation of forms and meanings 0: hard to imagine a related meaning or form.

Endurance of the concept $\frac{1}{2}$: Innovations on the Web tend to be short-lived.

Total score $1\frac{1}{2}$: doomed.

slackadem

Unless you're a student at Rice University, you probably won't have heard of this. In fact, not even all Rice students know of it. Here is how it was defined by students in a 1998 linguistics class at Rice: "A term used by science/engineering majors at Rice University for a person majoring in humanities or social sciences due to a perceived lack of work or effort put forth by the latter." They give this example of its use in conversation: "If you'll excuse me, I've got to study for a test. Not everyone can be a slackadem and watch TV all day."

Frequency 0: used by just a few.

Unobtrusiveness 1: combined from familiar words, but a little odd in leaving off the ending of *academic.*

Diversity of users 0: used by just one group in one place.

Generation of forms and meanings 0: if it were to spread, it might generate new meanings.

Endurance of the concept 2: Humanities and social sciences majors are likely to be around for a long time, as are science and engineering majors to look down on them.

Total score 3: unless it spreads to other campuses, not a chance.

so September 10

This term characterizes the activities or mindset of Americans just before the greatest calamity in American history. As many commentators have said, September 11, 2001, changed everything. Thus a proponent of "e-conferencing" declared in October 2001 that "face-to-face giant conferences held in big city hotels and convention centers now are so September 10," and May-May's Diary from Shanghai on November 17, 2001, explained: "If someone suggests something fun or extravagant to you, here is the correct response: 'Oh that's so September 10!!!'" The expression is said to have been invented by Bill Maher of ABC's *Politically Incorrect.*

Frequency 0: very few instances.

Unobtrusiveness 1: affected, but natural.

Diversity of users 1: a variety of sources for the few instances.

Generation of forms and meanings 1: both serious and frivolous meanings.

Endurance of the concept 0: the post–September 11 state

of high alert and high seriousness lasted only a few months.

Total score 3: let it go.

szhoosh

Famed window-dresser Simon Doonan invented this word and explained it in his 1999 book *Confessions of a Window Dresser:* To jazz up a display or the result of that action — "Szhoosh that wig up a bit" or "How's that for a bit of szhoosh?"

Frequency 0: just Doonan and friends.

Unobtrusiveness 1: a bit odd, but akin to words like *swoosh* and *zoom*.

Diversity of users 0: just the fashion world.

Generation of forms and meanings 1: both a verb and a noun.

Endurance of the concept 2: no reason *szhooshing* can't endure.

Total score 4: not likely to step out from behind the window glass.

weapons-grade

In February 2000 the software firm BeVocal announced, tongue-in-cheek, that "a large container of weapons-grade Costco Extra Spicy Salsa explodes in the BeVocal offices." Nowadays we also find references to "weapons-grade cryptography," "a weapons-grade pdf library," and even "weapons-grade Playstation 2," with a computer chip so powerful that an unfriendly country could use it to guide missiles. There have also been sightings of weapons-grade comedy, charisma, mascara, mozzarella, and hypocrites. But the most widespread recent use of *weapons-grade* was in reference to anthrax, after the anonymous mailings of fall 2001. All these are extensions of the original long-established meaning of *weapons-grade* to refer to enriched uranium or plutonium suitable for use in atomic and hydrogen bombs. Predictions for the extended meanings:

Frequency 2: widespread, especially with reference to anthrax.

Unobtrusiveness 2: natural extension of meaning of an established word.

Diversity of users 2: from serious discussions of military situations to jokes about salsa.

Generation of forms and meanings 1: no derivative forms, but the meanings of the word continue to extend.

Endurance of the concept 2: until all swords are beaten into plowshares.

Total score 9: We will have weapons-grade worries for the foreseeable future.

women of cover

"I see an opportunity at home when I hear the stories of Christian and Jewish women alike, helping women of cover, Arab American women, go shop because they're afraid to leave their home," President George W. Bush told U.S. State Department employees on October 4, 2001. At a press conference a week later, he repeated *women of cover* twice, and he continued to use that phrase in 2002. So far others haven't followed his example.

Frequency 1: When a president says it, the media notice.

Unobtrusiveness 1: like the familiar *women of color*, but *cover* is quite different from *color*, except in spelling.

Diversity of users 0: only the president.

Generation of forms and meanings 0: no new meanings or forms.

Endurance of the concept 2: As long as much of the world follows the Koran, there will be women who cover their heads for religious reasons.

Total score 4: not likely unless Bush attracts more of a linguistic following.

A score of 4 or less on the FUDGE scale indicates almost certain failure. With a score of 5 to 7, a word has a chance to hang on. Words with scores of 8, 9, or 10 are likely successes. Any survey of current newcomers, like the one above, will discover most scores to be toward the low end. In this collection of twenty words, only *weapons-grade* with a score of 9 and *ground zero* with 8 seem likely to succeed. *Desk rage*, at 7, is also a good candidate, especially because it can be easily re-created from the pattern *X rage*. *Chad*, with a current FUDGE score of 6, seems likely to endure, if mostly as a historical artifact. At 5, *clue stick, homeland,* and *she-eo* have a chance, but there's one additional obstacle: If a word scores 0 for Unobtrusiveness or Endurance, it's unlikely to succeed no matter how high its score otherwise. A 0 for Unobtrusiveness thus eliminates the too clever *she-eo*.

As this brief survey indicates, even the most notable of current new words face challenges to incorporating themselves in our general vocabulary. Looking back in 2042, the makers of dictionaries may pick out words of 2002 that were so successfully unobtrusive they escaped notice in their youth. There's a lesson here: There will always be room for more in our vocabulary, but if you want to create a successful new word, make it one that doesn't call attention to itself. And check it on the FUDGE scale before you launch it into the world.

10

A Word of Your Own

So after all this, you still want to plant a word of your own in the English language? Well, now you know what you have to do to give it a chance to grow. Take these steps:

1. Camouflage it.
2. Smuggle it in.
3. Talk it up.

And through it all, keep a straight face.

In other words, don't be clever. The more you show off your cleverness, the less likely the word is to be accepted by anyone else.

Instead, be sneaky. Spread your word without announcing it. Use it among friends and acquaintances. Like the cuckoo, plant your egg in the nests of others — your word in their vocabulary — so they will raise it as their own.

Don't be afraid to use it publicly. Not ostentatiously or awkwardly, but as if it's the most natural word in the world. Whenever you have a wide audience of listeners or readers, include it in your remarks. Put it in the articles and books and newsletters and bulletin board announcements you write. But do not do as the pundits and wits of the mass media do, patting yourself on the back and proclaiming your cleverness even as you propound your word. And whatever you do, do not hire a public relations firm to promote it. That would call too much attention to it. A regular word is not a brand name.

Above all, don't make your word a joke! Or if you must, pray that people won't get it. If they get the joke, they probably won't take the word.

Even if it's not for humorous effect, don't do anything to demonstrate your own brilliance and creativity. Such a demonstration rarely inspires admiration or emulation in others.

TELLING TALES

You can also help your word by making up a good story about it. Above all, be sure to claim that the word has been around for many years. Then, instead of having to persuade others to adopt something new, you'll have them eager to learn a word they think they've missed. This makes embarrassment work to your advantage. If people know a word is brand new, they may be too embarrassed to use it and possibly make fools of themselves. But if a word seems long established, they may be embarrassed not to use it and possibly make fools of themselves.

A good story will have the important effect of deflecting any suspicion that you may have made up the word. But how can you get others to believe that your word is long-lived? Choose a subject in which you're more expert than your listeners, use the word, and when they look puzzled, explain that this is the term everyone uses in that particular field.

Your story can also link the word to a favored group. "Favored" is a relative notion, of course, but you can follow the example of the myths about *OK* (its origins have been claimed to be Choctaw, Chickasaw, Haitian,

Greek, German, French, Finnish, Scottish, and African, among others) and say the word came from whichever group — ethnic, social, regional, occupational — your listeners would admire.

FULL CREDIT

But what about getting credit for your word? If you hide behind a story that credits someone long ago, how can you claim authorship once your word has succeeded?

Since you have read so far, I'll make a deal with you. Send me a letter with your word and its definition, along with any story you make up about it. Don't send anything as ephemeral as e-mail; make it a real old-fashioned letter on real paper, so its authenticity can't be questioned. I'll keep it in my registry of new words, and if it should succeed, I'll let know everyone know who should get the credit. I'll make a particular point of notifying the people who make the dictionaries, such as the authoritative *American Heritage Dictionary,* which, like this book, is published by Houghton Mifflin Company. Send the word to:

Allan Metcalf
English Department
MacMurray College
447 East College Avenue
Jacksonville, Illinois 62650

Of course, even with the best of planning, any new word has only a slim chance of spreading throughout our general vocabulary. If yours happens not to succeed, don't be too surprised or discouraged. I'll arrange for my registry of new words to be permanently archived, so that the words may be examined by future researchers and perhaps promulgated by them many years from now. In that case, you'll still get credit.

Good luck!

Appendix

American Dialect Society Words of the Year

Since 1990, the American Dialect Society has included in its annual meeting a vote on Words of the Year, the words that were most notable, prominent, and characteristic of the discourse of the year just past. At first the choices were restricted to new words, those that had not yet appeared in any dictionary. After a few years, however, it became evident that many apparently new words were actually not so new, and the most notable words of a given year were often not new at all, so the strict limitation to new words was lifted. But the emphasis on new words remains.

Although the society's members are watchful observers of our language, and their choices are assisted by the leading experts on new words, in retrospect the society's selections have often missed the significant and enduring new words of a given year. Why that should be is the subject of this book. The Introduction discusses the questions that arise from these choices.

2001

Word of the Year: *9-11, 9/11* or *September 11,* terrorist attacks on that date.

Most Likely to Succeed: *9-11.*

Most Useful (tie): *facial profiling,* using video "faceprints" to identify terrorists and criminals; and *secondhand speech,* cell phone conversations overheard in public places.

Most Creative: *shuicide bomber,* terrorist with bomb in shoes.

Most Unnecessary: *impeachment nostalgia,* longing for the superficial news of the Clinton era.

Least Likely to Succeed: *Osamaniac,* woman sexually attracted to terrorist Osama bin Laden.

Most Outrageous: *assoline,* methane used as fuel.

Most Euphemistic: *daisy cutter,* large bomb that explodes a few feet above the ground.

Most Inspirational: *Let's roll!* words of Todd Beamer to start the attack that foiled the hijackers of United Flight 93 on September 11.

2000

Word of the Year: *chad,* a small scrap of paper punched from a voting card.

Most Likely to Succeed: *muggle,* Harry Potter term for a non-wizard; a mundane, unimaginative person.

Most Useful: *civil union,* legal same-sex marriage.

Most Creative: *dot bomb,* a failed dot-com.

Most Unnecessary: *sudden loss of wealth syndrome* (the meaning is obvious).

Least Likely to Succeed: *kablokeys,* used in phrases like "It scared the kablokeys out of me."

Most Outrageous: *wall humping,* rubbing a thigh against a security card scanner to gain access without removing the card from one's pocket.

Most Euphemistic: *courtesy call,* an uninvited call from a telemarketer.

Brand New (coined during the year, not previously attested): *unconcede,* to rescind a concession, as presidential candidate Al Gore did on election night. (It was later discovered that candidate Bob Dole had *unconceded* the presidential election in 1996, and there have been occasional instances of this word going back several centuries.)

Also chosen in January 2000: Word of the Decade: *web*. Word of the Twentieth Century: *jazz*. Word of the Millennium: *she*.

1999

Word of the Year: *Y2K*, the year 2000.

Most Likely to Succeed and Most Useful: *dot-com*, a company operating on the Web.

Most Original: *cybersquat*, to register a Web address with the intention of selling it at a profit.

Most Unnecessary: *Milly*, dance commissioned by the city of Chicago for the millennium.

Most Outrageous: *humanitarian intervention*, use of military force for humanitarian purposes.

Most Euphemistic: *compassionate conservative*.

Brand New: *Pokemania*, obsession with Pokemon.

1998

Word of the Year: prefix *e-* for "electronic" as in *e-mail* and newly prominent *e-commerce*.

Most Likely to Succeed and Most Useful: *e-*.

Most Original: *multislacking*, playing at the computer when one should be working.

Most Unnecessary: the entire Monica Lewinsky word family, including *Big She* as a synonym for M. L., and the verb *Lewinsky*, to engage in what might be sexual relations.

Least Likely to Succeed: *compfusion*, confusion over computers.

Most Outrageous: *Ejaculation Proclamation*, the president's confession.

Most Euphemistic: *senior moment*, momentary lapse of memory due to age.

Brand New: -*agra* or -*gra* (from the drug name *Viagra*), suffix denoting substance prompting men to perform unusually, as in *Directra,* which causes men to ask for directions.

1997

Word of the Year: *millennium bug,* also known as *Y2K bug* or *Y2K problem,* that causes computers to think that the year after 1999 is 1900.

Most Likely to Succeed: *DVD,* Digital Versatile Disk, optical disk expected to replace CDs.

Most Useful (tie): -*[r]azzi,* an aggressive pursuer; and *duh* (with falling intonation), used to indicate someone else's stupidity.

Most Original: *prairie dogging,* popping one's head above an office cubicle for the sake of curiosity.

Most Unnecessary: *heaven-o,* replacement for "hello."

Most Outrageous: *Florida flambé,* fire caused by Florida electric chair.

Most Euphemistic: *exit bag,* bag placed over the head to assist in suicide.

Brand New: *El Nonsense,* illogical association of an event with El Niño.

1996

Word of the Year: *mom,* as in *soccer mom,* newly significant type of voter.

Most Likely to Succeed: *drive-by,* designating brief visits or hospital stays.

Most Useful: *dot,* used instead of "period" in e-mail and URL addresses.

Most Original: *prebuttal,* preemptive rebuttal.

Most Unnecessary: *Mexican hustle,* another name for the Macarena (which is Spanish, not Mexican).

Most Outrageous: *toy soldier,* land mine.

Most Euphemistic (tie): *urban camping,* living homeless in a city; and *food insecure,* said of a country where people are starving.

Most Controversial: *Ebonics,* African-American vernacular English.

1995

Word of the Year (tie): *World Wide Web* on the Internet; and *newt,* to make aggressive changes as a newcomer.

Most Likely to Succeed: *World Wide Web* and its variants *the Web, WWW, W3.*

Most Useful: *E.Q.* (for Emotional Quotient), the ability to manage one's emotions.

Most Original: *postal* or *go postal,* to act irrationally, often violently, from stress at work.

Most Unnecessary: *Vanna White shrimp,* large shrimp for the restaurant market.

Most Outrageous: *starter marriage,* a first marriage not expected to be the last.

Most Euphemistic: *patriot,* one who believes in using force of arms if necessary to defend individual rights against the government.

1994

Word of the Year (tie): *cyber,* pertaining to computers and electronic communication; and *morph,* to change form.

Most Promising: *Infobahn,* the Internet.

Most Useful: *gingrich,* to deal with government agencies, policies, and people in the manner of U.S. Speaker of the House Newt Gingrich.

Most Imaginative: *guillermo,* an e-mail message in a foreign language (the Spanish name *Guillermo* has the nickname *Memo*).

Most Trendy: *dress down day* or *casual day,* a workday when employees are allowed to dress casually.

Most Euphemistic: *challenged,* indicating an undesirable or unappealing condition.

Most Beautiful: *sylvanshine,* nighttime iridescence of certain forest trees.

1993

Word of the Year: *information superhighway,* network linking computers, television, telephone, and other electronic means of communication.

Most Likely to Succeed: *like* with a form of the verb *be* to indicate speech or thought.

Most Useful: *thing* premodified by a noun, for example, "a Chicago thing."

Most Imaginative: *McJob,* a generic, unstimulating, low-paying job.

Most Amazing: *cybersex,* sexual stimulation by computer communication.

Most Unnecessary: *mosaic culture,* to describe a multicultural society.

Most Outrageous: *whirlpooling,* assault of a female by a group of males in a swimming pool.

Most Euphemistic: *street builder,* a homeless person who constructs a shanty.

Most Unpronounceable: *Jurassosaurus nedegoapeferkimorum,* a new dinosaur.

1992

Word of the Year: *Not!* expression of disagreement with a previous statement.

Most Likely to Succeed: *snail mail, s-mail,* mail that is physically delivered, as opposed to e-mail.

Most Useful: *grunge,* a style of clothing.

Most Original: *Franken-,* genetically altered.

Most Amazing: *Munchhausen's syndrome by proxy,* illness fabricated by a caregiver about a person in his or her care in order to evoke sympathy for the caregiver.

Most Unnecessary: *gender feminism,* belief that sex roles are social, not biological.

Most Outrageous: *ethnic cleansing,* purging of ethnic minorities.

1991

Word of the Year: *mother of all —,* greatest, most impressive.

Most Likely to Succeed: *rollerblade,* skate with rollers in a single row.

Most Successful: *in-your-face,* aggressive, confrontational, flamboyant.

Most Original: *molecular pharming, pharming,* genetically modifying farm animals to produce human proteins for pharmaceutical use.

Most Amazing: *velcroid,* a person who sticks by the (U.S.) President, especially for photo opportunities.

Most Unnecessary: *massively parallel,* many small computers yoked together to process a program.

1990

Word of the Year: *bushlips,* insincere political rhetoric.

Most Likely to Succeed (tie): *notebook PC,* a portable personal computer weighing from 4 to 8 pounds; and *right-sizing,* adjusting the size of a staff by laying off employees.

Most Useful (tie): *technostupidity,* loss of ability through dependence on machines; and *potty parity,* equalization of toilet facilities for the sexes.

Most Original: *voice merging,* the oral tradition of African-American preachers using another's words.

Most Amazing: *bungee jumping,* jumping from a high platform with elastic cables on the feet.

Most Unnecessary: *peace dividend,* anticipated savings in military spending due to improved relations with Soviet Union (just before it collapsed).

Most Outrageous: *politically correct, PC,* adhering to principles of left-wing social concern in language use.

Index

Picture Credits